CW00729736

TRANSNATIONAL ORGANISED CRIME IN INTERNATIONAL LAW

There is extensive and detailed academic literature on the legal development of international crimes such as war crimes and crimes against humanity. However, not much attention has been paid to other serious crimes, including narcotics-related offences, human trafficking and money laundering, which do not necessarily amount to international crimes in the traditional sense. The purpose of this monograph is to fill this gap and offer a critical analysis of developments in the field of transnational organised crime under international law. The book is divided into two parts. Part I is entitled 'Norms, Principles and Concepts'. It traces the history of organised crime and explores key concepts and norms relating to the practice from a multi-disciplinary perspective. It then looks at legal obligations imposed upon states as well as non-state actors in relation to transnational organised crime. Part II illustrates how these norms, principles and obligations are translated and enforced in practice. This is done through case studies at the level of national law (Thailand, Serbia and the UK), regional law (European Union) and international law (United Nations).

Studies in International and Comparative Criminal Law: Volume 5

Studies in International and Comparative Criminal Law
General Editor: Michael Bohlander

Criminal law had long been regarded as the preserve of national legal systems, and comparative research in criminal law for a long time had something of an academic ivory tower quality. However, in the past 15 years it has been transformed into an increasingly, and moreover practically, relevant subject of study for international and comparative lawyers. This can be attributed to numerous factors, such as the establishment of ad hoc international criminal tribunals and the International Criminal Court, as well as to developments within the EU, the UN and other international organisations. There is a myriad of initiatives related to tackling terrorism, money laundering, organised crime, people trafficking and the drugs trade, and the international 'war' on terror. Criminal law is being used to address global or regional problems, often across the borders of fundamentally different legal systems, only one of which is the traditional divide between common and civil law approaches. It is therefore no longer solely a matter for domestic lawyers. The need exists for a global approach which encompasses comparative and international law.

Responding to this development, this new series will include books on a wide range of topics, including studies of international law, EU law, the work of specific international tribunals and comparative studies of national systems of criminal law. Given that the different systems to a large extent operate based on the idiosyncracies of the peoples and states that have created them, the series will also welcome pertinent historical, criminological and socio-legal research into these issues.

Editorial Committee:

Mohammed Ayat (ICTR, Kigali)
Caroline Fournet (Exeter)
Alex Obote-Odora (ICTR, Arusha)

Silvia Tellenbach (Freiburg)
Liling Yue (Beijing)

Robert Cryer (Birmingham)
Kaiyan Kaikobad (Brunel)
Dawn Rothe (Old Dominion University, VA)

Helen Xanthaki (IALS, London)

Volume 1: The German Criminal Code: A Modern English Translation
Michael Bohlander
Volume 2: Principles of German Criminal Law
Michael Bohlander
Volume 3: Crime, Procedure and Evidence in a Comparative and International Context: Essays in Honour of Professor Mirjan Damaska
Edited by John Jackson, Maximo Langer and Peter Tillers
Volume 4: Essays on International Criminal Law and International Criminal Procedure
Héctor Olásolo

Transnational Organised Crime in International Law

Tom Obokata

·H A R T·
PUBLISHING

OXFORD AND PORTLAND, OREGON
2010

Published in the United Kingdom by Hart Publishing Ltd
16C Worcester Place, Oxford, OX1 2JW
Telephone: +44 (0)1865 517530
Fax: +44 (0)1865 510710
E-mail: mail@hartpub.co.uk
Website: http://www.hartpub.co.uk

Published in North America (US and Canada) by
Hart Publishing
c/o International Specialized Book Services
920 NE 58th Avenue, Suite 300
Portland, OR 97213-3786
USA
Tel: +1 503 287 3093 or toll-free: (1) 800 944 6190
Fax: +1 503 280 8832
E-mail: orders@isbs.com
Website: http://www.isbs.com

© Tom Obokata 2010

Tom Obokata has asserted his right under the Copyright, Designs and
Patents Act 1988, to be identified as the author of this work.

All rights reserved. No part of this publication may be reproduced,
stored in a retrieval system, or transmitted, in any form or by any
means, without the prior permission of Hart Publishing, or as expressly
permitted by law or under the terms agreed with the appropriate
reprographic rights organisation. Enquiries concerning reproduction
which may not be covered by the above should be addressed to Hart
Publishing Ltd at the address above.

British Library Cataloguing in Publication Data
Data Available

ISBN: 978-1-84113-690-5

Typeset by Forewords, Oxford
Printed and bound in Great Britain by
TJ International Ltd, Padstow, Cornwall

Foreword

It is a pity that there isn't any international law in *The Wire*, the highly popular television series that is built around cops and the local gangsters in the city of Baltimore whom they are trying to put in jail. It is mainly about trafficking in drugs, but one set of shows also looks at human trafficking, prostitution, political corruption and systematic theft by workers in the city's dockyards. Regularly, the overworked Baltimore police try to enlist the interest of their federal counterparts, who have much better resources. Usually, they are told that their focus has switched to counter-terrorism, and away from the drug trade and human trafficking. It is post-11 September, after all.

Lurking in the background is 'the Greek', soft-spoken and avuncular, and his lieutenant, Vondas, who is usually clad in a charming newsboy cap. At one point, when the police make a series of arrests, the two are seen at the airport checking in for an international flight. Three years later, in the final series, they make a perfunctory reappearance. The two seem to be the local emissaries of a criminal multinational, but the show never lets us get behind their mysterious facade. If it did, we might find a new layer of activity, with international lawyers, Interpol and complex issues of mutual legal assistance.

Although the engagement of international law in the suppression of organised crime goes back more than a century, it has been through quite dramatic developments in the last decade or so. These comprise the subject matter of Tom Obokata's book. Now, the centrepiece is the Convention against Transnational Organized Crime, known generally as the 'Organised Crime Convention'. It was adopted in 2000, along with three Protocols which deal with human trafficking, smuggling of people and the international trade in firearms. As a result, the last decade has been particularly fertile, and it is time to take stock of the developments in a major monograph.

There has been much talk about the 'fragmentation' of international law. It is certainly true that many new areas have developed, with much interaction involving related fields. Human rights law is especially important here. Legal mechanisms to address various features of organised crime require close attention to human rights norms and standards. Indeed, human rights law probably owes a debt of gratitude to European mafias. With their wealthy resources for legal battles, they have taken fascinating challenges before the European Court of Human Rights, facilitating the further development of the law and the clarification of matters concerning due process and prison conditions.

The European Court of Human Rights will consider the importance of dealing with organised crime when it considers the acceptable limitations that may be imposed upon fundamental rights. In one ruling, its Grand Chamber said:

> Inherent in the whole of the Convention is the search for a fair balance between the demands of the general interest of the community and the requirements of the protection of the individual's fundamental rights. As movement about the world becomes easier and crime takes on a larger international dimension, it is increasingly in the interest of all nations that suspected offenders who flee abroad should be brought to justice. Conversely, the establishment of safe havens for fugitives would not only result in danger for the State obliged to harbour the protected person, but also tend to undermine the foundations of extradition.[1]

International law concerning organized crime also comes into contact with the discipline known widely as 'international criminal law'. The latter's primary concern is with international atrocity crimes, specifically genocide, crimes against humanity and war crimes. In some European languages, a distinction is made by changing the order of the words: *droit international pénal* and *droit pénal international*. The former concerns atrocity crimes such as genocide, while the latter is largely addressed to the suppression of organised crime through mutual legal assistance. In English, we more often make the distinction by speaking of 'transnational organised crime', underscoring the point that this is crime to be dealt with primarily through national prosecutions. International law intervenes to assist in the process because of the trans-border nature of the criminal activity.

This book contemplates the relevance of such a distinction. One explanation is that atrocity crimes are generally perpetrated by governments, whereas transnational crimes are the work of non-state actors. Atrocity crimes require internationalisation of prosecution because the investigating authorities and the courts that would normally be responsible are themselves often accomplices in the criminal acts. Organised crime seems different, because states are generally willing and able to prosecute such acts, but complications are imposed by the mafias themselves, with their skilled exploitation of the international environment.

This analysis works well as a general rule, but it has its limits. At the atrocity crime end of the spectrum, we have the phenomenon of non-state actors, such as rebel or guerrilla groups. They are the enemies of states and are in fact often trying to overthrow them. In some respects they resemble organised crime, and the legal problems have similarities. As for organised crime, sometimes it insinuates itself so deeply into the state that the boundaries become difficult to determine. Certainly, there is no willingness to prosecute because the relevant authorities are so corrupted.

There is a constituency that supports the addition of certain forms of organised crime, notably drug trafficking, to the subject matter of international criminal law, effecting its migration from the related but distinct area of transnational criminal law. When the Rome Statute of the International Criminal

---

[1] *Öcalan v Turkey* [GC], no 46221/99, Judgment, 12 May 2005, para 88.

Court was adopted, at the 1998 Rome Conference, proponents of such a view were unsuccessful in attaining this objective. Only a reference in the Final Act, adopted at the same time as the Statute of the Court, has kept the flame alive. There is a debate not only about the practical issues involved in the addition of such forms of organised crime, but also a more theoretical concern as to whether drug trafficking and similar acts belong to the same genus as genocide and the other international atrocity crimes.

One thing is certain: the international law governing organised crime is a close relative of the body of law applicable to the International Criminal Court and similar institutions. It provides a forum to address issues of more general concern, such as the scope of universal jurisdiction, immunities, statutory limitation and extradition. Tom Obokata's study, with its original and in some ways unique perspective, enriches our knowledge of the field.

Professor William Schabas OC MRIA
Galway, 28 February 2010

Acknowledgements

The completion of this monograph would not have been possible without assistance from a number of individuals and organisations. First, I would like to thank Brice Dickson at the QUB School of Law, who spent long hours reading and commenting on an earlier version of this monograph. I also wish to express my gratitude to Jean Allain (QUB) and Neil Boister (University of Canterbury, New Zealand) for their expert comments, as well as to Professor William Schabas (Irish Centre for Human Rights, Galway) for writing a foreword to this book.

I conducted field research to complete this monograph, and a number of people and organisations kindly offered their assistance. In particular, I would like to thank Professor Nenad Radovic (Academy of Criminalistic and Police Studies, Serbia), Lt Colonel Fatos Haziri (Kosovo Republic Police), Mr Uthai Arthivech (Office of the Attorney-General, Thailand), Major General Krerkphong Pukprayura (Royal Thai Police), Mr Matt Friedman (United Nations Inter-Agency Project on Trafficking), and Ms Anne Gallagher and her staff at the Asia Regional Trafficking in Persons Project.

Finally, I would like to thank the QUB School of Law for giving me some time off to complete this monograph.

Contents

Contents

Contents

Contents

Abbreviations

ACHR	American Convention on Human Rights
CCPCJ	Commission on Crime Prevention and Criminal Justice (UN)
CND	Commission on Narcotic Drugs (UN)
COMMIT	Co-ordinated Mekong Ministerial Initiative against Trafficking
COP	Conference of Parties (Organised Crime Convention)
CPS	Crown Prosecution Service (UK)
CRC	Convention on the Rights of the Child
EAW	European Arrest Warrant
ECHR	European Convention on Human Rights
ECJ	European Court of Justice
ECOSOC	Economic and Social Council (UN)
EDU	European Drug Unit
EEW	European Evidence Warrant
EJN	European Judicial Network
EU	European Union
EULEX	European Union Rule of Law Mission (Kosovo)
Europol	European Police Office
FATF	Financial Action Task Force
GRECO	Group of States against Corruption
HRA	Human Rights Act 1998 (UK)
ICCPR	International Covenant on Civil and Political Rights
ICESCR	International Covenant on Economic, Social and Cultural Rights
ICC	International Criminal Court
ICJ	International Court of Justice
ICL	international criminal law
ICPC	International Criminal Police Commission
ICTR	International Criminal Tribunal for Rwanda
ICTY	International Criminal Tribunal for the Former Yugoslavia
IHRL	international human rights law
ILO	International Labour Organisation
IMT	International Military Tribunal
INCB	International Narcotic Control Board
Interpol	International Criminal Police Organisation
IOM	International Organisation for Migration
KFOR	Kosovo Force (NATO)
KRP	Kosovo Republic Police
MNC	multi-national corporation
NATO	North Atlantic Treaty Organisation
NCB	National Central Bureau (Interpol)
NGO	non-governmental organisation
OAS	Organisation of American States
OSCE	Organisation for Security and Co-operation in Europe

PACE	Police and Criminal Evidence Act 1984 (UK)
PNR	Passenger Name Records
RICO	Racketeer Influenced and Corrupt Organisations Act 1970 (USA)
SOCA	Serious Organised Crime Agency (UK)
SOFA	Status of Force Agreement
TCL	transnational criminal law
TEU	Treaty on European Union
TFEU	Treaty on the Functioning of the European Union
UN	United Nations
UNIAP	United Nations Inter-Agency Project on Trafficking of Human Beings in the Greater Mekong Sub-region
UNICRI	United Nations Interregional Crime and Justice Research Institute
UNMIK	United Nations Interim Administration Mission in Kosovo
UNODC	United Nations Office of Drugs and Crime

Table of Cases

I. Regional/International Cases

Permanent Court of International Justice

International Military Tribunal

International Court of Justice

International Criminal Tribunal for the Former Yugoslavia

International Criminal Tribunal for Rwanda

Table of Cases

International Criminal Court

Extraordinary Chambers in the Court of Cambodia

Special Court of Sierra Leone

European Commission/Court of Human Rights

European Court of Justice

II. National Cases

Table of Cases

United States of America

Table of Regional and International Instruments

International Instruments

Regional Instruments

European Union

Treaties

Table of Regional and International Instruments

Joint Actions

Council of Europe

1

Introduction

1.1 The Rise of Organised Crime

Organised crime is not a modern or urban phenomenon.[1] It is deep-rooted in the history of all cultures and continues to evolve in line with political, social and economic changes.[2] Although systematic and comprehensive research on the evolution of organised crime around the globe is lacking,[3] individual case studies exist and it is possible to identify a trend through a comparative analysis. One of the most famous examples of organised crime or criminal groups is the Italian mafia. It was said to have emerged in the early nineteenth century 'when the Bourbon state in Sicily tried to curb the power of the traditional landowning aristocracy and encouraged the emancipation of the peasantry' by abolishing feudalism.[4] This created 'tensions between the central government and local landowners on the one hand, and between the latter and peasants on the other'. This led to the birth of a mafia which became adept at managing and resolving these tensions and conflicts.[5] To be specific, they provided protection for people, land, livestock and produce.[6] By the 1870s these 'mafias' were able to consolidate their organisational structures and activities, most notably in Palermo, Sicily.[7]

Detailed examination shows that organised crime and mafia type bodies are not purely an Italian phenomenon. Other, older counterparts to the Italian exist. For example, the contemporary Russian mafias have roots in fifteenth-century criminal associations formed by peasants fleeing serfdom.[8] This was promoted by a social institution known as *artel*, an arrangement which organised joint labour

---

[1] A Block, *East Side–West Side: Organized Crime in New York City, 1930–1950*, 2nd edn (New Brunswick, Transaction Publishers, 1995) 10.

[2] Ibid.

[3] L Paoli and C Fijnaut, 'Introduction to Part I: The History of Concept' in L Paoli and C Fijnaut (eds), *Organised Crime in Europe: Concepts, Patterns and Control Policies in the European Union and Beyond* (Dordrecht, Springer, 2006) 21.

[4] A Blok, *The Mafia of a Sicilian Village 1860–1960: A Study of Peasant Entrepreneurs* (Oxford, Basil Blackwell, 1974) 10.

[5] Ibid, 92.

[6] D Gambetta, *The Sicilian Mafia: The Business of Private Protection* (Cambridge, Harvard University Press, 1993) 91–99.

[7] G Fulvetti, 'The Mafia and the "Problem of the Mafia": Organised Crime in Italy 1820–1970' in Paoli and Fijnaut, above n 3, 60.

[8] Y Gilinskiy and Y Kostjukovsky, 'From Thievish Artel to Criminal Corporation: The History of Organised Crime in Russia' in Paoli and Fijnaut, above n 3, 184.

activities in agriculture, trade, construction and craft industries.[9] In time these associations evolved into more solid criminal organisations engaging in theft, burglary and robbery.[10] A similar trend was also evident in Germany during the Napoleonic wars, although terms such as gangs of robbers, crooks and bandits are used interchangeably.[11] Economic, political and social inequalities as well as other factors led to the growth of organised crime there.[12] In Turkey, where East meets West, organised crime and criminal groups also have a long history. Under the Ottoman Empire (1299–1922) people known as *kabadayi* emerged as an early example of organised crime groups. Similar to the Italian mafias, they sold protection, settled disputes and protected the poor against oppressive administrations.[13]

There are also prominent examples of organised crime and criminal groups in Asia. The Chinese criminal group Triad is a case in point. A secret society known as Tiandihui (the original name for Triads) was established in 1674 in the Fujian province of China as a mutual protection society in response to socio-economic conflicts among various ethnic groups.[14] After rebelling against the Qing dynasty in 1786, the Triads were declared illegal, thereby driving them underground.[15] With the passage of time, the Fujian people migrated to various parts of China, and this resulted in the spread of the Triads. Of particular significance was their growth in Hong Kong. Soon after the British colony was set up in 1842, Hong Kong became a major transit point for the flow of opium and Chinese labour, both of which were facilitated by the Triads.[16]

In seventeenth-century Japan the forerunners of the organised criminal group known as Yakuza emerged. Groups of individuals known as *machi-yakko*, or servants of the town, protected their towns from samurai criminal gangs who became prominent after centuries of civil war ended in 1604.[17] These *machi-yakko* were regarded as the heroes of the time[18] and were later associated with *tekiya* (street peddlers) and *bakuto* (gamblers).[19] *Tekiya* sustained themselves by organising legal sales of goods through portable stalls in markets and fairs held in various towns, while *bakutos* organised illegal gambling all around Japan.[20] It has been argued that of these two groups *bakutos* were the true ancestors[21]

[9] Ibid, 185.

[10] Ibid, 191.

[11] K Lange, '"Many a Lord is Guilty, Indeed for Many a Poor Man's Dishonest Deed": Gangs of Robbers in Early Modern Germany' in Paoli and Fijnaut, above n 3, 109–11.

[12] Ibid, 116–17.

[13] Y Yeşilgöz and F Bovenkerk, 'Urban Knights and Rebels in the Ottoman Empire' in Paoli and Fijnaut, above n 3, 203.

[14] YK Chu, *The Triads as Business* (London, Routledge, 2000) 12.

[15] Ibid, 7.

[16] Ibid, 14.

[17] D Kaplan and A Dubro, *Yakuza: Japan's Criminal Underworld* (Berkeley, University of California Press, 2003) 5.

[18] Ibid, 7.

[19] Ibid.

[20] Ibid, 10.

[21] P Hill, *The Japanese Mafia: Yakuza, Law and the State* (Oxford, Oxford University Press, 2003) 36.

because the term 'yakuza', which translated into the worst combination in a card game (8–9–3), was coined by them.[22] Similar to the Italian mafias, these Yakuza groups organised around families or hierarchical lines.[23]

In looking at the historical development of these major criminal groups globally, it is noticeable that early forms of organised crime and organised criminal groups emerged in response to oppressive governments or other malignant socio-economic forces, often with other external impetus. The result was associations that provided protection for disadvantaged groups or acted as intermediaries between public and governments. Therefore many of these groups were regarded as guardian angels of some sort and not necessarily criminals in the perception of oppressed people. The support of local populations undoubtedly helped these groups to grow and gain legitimacy.

How did the noble cause become the corrupt one? While is it difficult to generalise about all criminal groups in history, it may be inferred from the above analysis that they started recognising 'protection' as an important saleable commodity. In modern times this practice is known as extortion in many jurisdictions, where criminals demand financial or material benefits in return for 'protection' which is often not required in practice. This has been a common undertaking by the Italian mafias. Gambetta notes that the Italian mafia has been 'an industry which produces, promotes, and sells private protection'.[24] A similar trend was also recognised among the Japanese Yakuza,[25] the Chinese Triad[26] and the Turkish *kabadayi*.[27] What is apparent, then, is the gradual transformation of these groups from philanthropic organisations to business entities where profit became the main goal.

These groups gained a more criminal character when they started providing protection to criminals who sold illegal goods and services. The demand for such service was there because the governments were there to regulate, and not to provide protection over these illegal markets.[28] In the US, the emergence of mafias can be linked to the prohibition of alcohol in 1920s and 1930s. This resulted in the transfer of a specific commodity (alcohol) from the legitimate to illegitimate economy, and the mafias emerged to protect this market from the government.[29] A similar trend can be also seen in the aftermath of the break-up of the Soviet Union, when the subsequent transfer of property into private hands created a demand for protection services.[30] Once in the markets, these criminal

---

[22] Kaplan and Dubro, above n 17, 13.
[23] Ibid.
[24] Gambetta, above n 6, 1.
[25] Hill, above n 21, 37 and 40.
[26] Chu, above n 14, 12.
[27] Yeşilgöz and Bovenkerk, above n 13, 203.
[28] Hill, above n 21, 11.
[29] Ibid, 14.
[30] F Varese, *The Russian Mafia: Private Protection in a New Market Economy* (Oxford, Oxford University Press, 2001) ch 1.

groups and associations saw ample opportunities to make profits by providing illegal goods and services themselves.[31]

1.2   Contemporary Manifestation of Organised Crime

While many characteristics noted above are relevant to modern day organised crime and criminal groups, there are also some noticeable differences. For instance, globalisation has altered the ways in which organised crime flourishes and criminal groups operate. Globalisation refers to 'a process which transforms the spatial organization of social relations and transactions, generating transcontinental or interregional networks of interaction and the exercise of power'.[32] The principal driving force behind globalisation is the expansion of the global market economy. Globalisation has allowed capital, goods, services, people and information to move across borders with increasing speed, frequency and ease, contributing to the growth of the global markets and financial systems, multinational corporations and international trade.[33]

Although globalisation has produced some positive changes in how world affairs are conducted, it has also facilitated the growth of organised crime. In the word of Williams, transnational crime is the dark side of globalisation.[34] The historical examples of organised crime given above demonstrate that those groups initially emerged to deal with local problems. However, globalisation has enabled these criminals to operate beyond national borders thanks to improved transport capabilities. In other words, organised crime has become more transnational in nature. The Japanese Yakuza began travelling to South-East Asia in the late twentieth century to develop prostitution and sexual slavery in this region and in Japan.[35] Advances in communication, another consequence of globalisation, have allowed criminals to exchange information with anyone or any organisation in various parts of the world and to facilitate transnational co-operation. The Italian mafias are known for their collaborative networks with La Cosa Nostra in the US, the Colombian and Mexican drug cartels, and the Russian mafias.[36] Thanks to these extensive networks, the Italia mafias remain

---

[31] According to Hill, however, some groups emerged to provide illicit goods and services and not necessarily to provide protection. Above n 21, 15. See also Gambetta, above n 6, 251–52.

[32] D Held and A McGrew, 'Introduction' in D Held and A McGrew (eds), *Governing Globalization: Power, Authority and Global Governance* (Cambridge, Polity Press, 2003) 2.

[33] P Williams, 'Organizing Transnational Crime: Networks, Markets and Hierarchy' in P Williams and D Vlassis (eds), *Combating Transnational Crime: Concepts, Activities and Responses* (London, Frank Cass, 2001) 66–67.

[34] Ibid.

[35] Kaplan and Dubro, above n 17, 233.

[36] J Arquilla D Ronfeldt, *Networks and Netwars* (Santa Monica, RAND, 2001) 110.

one of the most powerful criminal groups in the world.[37] What is new or different about the contemporary manifestation of organised crime, then, is its scale and diversity.[38] A wide variety of individuals and criminal groups across the globe are involved in a range of criminal activities.

Another key point to note is the way in which management of risk is conducted in modern times. Criminals are now able to transfer criminal proceeds with a touch of a button, and technology such as internet banking has aided the accumulation and diversification of wealth while evading law enforcement actions.[39] This is further supported by offshore banks and tax havens such as Antigua and the Cayman Islands, where financial regulations are lax or non-existent, or there are strong bank secrecy rules protecting their clients.[40] In addition, in order to avoid law enforcement, criminal groups engage in 'jurisdictional shopping',[41] where they shift their activities to states and territories where their conduct is not properly prohibited or regulated.

In addition to these direct benefits to criminals and criminal groups, there are by-products of globalisation which have facilitated organised crime. For instance, it has created what Passas calls 'criminogenic asymmetries', defined as the structural discrepancies, mismatches and inequalities in the realms of economy, law, politics and culture.[42] These asymmetries, coupled with the growth of global trade and financial systems, have facilitated organised crime by fuelling the demand for illicit goods and services and generating incentives for individuals and organisations to engage in illegal activities.[43] In China the transition to a market economy has created uneven distribution of income and worsened poverty in certain rural areas, prompting criminal gangs such as the Triad to provide illicit goods and services.[44]

Another side effect of globalisation is the reduced ability of states to regulate transnational activities.[45] This is more evident in states in transition or developing states, as they lack the requisite capacity and/or resources. An appropriate is the situation of Central and Eastern European states at end of the cold war. Organised crime expanded in these states after the collapse of the one-party system within the Soviet bloc, which was said to be relatively effective in crime

---

[37] Ibid.

[38] Williams, above n 33, 58.

[39] C Fijnaut, 'Transnational Crime and the Role of the United Nations, in Its Containment through International Cooperation: A Challenge for the 21st Century' (2000) 8 *European Journal of Crime, Criminal Law and Criminal Justice* 119, 122–123.

[40] P Williams and G Baudin-O'Hayon, 'Global Governance, Transnational Organised Crime and Money Laundering' in Held and McGrew, above n 32, 132.

[41] N Passas, 'Cross-Border Crime and the Interface between Legal and Illegal Actors' in P Van Duyne, K Von Lampe and N Passas (eds), *Upperworld and Underworld in Cross-Border Crime* (Nijmegen, Wolf Legal Publishers, 2002) 27.

[42] N Passas, 'Globalisation, Criminogenic Asymmetries and Economic Crime' (1999) 1 *European Journal of Law Reform* 399, 402.

[43] Ibid.

[44] JH Mittelman and R Johnston, 'The Globalization of Organized Crime, the Courtesan state, and the Corruption of Civil Society' (1999) 5 *Global Governance* 103, 109.

[45] Passas, above n 42, 402.

prevention.[46] The newly independent states did not inherit the infrastructure or expertise on crime control, nor did they have adequate resources for such. The situation was exacerbated by corruption and undue influence by various industries keen to expand their business.[47] A similar problem is also evident in developing regions such as Asia, Africa and Latin America.

Furthermore, states are no longer the sole holders of power. Other, non-state actors, such as multi-national corporations (MNCs) and regional/international organisations such as the European Union and the United Nations, have become important players/stakeholders in international affairs.[48] The existence of these multiple actors has undoubtedly affected states' ability to monitor transnational activities, because it is extremely difficult, if not impossible, to pay attention to every single transaction. Rosenau once argued that, while these non-state actors lack the attributes of states, this is often an advantage rather than a disadvantage because they are able to institute actions which states cannot.[49] Organised criminal groups are among non-state actors which resonate well with Rosenau's analysis as they have been able to identify gaps in the markets, provide illegal goods and services to fill such gaps, and take advantage of loopholes in criminal justice systems to conduct their business.

Finally, a nexus between organised crime and terrorism has become more evident in modern times. Generally speaking, the key objectives of organised crime and terrorism are said to be different. While the main aim of organised crime is to maximise longer-term profits, that of terrorism is more political or ideological in that terrorists are interested in overthrowing a government or establishing a new state, for example.[50] As noted by some commentators, money is the goal of organised crime, while it is a tool for terrorist organisations in achieving political or ideological goals.[51] This distinction can be blurred at times, as organised criminal groups can become more ideological. Lal points to an example of South Asian criminal groups which have acquired ideological/religious predispositions.[52] Conversely, terrorists have increasingly been involved in organised crime to finance and sustain their activities. *Sendero Luminoso*, a terrorist organisation in Peru, is said to be representative of this.[53]

In any event, there is ample evidence of this link between organised crime

---

[46] Mittelman and Johnston, above n 44, 130.

[47] Passas, above n 41, 25.

[48] N Passas, 'Globalisation and Transnational Crime: Effects of Criminogenic Asymmetries' in Williams and Vlassis, *Combating Transnational Crime*, above n 33, 29–30.

[49] J Rosenau, *Turbulence in World Politics* (Princeton, Princeton University Press, 1989) 253.

[50] MC Bassiouni and E Vetere (eds), *Organized Crime: A Compilation of UN Documents 1975–1998* (New York, Transnational Publishers, 1998) xl –xli. See also A Leong, *The Disruption of International Organised Crime: An Analysis of Legal and Non-Legal Strategies* (Aldershot, Ashgate, 2007) 22.

[51] A Gómez-Céspedes and P Strangeland, 'Spain: The Flourishing Illegal Drug Haven in Europe' in Paoli and Fijnaut, above n 3, 390.

[52] R Lal, 'South Asian Organized Crime and Terrorist Networks' (2005) 49 *Orbis: Journal of World Affairs* 293, 294.

[53] A Jamieson, 'Transnational Organized Crime: A European Perspective' (2001) 24 *Studies in Conflict and Terrorism* 377, 379.

and terrorism. Organised criminal groups and terrorists sometime co-operate with each other in areas such as acquisition of illicit goods, trafficking routes and training of group members. The Revolutionary Armed Forces of Colombia (FARC)[54] is a good example as it works with drug cartels in the production and trafficking of cocaine.[55] The same trend can be seen in Pakistan and Afghanistan, where drug traffickers support the activities of Islamic terrorists,[56] and also in Northern Ireland, where paramilitaries fund their activities through organised crime.[57] Of particular concern in modern times is the trafficking and acquisition of weapons of mass destruction (WMDs). Trafficking of nuclear weapons has long been suspected of states such as North Korea, Iran and Libya.[58] Other forms of WMDs, such as chemical and biological weapons, also pose a threat to international peace and security. Readers might recall the sarin nerve gas attack on the Tokyo subway system in March 1995, which was carried out by a cult terrorist group, Aum Shinrikyo.[59] This and other incidents, such as the September 11 attacks in New York (2001), and the July 7 bombings London (2005) conducted by Al Quaeda, demonstrate the determination of terrorist and organised criminal groups in advancing their agenda. As such, there is an urgent need to ensure that they do not get possession of WMDs.

1.3   The Scope and Aim of This Book

The above analysis illustrates that organised crime has become more complex, dangerous and sophisticated over the course of time. From a practical point of view, this means that traditional law enforcement, which mainly takes place after a crime is committed and is therefore reactive in nature, is not adequate. In order to get ahead of criminals and criminal groups, states need to actively promote more proactive, intelligence-led law enforcement. Furthermore, as organised crime has become more transnational in modern times, it should no longer be regarded as a matter of purely domestic concern. In the era of globalisation, effective action against transnational organised crime requires a supranational framework to facilitate a high level of co-ordination and co-operation and to consolidate the efforts of all relevant actors, including states, international organisations and civil society. As with other issues of international importance, such as the protection of human rights, the prohibition of international crime, and

---

[54] *Fuerzas Armadas Revolucionarias de Colombia* [in Spanish].

[55] P Bibes, 'Transnational Organized Crime and Terrorism: Colombia, A Case Study' (2001) 17 *Journal of Contemporary Criminal Justice* 243.

[56] Lal, above n 52, 294.

[57] UK Home Office, 'One Step Ahead: A 21st Century Strategy to Defeat Organised Crime' (March 2004) 9.

[58] Lal, above n 52, 294.

[59] This resulted in 12 deaths and over 5,000 injuries. G Cameron, 'Multi-Track Microproliferation: Lessons from Aum Shinrikyo and Al Qaida' (1999) 22 *Studies in Conflict and Terrorism* 277, 277.

the maintenance of international peace and security, international law can play an important role in this regard. Indeed, the international community in the past has adopted various treaties to facilitate concerted effort to address some aspects of transnational organised crime. They include instruments on trafficking of drugs[60] and endangered species,[61] child pornography[62] and cyber crime,[63] to name but a few.

While these and other instruments have undoubtedly assisted states to implement measures against various forms of organised crime, some significant problems remain. These treaties are subject-specific and therefore have limited applicability. They are not necessarily suited to address new forms of criminality, and this requires states to adopt additional instruments in a piecemeal fashion in the future. The existence of multiple instruments also makes it difficult for states to keep track of various obligations, and this can result in delay in implementation of the core obligations so imposed. Furthermore, some of the instruments are geographically limited as they are adopted by the regional organisations such as the Council of Europe and the Organisation of American States. All of these factors have hindered a concerted response to transnational organised crime, and the value of a universal instrument applicable to all types of organised crime throughout the world has gradually been recognised.[64]

An important step was eventually taken when the United Nations adopted the Convention against Transnational Organised Crime (Organised Crime Convention), including three Protocols, in 2000.[65] The Convention provides for definitions, such as 'serious crime' and 'organised criminal group', to be utilised by states and the international community so as to promote and maintain consistency.[66] It also establishes a framework for international co-operation with detailed guidance on such issues as extradition and other mutual legal assistance in criminal matters.[67] However, the Organised Crime Convention is young compared to other branches of international law, such as international humanitarian law, international human rights law and international criminal law. Consequently the norms and principles arising, particularly those relating to the nature and extent of obligations imposed upon states and non-state actors, have yet to be thoroughly examined and articulated.

---

[60] Convention against Illicit Traffic in Narcotic Drugs and Psychotropic Substances 1988, 28 ILM 493.

[61] Convention on International Trade in Endangered Species of Wild Fauna and Flora 1973, 993 UNTS 243.

[62] Optional Protocol to the Convention on the Rights of the Child on the Sale of Children, Child Prostitution and Child Pornography, A/54/263 (25 May 2000); European Convention on the Protection of Children against Sexual Exploitation and Sexual Abuse 2007, ETS No 201.

[63] European Convention on Cybercrime 2001, ETS No 185.

[64] See, eg Report of the World Ministerial Conference on Organised Transnational Crime, A/49/748 (2 December 1994) 13 and the General Assembly Resolution A/RES/51/120 (12 December 1996).

[65] A/RES/55/25 (15 November 2000).

[66] Art 2.

[67] See, eg Arts 16 and 18.

This book aims to fill this gap and offers a critical analysis of the development of international law in relation to transnational organised crime, with particular reference to the Organised Crime Convention. The book is divided into two parts. Part I is entitled 'Concepts, Norms and Principles'. To begin with, Chapter 2 explores key concepts and theories relating to transnational organised crime from a multi-disciplinary perspective. Through an analysis of various definitions of organised crime and criminal groups incorporated into domestic, regional and international law, the chapter also examines how these concepts and theories are reflected or implemented in practice. Just as there are many conceptual and theoretical frameworks for understanding organised crime, a variety of definitions have been adopted at different levels. This demonstrates that perceptions of organised crime vary across the globe, and the key question becomes whether the Organised Crime Convention can alleviate this.

The next two chapters identify the key norms and principles arising from the Organised Crime Convention. This instrument belongs to an emerging branch of international law known as transnational criminal law, which obliges states to prevent and suppress organised crime at the national level through the adoption of appropriate legislative and law enforcement frameworks.[68] It should be noted from the outset that much of the analysis in these chapters is speculative, as the Organised Crime Convention is still at an early stage of development. Therefore references will be made to other relevant branches of international law, such as international criminal law and international human rights law, and this book examines how they might usefully supplement the development of transnational criminal law. The book does not provide a definitive answer to the question of how international law should develop in relation to transnational organised crime; rather, it is intended to facilitate further discussion and research.

Chapter 3 elucidates the key obligations imposed upon states in relation to transnational organised crime. In addition to an obligation to prohibit and punish organised crime and related offences such as inchoate offences (eg conspiracy), secondary participation and corruption, it will be shown that the main thrust of the Convention is the facilitation of intelligence-led law enforcement and international co-operation. This chapter examines the key related issues, such as special investigative techniques, extradition and other mutual assistance in criminal matters, including transfer of criminal proceedings and joint investigations. It also explores some of the main challenges facing states in implementing core obligations, such as the periods of limitation, diplomatic immunity and a lack of due regard for the rights of suspects and defendants.

Chapter 4 continues with the role and the position of non-state actors in the suppression and prevention of organised crime. Although states bear a primary obligation under international law, the co-operation of non-state actors, such as international organisations, MNCs and non-governmental organisations (NGOs), are essential in promoting an effective action against this criminality.

---

[68] N Boister, 'Transnational Criminal Law?' (2003) 14 *European Journal of International Law* 953.

That transnational criminal law and the Organised Crime Convention do not create rights and duties for non-state actors necessitates a move beyond the realm of international law to fully appreciate their position. In this regard, this chapter relies on the concept of 'global governance'. It will be shown that this concept supports the involvement of non-state actors, as it recognises the importance of non-legal instruments and arrangements which are more relevant for them. Furthermore, while national and international law remain vital in establishing criminal liability for individual criminals, criminal groups and legal persons, the concept of global governance also recognises other forms of accountability of a political, economic and administrative nature.

Part II of the book, 'Enforcement of Norms and Principles', explores how the relevant norms, principles and obligations explored in Part I are translated and enforced in practice. Chapter 5 presents national case studies of Thailand, Serbia (including Kosovo) and the UK. The chapter will analyse how these states in various stages of development respond to transnational organised crime in accordance with the Organised Crime Convention. Chapter 6 then looks at a regional response to transnational organised crime, as promoted by the European Union (EU). Key principles, such as approximation of national law, mutual recognition and availability, as well as the future prospect of the EU action against transnational organised crime in light of the Lisbon Treaty, will be analysed. Finally, various international responses to transnational organised crime will be explored in Chapter 7. This will examine the role to be played by international organisations, bodies and initiatives such as the Conference of Parties under the Organised Crime Convention, the United Nations Office of Drugs and Crime, the International Criminal Police Organisation and the United Nations Inter-Agency Project on Human Trafficking in relation to treaty monitoring, provision of technical assistance and promotion of international co-operation.

Part I

Concepts, Norms and Principles

2

Understanding Organised Crime
from a Multi-Disciplinary Perspective

2.1   Introduction

In this chapter various theories, concepts and definitions relating to organised crime will be explored. A theoretical foundation on organised crime will be focused on first, with particular reference to key criminological literature. It will be shown that, while there was a tendency within the academic and law enforcement communities, particularly in the US, to treat organised crime as a nationwide conspiracy committed by mafia-type hierarchically structured organisations, such perception has changed over time. Other aspects, such as the nature of their activities in illegal markets, have been examined in recent times. Whatever the stances one takes, it will be shown that there is no single way to describe organised crime, as it takes a variety of forms in practice.

The chapter will next examine legal definitions adopted at international and national and levels. Those given under the Organised Crime Convention will be analysed in the first instance, as these set a comprehensive international standard applying to a wide variety of criminalities. It will be shown that, while there are some conceptual difficulties, the definitions given under the Organised Crime Convention are wide enough to cover varied forms of organised crime, in line with its changing nature. The chapter will then explore the definitions adopted at the national level to understand whether they reflect international definitions given under the Organised Crime Convention. While some definitions employed after the adoption of the Convention reflect its substance, others do not, highlighting the difficulty in implementing international standards in practice due to political, cultural and social differences between states, as well as the principle of state sovereignty.

2.2 Concepts of Organised Crime from a Multi-disciplinary Perspective

It should be noted from the outset that it is difficult to give a precise definition of organised crime as a wide variety of views from different disciplines exists. However, certain characteristics of organised crime, which differentiate it from other types of crime, have been identified over the course of time. There are two main ways to understand organised crime: as a set of actors and as a set of activities.[1] While the organised nature of criminals or groups is a key point of analysis for the former, an emphasis is placed upon the organised nature of criminal activities in relation to the latter. What follows is an exploration of organised crime in these broad frameworks in an attempt to understand the nature and extent of organised crime from a multi-disciplinary perspective.

2.2.1 Organised Crime as a Set of Actors

This understanding of organised crime is perhaps more popular among the general public. When thinking of organised crime, they refer to large criminal organisations such as the Italian mafia and the Japanese Yakuza. Indeed, the term 'organised crime' was coined in the US at the end of the nineteenth century, when the New York Society for the Prevention of Crime used the term to describe gambling and prostitution.[2] At that time the term 'organised crime' was used to describe 'illegal business deals involving politicians, police officers, lawyers or professional thieves' and not gangsters or mafia-type criminal groups.[3] This changed in the 1950s, when the term was used to describe the Italian mafia in the US.

Within the discourse of organised crime as a set of actors, two main models have been advanced by politicians, law enforcement agencies and academics. The first is a corporate model, under which criminal organisations are regarded as entities having highly centralised and hierarchical corporate structures.[4] This model was widely accepted among the law enforcement and political communities in the US.[5] They were strongly influenced by the so-called 'alien conspiracy theory', which portrayed Italian mafia as 'a coherent and centralised international conspiracy of evil' that threatened the political, economic and legal systems of

---

[1] L Paoli and C Fijnaut, 'Organised Crime and Its Control Policies' (2006) 14 *European Journal of Crime, Criminal Law and Criminal Justice* 307, 308.

[2] M Woodiwiss, 'Transnational Organised Crime: The Strange Career of an American Concept' in M Beare (ed), *Critical Reflections on Transnational Organized Crime, Money Laundering and Corruption* (Toronto, University of Toronto Press, 2003) 5.

[3] Paoli and Fijnaut, above ch 1 n 3, 24.

[4] A Cohen, 'The Concepts of Criminal Organisation' (1977) 17 *British Journal of Criminology* 97, 98.

[5] L Paoli, 'The Paradoxes of Organized Crime' (2002) 37 *Crime, Law and Social Change* 51, 53.

the US.[6] This view was endorsed officially by the Congressional Committee on Inquiry, headed by Senator Estes Kefauver, in 1951.[7] This was followed by a report of the Katzenbach Committee entitled 'The Challenge of Crime in a Free Society' (1967), in which organised crime was viewed as a large criminal corporation supplying illegal goods and services.[8] The corporate model was further strengthened in the 1960s, when Joe Valachi, then a member of the Italian mafia, testified before the Senate Permanent Sub-Committee on Investigations and used a previously unheard-of name for this Italian mafia: La Cosa Nostra.[9] This subsequently became a household name in the US. Moreover, in the late 1960s, the Crime Commission under President Johnson described organised crime as:

> A society that seeks to operate outside the control of the American people and their governments. It involves thousands of criminals, working within structures as complex as those of any large corporation . . . Its actions are not impulsive rather the result of intricate conspiracies carried on over many years and aimed at gaining control over whole fields of activity in order to amass a huge profits.[10]

The corporate model widely accepted by the US influenced the government's response to organised crime for three decades. In a report entitled 'The Edge: Organized Crime, Business and Labor Unions' (1986), President Ronald Regan's Committee of Inquiry on Organised Crime asserted that an organised criminal group was 'a long-lasting hierarchical internal organization with a limited number of hard-core members, aimed at financial gain from illegal activities, and using the threat of violence, or actual violence, in order to achieve this goal'.[11]

Many have argued that the corporate model was a true reflection of some contemporary organised criminal groups. One of the leading scholars on La Cosa Nostra is Donald Cressey, who advised the Katzenbatch Committee noted above. In a book entitled *Theft of the Nation*, he described the basic structure of La Cosa Nostra in the US. According to Cressy, each mafia family had a hierarchical structure, headed by a boss whose main functions were to maximise profits through provision of illicit goods and services and to maintain order within the family.[12] Below the boss were several 'under-bosses', who were equivalent to vice presidents or deputy directors in corporations.[13] Under this level were 'lieutenants' or 'captains', who were the chiefs of operating units within a family. Finally there were more section chiefs and regular members (soldiers)

---

[6] M Woodiwiss, 'Transnational Organised Crime: The Global Reach of an American Concept' in A Edwards and P Gill (eds), *Transnational Organised Crime: Perspectives on Global Security* (London, Routldge, 2005) 15.

[7] Fijnaut, 'Organized Crime: A Comparison Between the United States of America and Western Europe' (1990) 30 *British Journal of Criminology* 321, 324.

[8] Ibid, 323.

[9] Paoli and Fijnaut, above n 1, 309.

[10] Woodiwiss, above n 6, 16.

[11] Fijnaut, above n 7, 323.

[12] D Cressey, *Theft of the Nation* (New York, Harper Collins, 1969) 113.

[13] Ibid.

under them.[14] The existence of hierarchical groups is also evident in Sicily. Like La Cosa Nostra, each individual mafia family has a hierarchical structure and all of them are bound together by what is known as 'the Commission', the highest decision-making body authorised to appoint bosses, approve new members, and settle disputes among families.[15] Further studies on organised criminal groups also suggest that groups such as the Russian mafia[16] and the Japanese Yakuza[17] have hierarchical, corporate like structures. Such an emphasis on the corporate structure of organised crime was shared by commentators in Western Europe to some extent.[18]

Although it seems obvious that some organised criminal groups represent the corporate model, it has been widely argued in recent times that the corporate model is too simplistic and does not reflect the reality of contemporary organised crime. Critics of the model dispute that organised crime is in many cases carried out by highly structured, hierarchical organisations.[19] These scholars advocate a so-called network model in which organised crime is understood to be carried out by a collection or network of individuals, small groups and departments, etc, collaborating with each other in various combinations.[20] This network model gained its prominence in the 1970s as an alternative form of a criminal organisation, influenced by scholarship in anthropology and political science.[21] One of the fiercest critiques of the corporate model comes from Pearce in *Crimes of the Powerful* (1976). He asserts that a mafia in Italy is a myth as its existence has never been proven conclusively.[22] Given that many studies have been conducted in relation to the Italian mafia[23] which demonstrate the existence of some type of organisational structures, this argument might be difficult to sustain. However, some argue that the Italian mafia and other groups operating in the US are based on network, rather than having strict hierarchy.[24]

In addition, the network model is suited to describe criminal organisations in other parts of the world. Contrary to a popular image, the Medellin and Cali cartels in Colombia consisted of 'loose combinations of relatively small, family

---

[14] Ibid, 114–15.

[15] Gambetta, above ch 1 n 6, 122.

[16] Gilinskiy and Kostjukovsky, above ch 1 n 8, 182.

[17] Hill, above ch 1 n 21, 66.

[18] Fijnaut, above n 7, 325.

[19] P Williams and R Godson, 'Anticipating Organized and Transnational Crime' (2002) 37 *Crime, Law and Social Change* 311, 332.

[20] G Bruinsma and W Bernasco, 'Criminal Groups and Transnational Illegal Markets' (2004) 41 *Crime, Law and Social Change* 79, 79.

[21] JS McIllwain, 'Organised Crime: A Social Network Approach' (1999) 32 *Crime, Law and Social Change* 301, 303.

[22] F Pearce, *Crimes of the Powerful: Marxism, Crime and Deviance* (London, Pluto Press, 1976) 117–21.

[23] Gambetta, above ch 1 n 6; Blok, above ch 1 n 4; J Dickie, *Cosa Nostra: A History of the Sicilian Mafia* (New York, Palgrave McMillan, 2004); L Paoli, *Mafia Brotherhoods: Organised Crime, Italian Style* (Oxford, Oxford University Press, 2003).

[24] Williams and Godson, above n 19, 331–32; McIllwain, above n 21, 309.

based cocaine manufacturing firms that merely joined forces in the early 1980s'.[25] The network model is also the dominant form of organised crime in European states such as the Netherlands[26] and Germany.[27] Furthermore, it has been noted that the Hong Kong Triad is largely organised through informal networks rather than formal structural organisations.[28] In view of all of these examples, it can be concluded that the network model is equally important in understanding organised crime and reflects the reality of organised crime today.

A question which might be asked here is why the network model has become dominant in modern times. One reason is that networks of criminals are able to respond quickly to a changing operational environment as they are fluid, flexible and adaptable. If they are dismantled, these networks can reorganise themselves quickly.[29] When the Cali cartel in Colombia was destroyed, other organisations formed a less concentrated network which continued global drug trafficking.[30] In comparison, hierarchical organisations do not have this flexibility and are easily detectable by law enforcement authorities. In this sense, Paoli notes that the illegality of goods and services prevents criminals from forming large-scale organisations.[31] Networks of organised criminals, then, have emerged because they have significant advantages over traditional hierarchical organisations. Another advantage of the network model is that it is not based on a long-term relationship. Unlike in a centrally organised structure, individual criminals do not have to show a life-time commitment and/or sacrifice their lives.[32] As a result, depending on opportunities, each illegal entrepreneur is free to look for other partners to maximise his/her own profits. This was said to be one of the reasons why Colombian trafficking organisations established an alliance with the Sicilian mafia.[33]

However, the network model has its disadvantages. Following from the point noted above, perhaps the key problem is that a strong bond might not exist among various actors, leading to competition rather than co-operation. In forming and maintaining a network, trust becomes a key element,[34] and this is promoted by a variety of 'relational ties'.[35] Some forge alliance purely out of economic interest or greed, in that they form a relationship to maximise profit. This may be seen where Colombian cartels worked closely with Russian mafias

---

[25] Paoli, above n 5, 68.
[26] Williams and Godson, above n 19, 332; P Klerks, 'The Network Paradigm Applied to Criminal Organisations: Theoretical Nitpicking or a Relevant Doctrine for Investigators? Recent Developments in the Netherlands' in A Edwards and P Gill (eds), Transnational Organised Crime, above n 6, 101.
[27] Paoli, above n 5, 67; Lange, above ch 1 n 11, 112–13.
[28] Chu, above ch 1 n 14, 7; Williams, above ch 1 n 33, 77; Kaplan and Dubro, above ch 1 n 17, 257.
[29] Paoli, above n 5, 67; Klerks, above n 26, 102.
[30] Williams and Godson, above n 19, 334.
[31] Paoli, above n 5, 64.
[32] Ibid, 76–77.
[33] Williams, above ch 1 n 33, 75.
[34] Ibid.
[35] McIllwain, above n 21, 305.

to open heroin and cocaine markets in Eastern Europe.[36] This alliance based on economic interests may work to an extent, but has caused some problems to some. Turkish drug traffickers in the past have used Albanian networks to transport heroin through the Balkan route to Europe.[37] However, because of the profits to be made from trading drugs, some Albanians went into business for themselves, pushing the Turks out of certain markets.[38] This shows that the network model does not necessarily provide for strong glue to hold the various actors together.

This is somewhat different for criminal organisations with hierarchical structures. A social/cultural analysis provides a useful framework to understand this. From a social perspective, ethnic or tribal ties, family relations, friendship and sharing a common geography (neighbourhood) strengthen the bonds between individuals and organisations.[39] The Italian mafia is a good example of groups formed on blood relations.[40] Another good example is Nigerian criminal organisations, which became prominent in the 1980s. They relied heavily on family and ethnic ties in diasporas and developed links between domestic and overseas bases.[41] Nigerian criminal gangs in London are said to take advantage of this.[42]

From a cultural perspective, rituals, codes, symbols and other shared norms and values are important factors in bringing people together. Some scholars, including Sutherland and Merton, argue that organised crime is a cultural phenomenon.[43] Chinese organised criminal groups, for instance, rely on the notion of 'guanxi', or reciprocal obligation or relationship, to bind groups together.[44] Groups such as the Triads additionally use specific oaths, rituals and other shared norms and values to facilitate a high sense of loyalty and brotherhood.[45] The Chinese groups have an additional advantage of sharing the same race/ethnicity and because of this are said to be more successful in making profits than other ethnic or non-ethnic groups.[46] A similar notion known as 'giri' is present among the Japanese Yakuza,[47] and initiation rituals and secret codes have also been employed by the Italian mafias[48] and criminal groups in Germany.[49] What becomes apparent is that both the corporate and network models are relevant in describing modern organised criminal groups.

---

[36] Mittelman and Johnston, above ch 1 n 44, 113.
[37] Williams, above ch 1 n 33, 75.
[38] Ibid.
[39] Klerks, above n 26, 102.
[40] McIllwain, above n 21, 305.
[41] Mittelman and Johnston, above ch 1 n 44, 111.
[42] Ibid. This is also the case in South Africa. See T Leggett, *Rainbow Vice: The Drugs and Sex Industries in the New South Africa* (London, Zed Books, 2002).
[43] Quoted in F Allum and J Sands, 'Explaining Organised Crime in Europe: Are Economists Always Right?' (2004) 41 *Crime, Law and Social Change* 133, 134.
[44] Williams and Godson, above n 19, 329–30.
[45] Ibid, 329.
[46] McIllwain, above n 21, 312.
[47] Kaplan and Dubro, above ch 1 n 17, 17.
[48] Fulvetti, above ch 1 n 7, 49–50.
[49] Lange, above ch 1 n 11, 130–131.

Finally, it is important to note that criminals in networks or hierarchical organisations are not the only participants in organised crime. Rather, organised crime is facilitated by 'a complex mix of actors with transnational criminal organisations playing a large but not exclusive role'.[50] To be specific, a wide variety of legitimate individuals and organisations become involved in crime directly or indirectly. Often these parties are unaware that they are part of criminal activities. Money laundering provides a good example of this, as money obtained through illegal activities is often transferred through various legitimate financial institutions before going back into the hands of the criminals. In other cases, individuals and organisations knowingly participate in crimes in co-operation with criminals. In trafficking of human beings, for example, individual brokers/ agencies, public officials and others are sometimes involved.[51] Consumers of illicit goods and services are also part of organised crime because the demand for goods and services promotes their supply. It is evident, therefore, that illicit and licit markets sit side by side and sometimes a clear distinction cannot be drawn.

The above analysis of organised crime as a set of actors and activities demonstrates that a wide variety of participants are involved in organised crime, and the corporate and/or network models are helpful to us in understanding how and why some criminals come together to commit a wide variety of criminal activities. They also help us identify the key individuals and organisations involved in organised crime. However, an emphasis on these sets of actors is not sufficient to understand organised crime itself, as it is difficult to know how these criminals operate to make profits. As a result, many in the academic and law enforcement communities also focus on the nature of activities conducted by criminals, to which this chapter now turns.

2.2.2   Organised Crime as a Set of Activities

If one chooses to focus on organised crime as a set of activities, the term 'organisation' refers to the 'structure of a chain of events, of an interaction process, in which different individuals and groups participate in different ways at different stages'.[52] It is the organised nature of illegal activities that is more important, regardless of the types of individuals, groups or organisations involved. To be more specific, organised crime is mainly regarded as illegal enterprises supplying contraband goods and services in illegal markets. This view gained force in 1960s and 1970s, when attention shifted from the criminal organisations to their activities.[53] Schelling's contribution may be regarded as a starting point,

---

[50] Williams, above ch 1 n 33, 81.
[51] On this, see T Obokata, *Trafficking of Human Beings from a Human Rights Perspective: Towards a Holistic Approach* (Leiden, Martinus Nijhoff Publishers, 2006).
[52] Cohen, above n 4, 98.
[53] Paoli and Fijnaut, above n 1, 310.

as his writing has influenced many scholars and was said to shape the modern understanding of organised crime.[54] In his view, the main purpose of organised crime is to provide the public with illicit goods and services in strong public demand.[55] His focus therefore was on the economic aspect of organised crime, and he argued that the economic analysis would allow the authorities to identify the incentives and disincentives to organised crime, evaluate the costs and losses, and restructure their laws and policies accordingly.[56] In other words, it would help them to understand the modus operandi regardless of the types of organisations they form.

Schelling's view has been shared and/or supported by many scholars in the US. Smith, for instance, views organised crime in terms of illegal enterprise in pursuit of profit.[57] Block and Chambliss also argue that organised crime 'should be defined as . . . those illegal activities involving the management and coordination of racketeering and vice'.[58] Williams and Godson[59] and Schloenhardt[60] also recognise a link between organised crime and the provision of illegal goods and services in the illegal markets, and argue that criminal organisations come into existence and flourish simply because of the dynamics of the illegal markets in which they operate.[61] By the 1980s, a consensus among American criminologists emerged that 'organised crime involved a continuing enterprise operating in a rational fashion and focused towards obtaining profits through illegal activities'.[62]

The enterprise theory of organised crime has become popular in Europe since the 1970s. Van Duyne, a Dutch scholar, asked: 'What is organized crime without organizing some kind of criminal trade; without selling and buying forbidden goods and services in an organizational context? The answer is simply nothing'.[63] Even in Italy, contemporary scholars focus more on the economic aspects of organised crime.[64] In this regard, Paoli and Fijnaut confirm that domestic legislation and working definitions in many European states reflect the enterprise theory of organised crime.[65] For instance, the Bundeskriminalamt, the German federal criminal police, refers to organised crime as 'the planned commission of

---

[54] Allum and Sands, above n 43, 134.

[55] T Schelling, 'What is the Business of Organized Crime?' (1971) 20 *Journal of Public Law* 71, 71; T Schelling, *Choice and Consequence* (Cambridge, Harvard University Press, 1984) 160.

[56] Ibid, 159.

[57] D Smith, *The Mafia Mystique* (New York, Basic Books, 1975) 335

[58] A Block and WJ Chambliss, *Organizing Crime* (New York, Elsevier, 1981) 13.

[59] Above n 19, 324.

[60] A Schloenhardt, 'Organised Crime and the Business of Migrant Trafficking: an Economic Analysis' (1999) 32 *Crime, Law and Social Change* 203, 206 and 208.

[61] See further M Findlay, *The Globalisation of Crime* (Cambridge, Cambridge University Press, 1999) 138–66; T Hellmann, *The Economics of Crime* (New York, St. Martin's Press, 1980).

[62] Paoli and Fijnaut, above n 1, 310.

[63] P Van Duyne, 'Organized Crime, Corruption and Power' (1997) 26 *Crime, Law and Social Change* 201, 203. The Dutch law enforcement officials and policy makers, however, have viewed organised crime in terms of criminal conspiracies. See Klerks, above n 26, 99.

[64] Paoli and Fijnaut, above ch 1 n 3, 31.

[65] Paoli and Fijnaut, above n 1, 312.

criminal offences determined by the pursuit of profit and power'.[66] The Polish police use the working definition: 'activities of groups that have been set up for making money with crime (no matter whether it relates to violent or economic offences), use of violence, blackmail and corruption, and aim at introducing illegal revenues into the legitimate economy'.[67]

Any discussion of the illegal markets cannot be divorced from that of the supply–demand dynamics. In general, organised crime does not flourish if there is no demand for illicit goods and services. Passas makes a legitimate point that illegal markets follow the rules of supply and demand more strictly than legitimate markets, mainly because they do not enjoy protection by states.[68] It is therefore apparent that consumers of illicit goods and services contribute to the growth of organised crime, and it is argued that this is what separates organised crime from ordinary crimes. According to Cressey, the basic distinction between the two is that the former offers a return to the general public while the latter is generally predatory[69] and does not satisfy the need of the customers. There-fore, it is argued, while no one would miss a burglar if he is arrested, organised criminals would be missed as they meet the public demand by providing goods and services.[70]

Depending on the demand, criminals will diversify their activities into a range of illicit products. The Chinese Snakehead and the Turkish mafia are just two examples of such entities which engage in multiple businesses.[71] It is important to note, however, that the availability of certain goods and services in the illegal markets depends largely on relevant national laws restricting those goods and services. Schloenhardt rightly points out in this regard that the prohibition of particular goods and services through national legislation creates illegal markets, and this serves as an incentive for organised criminals to get involved.[72] Further-more, international law has been said to have contributed to the growth of illegal markets and organised crime. The multilateral treaties on protection of human rights, slavery, drug and arms trafficking are examples of legal provisions that have promoted the creation of illegal markets.[73]

It has been suggested that criminals seek to monopolise certain illegal markets to maximise their profits.[74] This is said to be another difference between organ-ised crime and ordinary crimes in that ordinary criminals, such as burglars, do

---

[66] Bundeskriminalamt, 'Organised Crime: 2008 National Situation Report' (2009) 8.

[67] W Filipkowski, 'Organised Crime in Poland as the Field of Research and Its Contemporary Situation', paper presented at the Research Conference on Organised Crime (Frankfurt 2008) 2.

[68] N Passas, 'Globalization and Transnational Crime: Effects of Criminogenic Asymmetries' in Williams and Vlassis, above ch 1 n 33, 24.

[69] The President's Commission on Law Enforcement and Administration of Justice, 'Task Force Report: Organized Crime' (1967), Appendix A, 29; Cressey, above n 12, 72; Schelling, above n 55, 180.

[70] Schelling, ibid, 180.

[71] Williams and Godson, above n 19, 326; Schloenhardt, above n 60, 216.

[72] Schloenhardt, ibid, 207.

[73] P Arlacchi, 'The Dynamics of Illegal Markets' in Williams and Vlassis, above ch 1 n 33, 7.

[74] Schloenhardt, above n 60, 211.

not fight with each other to claim monopoly over certain markets.[75] This idea on monopoly, however, has been disputed by many because such a claim is not supported by empirical evidence.[76] In practice, it would be extremely difficult for the most criminal groups to enjoy monopoly over goods and services, because of the transnational nature of crimes and the numbers of actors involved. In relation to drug trafficking and distribution, for example, the drug markets have become so competitive that it is virtually impossible to monopolise.[77]

Another key aspect of organised crime from an economic perspective is that criminals seek to secure longer-term economic gain. Many actors and authors emphasise this point. For example, the profits gained through various activities are redistributed and invested in human and other resources through money laundering.[78] In so doing, criminals make rational decisions based on a cost–benefit analysis.[79] This is different from ordinary crimes, where the proceeds derived from simple theft, for instance, remain with and are used by the criminals themselves for the most part without diversification and investment.[80] In this sense, organised crime is no different from legitimate business, because both aim to maximise profits by providing goods and services accompanied by rational decision-making. As a result, it has been argued that economic theories and models used to analyse legitimate business are equally applicable to organised crime,[81] the key difference being that organised criminals are not bound by the rules and regulations imposed by states.[82]

In order to maximise profits, organised criminal groups also engage in risk management. This happens at various levels. To begin with, for criminal organisations, their employees pose a major threat due to their knowledge of the illegal activities. In order to prevent them from collaborating with law enforcement authorities, organised criminals use a wide variety of methods to constrain them. For instance, the imposition of discipline through threats and violence is frequently used so that individual criminals do nothing detrimental to the business as a whole.[83] They also reward employees by giving them higher status or higher wages.[84] Furthermore, following from the analysis of cultural/social models noted above, it is also worth noting that personal relationships or solidarity play a part in risk management. It is easier for groups who share the same ethnic, political, religious or other traits to build a sense of trust and

---

[75] Schelling, above n 55, 183.

[76] Reuter, *Disorganized Crime: The Economics of the Visible Hand* (Cambridge, MIT Press,1983) xi; Woodiwiss, above n 2, 23.

[77] Hill, above ch 1 n 21, 23; G Pearson and D Hobbs, 'Middle Market Drug Distribution', Home Office Research Study No 227 (2001) 11–12.

[78] Schloenhardt, above n 60, 206 and 226.

[79] Cressey, above n 12, 72.

[80] Schloenhardt, above n 60, 205.

[81] Ibid, 206.

[82] Williams, above ch 1 n 33, 70–71.

[83] Schelling, above n 55, 172; Schloenhardt, above n 60, 216; Hill, above ch 1 n 21, 72–73.

[84] Schloenhardt, ibid, 217.

therefore promote co-operation as opposed to competition.[85] Another way to minimise the risk is to keep the lower-level street criminals separate from the higher-level bosses so that the latter do not face enforcement action even when those belonging to the former are arrested.[86] Other methods of risk management include, but are not limited to, the incorporation of a legal section/department into the criminal organisation to find loopholes in criminal law and justice systems,[87] bribery, money laundering and intelligence gathering.[88]

While analysis of organised crime as a set of activities sheds light on how criminals operate in illegal markets, there are a few points to be noted. For instance, the existence of illegal markets does not necessarily depend on organised criminal groups. These groups are said to have existed before the formation and expansion of illegal markets in the trade of drugs, human beings and weapons. This is corroborated by the fact that the major criminal organisations explored in Chapter 1, such as the Japanese Yakuza, Chinese Triads and Sicilian Cosa Nostra in Italy, have existed for a long time without getting themselves involved in illegal markets. These markets have in fact grown in line with 'the development of economic regulation, protection, and social support initiated by the modern Welfare state and the development of international law at the beginning of the twentieth century'.[89] It is also worth noting that organised crime tends to flourish in states which suffer from political, economic and social instabilities, as they do not have solid legal and administrative frameworks to regulate licit and illicit markets. Furthermore, as noted above, criminals would not provide illicit goods and services without a strong demand for them. In reality, therefore, various factors contribute to the growth of illicit markets.

It should also be noted that organised crime permeates the licit economy. Many organised criminals invest the profits they acquire from sales of illicit goods and services in licit enterprises, ranging from restaurants to the import/ export business.[90] They also run successful legal businesses, including gambling, labour unions and race tracks.[91] The linkage with the licit economy is also facilitated through the corruption of politicians and civil servants and through money laundering, where the proceeds obtained through criminal activities are gradually integrated into the legitimate economy. Among others, Italy provides a good example of organised criminal groups playing a dominant role in construction and other legitimate enterprises through corruption.[92] This affirms the point expressed above that criminals and criminal groups are not the only actors who

[85] Arlacchi, above n 73, 8
[86] Schloenhardt, above n 60, 217.
[87] Cohen, above n 4, 107.
[88] Williams and Godson, above n 19, 336–338.
[89] Paoli, above n 5, 63.
[90] Paoli and Fijnaut, above n 1, 319.
[91] Cressy, above n 12, 123.
[92] Paoli and Fijnaut, above n 1, 320.

facilitate organised crime.[93] From a practical point of view, this makes it difficult for law enforcement authorities to tackle organised crime.

What becomes apparent in analysing organised crime from a multi-disciplinary perspective is that there is no single, accurate way of describing the practice. The key concepts explored in this chapter are applicable to one or more types of organised crime and criminal groups. Given the changing nature of the crime and groups, it is extremely difficult, if not impossible, to make any generalisation. From a legal point of view, this means that any legal definition adopted at national, regional and international levels must be flexible enough to include a wide variety of criminal organisations and their activities. Furthermore, it is also desirable to have some types of international standards for all to follow in order to promote effective co-operation. The next section will examine the extent to which these are achieved.

2.3 Legal Definitions of Organised Crime in National and International Law

2.3.1 Definitions of Organised Crime in International Law

2.3.1.1 General Discussion

Under international law, an attempt to define organised crime was made in the early 1990s. The Eighth Congress on the Prevention of Crime and the Treatment of Offenders, held in 1990, defined organised crime as 'the large-scale or complex criminal activities carried out by tightly or loosely organised associations and aimed at the establishment, supply and exploitation of illegal markets at the expense of the society'.[94] The Congress also identified the transnational nature and the use of violence as elements of organised crime.[95] This definition reflects the mixture of concepts explored earlier in that it describes organised crime both as the set of actors (criminal association) and as the set of activities (operation in illegal market). This definition, however, would not have applied to those crimes which were committed by individuals who were not part of criminal associations and which were not necessarily aimed at exploitation of illegal markets. Furthermore, organised crime had to be large in scale, and purely local activities probably would have been excluded under this definition.

---

[93] C Morselli and C Giguere, 'Legitimate Strengths in Criminal Networks' (2006) 45 *Crime, Law and Social Change* 185, 188–89. See also M Levi et al, 'Lawyers as Crime Facilitators in Europe: An Introduction and Overview' (2005) 42 *Crime, Law and Social Change* 117.

[94] A/CONF.144/7 (26 July 1990), para 12.

[95] Ibid, paras 12–13.

The next indicator is the Naples Political Declaration and Global Action Plan against Organized Transnational Crime,[96] adopted at the Ministerial Conference in 1994. While stopping short of adopting a definition, the Declaration identified six main characteristics of organised crime. They are (1) group organisation to commit crime; (2) hierarchical links or personal relations which permit leaders to control the group; (3) violence, intimidation and corruption used to earn profits or control territories or markets; (4) laundering of illicit proceeds to further criminal activity and to infiltrate the legitimate economy; (5) the potential for expansion into any new activities beyond national borders; and (6) co-operation with other organised transnational criminal groups. These characteristics emphasise the organised nature of a criminal group as it makes it clear that organised crime was to be committed by a group with hierarchical links or personal relations with a leader at the top. It is also worth noting that the transnational nature of organised crime was explicitly recognised under the Naples Political Declaration.

Further development came in Europe, when the EU adopted the Joint Action on Criminal Organisations[97] in 1998. Article 1 defined a criminal organisation as:

> a structured association, over a period of time, of more than two persons, in concert with a view to committing crimes which are punishable by deprivation of liberty or a detention order of a maximum of at least four years or more or a more serious penalty, whether such offences are an end in themselves or a means of obtaining material benefits and, where appropriate, of improperly influencing the operation of public authorities.

This definition is similar to the characteristics given under the Naples Political Declaration as the emphasis is placed upon a structured group. However, it goes further, stating that a criminal group must exist for some time, thus excluding groups formed randomly or on an ad hoc basis. In addition, a criminal conduct in question must attract serious penalties, effectively ruling out petty crimes. It is also worth noting that a crime does not necessarily have to be aimed at obtaining benefits and therefore the ambit is broader under this definition of a criminal organisation.

The most important instrument on organised crime, however, is the Organised Crime Convention, as this is a legally binding instrument that can be ratified by states in all parts of the world. The very first draft was proposed by the Government of Poland in 1996.[98] Two months later, the UN General Assembly recognised a need to develop an international convention to address organised crime, and requested the Secretary-General to invite views from Member States

---

[96] A/49/748 (2 December 1994), 9–10. This was endorsed by the General Assembly through the General Assembly Resolution A/RES/49/159 (23 December 1994).

[97] Joint Action 98/733/JHA on making it a criminal offence to participate in criminal organisation in the Member States of the European Union, OJ L351/1 (29 December 1998). See Chapter 6 for the EU action against organised crime.

[98] A/C.3/51/7 (1 October 1996).

on this issue and comment on the draft proposed submitted by Poland.[99] It further requested the Commission on Crime Prevention and Criminal Justice[100] to consider, as a matter of priority, the question of the elaboration of an international convention. In response to recommendations of the Commission and the UN Economic and Social Council, the General Assembly decided to establish an open-ended group of experts within the Commission to elaborate upon a preliminary draft.[101] Poland offered to host a meeting for this purpose, which was held in February 1998.[102] Later that year, the United Nations General Assembly adopted a Resolution to formally establish an Ad Hoc Committee to elaborate on the convention.[103] The Ad Hoc Committee held 11 meetings to elaborate on the Organised Crime Convention and its Protocols, and the final version was endorsed by the General Assembly in November 2000.[104]

It should be noted from the outset that the Organised Crime Convention itself does not provide a definition of organised crime.[105] Instead, organised crime is to be understood as a 'serious crime' committed by an 'organised criminal group'. According to Article 2:

> 'Organised criminal group' shall mean a structured group of three or more persons, existing for a period of time and acting in concert with the aim of committing one or more serious crimes or offences established in accordance with this Convention, in order to obtain, directly or indirectly, a financial or other material benefit.

This is a definition similar to that adopted by the EU noted above. The key difference is that criminal offences are to be committed for the purpose of obtaining financial or material benefits, whereas the definition under the Joint Action was wide enough to include crimes committed without obtaining these benefits.[106]

'A structured group' means 'a group that is not randomly formed for the immediate commission of an offence'.[107] This excludes groups formed in a course of a riot, for example. The key phrase then, is 'existing for a certain period of time'. During the drafting stage, some states suggested the inclusion of a provi-

---

[99] A/RES/51/120 (12 December 1996).

[100] This a functional commission established by the UN Economic and Social Council.

[101] A/RES/52/85 (12 December 1997).

[102] Report of the meeting of the inter-sessional open-ended intergovernmental group of experts on the elaboration of a preliminary draft of a possible comprehensive international convention against organized transnational crime, E/CN.15/1998/5 (18 February 1998).

[103] A/RES/53/111 (9 December 1998).

[104] A/RES/55/25 (15 November 2000).

[105] It should be noted, however, that the very first draft of the Organised Crime Convention contained a definition which provided 'group activities of three or more persons, with hierarchical links or personal relationships, which permits their leaders to earn profits or control territories or markets, internal or foreign, by means of violence, intimidation or corruption, both in furtherance of criminal activity and in order to infiltrate the legitimate economy'. A/AC.245/4 (18 December 1998).

[106] The Organised Crime Convention also covers participation in criminal organisation and this extends to other serious crimes. See Chapter 3 for details.

[107] Art 2(c).

sion explaining this phrase, while others opposed such an inclusion.[108] The latter view prevailed as the phrase was deleted from the draft presented at the Eighth Session of the Ad Hoc Committee.[109] In addition, *travaux préparatoires* provide that the term 'structured group' would apply to both groups with hierarchical structures and non-hierarchical groups.[110] Taking this into account, Article 2(c) stipulates that a structured group does not have formally defined roles for its members, continuity of its membership or a developed structure.[111] This means that criminals based on networks come under the definition, and therefore that the definition is flexible.

A 'serious crime' is defined as a 'conduct constituting an offence punishable by a maximum deprivation of liberty of at least four years or a more serious penalty'.[112] This wording is the same as the EU Joint Action noted above. During the early stages of drafting the Convention, there was no agreement as to the length of a maximum deprivation of liberty. The major reason for this was that linking seriousness with the length of deprivation of liberty would create a difficulty because each state had different perceptions about the nature and seriousness of a particular crime, which would lead to varying sentencing practices.[113] Although some states suggested that the focus should be placed upon the nature of the act rather than the severity of punishment,[114] a maximum of four years or more was included in the end as a compromise.[115] While acknowledging the national differences, this might be regarded as an international consensus on what constitutes a serious crime.

There are two key elements in these definitions of 'serious crimes' committed by 'organised criminal groups'. The first is the organised nature of a group, as opposed to the organised nature of a criminal activity. At the First Session of the Ad Hoc Committee, some states, including the US, emphasised the organised nature of crime itself by using the term 'organised criminal activity'. [116] There was no consensus as to whether or not the Convention should include the definition of 'organised crime', 'organised criminal activity' or 'organised criminal group'.[117] It was at this stage that the term 'structured group' was introduced, and at the end of the Second Session, the draft convention included 'organised criminal group' instead of 'organised crime'.[118] Therefore, the organised nature

---

[108] A/AC.254/4/Rev.2 (12 April 1999), 6; A/AC.254/4/Rev.3 (19 May 1999), 5; A/AC.254/4/Rev.5 (16 November 1999), 5.

[109] A/AC.254/4/Rev.7 (3 February 2000), 3.

[110] Interpretative notes for the official records (*travaux préparatoires*) of the negotiation of the United Nations Convention against Transnational Organized Crime, A/AC.254/37 (11 September 2000), para 4 (hereinafter Interpretative Notes).

[111] Art 2(c).

[112] Art 2(b).

[113] A/AC.254/4/Rev.1 (10 February 1999), 5.

[114] A/AC.254/4/Rev.2, above n 108, 5.

[115] Above n 109, 3.

[116] A/AC.254/5 (19 December 1998), 18.

[117] D McClean, *Transnational Organized Crime: A Commentary on the UN Convention and Protocols* (Oxford, Oxford University Press, 2007) 39.

[118] A/AC.254/4/Rev.2, above n 108.

of the groups, not of the crime itself, is the defining characteristic, and some states have made this point clear.[119]

Another key element is profit. This has been a subject of intense discussion among states participating in drafting. Azerbaijan, for instance, expressed a view that the commission of crime is a means to an end of obtaining profits.[120] The US further argued that this element of profits is important as it distinguishes organised crime from terrorism.[121] In relation to the types of profits, some states, including Belgium, stated that the application of the Convention should be limited to those crimes committed for financial or material benefits. Others, such as Turkey,[122] Uruguay and Egypt, thought that those committed for political and other purposes should also be included under the scope.[123] The former view has prevailed, as the definition of an 'organised criminal group' in the final text limits itself to crime committed for financial and material gain. However, not all forms of organised crime are financially or materially motivated. These include computer hacking and co-operative distribution of child pornography.[124] As a result, it was agreed in the end that the term 'financial or material gain' should be interpreted broadly to include such purposes as sexual gratification.[125] What may be noticed in looking at these definitions under the Organised Crime Convention is that they are broad enough to cover a wide variety of activities committed by different types of criminal groups. Therefore, it is submitted that they serve as good guidance for all of those concerned to follow.

2.3.1.2 The Transnational Nature of Organised Crime

While the above definitions are flexible, it is important to note that the application of the Organised Crime Convention is somewhat limited by the requirement of transnationality in Article 3(2). The concept of 'transnational crime' is not exactly a new one. In the 1950s, Jessup defined 'transnational law' to mean all laws which 'regulates action or events that transcend national frontiers'.[126] Applying this to organised crime, transnational organised crime affects more than one state, and this definition has been supported at the international level. At the Fifth United Nations Congress on the Prevention of Crime and the Treatment of Offenders in 1975, the concept of transnational crime was defined as the crime 'which spans the borders of two or more countries'.[127] In the early 1990s, the United Nations

---

[119] Above n 116, 4, 9, 10, 13 and 18; above n 113, 4–5; A/AC.254/5/Add.3 (8 February 1999), 9.
[120] A/AC.254/5/Add.17 (5 January 2000), 3.
[121] Above n 116, 19.
[122] Ibid, 15.
[123] A/AC.254/4/Rev.2, above n 108, 4–5.
[124] Above n 116, 19.
[125] Above n 110, para 3.
[126] PC Jessup, *Transnational Law* (New Haven, Yale University Press, 1956) 2.
[127] A/CONF.56/3 (1–12 September 1975), para 22. The United Nations Crime Prevention and Criminal Justice Branch in the 1970s coined the term to describe 'criminal phenomena transcending

further defined the term as 'offences whose inception, prevention and/or direct or indirect effects involved more than one country'.[128] The Naples Political Declaration noted above also recognises this element. Obviously the transnational nature of a crime is not just limited to organised crime. Fijnaut argues that the term 'transnational crime' is a 'container-type concept' in that it includes different types of crimes, including corporate crime (tax evasion, social security fraud, dumping of goods, etc) professional crime (serious theft, kidnapping, piracy, insurance fraud) and political crime (terrorist related offences, genocide, etc).[129] However, the term is fitting for organised crime because transnational crime are almost invariably organised.[130]

In any event, Article 3(2) of the Organised Crime Convention provides that:

an offence is transnational in nature if:
(a) It is committed in more than one state;
(b) It is committed in one state but a substantial part of its preparation, planning, direction or control takes place in another state;
(c) It is committed in one state but involves an organized criminal group that engages in criminal activities in more than one state; or
(d) It is committed in one state but has substantial effects in another state.

Subparagraphs (a), (b) and (d) are straightforward. Subparagraph (c) provides that 'transnational crime' includes an act committed within a state without any effect on other states if committed by a criminal group which operates abroad. This effectively expands the notion of 'transnational' as it applies not only to criminal activities, but also actors. However, this simultaneously means that crimes committed by local groups which do not operate beyond national borders fall outside of the Convention. This excludes organised burglary committed by a gang, for example, no matter how serious the crime may be in a given society or even if the gang fits the definition of 'a criminal group' under the Organised Crime Convention. Whether or not such instances deserve equal attention is subject to debate, but it might make sense to treat them as the examples of domestic crime over which states have exclusive jurisdiction and do not require international co-operation.

---

international borders, transgressing the laws of several states or having an impact on another country'. GOW Mueller, 'Transnational Crime: Definitions and Concepts' in Combating Transnational Crime' in Williams and Vlassis, above ch 1 n 33, 13.

[128] A/CONF.169/15/Add.1 (4 April 1995), para 9. In a similar vein, Bossard defines transnational crime as 'an activity that is considered a criminal offence by at least two countries'. A Bossard, *Transnational Crime and Criminal Law* (Chicago, University of Chicago Office of International Criminal Justice, 1990) 5.

[129] Fijnaut (2000), above ch 1 n 39, 120–22.

[130] Mueller, above n 127, 13.

2.3.1.3   'Transnational' and 'International' Crime

Sometimes the terms 'international crime' and 'transnational crime' are used interchangeably by the media and commentators to describe a conduct or activity which has international dimensions. Under international law, however, there is a distinction between these acts, and therefore a clarification should be made. It is mainly a question of the nature of crime in question. Under international law, international crimes are regarded as the concern of the international community as a whole, or *delicta juris gentium*. They are those conducts which threaten the international order or international values.[131] These offences are directly prohibited by international law, namely international criminal law (ICL), and establish an individual criminal responsibility.[132] Currently, the number of crimes which belong to this category is limited. Under the Rome Statute of International Criminal Court (Rome Statute),[133] the most recent example of ICL, only war crimes, crimes of aggression, crimes against humanity and genocide are regarded as belonging to this category.[134] Prohibition of these offences is firmly established in customary international law,[135] and constitutes *jus cogens*.[136] These crimes can be committed within the jurisdiction of one state, unlike the notion of 'transnational crime'.

One of the reasons why international crimes are said to shock the conscience of humanity and of the international community is perhaps because the human cost is very high. From a moral point of view, international crimes threaten the human life and dignity, and therefore offend fundamental human values.[137] As a result, international crimes can easily be regarded as inherently wrong or evil, or *mala in se*.[138] A further point to note is that international crimes are often committed on a massive scale. Take a crime against humanity, for instance. In order for a conduct to be recognised as such, it must be committed in a widespread and systematic manner.[139] Consequently, the human cost is likely to be

---

[131] Boister, above ch 1 n 68, 967. See also A Cassese, *International Criminal Law*, 2nd edn (Oxford, Oxford University Press, 2007) 11.

[132] EM Wise, 'The Obligation to Extradite or Prosecute' (1993) 27 *Israel Law Review* 268, 269. See Chapter 4 for the principle of individual criminal responsibility.

[133] A/CONF.183/9 (17 July 1998).

[134] Art 5.

[135] Customary international law is a source of international law stipulated under Art 38 of the Statute of the International Court of Justice and is generally binding on all states, unlike treaties which only bind those which ratify them. See, among others, I Brownlie, *Principles of Public International Law*, 6th edn (Oxford, Oxford University Press, 2003), 6–12.

[136] Under Art 53 of the Vienna Convention on the Law of Treaties 1969, 1155 UNTS 331, *jus cogens* is 'a peremptory norm of general international law is a norm accepted and recognized by the international community of states as a whole as a norm from which no derogation is permitted'. See further A Orakhelashvili, *Peremptory Norms in International Law* (Oxford, Oxford University Press, 2006) ch 2.

[137] W Schabas, 'International Crime' in D Armstrong (ed), *Routledge Handbook of International Law* (London, Routledge-Cavendish, 2008) 269.

[138] Ibid.

[139] Art 7 of the Rome Statute.

greater. Examples of this include the Nazi Holocaust, ethnic cleansing in the Balkans and genocide in Rwanda.

Transnational organised crime, in contrast, is not generally regarded as a crime of concern for the international community. It can affect interests of more than one state, but not all states which collectively constitutes the international community.[140] In other words, transnational organised crime is not regarded as being as serious as international crime. The crimes in this category are dealt with by an emerging branch of international law known as 'transnational criminal law' (TCL) which does not establish individual criminal responsibility in international law, nor does it prohibit a conduct directly.[141] Instead, TCL promotes indirect suppression of a crime through domestic criminal law by imposing obligations on states to enact legislation. Furthermore, prohibition of organised crime is not generally regarded as part of customary international law.[142] However, the last point may be open to question, because organised crime has been in existence for a long time in history, as noted in Chapter 1, and states have criminalised a variety of associated conducts in their domestic legislation.[143] Moreover, it may be argued that transnational organised crimes, such as money laundering, trafficking of drugs and other illicit goods, do not necessarily result in massive victimisation which offends the fundamental value of humanity as such. In summary, transnational organised crime may appropriately be termed as *mala prohibita*,[144] or conducts which are wrong because they are prohibited by law.

While these are valid points, a clear dividing line cannot be drawn in many cases in practice. In terms of the human cost, it may be true that some crimes, such as trafficking of cultural/national heritage, do not have a direct impact upon people and therefore it may be difficult to argue that they shock the conscience of humanity. Nevertheless, other forms of organised crime produce a large number of victims, and therefore the human cost is high. Trafficking of human beings is a good example. It has been estimated that approximately 800,000 people annually are trafficked worldwide for sexual and labour exploitation.[145] The same is true for drug trafficking. The victims in this process are not restricted to victims of violence inflicted by drug lords and other associated criminals; they also include those who use drugs, including persons who contract diseases such as HIV/AIDS, as well as individuals in the drug producing states who are forced to cultivate and process narcotics.[146] There-

---

[140] This reasoning has been applied, for instance, to piracy. Cassese, above n 131, 12.

[141] Boister, above ch 1 n 68.

[142] Ibid, 963.

[143] The sources of custom can derive from, among other things, policy statements, official manuals, legislation and judicial decisions. Brownlie, above n 135.

[144] Schabas, above n 137, 269.

[145] US Department of State, 'Trafficking in Persons Report 2009', available at www.state.gov/g/tip/rls/tiprpt/2009.

[146] T Obokata, 'Illicit Cycle of Narcotics from a Human Rights Perspective' (2007) 25 *Netherlands Quarterly of Human Rights* 159, 162.

fore, the human cost is certainly high for some of these crimes. The long-term effects of these crimes are also very serious, given the time need by victims to recover. In addition, the large number of victims worldwide also suggests that organised crime occurs more frequently and in a widespread manner. International crime is more sporadic and does not affect every single state. Moreover, some crimes, such as child pornography and sexual/labour exploitation, offend fundamental human values. Therefore the concept of *mala in se* is relevant for some forms of organised crime.[147]

It is submitted further that the argument that international crime affects the interest or value of the international community whereas organised crime does not is difficult to sustain. Organised crime threatens the rule of law, good governance, democracy and state sovereignty, as criminals resort to violence, intimidation, corruption and other means to achieve their aims. It goes without saying that these are the key principles for maintaining friendly relations and co-operation among states, as well as international peace and security. This is all the more so in cases where organised criminal groups co-operate actively with terrorists, as noted in Chapter 1. These are also the principles which must be actively respected and promoted if a state wishes to be recognised as a legitimate member of the international community. Therefore, it seems reasonable to argue that organised crime does affect the interest of the international community.

Essentially what constitutes a crime of concern for the international community as a whole is a political question as it is states which adopt international instruments and incorporate them into domestic legal systems. It is worth noting here that inclusion of drug trafficking and terrorism was discussed during the drafting stage of the Rome Statute.[148] The eventual exclusion of these crimes shows that the states did not consider them sufficiently serious or important when adopting the Rome Statute in 1998. However, the perceptions of states are not static and can change in line with the evolving nature of criminalities and the current trend of world affairs. This may be seen in various resolutions passed by the United Nations Security Council in recent times. For instance, it expressed its 'strong concern' about criminals and those involved in narcotics trading in Afghanistan[149] and threats to sub-regional stability in Liberia posed by 'drug trafficking, organised crime and illicit arms'.[150] It has also 'strongly condemned' violations of women's rights, including rape and

---

[147] Schabas, above n 137, 269.

[148] H Von Hebel and D Robinson, 'Crimes within the Jurisdiction of the Court' in RS Lee (ed), *The International Criminal Court: The Making of the Rome Statute* (The Hague, Kluwer Law International, 1999) 86; P Robinson, 'The Missing Crimes' in A Cassese, P Gaeta and J Jones (eds), *The Rome Statute of the International Criminal Court: A Commentary*, Vol I (Oxford, Oxford University Press, 2002) 497–525.

[149] Security Council Resolution 1890 (8 October 2009).

[150] Security Council Resolution 1885 (15 September 2009). See also Security Council Resolution 1840 (14 October 2008), in which the Council underscored that 'international illicit trafficking of persons, drugs and arms' affected the stability of Haiti. Acting under Chapter VII of the UN Charter, the Council in this resolution invited Member States to co-operate with Haiti to address these crimes.

other sexual violence in conflict and post-conflict situations,[151] and recruitment and kidnapping of children for their use as soldiers, as well as sexual and other forms of violence against them.[152] In addition, it reaffirmed that proliferation of nuclear, chemical and biological weapons, including trafficking of these weapons by non-state actors, constituted a threat to international peace and security.[153] Furthermore, at the 11th United Nations Congress on Crime Prevention and Criminal Justice, which took place in Bangkok in 2005, the delegates agreed that transnational organised crime presented one of the most serious security challenges facing the international community.[154] All of these demonstrate that various forms of organised crime can constitute a concern to the international community and threaten national and international peace and security. Therefore a clear line between 'international' and 'transnational' crime cannot be drawn in many cases.

2.3.2   Definitions of Organised Crime in National Law[155]

Having examined the definition adopted under international law, it is worth exploring the extent to which national legislation reflects international standards. In some states, organised crime is understood as a criminal offence committed by criminal groups, and they focus on the organised nature of the group. There are, however, discrepancies as to what constitute such a group. For instance in 1982, the Italian government introduced an offence of mafia-type criminal association through Act No 646, which modified the Criminal Code.[156] Under this law, a mafia-type association consists of three or more persons.[157] In Austria, a relevant law is the Austrian Criminal Code[158] as amended in 2002 and 2004. Its provisions make a distinction between regular criminal groups, such as common gangs and organised criminal groups. Section 278 (Kriminelle Vereinigung) defines a common gang as a structured group of more than two persons that is established over a period of time to commit one or more crimes listed in the Criminal Code. Section 278a (Kriminelle Organisation) further defines a criminal organisation as an 'entrepreneurial' group of a large number of persons established over a period of time which (i) aims at

---

[151] Security Council Resolution 1889 (5 October 2009); Security Council Resolution 1888 (30 September 2009).

[152] Security Council Resolution 1882 (4 August 2009).

[153] Security Council Resolution 1874 (12 June 2009); Security Council Resolutions 1810 (25 April 2008).

[154] Report of the Eleventh United Nations Congress on Crime Prevention and Criminal Justice, A/CONF.203/18 (17 May 2005), para 111.

[155] National legislation of the world explored in this book are taken from, among other sources, the International Money Laundering Information Network (www.imolin.org/imolin/index.html); Refworld (UNHCR website: www.unhcr.org/cgi-bin/texis/vtx/refworld/rwmain); World Law Guide (www.lexadin.nl/wlg/); Legislationline (OSCE: www.legislationline.org/).

[156] Paoli and Fijnaut, above ch 1 n 3, 34.

[157] Ibid.

[158] BGBI No60/1974.

the repeated and planned commission of serious crimes, (ii) has the objective to secure large profits or exert significant influence on the political or financial life through committing serious crime and (iii) seeks to corrupt or intimidate others.[159] One of the key differences here is the number of people involved in these groups. Under the Prevention of Organised Crime Act 1998[160] of South Africa, a criminal gang is defined as

> any formal or informal ongoing organisation, association or group of three or more persons, which has as one of its activities the commission of one or more criminal offences . . . and whose members individually or collectively engage in or have engaged in a pattern of criminal gang activity;

Finally, the French Penal Code provides for sections in relation to criminal association. Article 450-1 defines it as 'any group formed or any conspiracy established with a view to the preparation, marked by one or more material actions, of one or more felonies, or of one or more misdemeanours punished by at least five years' imprisonment'. It is evident that there are discrepancies as to the number of people thought necessary form to a criminal group/association.

In other jurisdictions, types of criminal activities are clearly spelled out. In California, organised crime is defined as 'crime which is of a conspiratorial nature and that is either of an organised nature and which seeks to supply illegal goods and services such as narcotics, prostitution, loan sharking, gambling, and pornography'.[161] Under the Crime Commission Act 2002 of Australia, 'serious and organised crime' is defined as an offence:

> that is a serious offence within the meaning of the Proceeds of Crime Act 2002, an offence of a kind prescribed by the regulations or an offence that involves any of the following: (i) theft; (ii) fraud; (iii) tax evasion; (iv) money laundering; (v) currency violations; (vi) illegal drug dealings; (vii) illegal gambling; (viii) obtaining financial benefit by vice engaged in by others; (ix) extortion; (x) violence; (xi) bribery or corruption of, or by, an officer of the Commonwealth, an officer of a state or an officer of a Territory; (xii) perverting the course of justice; (xiii) bankruptcy and company violations; (xiv) harbouring of criminals; (xv) forging of passports; (xvi) firearms; (xvii) armament dealings; (xviii) illegal importation or exportation of fauna into or out of Australia; (xix) cybercrime.[162]

One disadvantage of such legislation is that exhaustive lists hinder applying legal proscription to emerging and new forms of organised crime. This necessitates numerous time-consuming amendments and means limited suppression in the interim.

In addition, it is worth noting that organised crime can be committed for purposes other than financial or material benefits. The Control of Organised

---

[159] The Swiss Criminal Code also makes this distinction between common and organised criminal groups. E Symeonidou-Kastanidou, 'Towards a New Definition of Organised Crime in the European Union' (2007) 15 *European Journal of Crime, Criminal Law and Criminal Justice* 83, 98–99.

[160] Act No 121, Government Gazette No 19553.

[161] California Control of Profits of Organized Crime Act 1982, Penal Code Part 1, Title 7, 21; 186.

[162] Section 4(d).

Crime Act 1999 of the Indian state of Maharashtra defines organised crime as any continuing unlawful activity by an individual, singly or jointly, either as a member of an organised crime syndicate or on behalf of such syndicate, by use of violence or threat of violence or intimidation or coercion, or other unlawful means, with the objective of . . . *promoting insurgency*.[163]

Under the Nigerian Criminal Code, 'an unlawful society' is a group of 10 or more people which, among others, commits acts of violence and intimidation against the government.[164] A similar provision exists in the Pakistani Criminal Code, where it criminalises 'unlawful assembly'.[165] Furthermore, in Greece the definition of offences to be committed by a 'criminal group' include terrorist activities, such as hostage taking, hijacking, attacks on law enforcement and military authorities and use of explosives and weapons of mass destruction.[166] A link with terrorism is also recognised in Israel.[167]

Finally, specific definitions of organised crime or criminal group are not given in the national legislation of some states. In addition to Germany and Poland, noted above, Jamaica,[168] Vietnam[169] and the UK[170] belong to this category. Their law enforcement authorities have adopted working definitions instead. A lack of legal definitions has its advantage in that it allows law enforcement agencies to be more flexible in detecting and suppressing organised crime and related activities without the need to adopt or amend national legislation. There are, however, fundamental problems in not having a definition mandated by legislation. Different agencies in a given state, such as the police, special departments for organised crime and the customs office, can adopt different working definitions, which can lead to varied responses, making it difficult to facilitate inter-agency co-operation. The varied interpretations can also prevent effective co-operation at the regional and international levels. If a state chooses not to adopt a legal definition, it is essential that a working definition is followed by all concerned agencies to maintain consistency and coherence in law enforcement and international co-operation. A more serious problem is that a lack of definition goes against the principle of legality, which provides, among other things, that an offence must be clearly defined.

In analysing national legislation, several points emerge. To begin with, many of the definitions explored above are wide in scope and therefore are capable of addressing the various forms of organised crime explored earlier in this chapter.

---

[163] Section 2(e), Act No 30 (1999). Emphasis added. Some of the definitions noted above also do not focus on the economic aspect.

[164] Art 62. No definitions of 'organised crime' or 'criminal organisation' are given under the Code.

[165] Section 141, ACT XLV of 1986 as amended.

[166] Art 1 of the Law 1916 on the Protection of Society against Organised Crime 1990, Official Gazette of the Government of the Greek Republic, Vol. 1, No 187.

[167] Combating Criminal Organizations Law, 5763-2003.

[168] US Department of State, 'International Narcotics Control Strategy Report 2009', available at www.state.gov/p/inl/rls/nrcrpt/2009/vol1/index.htm.

[169] The Criminal Code does not include any definition. The government had not ratified the Organised Crime Convention as of 2009.

[170] See Chapter 5 for a case study of the UK.

These definitions are also flexible enough to cope with the changing nature of organised crime without a need to seek legislative amendments, which can take a very long time. This degree of flexibility is necessary in order to promote speedy responses. However, it is also apparent that the international standards set by the Organised Crime Convention are not necessarily reflected at the national level. Some of the laws mentioned above were adopted before the Organised Crime Convention, and yet any move to modify them in accordance with it cannot be seen in many jurisdictions. In relation to the laws adopted or amended after the adoption of the Organised Crime Convention, there still are discrepancies, and they are not necessarily in line with international standards.

This highlights the difficulty of implementing international standards on organised crime in practice. This is perhaps less so for international crimes as the prohibition regime has been established as customary law and all states are bound by it. Organised crimes, in contrast, are conducts regulated by treaties, and this leaves an option of not becoming a party to relevant instruments, such as the Organised Crime Convention. This is the weakness of TCL, and it will become apparent later in this book that this has much to do with the principle of state sovereignty where states are able to adopt legislation which reflects political, economic and social developments at the national level.

2.4   Conclusions

This chapter explored some of the major theories, concepts and legal definitions of organised crime and criminal groups from a multidisciplinary perspective. It is evident that a wide variety of views exist, and there is no single, accurate way to describe the phenomenon. This is also reflected in national legislation as discrepancies in the definitions of organised crime and criminal organisations are recognised in various parts of the world. The Organised Crime Convention can be used to lessen such discrepancies as it adopts common definitions such as 'serious crime' and 'criminal group'. Nevertheless, it has been shown that, while the majority of the states within the international community have signed or ratified the Convention, the adoption of common definitions is far from reality. All of these also show the fluid and complex nature of organised crime, because states would have no problem in adopting common definitions if the manifestation of organised crime were the same everywhere.

While the Organised Crime Convention is not strictly followed at the moment, it still reflects the will of the international community to consolidate its efforts to promote effective action against organised crime. As will be shown below, it can also be used to build mutual confidence and trust among states, and this can make it easier to facilitate international co-operation. The Convention is still a young instrument, only entering into force in September 2003. Given the sensitive nature of the subject matter, it will require extra time on the part of states to modify their legal and other frameworks to address organised crime. Therefore it is premature to conclude that the Organised Crime Convention is without any value. What can be said from the brief analysis above is that the definitions given under the Convention are broad enough to accommodate the complex nature of organised crime, and therefore can still be regarded as an important first step forward for addressing the practice in a more comprehensive way.

3

Obligations of States under International Law

3.1 Introduction

The purpose of this chapter is to explore the key obligations imposed upon states in addressing transnational organised crime. As TCL provides the main framework for policy implementation, this will be the main focus here, with particular reference to the Organised Crime Convention. It will also be shown that other branches of international law, such as ICL and international human rights law (IHRL), can usefully supplement TCL to effectively promote combat organised crime, and therefore will be analysed where appropriate. What becomes apparent in exploring the nature and extent of obligations is that, while the Organised Crime Convention provides a comprehensive framework to prohibit organised criminal activities and promote international co-operation, it is difficult to judge its efficacy given that it only came into force in 2003 and will need more time in operation before in-depth analysis is possible. What is evident is that TCL alone is not sufficient as it fails to address important issues such as the rights of defendants and suspects, as well as immunity and limitation periods. It is also an instrument primarily to promote a criminal justice response to organised crime through prosecution and punishment and international co-operation regarding criminal matters. It does not focus on other important areas, such as the causes and consequences of organised crime. Therefore other branches of international law also have an important role to play in suppression and prevention of transnational organised crime.

3.2 The Nature and Extent of Obligations under International Law

3.2.1 Prohibition of Organised Crime and Associated Acts

The main purpose of TCL is to promote indirect crime prevention at the national level. As will be shown below, the Organised Crime Convention and its Protocols[1] oblige states to criminalise various conducts related to organised crime. There are other pre-existing 'suppression conventions'[2] which oblige states to prohibit certain crime including trafficking of drugs,[3] cultural property,[4] endangered species,[5] nuclear materials,[6] offences relating to child pornography,[7] cyber crime[8] and counterfeiting.[9] However, as the Organised Crime Convention is not subject specific like these suppression conventions, its benefit is that it can be used to prosecute and punish a variety of criminal activities, provided that they are serious crimes committed by criminal groups as defined in the same Convention.

In addition to organised crimes themselves, states are obliged to prohibit participation in organised crime groups. Under Article 5(1)(a)(i) of the Organised Crime Convention, states must criminalise agreements to commit a serious crime for financial/material benefit. This is commonly known as an inchoate offence of conspiracy prevalent in common law jurisdictions. While this offence is recognised in some suppression conventions,[10] it is not in others. Therefore, the Organised Crime Convention fills this gap to ensure that conspiracy for all types of organised crime is punished. Article 5(1)(a)(ii) also criminalises participation in criminal and other activities of a criminal group with knowledge of either the aim and general criminal activity of such a group or its intention

---

[1] Protocol to Prevent, Suppress and Punish Trafficking in Persons and Protocol against the Smuggling of Migrant by Land, Sea and Air, A/RES/55/25 (15 November 2000); Protocol against the Illicit Manufacturing and Trafficking in Firearms, Their Parts and Components and Ammunition 2001, A/RES/55/255 (32 May 2001).

[2] These are crime control treaties concluded for the purpose of suppressing harmful behaviour by non-state actors. There are over 200 suppression conventions. Boister, above ch 1 n 68, 955.

[3] Drug Trafficking Convention 1988.

[4] Convention on the Means of Prohibiting and Preventing the Illicit Import, Export and Transfer of Ownership of Cultural Property 1970 (UNESCO Cultural Convention), 823 UNTS 231; Convention for the Protection of the World Cultural and Natural Heritage 1972, 11 ILM 1358; Convention on the Protection of Archaeological, Historical and Artistic Heritage of the American Nations 1976, 15 ILM 1350.

[5] Convention on Endangered Species.

[6] Convention on the Physical Protection of Nuclear Materials 1979, 18 ILM 1419; European Convention on the Protection of Environment Through Criminal Law 1998, ETS No 172.

[7] Optional Protocol to the CRC.

[8] European Convention on Cyber Crime.

[9] International Convention for the Suppression of Counterfeiting Currency 1929, 112 LNTS 371.

[10] See, eg Art 1(c)(iv) of the Drug Trafficking Convention 1988; Art 7(g) of the Convention on Nuclear Materials 1979; Art 3 of the Optional Protocol to the CRC.

to commit the crimes in question. Examples of this include arranging transport, knowing that it will be used to traffic prohibited items, or running a safe house for criminals. This may be regarded as a form of joint criminal enterprise. Simply put, joint criminal enterprise is established where several persons having a common purpose embark on criminal activity that is then carried out either jointly or by some members of this plurality of persons.[11] The main difference between conspiracy and joint criminal enterprise is that the former stands as soon as criminals reach an agreement, whereas the latter requires concrete crimes to be committed.[12] In any event, it must be demonstrated that he/she has knowledge of the nature of the criminal group, and therefore mere membership of such a group is not sufficient for conviction.[13] In addition, Article 5(1)(b) obliges states to prohibit secondary participation, such as aiding, abetting or counselling the commission of a serious crime.

The rationale for this inclusion of participation in a criminal group was expressed by the European Parliament when it was considering the issue of organised crime:

> Making participation in a criminal organisation a criminal offence thus serves primarily the purpose of exposing to criminal penalties those persons who contribute substantively to the operation of a criminal organisation without themselves directly committing any criminal offence. They include primarily the members at 'leadership and advisory level' within the criminal organisation and also those individuals who act as protectors, advisers and promoters in the police force, the legal system, or in the political and economic world to set up what can amount to a 'buffer zone' around the criminal organisation.'[14]

There is, however, a major problem with Article 5 of the Organised Crime Convention, conspiracy in particular. Sometimes an act can be very remote from the actual commission of a crime. For instance, some individuals can simply agree to traffic narcotics and be held liable even when they do not actually commit the offence itself. It has been pointed out that this runs the risk of undermining the principle *nullum crimen sine actus*,[15] which provides that the actual commission of act is necessary for prosecution and punishment. This point was debated among states while drafting the Organised Crime Convention, because some Member States did not criminalise offences such as conspiracy

---

[11] *Prosecutor v Tadic*, IT-94-1-T, Appeal Judgment (15 July 1999), para 190.

[12] See Separate Opinion of Judge Hunt in *Prosecutor v Milutinovic, Sainovic and Ojdanic, Decision on Dragoljib Ojdanic's Motion Challenging Jurisdiction—Joint Criminal Enterprise*, IT-99-37-AR72 (21 May 2003), para 23. In practice, however, these two overlap. In most states of the US, conspiracy requires an overt act in furtherance of a common plan or agreement. A Danner and J Martinez, 'Guilty Associations: Joint Criminal Enterprise, Command Responsibility and the Development of International Criminal Law' (2005) 93 *California Law Review* 75, 119.

[13] *Prosecutor v Brdanin*, IT-99-36-T, Trial Judgment (1 September 2004), para 263.

[14] Doc A4-0349/97 (5 November 1997), quoted in V Mitsilegas, 'Defining Organised Crime in the European Union: The Limits of European Criminal Law in an Area of 'Freedom, Security and Justice" (2001) 26 *European Law Review* 565, 572.

[15] Ibid.

in their jurisdiction.[16] The matter was eventually settled when the phrase 'in accordance with the fundamental legal principles of its domestic legal system' was inserted to allow some leeway for each state.[17] This reflects the principle of state sovereignty, and the offence of conspiracy might not be punished in some states in practice. A recent report submitted to the Conference of Parties established by the Organised Crime Convention reveals that most states which submitted their responses do have related pre-existing legislation or have since criminalised these conducts.[18]

In addition, states are under an obligation to prohibit other acts associated with organised crime. Of particular importance is money laundering.[19] Article 6 provides the definition of money laundering,[20] and a point to note is the term 'intentionally'. This excludes money laundering committed through negligence or without knowledge. Therefore, if financial institutions and banks are not aware they are being used for money laundering, they should not be held liable. This is in line with the general principle of criminal law: *actus non facit reum nisi mens sit rea*.[21] Article 7 then obliges states to take action against money laundering. For instance, states are to institute a supervisory mechanism over financial institutions to deter and detect instances of money laundering.[22] It also obliges them to 'consider' adopting measures to detect and monitor the flow of cash beyond national borders, such as the imposition of a reporting obligation on individuals and financial institutions.[23] This last point on reporting obligations is worth noting as it demonstrates that TCL as represented by the Organised Crime Convention indirectly imposes an obligation on non-state actors to co-operate with the authorities through national law.[24]

These provisions on money laundering are strengthened by Articles 12 and 13, which deal with freezing, confiscation and seizure of criminal proceeds/assets, as well as facilitation of international co-operation for these purposes. These measures are important because they can deter future commission of organised crime by hindering profit making and retention. Article 14 of the Organised

---

[16] Above ch 2 n 108, 8.

[17] Ibid, 7.

[18] CTOC/COP/2005/2/Rev.2 (25 August 2008), para 6.

[19] Also listed under Art 3(1)(b) of the Drug Trafficking Convention 1988; European Convention on Laundering, Search, Seizure, and Confiscation of the Proceeds from Crime 1990, ETS No 141; European Convention on Laundering, Search, Seizure, and Confiscation of the Proceeds from Crime and on the Financing of Terrorism 2005, ETS No 198.

[20] Under Arts 6(1)(a)(i), money laundering is defined as '[t]he conversion or transfer of property, knowing that such property is the proceeds of crime, for the purpose of concealing or disguising the illicit origin of the property or of helping any person who is involved in the commission of the predicate offence to evade the legal consequences of his or her action'. The act also includes (under Art 6(1)(a)(ii)) '[t]he concealment or disguise of the true nature, source, location, disposition, movement or ownership of or rights with respect to property, knowing that such property is the proceeds of crime'.

[21] It is a Latin phrase which translates as 'an act does not make a man guilty of a crime, unless his mind be also guilty'.

[22] Arts 7(1)(a) and (b).

[23] Art 7(2).

[24] See Chapter 4 for the position of non-state actors.

Crime Convention further allows states to dispose of the proceeds of crime in accordance with domestic law. They can be used, for example, to compensate victims, invest in technology to detect organised crime or provide assistance to states lacking in capabilities to combat organised crime. A point to note, however, is that the Convention does not restrict the rules relating to diplomatic or state immunity, or those of international organisations.[25] Under the Vienna Convention on Diplomatic Relations 1961,[26] for instance, any property found within the premises of a diplomatic mission is immune from search and requisition.[27] The same rule is also stipulated under the Convention on the Privileges and Immunities of the United Nations 1946.[28] These existing rules may cause difficulties when diplomatic agents or personnel of international organisations commit money laundering.

Two more related offences are criminalised under the Organised Crime Convention. They are corruption[29] and obstruction of justice under Articles 8 and 23 respectively. A provision on corruption was not included in the first draft[30] but, along with the proposals from the US and Uruguay, it was included in the second one.[31] Simply put, corruption involves giving and receiving of 'an undue advantage'. While some states expressed the view during the drafting stage that this term should be clarified or rephrased,[32] the final version retained the same language. Unfortunately, the *travaux préparatoires* do not provide any guidance on the meaning, and therefore it remains unclear. Another problem is that Article 8 only applies to public officials of state parties and not private entities such as MNCs. Furthermore, Article 8 obliges states only to 'consider' establishing an offence of corruption involving foreign officials and personnel of international organisations. The weakness evident in this wording is perhaps due to the immunity granted to them, as explained above. The measures for prevention, detection and punishment of corruption are to be left to states to decide in accordance with their legal systems under Article 9. It is unfortunate that Article 9 is too general and does not provide detailed guidance on how to tackle the root causes of corruption, such as low salaries among public/law enforcement officials, the deep-rooted culture of corruption, and other factors conducive to the growth of corruption. Without effective measures addressing these, the problem of corruption will continue to exist. All of these demonstrate that the Organised Crime Convention on its own is not sufficient to combat corruption.

---

[25] Interpretative Notes, above ch 2 n 110, para 20.
[26] 500 UNTS 95.
[27] Art 22(3).
[28] Art II, ss 2 and 3, 1 UNTS 15.
[29] See also United Nations Convention against Corruption 2003, A/RES/58/4 (31 October 2003); European Criminal Law Convention on Corruption 1999, ETS No 173; Inter-American Convention against Corruption 1996, 35 ILM 724; African Union Convention on Preventing and Combating Corruption, 43 ILM 5.
[30] A/AC.254/4 (15 December 1998).
[31] Above ch 2 n 113, 11.
[32] A/AC.254/4/Rev.4 (19 July 1999), 13.

The UN Corruption Convention does, however, address some of these problems. For instance, states are obliged to criminalise giving undue advantage to foreign officials and the personnel of international organisations,[33] and to take measures against corruption involving private sectors.[34] In relation to prevention, states are to establish effective anti-corruption policies (Article 5) and an independent body responsible for implementation (Articles 6), to strengthen the systems for recruitment, retention and promotion in the public sector (Article 7), to create codes of conduct for public officials (Article 8) and to work closely with the private sector (Article 12). It is encouraging that, of the state parties which submitted implementation reports, 78% claim to have adopted action plans and other corruption prevention strategies.[35] In Latvia, for example, members of civil society participate in developing policies on corruption to promote transparency, and diplomats in the UK must undergo training on corruption to achieve promotion.[36] States such as Fiji, Morocco, Pakistan and Rwanda have established independent bodies to deal with corruption.[37]

As to obstruction of justice, Article 23 obliges states to criminalise the use or threat of force or intimidation or giving an undue advantage to induce false testimony, or interfere with the production of evidence or the official duties of judicial or law enforcement authorities. It goes without saying that effective action against obstruction of justice is fundamental to preserving the rule of law and the integrity of justice. Its importance is heightened by the need to protect witnesses and other participants of the criminal justice processes. This is an offence which previously has been overlooked in other suppression conventions, and therefore the Organised Crime Convention marks an important step forward. Most states have legislation criminalising the obstruction of justice,[38] and Article 23 is supplemented by the UN Corruption Convention, which also has a provision on this.[39]

While imposing obligations on states to enact national legislation to prohibit and punish the organised crime and associated acts noted above is an important first step, simply utilising domestic criminal law is problematic for two reasons. First, each jurisdiction defines an offence according to its political, cultural and social traditions. The definitions of organised crime explored in Chapter 2 illustrate this. The practical effect of variation is that certain acts may be regarded as offences in some jurisdiction but not in others. Secondly, the level of punishment also varies internationally. This means that some criminals are punished

---

[33] Art 16.

[34] Art 21.

[35] Self-assessment of the implementation of the United Nations Convention against Corruption, CAC/COSP/2008/2 (7 December 2007), para 30.

[36] Ibid, para 33 and 35.

[37] Compliance with the United Nations Convention against Corruption: Report of the Secretariat, CAC/COSP/2009/9 (9 September 2009), paras 35 and 36.

[38] Implementation of the United Nations Convention against Transnational Organized Crime: Consolidated Information Received from States for the First Reporting Cycle, CTOC/COP/2005/2/Rev.2 (25 August 2008), paras 23–26 (hereinafter Implementation Report 2008 No 1).

[39] Art 25.

more severely than others. Consequently, many instances of organised crime may not be punished properly, depending on where the criminals are arrested, prosecuted and sentenced.

Another important function of TCL, then, is to reduce such instances of variations and inconsistency by promoting a degree of harmonisation or approximation of substantive criminal law among Member States. This is done through the adoption of common definitions of various criminal offences. Relevant Articles under the Organised Crime Convention include Article 2 (Use of Terms), Article 6 (Money Laundering) and Article 8 (Corruption). Trafficking and Smuggling Protocols also provide definitions of these practices.[40] These do not mean that states will use the same definitions to counter organised crime. Once again, the contrary was shown in the previous chapter. This is heightened by the principle of state sovereignty, explicitly recognised under Article 4 of the Organised Crime Convention, which can be used as a justification for non-compliance. However, it is to be noted simultaneously that such terms set a minimum threshold for all Member States. A good example is the definition of 'serious crime', which is regarded as conduct that carries a sentence of at least four years' imprisonment. Furthermore, for those states which have not adopted any definition of organised crime or criminal groups, the Organised Crime Convention is likely to be used as a template or model to enact national legislation, particularly when they have ratified it. Therefore, TCL can still promote a degree of harmonisation for effective co-operation.

While it is apparent that TCL plays a key role in obliging states to prohibit and punish organised crime, this obligation is strengthened by other branches of international law. ICL is one example. This branch of international law becomes relevant when a crime can be considered 'international crime'. It has been argued elsewhere that trafficking of human beings can be regarded as a crime against humanity in certain circumstances[41] and, given that some aspects of organised crime have been regarded as affecting the interest of the international community or international peace and security, there is a prospect in the future of elevating other crimes to the status of *delicta juris gentium*. While the involvement of international penal tribunals such as the International Criminal Court (ICC) is recognised under ICL, the primary obligation to prosecute and punish is still imposed upon states based on the principle of complementarity.[42] This is stipulated in Article 17 of the Rome Statute,[43] which provides that the ICC will find a case inadmissible if it is being investigated at the national level.

Another branch of law which imposes an obligation to prohibit organised crime is IHRL. This branch of law is relevant where organised crime can be

---

[40] Arts 3 respectively.

[41] T Obokata, 'Trafficking of Human Beings as a Crime against Humanity: Some Implications for the International Legal System' (2005) 54 *International and Comparative Law Quarterly* 445.

[42] JT Holmes, 'The Principle of Complementarity' in RS Lee (ed), *International Criminal Court*, above ch 2 n 148, 41.

[43] Above ch 2 n 133.

regarded simultaneously as a violation of human rights. Crimes such as child prostitution and pornography, sexual/labour exploitation and illicit production, trafficking and consumption of narcotics[44] are some examples of crimes which entail human rights implications. Unlike ICL, which imposes obligations on individuals not to commit international crime, IHRL does not strictly create legal obligations upon non-state actors such as organised criminal groups. This does not exclude the application of IHRL, as it has been widely recognised that states can be held liable for the acts of non-state actors in certain circumstances. For instance, an obligation to investigate, prosecute and punish private acts which violate human rights has long been established,[45] and this is explicitly provided for in instruments such as the Optional Protocol to the CRC.[46] In addition, the United Nations Convention on the Law of the Sea 1982, while not an instrument to promote criminal justice or human rights, obliges states to suppress trafficking of slaves and drugs on the high seas.[47] Therefore, TCL can usefully be supplemented by these branches of international law.

Before concluding this section, it might be asked whether prohibition of organised crime may be regarded as part of customary international law. As noted in Chapter 2, prohibition of international crime has been established as part of customary international law and therefore all states are required to prosecute and punish, despite some not being parties to the Rome Statute. This means that there has been consistent state practice followed by *opinion juris* or a sense of legal obligation on the part of states to prosecute and punish international crime. Is this also the case for organised crime? Arguably development of the law on organised crime is as long as that on international crime, as states have prohibited the practice one way or another throughout history, and some of the international instruments noted have existed for a long time. However, it is submitted that there is currently no strong evidence of state practice and *opinion juris* on the prohibition of organised crime per se, mainly for the reason that states have different understandings of what organised crime is. If a particular conduct is not recognised as organised crime, then it is not prosecuted or punished as such. As a result, it becomes difficult to say state practice is consistent. Whether prohibition of organised crime can be regarded as customary law therefore will depend on the extent to which states will be able to share common understanding in the future, and it is submitted that the Organised Crime Convention can play an important role in this regard.

---

[44] Obokata, ch 2 n 146; S Takahashi, 'Drug Control, Human Rights and the Right to the Highest Attainable Standard of Health: By No Means Straightforward Issues' (2009) 31 *Human Rights Quarterly* 748.

[45] *Velasquez Rodriguez v Honduras* before the Inter-American Court of Human Rights, Ser C, No 1 (1988), para 176. See also D Shelton, 'Private Violations, Public Wrongs, and the Responsibility of states' (1989) 13 *Fordham International Law Journal* 1, 24; N Roht-Arriaza, 'State Responsibility to Investigate and Prosecute Grave Human Rights Violations in International Law' (1990) 78 *California Law Review* 449, 489–504.

[46] Arts 1, 3, and 4.

[47] Part VII, 1833 UNTS 396.

3.2.2   Criminal Jurisdiction over Organised Crime

In prosecuting and punishing transnational organised crime, one of the necessary first steps which must be taken is to establish criminal jurisdiction. The Organised Crime Convention provides detailed guidance on this. Consistent with the principles of international law, particularly state sovereignty, the main basis for the exercise of jurisdiction is territory.[48] That is to say, a state in which organised crime is committed has the primary jurisdiction to prosecute and punish, as recognised in Article 15(1)(a) of the Organised Crime Convention. An extension of this is the flag principle, which allows a state to exercise jurisdiction over a vessel or aircraft flying its flag as though forming part of its territory.[49] As the term 'shall establish' suggests, the exercise of criminal jurisdiction on these bases is mandatory and therefore these principles have primacy over others noted below.

Given the transnational nature of organised crime, it might be difficult to establish criminal jurisdiction solely on the territorial and flag principles when it also occurs in another state and/or criminal groups operate in another state. In order to deal with this situation, the exercise of other types of jurisdiction has been recognised under the Organised Crime Convention. There is, for instance, the passive personality principle, whereby a state can exercise jurisdiction if a crime is committed against its nationals.[50] This has been recognised, for example, in Argentina, Ecuador, Egypt, Indonesia and Sweden.[51] Another relevant principle is that of nationality (also known as the active personality principle), which allows states to try their own offending nationals.[52] The exercise of jurisdiction on this basis is recognised in states including Albania,[53] Azerbaijan,[54] France,[55] Poland[56] and the UK[57] in relation to some offences.

In addition, there is another dimension to the exercise of jurisdiction. Article 15(2)(c) provides:

> 2. Subject to article 4 of this Convention, a state Party may also establish its jurisdiction over any such offence when:
>
> . . .

[48] *SS Lotus* (1927) PCIJ Reports Series A, No 10. MC Bassiouni, 'Universal Jurisdiction for International Crimes: Historical Perspectives and Contemporary Practice' (2001) 42 *Virginia Journal of International Law* 81, 90.

[49] Art 15(1)(b).

[50] Art 15(2)(a).

[51] Implementation Report 2008 No 1, above n 38, para 31. See also A Calica, 'Self-Help is the Best Kind: The Efficient Breach Justification for Forcible Abduction of Terrorists' (2004) 37 *Cornell International Law Journal* 389, 400.

[52] Art 15(2)(b). This Article also allows prosecution of a stateless person whose habitual residence is located in the state concerned.

[53] Art 6 of the Albanian Criminal Code, cited in UNODC, 'Legislative Guide to the Implementation of the United Nations Convention against Transnational Organised Crime' (2004) 113.

[54] Art 12(1) of the Azerbaijan Criminal Code.

[55] Art113 of the French Criminal Code.

[56] Art 109 of the Polish Penal Code.

[57] S 5 of the Asylum and Immigration (Treatment of Claimants, etc) Act 2004.

(c) The offence is:

    (i) One of those established in accordance with article 5, paragraph 1, of this Convention and is committed outside its territory with a view to the commission of a serious crime within its territory;

    (ii) One of those established in accordance with article 6, paragraph 1(*b*)(ii), of this Convention and is committed outside its territory with a view to the commission of an offence established in accordance with article 6, paragraph 1(*a*)(i) or (ii) or (*b*)(i), of this Convention within its territory.

In a sense, this is similar to the effect principle, whereby criminal jurisdiction may be established if an act committed abroad has some kind of impact on a given state. This is recognised in, among others, Azerbaijan,[58] Georgia,[59] Germany[60] and the UK.[61] It should be noted, however, that Articles 5(1) and 6(1)(b)(ii) relate to inchoate offences and secondary participation in the commission of serious crimes and money laundering. Therefore, the principle does not apply to the actual commissioning of serious crimes or money laundering. A difficulty in applying this type of jurisdiction is that the harm may be intended but no harmful effect actually occurs in relation to inchoate offences.[62] This raises an issue of *nullum crimen sine actus*, as noted above.

Finally, a question may be asked whether or not there is a legal basis to rely upon universal jurisdiction over organised crime in general. Simply put, universal jurisdiction allows any state to apply its laws to punish an offence even when the state has no territorial or nationality links with the offence in question.[63] Whether or not this principle should be applied over organised crime may be answered by looking at the main rationale behind its exercise. It is often thought that the universality principle is justified because the international community has a strong interest in suppressing a particular conduct.[64] Its exercise over international crimes is a good example, because they shock the conscience of the international community. It then follows that every state has an interest in preserving world order by punishing such behaviour.[65] The prohibition of these conducts is also established as a matter of customary law and regarded as *jus cogens* crimes and/or crimes which establish *erga omnes* obligations.[66] More recently, the Princeton Principles on Universal Jurisdiction (2001), adopted by leading scholars of international law, affirmed that 'universal

---

[58] Art 12(2).

[59] Art 5 of the Georgian Criminal Code.

[60] Ss 5 and 6 of the German Criminal Code 1998, Federal Law Gazette I 945, 3322.

[61] See, eg *Liangstriprasert v Government of the United States* [1991] 1 AC 225; *R v Jamshid Hashemi Naini* [1999] 2 Cr App R 398; *HM Advocate v Al-Megrahi (Abdelbaset Ali) (No 1)* 2000 JC 555.

[62] CL Blakesley, 'United States Jurisdiction over Extraterritorial Crime' (1982) 73 *Journal of Criminal Law and Criminology* 1109, 1145.

[63] American Law Institute, 'Restatement of the Law (Third), Foreign Relations Law of the United States', 2 American Law Institute (1987), § 404 (Restatement).

[64] Bassiouni (2001), *Universal Jurisdiction*, above n 48, 96.

[65] Ibid, 88; Restatement, above n 63.

[66] KC Randall, 'Universal Jurisdiction under International Law' (1988) 66 *Texas Law Review* 785, 831.

jurisdiction is criminal jurisdiction based solely on the nature of the crime'.[67] If this line of reasoning is accepted, universal jurisdiction is not appropriate for organised crime, because the practice is not strictly regarded as the crime of concern for the international community, as noted in the previous chapter.

However, the nature of a crime is not the sole justification for the exercise of universal jurisdiction, and there is scope for its application to organised crime. This might be understood better in looking at the exercise of jurisdiction over piracy, which contributed to the initial development of universal jurisdiction. Piracy was traditionally regarded as an offence against the law of nations.[68] It was thought that this, coupled with the idea that piracy constituted *hostis humani generis* (enemy of mankind), facilitated the development of universal jurisdiction over the practice.[69] It was thought that all states had an interest or a right to punish acts of piracy, and one way to do so was to allow the exercise of universal jurisdiction.[70] In looking at this development, one would notice that similar reasoning applies to international crime.

Nevertheless, a closer look at the development of universal jurisdiction over piracy reveals another basis for justifying universal jurisdiction. The Harvard Law School, whose effort contributed to the adoption of the Convention on the High Seas 1958 and later the United Nations Convention on the Law of the Sea 1984, noted that piracy required a special, common basis of jurisdiction because it was frequently committed by foreigners outside the territorial and other ordinary jurisdictions of the prosecuting state.[71] Coupled with this is the concept of *mare liberum*, developed by Hugo Grotius, which stated that seas could belong to no state and therefore all states were free to travel thereupon.[72] For these reasons, it was difficult for states to assert jurisdiction over pirates. Universal jurisdiction thus provided an effective avenue to ensure pirates could be punished. In this regard, it has been noted by commentators that universal jurisdiction was exercised over piracy not because pirates were regarded as *hostis*

---

[67] Principle 1.1. Under Principle 2, serious crimes include piracy, slavery, war crimes, crimes against peace, crimes against humanity, genocide and torture. Reprinted in S Macedo (ed), *Universal Jurisdiction: National Courts and the Prosecution of Serious Crimes under International Law* (Philadelphia, University of Pennsylvania Press, 2004) 21–25.

[68] Piracy Act—15th Congress, 2nd Session, ch 77, 3 Stat 510 (1819). See also *United States v Smith* 18 US 153, 162(1820); Restatement, above n 63.

[69] This phrase was first used to describe piracy by Sir Lord Cork in 1797. JM Goodwin, 'Universal Jurisdiction and the Pirate: Time for an Old Couple to Part' (2006) 39 *Vanderbilt Journal of Transnational Law* 973, 991. See also *The SS Lotus*, above n 48, para 65; *United States v Brig Malek Adhel* 43 US 210, 232(1844); *Filartiga v Pena-Irala* 630 F 2d 876, 890 (2d Cir 1980).

[70] Y Dinstein, 'Criminal Jurisdiction over Aircraft Hijacking' (1972) 7 *Israel Law Review* 195, 197. However, Goodwin argues that labelling piracy as *hostis humani generis* does not necessarily provide justification for the exercise of universal jurisdiction as it was not regarded as such historically. Ibid, 989–95.

[71] JF Bingham, 'Codification of International Law: Part IV: Piracy' (1932) 26 *American Journal of International Law Supplement* 739, 760. See also M Halberstam, 'Terrorism on the High Seas: The Achille Lauro, Piracy and the IMO Convention on Maritime Safety' (1988) 82 *American Journal of International Law* 269, 288.

[72] Goodwin, above n 69, 988.

humani generis[73] but because it was easy for pirates to evade the jurisdiction of any state on the high seas.[74] Bassiouni succinctly summarises all of these by stating that 'conduct that is universally condemned does not necessarily imply that universal jurisdiction is applicable to such conduct'.[75] All of these ideas on universal jurisdiction resonate well with organised crime, because many of them take place beyond ordinary jurisdictions of states, such as on the high seas,[76] airspace or cyber/electronic space, where it is difficult to apply traditional territorial or nationality principles. Under this justification, organised crime does not have to be regarded as *delicta juris gentium*.

Another valid justification for universal jurisdiction over organised crime is that there is no international penal tribunal to prosecute and punish it, except when some activities can be elevated to the status of international crime, as noted above. One benefit of an independent international penal tribunal such as the ICC is that it can exercise jurisdiction in order to make sure that perpetrators do not go unpunished when a state is unable or unwilling to prosecute and punish core international crimes. However, there is no mechanism of last resort for organised crime at the international level. This forced states to resort to universal jurisdiction for piracy in the past,[77] and there is no reason why the same reasoning should not apply to organised crime.

Another justification for universal jurisdiction over organised crime is the idea of 'common interest'. The Harvard Research Group noted that universal jurisdiction over piracy was justified because all states had an interest in the safety of commerce.[78] This is obviously different from saying that universal jurisdiction was justified because pirates were *hostis humani generis*. In other words, what matters is that the conduct affects the interest of all states, and not necessarily the nature of a crime in question. This reasoning should apply to organised crime because the adoption and ratification of the Organised Crime Convention demonstrates that there is a common interest among states and the international community in its prevention and suppression. This common interest is expressed in the Preamble of the Organised Crime Convention: 'Determined to deny safe havens to those who engage in transnational organized crime by prosecuting their crimes wherever they occur and by cooperating at the international level'.

---

[73] *Ibid*, 994. Kontrovich also argues that piracy can only be *hostis humani generis* when it entails wilful disregard for essential order and welfare of human society. E Kontrovich, 'The Piracy Analogy: Modern Universal Jurisdiction's Hollow Foundation' (2004) 45 *Harvard International Law Journal* 183, 236.

[74] V. Lowe, 'Jurisdiction' in M Evans (ed), *International Law*, 2nd edn (Oxford, Oxford University Press, 2006) 348; YS Kraytman, 'Universal Jurisdiction: Historical Roots and Modern Implications' (2005) 2 *BSIS Journal of International Studies* 94, 103.

[75] Bassiouni (2001), *Universal Jurisdiction*, above n 48, 94.

[76] See, eg *Regina v Charrington and Others* (unreported), which was about the British authority seizing a Maltese vessel importing 14 tons of cannabis. W Gilmore, C. Warbrick, and D McGoldrick, 'Drug Trafficking at Sea: The Case of R Charrington and Others' (2000) 49 *International and Comparative Law Quarterly* 477.

[77] Bingham, above n 71, 756; Restatement, above n 63.

[78] ED Dickinson, 'Codification of International Law: Part II: Jurisdiction with Respect to Crime' (1935) 29 *American Journal of International Law Supplement* 435, 566.

It was also shown in the previous chapter that some organised crime has impact upon international peace and security. However, the International Court of Justice (ICJ) was cautious when elaborating upon the legal nature of an 'interest' of the international community. It stated:

> humanitarian considerations may constitute the inspiration basis for rules of law . . .
> Such considerations do not, however, in themselves amount to rules of law. All states
> are interested—have an interest—in such matters. But the existence of an 'interest'
> does not itself entail that this interest is specifically juridical in character.[79]

In relation to international crimes, it may be argued that an 'interest' of the international community has attained a juridical character as their prohibition is firmly established by customary international law and constitutes *jus cogens*, as noted in Chapter 2. As to organised crime in general, while no such legal basis can be found as yet, the legal character of an 'interest' of the international community can arguably be found in numerous conventions and treaties that have been adopted over the course of time.

A state may also exercise universal jurisdiction on the basis of the presence of foreign suspects who commit crimes outside its territory. This is regarded as 'universal' jurisdiction in the sense that the state in which the suspect is found has no territorial or nationality connections with the offences in question. In the modern context, the exercise of universal jurisdiction on this basis is reflected in the principle of *aut dedere aut judicare*.[80] This phrase is a modern version of that used by Hugo Grotius, '*aut dedere, aut punire* (extradite or punish)',[81] and is the cornerstone of indirect control of crimes.[82] This principle holds that if a state does not extradite an offender to a requesting state, then the non-extraditing state must exercise jurisdiction to prosecute him/her. Reydams calls it 'the co-operative general universality principle' or a form of bilateral co-operation in criminal matters.[83] This is regarded as a subsidiary form of universal jurisdiction as its application is limited to cases where the surrender of a suspect to the territorial/nationality state is not possible.[84] It is to be emphasised that under this notion of universality a prosecuting state has no jurisdiction over a foreign national if he/she is not present in its territory.

In any event, the principle of *aut dedere aut judicare* is recognised under Articles 15 and 16 of the Organised Crime Convention and in other suppression

---

[79] *South West Africa Case (Second Phase)* (1966) ICJ Reports 6, para 50.

[80] Dickinson above n 78, 574. See also AR Carnegie 'Jurisdiction over Violations of the Laws and Customs of War' (1963) 39 *British Yearbook of International Law* 402, 405; A Cassese, 'Is the Bell Tolling for Universality? A Plea for a Sensible Notion of Universal Jurisdiction' (2003) 1 *Journal of International Criminal Justice* 589, 592–93.

[81] Wise, above ch 2 n 132, 276.

[82] MC Bassiouni, 'The Penal Characteristics of Conventional International Criminal Law' (1983) 15 *Case Western Reserve Journal of International Law* 27, 35.

[83] L Reydams, *Universal Jurisdiction: International and Municipal Legal Perspectives* (Oxford, Oxford University Press, 2004) 29.

[84] Dickinson, above n 78, 574; Carnegie, above n 80, 405.

conventions.[85] It is worth noting that the nature of obligation depends on the nationalities of offenders. Under Article 15(3), if a state does not extradite its nationals, then it must establish criminal jurisdiction over them. This, in effect, is the exercise of the nationality principle as noted above, and the use of 'shall' illustrates that the principle has a stronger legal force. Nevertheless, Article 15(4) provides that states 'may' establish criminal jurisdiction over other nationals, suggesting that prosecution is not mandatory. Such a provision can also be seen in other treaties.[86] Therefore, universal jurisdiction over foreign nationals is not mandatory, and this will inevitably limit its application over organised crime. While some argue that the principle of *aut dedere aut judicare* constitutes customary international law,[87] the extent to which state practice reflects this principle is not clear.[88] Bassiouni notes that such a position may be supported when the only available means for suppression is indirect enforcement at the national level.[89]

Finally, aside from the *aut dedere aut judicare* principle, the Organised Crime Convention does not deny the possibility of universal jurisdiction. Article 15(6) thereof stipulates, for instance, that it 'does not exclude the exercise of any criminal jurisdiction established by a State Party in accordance with its domestic law'. Bassiouni argues that a provision such as this, which is also found in other international instruments,[90] implicitly authorises the exercise of universal jurisdiction.[91] In this regard, the following passage in the Preamble of the Organised Crime Convention is once again worth noting: '*Determined* to deny safe havens

---

[85] This principle appears, among other treaties, in Convention on Illicit Traffic in Dangerous Drugs 1936, 198 LNTS 299; International Convention for the Suppression of Unlawful Seizure of Aircraft 1970, 860 UNTS 105; Convention for the Suppression of Unlawful Acts against the Safety of Civil Aviation 1971, 974 UNTS 178; International Convention on Prevention and Punishment of Crimes against Internationally Protected Persons 1972, 1035 UNTS 167; International Convention against the Taking of Hostages 1979, 1316 UNTS 205; Convention on the Physical Protection of Nuclear Materials 1979; Convention against Torture and Other Cruel, Inhuman or Degrading Treatment or Punishment 1984; 1465 UNTS 85; Convention for the Suppression of Unlawful Acts against the Safety of Maritime Navigation 1988,1678 UNTS 221; Drug Convention 1988; International Convention against the Recruitment, Use Financing and Training of Mercenaries 1989, 29 ILM 89.

[86] Wise, above ch 2 n 132, 274.

[87] Dissenting Opinion of Judge Weeramantry in *Case Concerning Questions of Interpretation and Application of the 1971 Montreal Convention Arising from the Aerial Incident at Lockerbie (Provisional Measures)* (1992) ICJ Reports 114. Bassiouni goes further to state that it constitutes *jus cogens*. MC Bassiouni, *International Extradition: United States Law and Practice*, 2nd edn (New York, Oceania Publications, 1987) 22. See further MC Bassiouni and EM Wise, *Aut Dedere, Aut Judicare: The Duty to Extradite or Prosecute in International Law* (Dordrecht, Matinus Nijhoff Publishers,1995); C Enache-Brown and A Fried, 'Universal Crime, Jurisdiction and Duty: The Obligation of *Aut Dedere Aut Judicare* in International Law' (1997) 43 *McGill Law Journal* 613, 629.

[88] Wise, above ch 2 n 132, 282; T Meron, *Human Rights and Humanitarian Norms as Customary Law* (Oxford, Clarendon Press, 1989) 61; RB Lillich and JM Paxman, 'State Responsibility for Injuries to Aliens Occasioned by Terrorist Activities' (1977) 26 *American University Law Review* 217, 300.

[89] Bassiouni, above n 82, 34.

[90] Such as Art 36(4) of the Single Convention on Narcotic Drugs 1961, 520 UNTS 151; Art 22(5) of the Convention on Psychotropic Substance 1971, 1019 UNTS 175.

[91] Bassiouni, above n 87, 125.

to those who engage in transnational organized crime by prosecuting their crimes wherever they occur and by cooperating at the international level'.

During the drafting stage of the Convention, some states expressed concern over Article 15(6) as it could be interpreted as authorising extraterritorial jurisdiction.[92] As a result, Mexico, along with other states, proposed to include the phrase 'this Convention does not allow extraterritorial application of domestic law'.[93] However, it was stressed simultaneously that the principle of territorial integrity and non-intervention, as reflected in Article 4 of the Organised Crime Convention, would be applicable to any principle of jurisdiction,[94] meaning that the territoriality principle remains the most important form of jurisdiction. Therefore, while the exercise of universal jurisdiction remains a possibility, it is an exception rather than a norm.

In looking at state practice, it will become apparent that domestic legislation does allow the exercise of universal jurisdiction for some crimes. Section 64 of the Austrian Criminal Code provides for universal jurisdiction over offences such as human trafficking, counterfeiting, participating in criminal organisations, child pornography and other offences established in accordance with international treaties. Similarly, the Azerbaijan Criminal Code establishes universal jurisdiction over terrorism, narcotics trafficking and counterfeiting of currencies.[95] In addition, the Japanese Penal Code of 1907 as revised provides for universal jurisdiction over counterfeiting of currencies and official documents and offences established by an international treaty.[96] Spain exercises universal jurisdiction over counterfeiting of foreign currencies, crimes relating to prostitution and illegal drug trafficking.[97] Finally, the Criminal Justice (International Co-operation) Act 1990 of the UK allows the authorities to exercise jurisdiction over foreign ships trafficking drugs at seas.[98] All of these examples show that universal jurisdiction is recognised for some crimes at the domestic level in practice.

The establishment of criminal jurisdiction over organised crime is also strengthened by ICL and IHRL when a conduct is regarded as an international crime or a violation of human rights. In relation to ICL, states have a primary obligation to prosecute and punish, and therefore all the principles of criminal jurisdiction noted above are relevant. The ICC can also exercise jurisdiction when states are not willing or able to deal with it at the national level. Of particular relevance is the Rome Statute, which provides that the Court may exercise jurisdiction if:

one or more of the following States are Parties to this Statute or have accepted the

---

[92] Above ch 2 n 108, 18.
[93] A/AC.254/4/Rev.4 (19 July 1999), 20.
[94] Ibid.
[95] Art 12(3).
[96] Arts 2 and 3.
[97] *Sentencias del Tribunal Supremo espahiol en el caso del Gral Chileno Herndn Julio Brady Roche* Sentencia No 319/2004, 39–40. Available at www.derechos.org/nizkor/chile/juicio/brady. html.
[98] Ss 19–21.

jurisdiction of the Court in accordance with paragraph 3:

(a) The State on the territory of which the conduct in question occurred or, if the crime was committed on board a vessel or aircraft, the state of registration of that vessel or aircraft;

(b) The State of which the person accused of the crime is a national.[99]

The basis of such jurisdiction is therefore territoriality and nationality. It is important to emphasise that states must be parties to the Rome Statute or have accepted its jurisdiction without becoming parties.[100] The exception is where the United Nations Security Council refers a case to the ICC.[101] Beyond this, however, ICL does not provide for detailed guidance.

In relation to IHRL, human rights obligations of states generally extend over individuals within a state's territory and subject to its jurisdiction.[102] As the flag principle is a recognised principle of jurisdiction exercised by states, it can be assumed that the human rights obligations can be extended over vessels and aircraft. This has been recognised in Europe at least.[103] Skogly argues in this respect that there can be an extraterritorial obligation to protect individuals abroad from human rights violations that could be attributed to actions committed by third parties over which the state has jurisdiction.[104] Furthermore, IHRL often places an obligation on states to protect not only its nationals, but also foreigners.[105] Therefore, they must prosecute and punish criminals who victimise foreign nationals in their territories and jurisdiction.

In addition, it has been held in the past that IHRL applies to the territories where states have 'effective control'. This may be established on the basis of deci-

---

[99] Art 12.

[100] Art 12(2).

[101] Art 13(b).

[102] Art 2(1) of the International Covenant on Civil and Political Rights 1966 (ICCPR), 999 UNTS 171. Similar wording can be found in Art 1 of the European Convention on Human Rights 1950 (ECHR), ETS No 5; Art 1 of the American Convention on Human Rights 1969 (ACHR), 1144 UNTS 123.

[103] *Cyprus v Turkey* (1982) 4 EHRR 482. The European Commission on Human Rights noted that nationals of a state, including ships and aircrafts, were partly within its jurisdiction wherever they might be (136). In *Bankovic v Belgium* (2001) 11 *BHRC* 35, the European Court of Human Rights, while maintaining that the territory is the primary basis for jurisdiction, recognised the validity of the flag and other principles in exceptional cases (para 59). See also T Meron, 'Extraterritorial Application of Human Rights Treaties' (1995) 89 *American Journal of International Law* 78, 81.

[104] S Skogly, *Beyond National Borders: States' Human Rights Obligations in International Cooperation* (Antwerp, Intersentia, 2006) 70.

[105] The ICCPR provides in this regard that '[e]ach State Party to the present Covenant undertakes to respect and to ensure to all individuals within its territory and subject to its jurisdiction the rights recognized in the present Covenant'. The Human Rights Committee made it clear through General Comment No 15 (Status of Aliens) that 'each one of the rights of the Covenant must be guaranteed without discrimination between citizens and aliens'. This is affirmed again in General Comment No 31 (The Nature of states Obligations), para 10. *Compilation of General Comments and General Recommendations Adopted by Human Rights Treaty Bodies*, HRI/GEN/1/Rev.7 (12 May 2004). See also the International Convention on the Protection of the Rights of All Migrant Workers and Members of Their Families 1990, A/RES/45/158 (18 December 1990) (Migrant Workers' Convention).

sions taken in *Cyprus v Turkey*,[106] *Loizidou v Turkey*,[107] *Bankovic v Belgium*,[108] *Armando Alejandre Jr and Others v Cuba*[109] and *Lopez Burgos v Uruguay*.[110] A contemporary example of this would be crimes such as human trafficking committed by soldiers in conflict/post conflict zones. If a state in question still retain controls over such zones, there is a basis for establishing international obligation and accountability for acts committed by its agents. As will be shown in Chapter 5, this has been one of the problems prevalent in Kosovo, where personnel of peacekeeping forces have been implicated of human trafficking, prostitution and other forms of organised crime. In any event, IHRL is only relevant where organised crime is regarded as a violation of human rights simultaneously.

3.2.3   Special Investigative Techniques and Intelligence-Led Law Enforcement

The transnational nature of organised crime and sophisticated techniques employed by organised criminal groups mean that traditional law enforcement, which mainly takes place after a crime is committed, is not sufficient. What is necessary is intelligence-led law enforcement, which might be defined as 'a strategic, future-oriented and targeted approach to crime control, focussing upon the identification, analysis and management of persisting and developing problems or risks'.[111] Compared to traditional law enforcement, which is more reactive in nature, such intelligence-led law enforcement may be regarded as more proactive as authorities are often required to act before a particular crime is committed. In order to achieve this, however, states may need to confer special powers upon their law enforcement authorities. Such measures have already been taken in relation to terrorism and, given the serious nature of many forms of organised crime, similar measures may be justified, provided that they comply with the pertinent human rights norms and principles. The Organised Crime Convention elaborates upon some of the measures to be taken in this regard. Article 20, for instance, provides for the use of controlled delivery. Article 2(i) defines this as

> the technique of allowing illicit or suspect consignments to pass out of, through or into the territory of one or more states, with the knowledge and under the supervision of their competent authorities, with a view to the investigation of an offence and the

---

[106] Above n 103.

[107] Preliminary Objections, Series A no 130 (1995) 20 EHRR 99, para 62.

[108] Above n 103.

[109] 'Inter-American Commission on Human Rights', IACHR Report No 86/99, Case No 11.589 (29 September 1999), para 25.

[110] Human Rights Committee, Communication No52/1979, CCPR/C/13/D/52/1979 (29 July 1981).

[111] M Maguire, 'Policing by Risks and Targets: Some Dimensions and Implications of Intelligence-Led Crime Control' (2000) 9 *Policing and Society* 315, 316.

identification of persons involved in the commission of the offence.

This method is often employed in the investigation and prosecution of drug-related offences.[112] The Convention also obliges states to consider allowing other techniques, such as electronic surveillance and undercover operations. These measures are facilitated in states including Algeria, Benin, Kuwait, Spain and Turkey.[113] These measures are supplemented by Article 28, which touches upon collection, analysis and sharing of intelligence on organised crime. In the spirit of international co-operation, states are encouraged to conclude bilateral or multi-lateral agreements to facilitate overseas investigations.[114]

A note of caution is that some of these measures can impact upon the rule of law and administration of justice. For instance, there is a fine line between undercover operations and entrapment. This has been recognised in Europe. Under English law, for instance, entrapment is regarded as an act of 'causing someone to commit an offence in order that he should be prosecuted'.[115] Put differently, the law enforcement authorities such as the police would be acting as *agents provocateurs*. This may be distinguished from merely providing an opportunity for a person to commit a crime, of which he or she freely takes advantage.[116] It was recognised in the past that undercover operations could be regarded as violations of human rights. In *Teixeira de Castro v Portugal*, the European Court of Human Rights held that, while the use of special investigative techniques such as undercover operations do not automatically result in violations of the right to a fair trial, Portugal was in breach of this right as the applicant's conviction for drug-related offences was instigated by police officers when they offered to buy illegal drugs.[117] Nevertheless, what constitutes instigation or voluntary acts on the part of a suspect is not entirely clear. In *Teixeria*, the defendant arguably had an opportunity to not provide drugs and therefore his act could have been regarded as voluntary. If this line of reasoning were to be accepted, then a different finding could be reached.[118] The safeguards in such

---

[112] GD Lee, *Global Drug Enforcement: Practical Investigative Techniques* (Boca Raton, CRC Press, 2004) 255.

[113] Implementation Report 2008 of the United Nations Convention against Transnational Organized Crime: Consolidated Information Received from States for the Second Reporting Cycle, CTOC/COP/2006/2/Rev.1 (1 September 2008), para 27 (hereinafter Implementation Report 2008 No 2). However, Chad, Comoros, the Congo, Egypt, Guatemala, Indonesia, Trinidad & Tobago and Tunisia reported that their legislation did not allow any of these measures.

[114] Arts 20 and 27.

[115] *R. v Loosely* [2001] UKHL 53, para 36.

[116] Ibid, para 53, citing Lord Bingham in *Nottingham City Council v Amin* [2000] 1 WLR 1071 at 1075.

[117] (1998) 28 EHRR 101. In this case, police officers were not authorised to conduct undercover operations in the first instance. This case was affirmed in, among others, *Ramanauskas v Lithuania*, Application Number 74420/01 (2008). Another factor to consider is whether there has been any good reason to suspect that the defendant has been involved in a criminal activity.

[118] In *Ludi v Switzerland* (1992) 15 EHRR 173 the European Court found no violation of Art 8 on a similar fact as the Portuguese case. The Court distinguished the former from the latter on the ground that the undercover operation was authorised by an investigative judge and that the officer was sworn in. If one is to accept reasoning, any operation could be justified if it was supervised by

cases include a stay of proceedings, which is recognised in England.[119] Nevertheless, such power can be discretionary,[120] and if the fairness of proceedings is not affected, then such an investigative technique may be resorted to.

Another area of concern is surveillance operations and the right to privacy. There is no doubt that the use of such is sometimes necessary to prevent and suppress organised crime. In Europe a right to privacy is recognised as qualified[121] and can be restricted on grounds of public safety, national security or prevention of crime.[122] However, even if this is the case, the use of such methods must be established by law and guided by detailed and clear rules.[123] This was highlighted at the international level by the Human Rights Committee, a supervisory organ of the International Covenant on Civil and Political Rights (ICCPR):

> Even with regard to interferences that conform to the Covenant, relevant legislation must specify in detail the precise circumstances in which such interferences may be permitted. A decision to make use of such authorized interference must be made only by the authority designated under the law, and on a case-by-case basis.[124]

Furthermore, such action should be supervised by a judicial or independent body.[125] Short of this, such measures can be regarded as a breach of the right to private and family life. It is also worth noting that one can claim to be a victim of human rights violation even when surveillance measures are not applied to one directly.[126] As the instrument to promote a criminal justice response, TCL as represented by the Organised Crime Convention does not sufficiently cover these issues. It is therefore evident that it should be assisted by, among others, IHRL, which provides the norms and principles in this area.

3.2.4   Mutual Assistance in Criminal Matters

3.2.4.1   Extradition

Another important aspect of TCL is the facilitation of international co-operation to suppress and punish transnational organised crime. Given the global nature of organised crime, prohibition and prosecution at the national level is not enough. States must be able to co-operate with each other to facilitate prosecution and

---

a judge. In any event, the Court's reasoning relates to the procedural aspects and it did not explain the difference between incitement and voluntary act.

[119] Above n 115, paras 39–42. See also *Edwards and Lewis v United Kingdom* (2004) 40 EHRR 593.

[120] Ibid.

[121] Art 8 of the ECHR.

[122] *Ludi v Switzerland*, above n 118, para 39.

[123] *Kruslin v France* (1990) 12 EHRR 547; *Kopp v Switzerland* (1999) 27 EHRR 91; *Valenzuela v Spain* (1998) 28 EHRR 483.

[124] General Comment No 16 on Art 17 (Right to Privacy, Family and Correspondence)(1988), in Compilation of General Comments, above n 105.

[125] *Dumitru Popescu v Romania*, Application No 71525/01 (2007), paras 70–73.

[126] *Klass v Germany* (1979–80) 2 EHRR 214.

punishment. A key measure to promote international co-operation in preventing and suppressing organised crime is extradition. Simply put, it is a process of handing over a suspect/criminal from one jurisdiction to another. This is facilitated mainly by bilateral and/or multilateral treaties.[127] International instruments touching upon various types of organised crime, such as counterfeiting and drug trafficking, also have provisions on extradition.[128] As the consolidated version of these relating to organised crime, the Organised Crime Convention provides detailed guidance on extradition under Article 16. The benefit of this provision is that it applies to all regions of the world, unlike the geographically limited regional treaties. Furthermore, it applies to almost all instances of organised crime, and therefore does not limit itself to the particular crimes stipulated under subject-specific conventions. At the time of ratification or accession, states can choose to use the Organised Crime Convention as a legal basis to facilitate extradition in the absence of the pre-existing treaties on extradition.[129] However, it has been pointed out recently that some states do not use the Convention as a legal basis, nor do they have any bilateral agreements with others.[130] This inevitably makes it difficult to extradition in practice.

There are several key principles relating to extradition. The first is the principle of reciprocity. This means that a state will honour a request for extradition if it asks others to honour the same request.[131] While Article 16 of the Organised Crime Convention does not specifically provide for this, the principle can be inferred because the Convention is designed to promote mutual recognition and confidence. The second principle is double criminality. It provides that the conduct for which extradition is sought must be an offence both in the requesting and requested states. This reflects the principle of *nulla poena sine lege* (no crime without law). This is recognised in Article 16(1) of the Organised Crime Convention, although some states, such as Afghanistan, Guatemala and Honduras, do not recognise it at all.[132] The third principle is the political offence exception, providing for the refusal of extradition if the offence in question is political in nature.[133] This principle is recognised in, among others, Brazil,

---

[127] See, eg Inter-American Convention on Extradition 1981, 20 ILM 723; European Convention on Extradition 1957, ETS No 24; Convention on Simplified Extradition Procedures between the Member States of the European Union 1995, OJ C78/2 (30 March 1995); Convention Relating to Extradition between the Member States of the European Union 1996, OJ C313/12 (23 October 1996). In the context of the European Union, the traditional procedure was replaced by the European Arrest Warrant. See Chapter 6 for details.

[128] Bassiouni and Wise, above n 87, 11–19.

[129] As of August 2008, 23 states have notified the secretariat that they would use the Convention as a legal basis. CTOC/COP/2008/5 (12 August 2008), para 27.

[130] Meeting of the open-ended working group of government experts on international cooperation: Report of the Chairperson, CTOC/COP/2008/18 (18 February 2009), para 10.

[131] G Gilbert, *Aspects of Extradition Law* (Dordrecht, Martinus Nijhoff Publishers, 1991) 17–19.

[132] Implementation Report 2008 No 1, above n 38, para 61.

[133] See, eg Art 3 of the European Extradition Convention. For the discussion of this concept, see C van den Wijngaert, *The Political Offence Exception to Extradition* (Deventer, Kluwer Law International, 1980).

China, Congo, Iceland and Tunisia.[134] While the notion of political offence is vague and varies between states,[135] it suffices to state that this does not apply to organised crime as it is committed mainly for economic reasons. Even where organised crime has a strong nexus with terrorism, it has been widely accepted that the latter is not to be regarded as a political offence.[136] To strengthen this, Article 16(3) makes it clear that each offence covered in the Convention is to be regarded as extraditable. Finally, there is a rule of speciality, under which a person who has been extradited may be prosecuted only for the offence listed in the extradition request.[137] It is apparent that many of these principles are designed to protect the rights of suspects and defendants.

There are several other points to be noted in relation to Article 16 of the Organised Crime Convention. The principle of *aut dedere aut judicare* is explicitly recognised. As noted above, this principle becomes relevant particularly when states do not extradite their nationals.[138] This is common in civil law states, while common law states such as the UK allow for the extradition of their own nationals. The facilitation of simplified procedure for extradition is also provided for, and a good example of this is the system of the European Arrest Warrant within the EU. In addition, Article 16(14) provides that:

> Nothing in this Convention shall be interpreted as imposing an obligation to extradite if the requested state Party has substantial grounds for believing that the request has been made for the purpose of prosecuting or punishing a person on account of that person's sex, race, religion, nationality, ethnic origin or political opinions or that compliance with the request would cause prejudice to that person's position for any one of these reasons.

This reflects the well-established principle of *non-refoulement*, which is widely recognised under IHRL. Traditionally applicable to those recognised as refugees under the Convention Relating to the Status of Refugees 1951,[139] the principle has been expanded to apply to other situations, including cases where a suspect

---

[134] Implementation Report 2008 No 1, above n 38, para 62.

[135] Gilbert, above n 131; Chapter 6.

[136] See, eg Security Council Resolution 1373 (2001); Art 1 of the European Convention on Suppression of Terrorism 1977, ETS No 90; Art 11 of the International Convention for the Suppression of Terrorist Bombing 1997, 37 ILM 249; Art 14 of the International Convention for the Suppression of Financing of Terrorism 1999, 39 ILM 270. It should be noted some treaties provide that armed struggles for self-determination and liberation against foreign occupation or colonisation are not to be regarded as political offences. See, eg Art 3(1) of the Organisation of African Unity (OAU) Convention on the Prevention and Combating of Terrorism 1999, OAU Doc AHG/Dec 132 (V).

[137] Gilbert, above n 131, 106–07.

[138] They include: Algeria, Angola, Austria, Azerbaijan, Belarus, Belgium, Benin, Bosnia and Herzegovina, Brazil, Bulgaria, Burkina Faso, Burundi, Cambodia, Cameroon, Cape Verde, Central African Republic, Chad, China (mainland), Comoros, Congo, Costa Rica, Côte d'Ivoire, Croatia, Cyprus, Djibouti, Egypt, France, Gabon, Germany, Greece, Honduras, Kazakhstan, Kuwait, Madagascar, Mali, Moldova, Morocco, Myanmar, Niger, Poland, the Russian Federation, Sao Tome and Principe, Switzerland, Tajikistan, the former Yugoslav Republic of Macedonia, Togo, Tunisia, Turkey, Ukraine and Uzbekistan. Implementation Report 2008 No 1, above n 38, para 65.

[139] Art 33, 189 UNTS 150. It should be noted that 'membership to a particular social group' is not included under the Organised Crime Convention.

faces a risk of being subjected to the death penalty. Once again, it becomes apparent that TCL is strengthened by other branches of international law.

Despite the fact that the system of extradition has been firmly established in domestic and international law, some states ignore this and resort to irregular rendition and abduction to bring suspects into their domestic jurisdictions. The current state of affairs is that such actions are held to be justified under certain circumstances based on the doctrine of *male captus bene detentus*. This allows a court to exercise jurisdiction over an accused person regardless of how that person has come into its jurisdiction. While it is common knowledge that forcible abduction and irregular rendition have been relied upon in recent times to interrogate terror suspects, the methods have also been used to transfer those suspected of organised crime. An often cited example of this is *United States v Alvarez-Machain*.[140] The defendant was accused of torturing and killing an agent of the US Drug Enforcement Administration. Instead of facilitating a formal transfer through a bilateral extradition agreement, Alvareaz-Machain was abducted from Mexico and brought to the US to stand trial. The US Supreme Court affirmed the doctrine of *male captus bene detentus* and held that the procedural safeguards satisfied the requirements of due process of law. This decision has been criticised as the US Supreme Court undermined the integrity of the established international legal regime relating to extradition.[141] It also breaches the customary principle of state sovereignty as stipulated, among others, in Article 2 of the United Nations Charter.[142] The decision was also criticised because it breaches fundamental human rights, including the right to liberty and security of the person.[143] However, reliance on forcible abduction has intensified recently in the name of war on terror.[144] While the degree of threat posed by terrorists and organised criminal groups might be different, the increasing nexus between these criminalities may justify states in using forcible abduction to bring organised criminals to justice.

Despite these criticisms, developments in this area of law reveal that the doctrine of *male captus bene detentus* can be upheld under certain circumstances. In deciding whether or not forcible abduction is permissible, states and international organisations alike strike a balance between individual rights and the interest of the society or community in crime prevention. This was

---

[140] *United States v Alvarez-Machain* 504 US 655 (1992). See also *Sosa v Alvares-Machain* 542 US 692 (2004), in which the US Supreme Court rejected an argument that prohibition on arbitrary detention is part of customary law.

[141] R Rayfuse, 'International Abduction and the United States Supreme Court: The Law of the Jungle Reigns' (1993) 42 *International and Comparative Law Quarterly* 882.

[142] See also *SS Lotus*, above n 48, para 18; L Henkin, 'A Decent Respect to the Opinions of Mankind' (1992) 25 *John Marshall Law Review* 215, 231.

[143] Rayfuse, above n 141, 890–91. See also Organisation of American States, 'Legal Opinion on the Decision of the Supreme Court of the United States', 4 Crlm LF 119, 124 (1993); Meron, *Extraterritorial Application*, above n 103, 80.

[144] See, eg Amnesty International, 'State of Denial: Europe's Role in Rendition and Secret Detention' (2008).

touched upon, for example, in *Prosecutor v Dragan Nikolic*.[145] In this case, the Trial Chamber of the International Criminal Tribunal for the Former Yugoslavia (ICTY) in the first instance stated that:

[I]n a situation where an accused is very seriously mistreated, maybe even subjected to inhuman, cruel or degrading treatment, or torture, before being handed over to the Tribunal, this may constitute a legal impediment to the exercise of jurisdiction over such an accused.[146]

However, the Appeal Chamber of the ICTY in the same case stressed the importance of striking a fair balance between the rights of defendant and the interest of the international community in prosecuting serious violations of international (humanitarian) law.[147] It seems that, following the classic cases of *Eichmann* in Israel[148] and *Fédération Nationale des Déportés et Internés Résistants et Patriots v Barbie* in France,[149] if the crime in question is of a grave nature (such as international crime), this might justify the use of forcible abduction.[150] Some commentators support this position.[151] This reasoning perhaps could also apply to terror suspects, as it has been recognised widely that terrorism is a threat to international peace and security.

The question then arises whether or not forcible abduction can be justified for organised crime. On the one hand, the above jurisprudence of the ICTY seems to suggest that if the crime in question is not as serious as international crime, then abduction is not justified. Nevertheless, the same reasoning of the ICTY can apply to organised crime. The European Court of Human Rights, in *Ocalan v Turkey*, noted in this regard that

Inherent in the whole of the Convention is the search for a fair balance between the demands of the general interest of the community and the requirements of the protection of the individual's fundamental rights. As movement about the world becomes easier and crime takes on a larger international dimension, it is increasingly in the interest of all nations that suspected offenders who flee abroad should be

---

[145] *Prosecutor v Dragan Nikolic*, Decision on Defence Motion Challenging the Exercise of Jurisdiction by the Tribunal, IT-94-2-PT (9 October 2002).

[146] Ibid, para 114. The Trial Chamber eventually found that there was no such serious mistreatment and therefore exercised its jurisdiction. See also *Prosecutor v Jean-Bosco Barayagwiza*, ICTR-97-19, Appeal Judgment (3 November 1999), para 74.

[147] *Prosecutor v Dragan Nikolic*, Decision on Interlocutory Appeal Concerning Legality of Arrest, IT-94-2/AR73 (5 June 2003), para 30.

[148] *Public Prosecutor v Eichmann* (1962) 36 ILR 277.

[149] (1983) 78 ILR 125.

[150] *Decision on Interlocutory Appeal*, above n 147, para 24. See also the Office of Co-Investigating Judges (Extraordinary Chambers in the Court of Cambodia), *Order of Provisional Detention* (Kaing Guek Eav alias Duch) (31 July 2007), para 21.

[151] R Higgins, *Problems and Process: International Law and How We Use It* (Oxford, Oxford University Press, 1995) 72; G Sluiter, 'Due Process and Criminal Procedure in the Cambodian Extraordinary Chambers' (2006) 4 *Journal of International Criminal Justice* 314, 317–18; C Ryngaert, 'The Doctrine of Abuse of Process: A Comment on Cambodia Tribunal's Decisions in the Case against Duch (2007)' (2008) 21 *Leiden Journal of International Law* 719, 731; M Scharf, '*The Prosecutor v Slavko Dokmanovic*': Irregular Rendition and the ICTY' (1998) 11 *Leiden Journal of International Law* 369, 381.

brought to justice. Conversely, the establishment of safe havens for fugitives would not only result in danger for the state obliged to harbour the protected person, but also tend to undermine the foundations of extradition.[152]

While this case concerned an applicant who was the leader of the PKK, which is regarded as a terrorist organisation by many, the Court did not make a distinction between types of crime. It would also be arbitrary to maintain that states do not have any interest in suppressing organised crime if they collectively adopted the Organised Crime Convention and other pertinent instruments. As a result, an argument may be made by the law enforcement authorities that forcible abduction is justified in the interest of crime prevention. It is true that Article 4(2) of the Organised Crime Convention prohibits a state from exercising jurisdiction in another state. However, if the latter state consents to such exercise of jurisdiction, then forcible abduction can be facilitated. The European Court noted in this regard that 'an arrest made by the authorities of one state on the territory of another state, without the consent of the latter, affects the person concerned's individual rights to security'.[153] The Court also held that the consent would be regarded as a form of co-operation carried out in accordance with national and international law.[154] In other words, forcible abduction may be accepted as the 'extradition in disguise',[155] and this line of reasoning would be supported to combat organised crime.[156] Such an act threatens the very existence of the extradition procedures adopted by states and can negatively impact upon the friendly relations among states.

It is encouraging to see, however, that national courts have set aside criminal proceedings based on the principle of 'abuse of process'[157] in order to avoid gross injustice. This was stipulated in *Bennet v Horseferry Road Magistrates Court*,[158] concerning a New Zealand national arrested in South Africa and forcibly transferred to the UK to stand trial. Lord Bridge of the House of Lords stated that:

> When it is shown that the law enforcement agency responsible for bringing a prosecution has only been enabled to do so by participating in violations of international law and of the laws of another state in order to secure the presence of the accused within the territorial jurisdiction of the court, I think that respect for the rule of law demands that the court takes cognisance of that circumstance.[159]

Similar decisions have been reached in other common law jurisdictions,

---

[152] (2005) 41 EHRR 45, para 88.

[153] Ibid, para 85. See also *Bozano v France* (1986) 9 EHRR 297.

[154] *Ibid*, paras 86, 93–99.

[155] Judgment of the Chamber on *Ocalan v Turkey*, delivered on 12 Mach 2003, para 91.

[156] A Künzuli, '*Öcalan v Turkey*: Some Comments' (2004) 17 *Leiden Journal of International Law* 141, 149.

[157] C Warbrick, 'Judicial Jurisdiction and Abuse of Process' (2000) 49 *International and Comparative Law Quarterly* 489, 490.

[158] [1993] 3 All ER 138.

[159] Ibid, 155.

including Australia,[160] Canada,[161] New Zealand[162] and South Africa.[163] The principle of abuse of process was also upheld at the international level in the *Nicolic* Trial Chamber case[164] and *Prosecutor v Barayagwiza*[165] before the International Criminal Tribunal for Rwanda (ICTR). Coupled with this is a human rights argument which treats forcible abduction as a clear violation.[166] The House of Lords in this regard held that there was a duty to 'oversee executive action and to refuse to countenance behaviour that threatens either basic human rights or the rule of law'.[167] Germany takes a similar approach.[168] At the international level, it has been argued that, even with the consent of a state, forcible abduction constitutes a violation of peremptory norms of human rights.[169]

There are a few points to be noted. First, it has been held that the abuse of process must be such as to make it repugnant to the rule of law or be tainted with gross violation of the rights of the individual.[170] The Extraordinary Chambers in the Court of Cambodia listed torture and similar serious mistreatment as examples for invoking the principle of abuse of process.[171] The ICTY spoke of 'the egregious nature' of such treatment.[172] What becomes apparent, then, is that it would be difficult to cross this threshold to invoke the principle. Furthermore, most of the aforementioned cases at the national and international levels ruled that courts should stay criminal proceedings if the public officials/authorities as well as the organs of the international penal tribunals were directly involved in abduction. This means that if forcible abduction was carried out by non-state actors, then the court may still exercise jurisdiction over the suspect.[173] This was

---

[160] *Levinge v Director of Custodial Services* 9 NSWLR 546.

[161] *Keyowski v Her Majesty The Queen* [1988] 1 SCR 657; *R v Jewitt* [1985] 2 SCR 128; *O'Connor v The Queen* [1995] 4 SCR 411.

[162] *Regina v Hartley* 2 NZLR 199 (1978); *Moevao v Dept of Labour* [1980] 1 NZLR 464.

[163] *State v Ebrahim* 1991 (2) S.A. 533.

[164] Above n 145, paras 106–15.

[165] Above n 146, paras 73–77.

[166] *Canon Garcia v Ecuador*, Communication No 319/1988, CCPR/C/43/D/319/1988 (6 November 1991), in which the Human Rights Committee held that abduction of Colombian national by the US DEA was a breach of Art 9 of the ICCPR. The UN Working Group on Arbitrary Detention also ruled that Alvarez-Machain's detention was arbitrary, E/CN.4/1994/27 (17 December 1993), paras 139–40. Other cases include: *Almeida de Quinteros and Quinteros Almeida v Uruguay*, Communication No 107/1981, CCPR/C/19/D/107/1981 (21 July 1983); *Celiberti de Casariego v Uruguay*, Communication No 56/1979, CCPR/C/13/D/56/1979 (29 July 1981). See further J Paust, 'After *Alvarez-Machain*: Abduction, Standing, Denials of Justice, and Unaddressed Human Rights Claims' (1993) 67 *St. John's Law Review* 551.

[167] Above n 158, 150. It is worth noting that the UK traditionally supported the rule of *male captus bene detentus*. See *Ex parte Scott* (1829) 109 Eng Rep 166 (KB); *R v Sattler* (1858) Eng Rep 111 (KB).

[168] Bundesverfassungsgericht, Decision of 17 July 1985—2 BvR 1190/84, in *EuGRZ* 1986, 18-2.

[169] HA Blackmun, 'The Supreme Court and the Law of Nations' (1994) 104 *Yale Law Journal* 39, 41–42.

[170] *Prosecutor v Lubanga, Judgment on the Appeal of Mr Thomas Lubanga Dyilo against the Decision on the Defence Challenge to the Jurisdiction of the Court Pursuant to Art 19(2)(a) of the Statute of 3 October 2006*, Case No ICC-01/04–01/06 (OA4) (14 December 2006), paras 30 and 31.

[171] Above n 150, para 21.

[172] Above n 145, para 114.

[173] Above n 160; A Sridhar, 'The International Criminal Tribunal For the Former Yugoslavia's

affirmed in *Stocke v Germany*[174] by the European Court of Human Rights. This finding further suggests that courts can exercise jurisdiction over a suspect even when trickery is used.[175] Finally, measures such as the stay of criminal proceedings are discretionary, and therefore the judiciary would not be held liable for not exercising this. To summarise, although the principle of *male captus bene detentus* has been challenged on the grounds of human rights violation and the abuse of process in recent times, it is still an accepted principle of law. Therefore states can rely on it to bring criminals to justice. This, in turn, can cast some doubts on the effectiveness of a legal framework established by TCL as it does not oblige states to refrain from forced abduction.

3.2.4.2 Other Mutual Legal Assistance

Another important part of TCL is the provision relating to mutual legal assistance in criminal matters other than extradition. The transnational nature of organised crime makes it necessary to establish a comprehensive legal framework to facilitate mutual legal assistance in law enforcement and other areas. In looking at the provision of the Organised Crime Convention, it may be concluded that it does provide a basic framework. Traditionally, mutual legal assistance was facilitated through a comity-based system of requests for assistance known as 'Letters Rogatory' and was mainly concerned with collection of evidence to facilitate investigation and prosecution of offenders.[176] Compared to co-operation in civil and commercial matters, the development of the framework in relation to co-operation in criminal issues has been very slow.[177] This is understandable given the sensitive nature of the subject matter. Today, mutual legal assistance is provided bilaterally[178] or multilaterally[179] through international treaties and the Organised Crime Convention is the latest attempt to bind most states. Its benefit is also that the assistance is to be facilitated for different types of organised crime, unlike many of the pre-existing conventions, which are subject specific.

Mutual legal assistance is important as it can ameliorate the difficulty in achieving international co-operation through approximation of national laws and legal systems. There is no doubt that approximation of national substantive

Response to the Problem of Transnational Abduction' 42 (2006) *Stanford Journal of International Law* 343, 349–350.

[174] (1991) 11 EHRR 46.

[175] Sridhar, above n 173, 349.

[176] R Cryer et al, *An Introduction to International Criminal Law and Procedure* (Cambridge, Cambridge University Press, 2008) 86.

[177] D McClean, *International Judicial Assistance* (Oxford, Clarendon Press,1992) 124.

[178] See, eg Mutual Legal Assistance in Criminal Matters (Australia) Order 1999 (Hong Kong); Mutual Assistance in Criminal Matters (Malaysia) Regulations 2006 (Australia).

[179] European Convention on Mutual Assistance in Criminal Matters 1959, ETS No 30; Inter-American Convention on Mutual Assistance in Criminal Matters 1992, OASTS No 75. See D McClean, *International Co-operation in Civil and Criminal Matters* (Oxford, Oxford University Press, 2002) ch 6.

and procedural laws will make it easier for all states to co-operate as states would be guided by the same standards. As noted above, this is to some extent facilitated by the Organised Crime Convention through, among others, the adoption of common definitions. However, it was also shown that this is not the case in practice. The benefit of mutual legal assistance is that it is not conditional upon having uniform standards. Rather, it is facilitated through mutual recognition of national laws and procedures. That is to say, a state will respect a decision made by another despite differences and will implement it at the domestic level as far as possible. From the viewpoint of states, mutual recognition may be a preferred option over the approximation of national laws as it does not necessarily require them to substantially modify their legislative and law enforcement frameworks. This is the principle being widely promoted at the European level,[180] but the Organised Crime Convention goes further to promote it widely at the international level.

In looking at a pertinent provision, Article 18, it becomes apparent that the principle of mutual recognition is recognised to some extent. Some of the measures to be taken in this regard are effecting the services of judicial documents, executing searches, and seizing and freezing assets.[181] These may be regarded as examples of mutual recognition of judicial decisions as a court in one jurisdiction executes the orders and decisions issued by another state. Of those states which have complied with the reporting obligation,[182] most have stated that they facilitate these types of assistance. The principle can also be seen in other provisions, such as Articles 13 (execution of confiscation or freezing orders), 21 (transfer or criminal proceedings) and 22 (criminal record). This principle of mutual recognition is further augmented by exchange of authorities stipulated under Articles 19 (joint investigations)[183] and 27 (law enforcement co-operation)[184] which are designed to co-ordinate law enforcement activities among state parties.

There are, however, a number of obstacles in realising the principle of mutual recognition. For instance, Article 18 mainly applies to states which are not part of any prior instruments in relation to mutual legal assistance. In other words, if states are part of bilateral or multilateral treaties, then these instruments take precedence over the Organised Crime Convention.[185] Mutual assistance can also be refused on grounds of state sovereignty and public order under the same

---

[180] See Chapter 6 for details.

[181] Other measures under the same Article include, but are not limited to, examining objects and sites, providing information, evidentiary items and expert evaluations, providing originals or certified copies of relevant documents and records, identifying or tracing proceeds of crime, property, instrumentalities or other things for evidentiary purposes, and facilitating the voluntary appearance of persons in the requesting state Party.

[182] Implementation Report 2008 No 1, above n 38, para 77.

[183] This is facilitated in states such as Bulgaria, Burundi, Cameroon, Kazakhstan, Paraguay, Trinidad & Tobago and Zimbabwe. Implementation Report 2008 No 2, above n 113, para 37.

[184] The measures to be adopted include establishing channels of communication, intelligence sharing, and exchange of personnel.

[185] Art 18(7).

Article. This applies to states including Côte d'Ivoire, Croatia, Gabon, Malta and Mauritius.[186] A provision such as this has existed in treaties on mutual legal assistance for a long time as states are generally still reluctant to provide certain kinds of evidence, particularly when it contains national security information or other state secrets.[187] Also, the ambit of 'public order' is wide so that states can refuse to co-operate on for a variety of reasons.[188] Despite these shortcomings, the Organised Crime Convention is still an important step forward as it can start building mutual confidence and understanding among states for better co-operation.

An obligation to co-operate can also be facilitated by other branches of international law. For instance, if particular conduct crosses the threshold of international crime, ICL imposes an obligation to co-operate with the ICC. There is a general duty to co-operate under Article 86, and co-operative measures include surrender of offenders (Article 89), search and seizure of assets, and facilitating the voluntary appearance of witnesses and experts (Article 93). An obligation to co-operate can also be promoted by IHRL. Article 1(3) of the United Nations Charter provides that one purpose of the United Nations is to 'achieve international co-operation . . . in promoting and encouraging respect for human rights and for fundamental freedoms'. This provision can be taken as requiring the promotion of international co-operation in criminal matters as part of the obligation to investigate, prosecute and punish conducts by non-state actors. Finally, if and when some aspects of organised crime can be regarded as threats to international peace and security as noted in the previous chapter, the United Nations Security Council can impose binding obligations on states to co-operate under Chapter VII of the United Nations Charter.

3.2.5 Prevention of Organised Crime

A criminal justice response with a focus on prosecution and punishment of offenders is not sufficient to address organised crime. While it may deter criminals from future criminality, given the amount of profits they can make, criminals often offend repeatedly and therefore their prosecution and punishment do not necessarily contribute to this aim. The main reason why organised criminals supply illicit goods and services is because there exists strong demands for drugs, sexual services, cultural goods, endangered species and so forth. Therefore, demand reduction should be a vital part of any comprehensive framework. This can be achieved through awareness-raising at the national level so that the general public is better educated about the impact of illicit goods and services, and is recognised under Article 31(5) of the Organised Crime Convention.

---

[186] Implementation Report 2008 No 1, above n 38, para 83.
[187] R Currie, 'Human Rights and International Mutual Legal Assistance: Resolving the Tension' (2000) 11 *Criminal Law Forum* 143, 160.
[188] Ibid, 161.

However, the Convention does not go so far as to oblige states to take more concrete measures, and this is a major weakness.

One way to address the demand for illicit goods and services would be to impose severe penalties. This would deter potential clients from purchasing illicit goods and services in the future. In states where strict penalties are not imposed, the likely outcome is that the demand will remain high, and this makes it more likely that organised criminal groups will get involved. In the UK, for example, prostitution itself is not criminalised, and this has maintained the existence of the sex industry and human trafficking. It is worth noting in this respect that 80% of sex workers in London are foreign nationals, many of whom have been trafficked.[189] In the Netherlands, it is widely known that possession and consumption of cannabis are tolerated. However, as they remain criminal offences, the involvement of organised crime still continues.[190] One way to solve this, then, is to impose severe penalties for those who purchase sexual services, child pornography, illegal narcotics and so on. This can prevent actual/potential consumers from purchasing these goods and services.

While this is a sensible option, experience shows that prohibition can drive activities underground, making the problem worse in many cases. This helps organised crime to flourish and it becomes more difficult for law enforcement authorities to suppress it. A comprehensive approach, then, would also include action to reduce supply at the same time. Many people produce illegal drugs or become prostitutes due to poverty and a lack of economic opportunities in their states of origin.[191] If these individuals can find alternative ways to earn their living, this can reduce the need to engage in illegal activities. Therefore, good poverty reduction, employment and alternative development[192] strategies must be incorporated into a comprehensive framework. In many cases, states where illicit goods and services originate lack an ability to effectively implement these measures. The Organised Crime Convention therefore obliges states to provide financial, technical and other assistance to developing states under Article 30. The Article also recognises the role to be played by regional and international organisations in this regard, and Article 31 provides for participation in international projects developed by these and other organisations.

---

[189] UK Parliamentary Home Affairs Committee, 'The Trade in Human Beings: Human Trafficking in the UK' (May 2009), 15.

[190] International Narcotics Control Strategy Report 2009, above ch 2 n 168.

[191] Obokata, above ch 2 n 146.

[192] This is a strategy adopted for illicit cultivation of narcotics, and has been defined by the United Nations General Assembly as a 'process to prevent and eliminate the illicit cultivation of plants containing narcotic drugs and psychotropic substances through specifically designed rural development measures in the context of sustained national economic growth and sustainable development efforts in countries taking action against drugs, recognizing the particular socio-cultural characteristics of the target communities and groups, within the framework of a comprehensive and permanent solution to the problem of illicit drugs'. A/RES/S-20/4 (10 June 1998).

3.3 Key Legal Challenges Facing Effective Implementation of Obligations

3.3.1 Periods of Limitations for Organised Crime

One of the major challenges facing the prosecution and punishment of organised crime is the existence of statutes of limitations in many jurisdictions. Generally speaking, the law enforcement authorities are not able to initiate prosecution after a passage of a certain period of time under this rule. This is also known as a period of limitation in civil law states where it is recognised under their Criminal Codes. The main reason for retaining this rule is to ensure fairness in criminal procedure. As time passes, it becomes difficult for the accused as well as the authorities to prepare a case due to loss of memory on the part of witnesses and of other evidence. This not only affects a defendant's right to a fair trial, but also casts doubt on the credibility of the administration of justice.

While this is an important point to recognise, the rule on the period of limitation can be taken advantage of by criminals, as they can escape abroad or go into hiding until a period of limitations expires. The Organised Crime Convention takes this into consideration and obliges states to establish a long limitation period for offences covered under it.[193] It further provides that a period should be longer if the offender has evaded the administration of justice. It should be noted that long periods for serious offences (ie 10 years or longer) are recognised in many states, including Estonia,[194] Ethiopia,[195] Finland,[196] Germany[197] and Indonesia,[198] and that they apply to various forms of organised crime. Therefore, it may be that most cases of organised crime are prosecuted and punished within the timeframes provided under relevant domestic legislation. It is also worth noting that states such as the UK[199] and New Zealand[200] recognise limitations periods only for minor offences. Therefore, serious crimes, including organised crime, can be prosecuted even after a long lapse of time. Furthermore, in relation to international crime, Article 29 of the Rome Statute explicitly provides that statutory limitations do not apply to crimes stipulated under it.[201]

---

[193] Art11(5).

[194] 10 years for crimes carrying imprisonment of five years or longer under the Chapter 6 of Estonian Criminal Code, RT I 2001, 61, 364 (consolidated text RT I 2002, 86, 504).

[195] 15 years for serious crimes of minimum imprisonment of between five to ten years under Art 217 of the Criminal Code, Proclamation No414/2004.

[196] Ten years for crimes carrying imprisonment of two to eight years under Chapter 8 of the Finnish Criminal Code, 39/1889, as amended in 2008.

[197] Ten years for crimes carrying imprisonment of five to ten years under Art 78 of the German Criminal Code.

[198] Twelve years for a crime carrying imprisonment of three years or longer under Art 78 of the Indonesian Criminal Code 1952

[199] S 127 of the Magistrates Court Act 1980.

[200] S 10B of the Crimes Act1961 as amended.

[201] See also: Convention on the Non-Applicability of Statutory Limitations to War Crimes and

However, some types of organised crime are not regarded as serious. An offence of corruption among public officials in Japan, for example, carries a maximum of two years' imprisonment.[202] In Russia, punishment for human trafficking and the use of slave labour is imprisonment for a maximum of five years,[203] and in Vietnam, people who illegally export or import goods such as precious metal, gem stones and cultural/historical goods are punished with the maximum of 2–5 years' imprisonment, depending on the value of such goods.[204] The periods of limitation for these less serious offences are shorter, and they create ample opportunities for evasion of liability. Another dimension of these limitations is their impact on international co-operation, and extradition in particular. The UK does not have a statute of limitations on serious offences, as noted above. Thus, if it wishes to make a request for extradition to another state, it will have to make sure that the period of limitation has not expired in the requested state—otherwise extradition cannot be carried out due to the principle of double criminality. Obviously such an instance can be solved through bilateral agreements, but this highlights some of the practical difficulties in implementing international co-operation.

3.3.2 Immunity of Government Officials and Diplomats

Another challenge is immunity granted to government officials and diplomats serving in foreign states. This occasionally becomes an issue when the agents of states abroad become part of organised crime, although it should be stated from the outset that such instances are rare. A recent example of this is a case concerning a domestic worker working for a diplomatic mission in London who became a victim of slavery.[205] Similar cases of abuses against domestic workers working for diplomats have been reported in the US.[206] In simple terms, immunity gives procedural protection from adjudication and enforcement at a national level, although it confers no substantive exemption from local law.[207]

Crimes against Humanity 1968, 754 UNTS 73; European Convention on Non-Applicability of Statutory Limitations to Crimes against Humanity and War Crimes 1974, ETS No 82.

[202] Art 193 of the Japanese Penal Code. Trafficking of human beings also carries a maximum of five years' imprisonment under Art 226(2), which is substantially lower than other jurisdictions such as the UK, where it is published by the maximum imprisonment of 14 years. See Sexual Offences 2003.

[203] Arts 127(1) and (2) of the Russian Criminal Code, NO. 63-FZ (1996).

[204] Art 154 of the Vietnamese Penal Code.

[205] 'Diplomat's Nanny Lift Lid on Modern Slavery,' The Independent (9 August 2009).

[206] US Government Accountability Office, 'US Government's Efforts to Address Alleged Abuse of Household Workers by Foreign Diplomats with Immunity Could Be Strengthened', report to the Subcommittee on Human Rights and the Law, Committee on the Judiciary, US Senate (July 2008). See also See the website of the American Civil Liberties Union at www.aclu.org/womensrights/employ/domesticworkers.html.

[207] A Reinisch, *International Organisations before National Courts* (Cambridge, Cambridge University Press, 2000) 13; F Rawski, 'To Waive or Not to Waive? Immunity and Accountability in UN Peacekeeping Operations' (2002) 18 *Connecticut Journal of International Law* 103, 106; E Denza,

This means that individuals and organisations must still obey the applicable laws, although they are exempt from the judicial process to enforce those laws.[208] Jurisdictional immunity derives from the customary international law of state or sovereign immunity, which has prevented states from exercising control over the public acts of other states.[209] To be more precise, domestic courts and tribunals did not exercise civil or criminal jurisdictions over all acts of foreign states and their agents.[210]

This was later modified to apply only to official or public acts of governments.[211] This is commonly referred to as functional immunity or immunity *ratione materiae.*[212] It applies not only to high-ranking public officials, but also to low-ranking public officials and those acting on behalf of the state. Furthermore, this type of immunity does not cease at the end of the discharge of official functions because the act is legally attributable to the state and therefore liability may only be incurred by the state.[213] Therefore, former heads of state and diplomats, for instance, continue to enjoy immunity *ratione materiae* even after they leave office for acts performed in an official capacity.[214] However, immunity *ratione materiae* can be waived by the sending states as it operates only as a procedural bar to jurisdiction.[215]

The immunity *ratione materiae* does not pose much difficulty in the prosecution of organised crime because criminal conduct generally is regarded as an act of private nature and not an official or public act. In *Jimenez v Aristeguieta,*[216] the accused used his position as the former President of Venezuela to commit financial crimes for his personal benefit. His claim for immunity was rejected. In a similar vein, in *United States v Noriega,*[217] it was held that the acts of drug-

---

Diplomatic Law: Commentary on the Vienna Convention on Diplomatic Relations (Oxford, Oxford University Press,1998) 256.

[208] Reinisch, ibid, 14.

[209] D Akande, 'International Law Immunities and the International Criminal Court' (2004) 98 *American Journal of International Law* 407, 409. The rule was said to be recognised in *The Shchooter Exchange v McFaddon* 11 US 166 (1812). See H Fox, 'International Law and Restraints on the Exercise of Jurisdiction by National Courts of states' in M Evans (ed), *International Law*, 2nd edn (Oxford, Oxford University Press, 2006), 365. Orakhelashvili, however, argues that there is not enough evidence to support a claim that state immunity is established in customary international law. Above ch 2 n 136, 337.

[210] They include Brazil, China, Japan, Poland and Thailand. Brownlie, above ch 2 n 135, 323–24.

[211] See International Convention for the Unification of Certain Rules Concerning the Immunities of Government Vessels 1926, 176 LNTS 199; European Convention on State Immunity 1972, ETS No 74; *Empire of Iran Case* (1963) 45 ILR 57 (German Federal Constitutional Court 1963); *The Philippine Admiral* [1977] AC 373 (UK Privy Council); *Trendtex Trading Corporation v Central Bank of Nigeria* [1977] 1 QB 529 (UK Court of Appeal); *I Congreso del Partido* [1983] 1 AC 244 (UK House of Lords). See further MA Tunks, 'Diplomats or Defendants? Defining the Future of the Head-of-state Immunity' (2002) 52 *Duke Law Journal* 651; Fox, above n 209, 374.

[212] I Bantekas and S Nash, *International Criminal Law* (London, Routledge-Cavendish, 2007) 39.

[213] Akande, above n 209, 266.

[214] C Wickremasinghe, 'Immunities Enjoyed by Officials of states and International Organisations' in M Evans (ed), *International Law*, 2nd edn (Oxford, Oxford University Press, 2006) 408.

[215] Ibid, 397.

[216] 1 F 2d 547, 552 (5th Cir 1962), cert denied, 373 US 914 (1963).

[217] 746 F.Supp 1506, 1511 (SD Fla 1990).

trafficking committed by a leader of a county did not constitute a sovereign act. The same reasoning also applies to violations of human rights, such as torture, enslavement, unlawful killing and rape,[218] some of which are relevant to the commission of organised crime. It has been argued in this respect that there is an emerging international rule whereby immunity from national criminal jurisdiction is excluded in all cases of serious human rights violations, regardless of where they have been committed.[219]

There is another type of immunity known as personal immunity or immunity *ratione personae*. This type of immunity is granted on the basis of customary and treaty law,[220] and is based on the official status of the persons concerned. It is available to a limited number of individuals—heads of states and governments, and senior members of the cabinet, such as foreign ministers, diplomatic and consular agents.[221] These individuals enjoy absolute immunity from criminal jurisdiction regardless of whether the acts in question were performed in an official or private capacity while they were in office.[222] As this type of immunity is attached to the office, it ends with the termination of the agent's official duties.[223] A concrete example of immunity *ratione personae* is that given to diplomats. To begin with, the detailed rule on diplomatic immunity is laid down by the Vienna Convention on Diplomatic Relations 1961. Article 31 provides that a diplomat 'shall enjoy immunity from the criminal jurisdiction of the receiving state'. This article grants absolute or complete immunity from criminal jurisdiction, which has been supported since the sixteenth century and has acquired the status of customary law.[224]

Diplomatic immunity, as with the doctrine of state immunity, is procedural in character and does not affect any underlying substantive liability.[225] It gives protection from a legal process of adjudication and enforcement but confers no substantive exemption from local law.[226] As noted, immunity extends to official and private acts of diplomats while on assignment in the receiving states.[227] When their immunities *ratione personae* come to an end, they are still covered by immunities *ratione materiae* in that their acts performed in an official

---

[218] *Pinochet (No 3)* [2000] 1 AC 147; Orakhelashvili, above ch 2 n 136, 323–25.

[219] Bantekas and Nash, above n 212, 42; LM O'Connell, 'State Immunity, Human Rights and Jus Cogens: A Critique of the Normative Hierarchy Theory' (2003) *American Journal of International Law* 741, 746.

[220] Cassese, above ch 2 n 131, Chapter 14.

[221] *Case Concerning the Arrest Warrant of 11 April 2000* (2002) ICJ Reports 3, para 51; Bantekas and Nash, above n 212, 39; Akande, above n 209, 411.

[222] Ibid, paras 54–55; Tunks, above n 221, 676; Wickremasinghe, above n 214, 397. See also *Gaddafi* (2001) 125 ILR 456; *HSA et al v SA* 42 ILM 596; *Tachiona v Mugabe* 169 F Supp 2d 259, 288, 296–297 (SDNY 2001); *Saltany v Reagan* 702 F Supp 319, 320 (DDC 1988).

[223] Bantekas and Nash, above n 212, 39.

[224] Denza, above n 207, 230 and 232.

[225] Ibid, 256.

[226] Reinisch, above n 207, 13.

[227] VL Maginnis, 'Limiting Diplomatic Immunity: Lessons Learned from the 1946 Convention on the Privileges and Immunities of the United Nations' (2002–2003) 28 *Brooklyn Journal of International Law* 989, 990.

capacity are attributable not to themselves but to their states.[228] Article 39(2) of the Vienna Convention provides that a diplomatic agent enjoys continuing immunity for acts performed in his official capacity, and this is effective in a receiving state even after the termination of diplomatic status. The problem of diplomatic immunity, then, is that if they become part of organised crime, they cannot legally be held liable.

The importance of diplomatic immunity is also recognised in the Organised Crime Convention. To begin with, the premises of diplomatic missions, including private residences of diplomatic agents, are inviolable and the agents of receiving states may not enter them without the consent of the heads of missions.[229] This is implicitly reflected in Article 4 of the Organised Crime Convention on state sovereignty as these premises are regarded as territories of the sending states, which retain authority over them. *Travaux préparatoires* on Article 12 (confiscation of proceeds of crime) further indicate that 'it is not the intention of the Convention to restrict the rules that apply to diplomatic or state immunity, including that of international organizations'.[230] It should be stressed that under the Vienna Convention any property found within the premises of a diplomatic mission is immune from search and requisition.[231] The inviolability of archives and documents, diplomatic bags, and courier and official correspondence is also recognised.[232] All of these make it difficult to conduct effective law enforcement activities against diplomatic agents when they are suspected of being involved in organised crimes. In addition, in relation to the offence of corruption, Article 8(2) obliges states to 'consider' adopting measures to criminalise corruption involving foreign public officials or international civil servant. This obligation can be fulfilled as long as states consider measures without implementing them. The obligation therefore is weak, with the possible result that diplomats are not properly prosecuted and punished.

While these examples make it look as if diplomats are untouchable, there are several ways to hold them accountable if diplomatic immunity is abused. First, as noted above, immunity *ratione personae* of diplomatic agents can be waived by the sending states. Article 32 of the Vienna Convention in this respect authorises sending states to do so,[233] thereby subjecting their diplomats to the jurisdiction of receiving states. It is a common practice that receiving states request waiver of immunity to sending states of diplomats who commit criminal offences. In *Gustavo JL and Another*,[234] for example, the Supreme Court of Spain rejected the argument that a diplomat at the Embassy of Colombia could not be tried for drug trafficking offences even after dismissal from his post and

---

[228] Wickremasinghe, above n 214, 403.

[229] Arts 22(1) and 30 of the Vienna Convention.

[230] Interpretative Notes, above ch 2 n 110, para 20.

[231] Art 22(3).

[232] Arts 24 and 27.

[233] The right of sending states to waive immunity is part of customary international law. *Arrest Warrant Case*, above n 221, para 52.

[234] (1991) 86 ILR 517.

waiver of immunity. Similarly, in *United States v Guinand*[235]a staff member of the Peruvian Embassy was charged with distribution of cocaine following his dismissal from the Embassy. Finally, in the case *Deputy Commissioner McMahon v Kevin McDonald*, the immunity of an administrative staff who sold Irish passports illegally was waived by the Irish government and was eventually convicted in England.[236]

However, all of these examples do not mean that sending states have a duty to do so, because the waiver is an option rather than a mandatory obligation.[237] Because of this, some argue that waivers are an ineffective tool in practice, as states are unwilling to waive immunity to allow their diplomats to face criminal charges.[238] There are examples to support this. In *Ahmed v Hoque*,[239] the court dismissed the claim made by a plaintiff who was enslaved by his employer, the Economics Minister for the Permanent Mission of Bangladesh, on a ground of diplomatic immunity. In *Tabion v Mufti*,[240] where a plaintiff, a Filipino national, complained of low wages and long hours working for the first secretary of the Jordanian Embassy in Washington DC, the Court held that 'day-to-day living services such as domestic help were not meant to be treated as outside of diplomats' official functions', and therefore Article 31(c) did not apply. These cases came before the courts of receiving states as the sending states did not waive the immunity granted to these officials.

If the sending states are not willing to waive immunity, the receiving states can declare diplomats *persona non grata* (not acceptable) under Article 9 of the Vienna Convention. This obliges sending states to recall their own diplomats or terminate their functions. If sending states refuse to do so, receiving states can refuse to recognise them as members of the diplomatic mission. This declaration is used for diplomats who engage in such conducts as espionage, terrorism or other subversive activities, but can also be used for other serious criminal offences.[241] The UK, for example, resorts to Article 9 in cases involving violent crimes, drug trafficking, firearm offences, serious sexual offences, fraud and other serious offences.[242] An example of this is the expulsion of four Russian diplomats who refused to co-operate with the investigation of the murder of Alexander Litvinenko in 2007.[243] Once they are sent home, they can be prosecuted in accordance with the domestic law of states. In this regard, Article 31(4) provides that the immunity of a diplomatic agent from the jurisdiction of the receiving state does not exempt him from the jurisdiction of the sending

---

[235] 88 F Supp 774, 775(DDC 1988).
[236] Denza, above n 207, 276.
[237] Maginnis, above n 227, 1003.
[238] Ibid. See also G McClanahan, *Diplomatic Immunity: Principles, Practice, Problems* (London, C Hurt and Co, 1989), 137.
[239] WL 1964806 (SDNY 2002).
[240] 73 F 3d 535 (1996).
[241] Maginnis, above n 227, 1003; Denza, above n 207, 63–67.
[242] 'Review of the Vienna Convention' (Cmnd 9497, 1985), paras 60–71.
[243] Available at news.bbc.co.uk/1/hi/uk_politics/6902046.stm.

state. Denza notes that sending states are likely to initiate criminal proceedings at home against their diplomats who committed serious crimes.[244]

Finally, immunity for commission of international crime is worth mentioning as some forms of organised crime can be elevated to that status, as noted elsewhere. The general position is that those who are accused of international crimes enjoy immunities *ratione personae*, but not immunities *ratione materiae*, before domestic courts and tribunals because of the principle of individual criminal responsibility under which the official position of individuals does not exempt them from responsibility for acts which are crimes under international law.[245] A violation of *jus cogens* norms, which include prohibition of international crime, is not a sovereign act and therefore should not attract immunity.[246] From a different angle, it has been said that universal jurisdiction displaces the immunity *ratione materiae* because the latter cannot coexist with the former, which permits domestic courts to exercise jurisdiction over certain international crimes committed in an official capacity.[247] Finally, individuals are only entitled to personal immunities vis-à-vis the authorities of the state and therefore they cannot be relied upon at international tribunals such as the ICC. Such an argument has been supported at the national and international levels. The ICJ, in the *Arrest Warrant Case*, held that 'the immunities enjoyed under international law does not prevent one from being prosecuted before international criminal courts where they have jurisdiction'.[248] A similar view was also taken by the Special Court of Sierra Leone, created under a treaty between the United Nations and Sierra Leone to prosecute those who committed serious international crimes, in prosecuting the former head of state of Liberia Charles Taylor.[249] This is affirmed in Article 27(2) of the ICC Statute.[250] Ratification of the ICC Statute, therefore, constitutes a waiver of national and international law immunities by state parties, even in their own states. This provision has already been incorporated into domestic legislations of Canada, Ireland, Malta, New Zealand and the UK.[251]

---

[244] Above n 207, 267.

[245] Akande, above n 209, 415; Art 7(2) of the ICTY Statute, Security Council Resolution 827 (1993); Art 6(2) of the ICTR Statute, Security Council Resolution 955 (1994); Art 27(1) of the Rome Statute Art 27(1).

[246] Orakhelashvili, above ch 2 n 136, 325. See also Joint Separate Opinion of Judges Higgins, Kooijmans and Buergenthal of the ICJ in the *Arrest Warrant Case*, in which they stated that international crimes are not covered by the immunities *ratione materiae* of former state officials. Above n 221.

[247] Akande, above n 209, 415. This was the reasoning adopted by most judges in *Pinochet (No 3) Case*, above n 218.

[248] Above n 221, para 61.

[249] *Prosecutor v Charles Taylor, Decision on Immunity from Jurisdiction*, No SCSL-03-01-I (31 May 2004).

[250] It provides: 'Immunities or special procedural rules which may attach to the official capacity of a person, whether under national or international law, shall not bar the Court from exercising its jurisdiction over such a person'.

[251] Akande, above n 209, 420 and 425.

3.3.3   Protection of Human Rights of Suspects/Defendants

As has been shown, TCL as represented by the Organised Crime Convention provides a comprehensive framework for addressing organised crime. Nevertheless, the primary focus is placed upon prosecution and punishment, and the rights of suspects and defendants are not sufficiently provided for. In addition to some of the issues raised above, there are other pertinent human rights issues in relation to suspects and defendants. During the course of investigation of organised crime, instances of arbitrary detention, torture and ill treatment, the breach of the principle of non-discrimination and even extrajudicial killings have been widely reported.[252] These are clear breaches of established human rights norms and principles.

Also pertinent is the excessive form of punishment, namely the death penalty. This punishment is imposed for drug-related offences in some jurisdictions[253] and raises a set of human rights issues. The death penalty per se is not a violation of human rights. Article 6(2) of the ICCPR provides that the death penalty may be imposed for the most serious crimes.[254] The parties to the Second Optional Protocol to the International Covenant on Civil and Political Rights, Aiming at the Abolition of the Death Penalty 1989,[255] as well as to Protocols 6 and 13 to the European Convention on Human Rights (ECHR)[256] have agreed to abolish the death penalty. The Second Optional Protocol, however, is not compulsory, and only 72 states are parties to it at this point.[257] Moreover, it is difficult to state that abolition of the death penalty has spread beyond Europe. All of these examples suggest that abolition itself is not as yet a universal concept under IHRL.

This does not mean that the death penalty does not raise any human rights concerns. It has been held to the contrary in the past. One often cited decision in this regard is *Soering v United Kingdom*.[258] In this case, the European Court of Human Rights held that:

> The manner in which it (death penalty) is imposed or executed, the personal circumstances of the condemned person and a disproportionality to the gravity of the crime committed, as well as the conditions of detention awaiting execution, are examples of factors capable of bringing the treatment or punishment received by the condemned person within the proscription under Article 3.[259]

---

[252] Obokata, above ch 2 n 146.

[253] International Narcotics Control Strategy Report 2009, above ch 2 n 168. These states include Iran, Laos, Saudi Arabia, Singapore, Syria, Thailand, UAE and Vietnam.

[254] Art 6(2).

[255] 9 ILM 1464.

[256] Protocol No 6 to the Convention for the Protection of Human Rights and Fundamental Freedoms Concerning the Abolition of the Death Penalty, ETS No 114; Protocol No 13 to the Convention for the Protection of Human Rights and Fundamental Freedoms, Concerning the Abolition of the Death Penalty in All Circumstances, ETS No 187.

[257] As of December 2009.

[258] (1989) 11 EHRR 439.

[259] Ibid, para 104.

In examining the so-called 'death row phenomenon', whose characteristics included the excessive waiting time until the execution, the mental anguish associated with it, and sexual and physical abuse in prison, the European Court stated that the extradition of Soering from the UK to the state of Virginia in the US would give rise to a breach of Article 3.[260]

Another important aspect of the death penalty is *non-refoulement* or non-return, and this was explored in *Judge v Canada* before the Human Rights Committee. In this case, the Committee expressed the opinion that

> For countries that *have* abolished the death penalty, there is an obligation not to expose a person to the real risk of its application. Thus, they may not remove, either by deportation or extradition, individuals from their jurisdiction, if it may be reasonably anticipated that they will be sentenced to death, without ensuring that the death sentence would not be carried out.[261]

In examining the position of Canada, which has abolished the death penalty, the Committee stated that 'by deporting him to a country where he was under sentence of death, Canada established the crucial link in the causal chain that would make possible the execution of the author', and therefore would violate the right to life under Article 6.[262] The same Committee has stated further that the death penalty can constitute arbitrary deprivation of life where it is imposed without regard being paid to the defendant's personal circumstances or the circumstances of a particular offence.[263]

Finally, it is to be noted that international law, IHRL, is a living instrument, and therefore should be interpreted in light of the present day conditions. Applying this to the death penalty, it has been noted by the European Court of Human Rights that the law on the death penalty has undergone a considerable evolution over the course of time.[264] The Court continued that, while Article 2 of the ECHR permits the death penalty, in looking at the development within Europe, the practice of the death penalty has come to be regarded as unacceptable. As more and more societies move towards the abolition of the death penalty, such a position might eventually spread to the rest of the world in the future.

---

[260] Ibid, paras 109–11.

[261] *Judge v Canada*, Communication No 829/1998, CCPR/C/78/D/829/1998 (5 August 2002), para 10.4. In this case, the Human Rights Committee reversed the decision made in *Kindler v Canada*, Communication No 470/1991, CCPR/C/48/D/470/1991 (30 July 1993). In *Kinder*, the Committee held that deportation of a person from a country which had abolished the death penalty to a country where he/she was under the sentence of death did not, per se, amount to a violation of Art 6 of the Covenant. In adopting a different decision in *Judge*, the Committee recognised that the Covenant should be interpreted as a living instrument and the rights protected under it should be applied in context and in light of present day conditions.

[262] Ibid, para 10.6.

[263] *Thompson v St Vincent & The Grenadines*, Communication No 806/1998, CCPR/C/70/D/806/1998 (5 December 2000); *Kennedy v Trinidad & Tobago*, Communication No 845/1998, CCPR/C/74/D/845/1998 (26 March 2002); *Carpo and Others v Philippines*, Communication No 1077/2002, CCPR/C/77/D/1077/2002 (28 March 2003).

[264] *Ocalan v Turkey*, above n 152.

Another key issue is expulsion of foreign criminals after they serve their sentences. It should be noted from the outset that a state has a right to control entry and expulsion of foreign nationals in accordance with domestic and international law, as part of the principle of state sovereignty.[265] Therefore, expulsion per se is not a violation of human rights.[266] However, under certain circumstances, such a practice may constitute human rights violations and therefore states are obliged to refrain from returning individuals. For instance, Article 3 of the Torture Convention prohibits states from returning an individual if there are substantial grounds to believe that he/she would be tortured.[267] This principle applies even to those who are accused of committing serious crimes such as terrorism[268] and, by extension, would apply to those who commit organised crime. The risk of ill-treatment must be real and, short of this, expulsion would not breach relevant human rights principles. This was the case for a Colombian national who was convicted of narcotics trafficking in France and awaiting deportation.[269]

It is important to note that ill-treatment does not have to come from human agents. Hence, in *D v United Kingdom*, the applicant who was detained in the UK for possession of drugs and was suffering from HIV/AIDs successfully argued that his return to St Kitts would breach Article 3 of the ECHR as there was no adequate health facility there.[270] This issue of expulsion arises in other contexts. For instance, in *Mehemi v France*,[271] the applicant successfully argued that his expulsion to Algeria and permanent exclusion from France as a result of his conviction for narcotics trafficking would be a breach of Article 8 of the ECHR, given his strong tie with his family and France.[272] Finally, it has also been held that if there is a danger of a suspect's right to a fair trial being denied, expulsion might not be carried out.[273]

What becomes apparent is that there are a wide variety of human rights issues in relation to the treatment of suspects and defendants, and a failure to address these raises a set of problems. First and foremost, states and the international community run the risk of losing legitimacy in their action against organised crime and of undermining the established legal and institutional framework to protect and promote human rights at the international level. This has been

---

[265] *Saadi v Italy* (2008) 24 BHRC 123, para 124.

[266] General Comment No 15, above n 105.

[267] See also *Soering v United Kingdom*, above n 258. Such a risk can come from non-state actors, when a state is unwilling or unable to protect the victim sufficiently. *D v United Kingdom* (1997) 24 EHRR 423, para 49.

[268] *Chahal v United Kingdom* (1996) 23 EHRR 413.

[269] *HLR v France* (1997) 26 EHRR 29.

[270] Above n 267, para 53. However, in *N v United Kingdom*, the Court, while supporting the reasoning in *D v United Kingdom*, held that 'aliens who are subject to expulsion cannot in principle claim any entitlement to remain in the territory of a Contracting state in order to continue to benefit from medical, social or other forms of assistance and services provided by the expelling state'. Application No 26565/05 (2008), para 42.

[271] (2000) 30 EHRR 739.

[272] See also *Amrollahi v Denmark*, Application No 56811/00 (2002).

[273] *Soering v UK*, above n 258, para 113.

pointed out in the context of terrorism,[274] and there is no reason why the same reasoning cannot be applied to action against organised crime. It will further undermine the rule of law and administration of justice at the national level. All of these are counterproductive in the prevention and suppression or organised crime. Those involved in criminal activities serve as valuable sources of information and evidence; their co-operation is essential for prosecution and punishment. If states are not able to protect and promote their human rights, it will become rather difficult to seek active co-operation. This can also incite further animosity towards the authorities, and it becomes more likely that criminals will resort to violence and intimidation.

It should be noted that there are some provisions in the Organised Crime Convention which are designed to protect the rights of defendants. Unfortunately the wording used in them is weak and they therefore do not place firm obligations on states. For example, in relation to extradition, Article 15(16) provides that:

> Nothing in this Convention shall be interpreted as imposing an obligation to extradite if the requested state Party has substantial grounds for believing that the request has been made for the purpose of prosecuting or punishing a person on account of that person's sex, race, religion, nationality, ethnic origin or political opinions or that compliance with the request would cause prejudice to that person's position for any one of these reasons.

On the face of it, this provision reflects the principle of *non-refoulement*, as noted above. However, the actual obligation relates to interpretation, and the provision itself does not go so far as to oblige states not to extradite. Article 16(13) also provides that fair treatment should be guaranteed during the extradition proceedings. However, such treatment is to be provided in accordance with domestic law and not the established international norms and principles.

There are other examples of weak provisions to protect and promote human rights. Article 11(3), on prosecution, adjudication and sanctions, refers to the rights of the defence in making decisions on the conditions attached to temporary release. However, the emphasis is placed upon ensuring the presence of suspects in criminal proceedings and not on the protection of their rights. In addition, the use of the term 'may' in relation to a refusal of mutual legal assistance on the ground of the absence of double criminality as stipulated under Article 18(9) suggests that it would be discretionary as opposed to mandatory. In striking a balance between the need for criminal justice and the human rights of suspects or defendants, therefore, the Organised Crime Convention favours the former. Thus, in order to promote full realisation of the rights of defendants and suspects, TCL as represented by the Organised Crime Convention must be

---

[274] See, eg P Hoffman, 'Human Rights and Terrorism' (2004) 26 *Human Rights Quarterly* 932; J Fitzpatrick, 'Speaking Law to Power: The War against Terrorism and Human Rights' (2003) 14 *European Journal of International Law* 241; M Ratner, ' Moving Away from the Rule of Law: Military Tribunals, Executive Detentions and Torture' (2003) 24 *Cardozo Law Review* 1513; K Roth 'Human Rights as a Response to Terrorism' (2004) 6 *Oregon Review of International Law* 37.

supplemented by IHRL and ICL, which also protect the rights for defendants or suspects.[275]

3.4 Conclusions

This chapter analysed some of the key obligations imposed upon states in relation to organised crime. It showed that TCL generally provides a comprehensive framework to address the practice by obliging states not only to prohibit and punish organised crime and related practices, such as inchoate offences, but also to facilitate international co-operation and some measures to prevent organised crime. The previous instruments are either subject specific and/or geographically limited, and the Organised Crime Convention improves this as it applies to various aspects of organised crime in all parts of the world. As such, it is reasonable to conclude that TCL as represented by the Organised Crime Convention marks an important step forward in consolidating the efforts of the international community to promote effective action against organised crime.

However, there are various problems associated with the current legal framework. For instance, the protection of state sovereignty is at the forefront of TCL as represented by the Organised Crime Convention. This is an inevitable feature in order to secure participation by as many states as possible, and given the national security implications arising from organised crime. Yet the same reasoning applies to other conduct, such as terrorism, international crime and gross violation of human rights. In those contexts, states are more willing to set aside the principle of state sovereignty to seek effective suppression and international co-operation. This clearly demonstrates that organised crime is not yet regarded as sufficiently important within the international legal system, and it will take some time for the prohibition of organised crime to attain a firmer legal status such as that of customary international law. In addition to a lack of common understanding of organised crime, perhaps this is due to the fact that organised crime not only produces vast amounts of profits for the criminals, but also brings income to those who produce goods and services. Therefore, states, particularly developing ones, may be reluctant to cut such convenient sources of income.

Another point to note is TCL's lack of due regard for the protection and promotion of the human rights of suspects and defendants. All suppression conventions, including the Organised Crime Convention, represent a criminal justice response to crimes stipulated under them, in that their focus is placed upon prosecution and punishment of offences and offenders through national law. While such an approach is necessary, it has been argued above that the international community cannot legitimately suppress the practice without having

---

[275] See, eg Arts 66 and 67.

regard to the human rights of suspects and defendants. The key principles and norms on this have been firmly established under international law, and the international community could have incorporated them into the Organised Crime Convention to demonstrate that they take human rights seriously in any action against organised crime. This has been done in relation to ICL, where the rights and suspects and defendants are recognised as important and guaranteed under the Rome Statute, for example. The same could have been the case for organised crime. The international community therefore missed a valuable opportunity in this regard.

It follows from the above that TCL on its own is not sufficient to address organised crime. In other words, a criminal justice response alone does not solve the problem. An effective response to the practice requires a holistic approach which addresses not only crime but also wider issues, such as the causes of organised crime, the supply and demand dynamics, and the human rights of suspects and defendants. While TCL is suitable for obliging states to criminalise a variety of activities related to organised crime, it has been shown above that it fails to deal with these key issues. It must be supplemented by other branches of international law such as IHRL, which can assist TCL to facilitate a holistic approach to organised crime.[276] Also, states alone are not capable of preventing and suppressing organised crime. They must be assisted by regional and international organisations, corporate entities such as banks and financial institutions, as well as members of civil society at the national/local level who possess good expertise on the subject. The next chapter provides a detailed analysis of the position and the role of non-state actors in the prevention and suppression or transnational organised crime.

---

[276] On this, see Obokata, above ch 2 n 51.

4

The Role of Non-state Actors in Suppression and Prevention of Organised Crime

4.1 Introduction

In this chapter, the role of non-state actors in suppressing and preventing organised crime will be examined. While states are the key actors under international law in combating transnational organised crime, as noted in Chapter 3, they often cannot do so without assistance or co-operation from non-state actors, such as international organisations, MNCs and NGOs. However, international law mainly regulates the conduct of states, and TCL as represented by the Organised Crime Convention is no exception as it does not create rights and obligations for non-state actors. In order to fully appreciate their contribution, this chapter goes beyond the realm of international law and explores the concept of global governance. This aids understanding the status of non-state actors by challenging the traditional state-centric notion of world order and supports the involvement of other relevant actors in governance over issues of international importance, such as transnational organised crime. Furthermore, it recognises the importance of non-legal instruments and arrangements to facilitate effective action against this criminality, which are more relevant to these actors.

The chapter begins with an examination of the concept of global governance, with particular reference to its key principles of participation and accountability. It then applies such to governance over transnational organised crime in order to articulate the role of relevant actors. It will be shown that actors such as international organisations, MNCs and NGOs, as well as witnesses and victims of organised crime, make valuable contributions to the prevention and suppression of transnational organised crime. Furthermore, various forms of accountability are available to address non-compliance by these actors. In terms of legal accountability, this chapter focuses on the criminal liability of individual criminals, criminal organisations, legal persons and international organisations. It also explores non-legal forms of accountability of a political, economic and administrative nature and highlights their relevance to transnational organised crime. Finally, the chapter re-examines the notion of the 'international community' and argues that its membership should be extended to all relevant actors.

4.2 The Role of Non-state Actors in Prevention and Suppression of Organised Crime

4.2.1 The Concept of Global Governance

'Global governance' is a concept which attempts to explain how world affairs should be governed in an era of globalisation.[1] It is relevant for the discussion of transnational organised crime as it assists in understanding the role of various actors in prevention and suppression. Although a wide variety of views exist and consensus is elusive, some key characteristics can be identified. A starting point is to understand the idea of 'governance'. Keohane defines it as 'the making and implementation of rules and the exercise of power within a given domain of activity'.[2] Rosenau notes in a similar vein that governance consists of 'rule systems, of steering mechanisms through which authority is exercised in order to enable systems to preserve their coherence and move towards desired goals'.[3] In short, governance is about making rules and implementing them.

Two of the key principles of good governance are participation and accountability.[4] Participation is closely linked to the right of individuals to present views and be heard in decision-making.[5] The right to participate applies to those who formally make and implement decisions. At the domestic level, the central agents in this regard are the legislative and executive branches. It is also interpreted as including those affected by those decisions.[6] This is an important point to recognise, as a good decision cannot be made without consultation and feedback from those who are likely to be affected. It has been argued that the right to participate should be extended to those who are not affected directly yet have particular expertise or interest in representing affected individuals and organisations, such as lobby groups, NGOs and community-based organisations.[7] In

---

[1] Held and McGrew, above ch 1 n 32, 8.

[2] R Keohane, 'Global Governance and Democratic Accountability' in D Held and M Koeing-Archibugi (eds), *Taming Globalization* (Cambridge, Polity Press, 2003) 132.

[3] J Rosenau, 'Governance in a New Global Order' in Held and McGrew, above ch 1 n 32, 72.

[4] N Woods, 'Good Governance in International Organizations' (1999) 5 *Global Governance* 39, 41.

[5] B Kingsbury, N Krisch and RB Stewart, 'The Emergence of Global Administrative Law' (2005) 68 *Law and Contemporary Problems* 15, 38.

[6] Woods, above n 4, 43–44.

[7] Kingsbury et al, above n 5, 38.

any area of decision-making in the contemporary world these actors exercise enormous influence.

In examining the idea of participation in global governance, a key point to stress from the outset is that it is not based on the traditional or Westphalian state-centric conception of world order. Although states remain the primary actors,[8] participation by a wide variety of bodies, including international organisations, NGOs, MNCs and financial institutions, is regarded as equally important.[9] This was made clear by the United Nations Commission on Global Governance in its report 'Our Global Neighborhood', which states that global governance is 'the sum of the many ways individuals and institutions, public or private, manage their common affairs'.[10]

Participation of multiple actors in global governance means there are various decision-making processes at the international, regional and national levels. Global governance therefore represents 'a broad, dynamic, complex process of interactive decision-making that is constantly evolving and responding to changing circumstances'.[11] As a result, unlike domestic governance, there is no central authority to govern all. Global governance is characterised by 'reconfiguration or relocation of authority between different layers or infrastructures of governance: the suprastate (such as UN), the regional (EU, etc), the transnational (civil society and business network), and the substate (community associations and local governments), and in between these layers, there are national governments'.[12] Global governance is not to be confused with the idea of 'global government' as it does not necessarily advocate the creation of 'a global central public body' to legislate for the international community as a whole,[13] although some commentators do support such a development.[14]

The lack of a core authority renders decision-making in global governance less centralised. At the domestic level, authority is exercised in a relatively organised manner in that there are unitary and hierarchical structures of decision-making and administration.[15] At the global level, however, regulatory and administrative systems are much more disorganised with 'decision making, participatory

---

[8] Rosenau, above n 3, 73.

[9] Held and McGrew, above ch 1 n 32, 3–4.

[10] Commission on Global Governance, 'Our Global Neighbourhood' (Oxford, Oxford University Press, 1995) 2. The former Secretary-General Kofi Anan also stated that the 'international public domain must be opened up further to the participation of the many actors whose contributions are essential to managing the path of globalisation'. K Annan, 'We the Peoples: The Role of the United Nations in the 21st Century' (2000).

[11] Ibid, 4.

[12] Held and McGrew, above ch 1 n 32, 9 and 10.

[13] L Finkelstein, 'What is Global Governance?' (1995) 1 *Global Governance* 367, 367; Held and McGrew, ibid, 9–10.

[14] D Held, *Democracy and the Global Order: From the Modern State to Cosmopolitan Governance* (Cambridge, Polity Press, 1995) 273; R Falk and A Strauss, 'On the Creation of a Global Peoples Assembly: Legitimacy and the Power of Popular Sovereignty' (2000) 36 *Stanford Journal of International Law* 191.

[15] N Krisch, 'The Pluralism of Global Administrative Law' (2006) 17 *European Journal of International Law* 247, 256.

procedures and review often taking place in different sites at the same time and with no formal connection among them'.[16] Rosenau summarises the nature of global governance as 'an extensive disaggregation of authority'.[17] The key to the success of global governance, then, is active co-operation and/or co-ordination to maintain consistency.

The second principle of good governance, accountability, requires decision-makers to communicate the nature and extent of decisions and implementation to stakeholders.[18] This means, among other things, that there needs to be a system or procedure in place to promote transparency and flow of information.[19] Kingsbury et al rightly observe that transparency and access to information are important foundations for the effective exercise of participation.[20] Also, in order to promote the smooth governance, it is essential to establish mechanisms of accountability for non-compliance. In this sense, accountability means 'to have to answer for one's action or inaction', and 'to be exposed to potential sanctions'.[21] Finally, there should also be a system where those affected by the decisions can seek a remedy in the event of breach of rules and decisions.

In contrast to domestic governance, the multiple levels of decision-making in global governance mean that accountability must be addressed on multiple levels. Accountability occurs not only nationally, but regionally and internationally as well, depending on the participants and issues at stake. For instance, states are the key subjects under international law and therefore the best place for accountability might be at the international level, before the ICJ and the Security Council, for example. As international organisations are frequently not subjected to the domestic jurisdiction of national courts and tribunals due to immunity,[22] an international forum may also be appropriate.

Nevertheless, nothing in the concept of global governance prevents the issue of accountability from being addressed at other levels. Indeed, accountability may be better addressed regionally and nationally based on the principle of subsidiarity. Simply put, this principle provides that a matter should be dealt with at the lowest level possible, with others stepping in only when this is not possible. This is a principle firmly established within the context of the EU,[23] for example. There are two key reasons in support of this arrangement. First, not all actors can participate in the formal decision-making at the international level. Secondly, for those affected by particular decisions, the remoteness might make it difficult to achieve a sense of justice being done. A member of civil

---

[16] Ibid.

[17] Rosenau, above n 3, 75.

[18] Woods, above n 4, 44.

[19] Ibid.

[20] Kingsbury et al, above n 5, 38.

[21] R Oakerson, 'Governance Structures for Enhancing Accountability and Responsiveness' in JL Perry (ed), *Handbook of Public Administration* (San Francisco, Jossey-Bass, 1996) 114.

[22] See below for details.

[23] Art 5(3) of the Treaty on European Union as revised by the Lisbon Treaty, OJ C115/1 (9 May 2008).

society, for instance, might feel that justice is done when the issue of account-ability is addressed at the national level. The key point to stress in relation to accountability, then, is that it should take place at the level where the issue is most relevant.

Multiple levels of accountability are also desirable for the reason that one actor at one level can serve as a check against another actor at a different level.[24] For instance, domestic institutions (governmental or non-governmental) can monitor the activities of international financial institutions operating on an international plane, while organisations such as the United Nations can monitor the implementation of treaty obligations imposed upon states. Such a reciprocal arrangement is desirable not only to promote transparency among diverse stake-holders, but also to establish dialogue among concerned parties. Such interaction can also help prevent conflicting rules emerging simultaneously at different levels by forcing actors to pay attention to what others are doing.

Equally important is the style of accountability. One good example is legal accountability. This brings those responsible for breach of decisions/rules before national, regional or international courts and tribunals. In any system of govern-ance, legal accountability is desirable for three reasons. First, competent tribunals can clarify the existing rules and regulations for all of those concerned so that they can understand them without difficulty. Secondly, legal accountability discourages breaching obligations. Naming, shaming and even punishing can deter rule-breakers and others from doing the same in the future. Harlow further notes that the rule of law, which is central to legal accountability, ensures due process of law for alleged offenders.[25] Finally, through legal accountability, those affected by decisions have a forum to have their voice heard and seek redress depending on the types of breaches suffered.

There are other types of accountability which might be more effective, depending on the types of issues and actors. Keohane argues in this regard that an analogy with domestic governance and accountability should not be made.[26] This suggests that different systems of accountability may be more appropriate in global governance. Indeed, there are other viable ways to hold various non-state actors accountable. These are political, administrative and economic accountability. Examples of these forms of accountability include holding elec-tions, dismissal of high ranking officials, enforcing of internal rules/guidelines, involving independent complaints bodies such as ombudsman institutions, imposing fines and restricting resource allocation. Other effective mechanisms of holding non-state actors accountable include publicity and public condemna-tion of rule-breaching. These measures may sometimes be more effective than seeking legal accountability, which can consume much time as well as human and financial resources. Furthermore, non-legal routes are often more informal,

---

[24] Kingsbury, Kirsch and Stewart, above n 5, 31.
[25] C Harlow, 'Global Administrative Law: The Quest for Principles and Values' (2006) 17 *European Journal of International Law* 187, 190.
[26] Keohane, above n 2, 137.

and this might make it easier to achieve resolution. In summary, it may be argued that global governance not only recognises the role of non-state actors but also offers a flexible way to deal with issues of global importance.

4.2.2 Global Governance over Transnational Organised Crime

4.2.2.1 Decision-Making and Participation

Having explored the basic ideas behind global governance, it is now necessary to consider its relevance to transnational organised crime. To begin with, any rule or decision made should relate to prevention and suppression of transnational organised crime. There is no doubt that the Organised Crime Convention, other suppression conventions, ICL and IHRL adopted at the regional and international levels embody such rules. The domestic legislation and policies aimed at suppressing and preventing organised crime as well as facilitating international co-operation and mutual legal assistance are also pertinent. Further, as a decision or rule does not necessarily have to be legally enforceable under the concept of global governance, non-legal decisions and arrangements are also important. One good example is the Global Compact, which is relevant for organised crimes such as human trafficking and sexual/labour exploitation. The main purpose of this voluntary initiative is to bring together governments, companies, workers, NGOs and the United Nations to promote 10 universal principles in the areas of human rights, labour, environment and anti-corruption.[27] The Global Compact is not a regulatory instrument as it does not formally police, enforce or measure the behaviour or actions of companies. Rather, it relies 'on public accountability, transparency and the enlightened self-interest of companies, labour and civil society to initiate and share substantive action in pursuing the principles upon which the Global Compact is based'.[28] The codes of conduct adopted by MNCs to uphold relevant labour standards,[29] decisions without legal effect,[30] and policies or strategies developed by relevant organisations such as the United Nations[31] should also be regarded as part of the overall decision to prevent and suppress transnational organised crime.

---

[27] Available at www.unglobalcompact.org/AboutTheGC/index.html.

[28] Ibid.

[29] Philip Morris International, available at www.philipmorrisinternational.com/global/downloads/ci/code.pdfm; Nike, available at www.nikebiz.com/responsibility/documents/Nike_Code_of_Conduct.pdf; GAP, available at www.gapinc.com/public/documents/code_vendor_conduct.pdf; the Code of Conduct for Multinationals adopted by the International Labour Organisation, available at http://actrav.itcilo.org/actrav-english/telearn/global/ilo/guide/main.htm.

[30] See, eg '40 Recommendations on Money Laundering' (2003), adopted by the Financial Action Task Force (an inter-governmental body which develops and promotes standards and policies to combat money laundering and terrorist financing), available at http://fatf-gafi.org/dataoecd/7/40/34849567.PDF; the Global Plan for Recovery and Reform (April 2009) adopted by the leaders of G20 states, which include its position on bank secrecy, available at www.g20.org/Documents/final-communique.pdf.

[31] See, eg the Naples Declaration, as described in Chapter 2.

In terms of participation in governance over transnational organised crime, it is important to acknowledge that states remain the key actors. At the international and regional levels they have the power to conclude international instruments relating to transnational organised crime. They are also primarily responsible for facilitating international co-operation and mutual legal assistance. At the domestic level, states enact domestic legislation and law enforcement agencies implement it. However, it is also evident that states are not the only actors which engage in the suppression and prevention of organised crime. International organisations such the United Nations Office of Drugs and Crime (UNODC) and the International Criminal Police Organisations (Interpol) play an important role in setting and promoting international standards, providing technical and legal assistance, and facilitating international co-operation.[32] The United Nations Human Rights Council has also established or maintained independent special procedures, some of which have relevance to organised crime.[33] It was also noted earlier that the co-operation of MNCs, financial institutions and other legal persons is essential as these bodies often come into contact with organised crime directly or indirectly. Finally, members of civil society, such as Transparency International,[34] the Alliance on Crime Prevention and Criminal Justice,[35] and human rights organisations such as Amnesty International and the Human Rights Watch, contribute to the development of effective action against transnational organised crime as they can lobby states, report any cases of breach of rules and decisions and mobilise public opinion.

It is important to stress that international law directly or indirectly facilitates participation of concerned actors to prevent and suppress transnational organised crime. The Organised Crime Convention has provisions which oblige states to facilitate co-operation with non-state actors such as financial institutions and international organisations in relation to money laundering, economic and development assistance, training and technical assistance and prevention.[36] The Conference of Parties established under Article 32 of the Organised Crime Convention, which is tasked with monitoring implementation of the Convention, meets on a regular basis, and its sessions are observed by international organisations and NGOs to promote transparency.[37] In addition, the Single

---

[32] See Chapter 7 for more details on activities of international organisations.

[33] They include Working Group on Arbitrary Detention, Working Group on Enforced or Involuntary Disappearances, Special Rapporteur on Trafficking in Persons, Special Rapporteur on Contemporary Forms of Slavery, Special Rapporteur on Independence of Judges and Lawyers, Special Rapporteur on Sales of Children, Child Prostitution and Child Pornography, and Special Representative on Human Rights and Transnational Corporations and Other Business Enterprises.

[34] www.transparency.org/.

[35] www.cpcjalliance.org/.

[36] Arts 7, 29, 30 and 31.

[37] Rules 14–17 of the *Rules of Procedure for the Conference of Parties to the United Nations Convention against Transnational Organised Crime* (2005). Its first session was observed by international organisations such as the Organisation for Security and Co-operation in Europe (OSCE), the Council of Europe, the International Organisation for Migration (IOM) and the Organisation of American States (OAS), as well as NGOs such as the Asian Crime Prevention Foundation, the International Council of Women, the International Human Rights Law Group and the International Council

Convention on Narcotic Drugs 1961 established a non-governmental mechanism known as the International Narcotics Control Board, the key task of which is to monitor the implementation of obligations established by the Convention and other narcotics treaties.[38]

There are other means by which participation of relevant non-state actors are facilitated. Article 71 of the United Nations Charter authorises the Economic and Social Council (ECOSOC) to make suitable arrangements for consultation with NGOs, and ECOSOC has done this by granting 'consultative status' to them.[39] Once granted, NGOs can attend meetings held by ECOSOC and its subsidiary bodies, such as the Commission on Crime Prevention and Criminal Justice and the Commission on Narcotic Drugs, submit written statements, make oral presentations and undertake special studies.[40] In the area of transnational organised crime, the relevant NGOs with consultative status include Amnesty International, the Asia Crime Prevention Foundation, the Human Rights Watch, the International Harm Reduction Association and Transparency International.[41]

Participation of non-state actors is also supplemented by IHRL when criminal activities have human rights implications. The role to be played by parents and family,[42] legal guardians or local community,[43] media,[44] NGOs and international organisations,[45] as well as educational institutions,[46] in the promotion and protection of human rights are recognised under legally binding instruments. Regional human rights courts, such as the European, Inter-American and African Courts of Human Rights, and bodies established by human rights treaties, including the Human Rights Committee and the Committee against Torture, also monitor the implementation of states' obligations, some of which are relevant for transnational organised crime, as noted in Chapter 3.

Two more categories of individuals should be regarded as important participants in governance over transnational organised crime. The first is the witnesses of organised crime. While not decision-makers per se, they provide valuable testimonies and evidence to bring criminals to justice, thereby contributing to prevention and suppression of organised crime. Given the danger to their physical and mental well-being, sufficient protection must be afforded in order to secure their participation in criminal proceedings. The Organised Crime

---

for Alcohol and Addiction. Report of the Conference of Parties to the United Nations Convention against Transnational Organised Crime on Its First Session, held in Vienna from 28 June to 8 July 2004, CTOC/COP/2004/6 (23 September 2004).

[38] Art 9.

[39] See ECOSOC Resolutions 1296 (XLIV) (23 May 1968) and 1996/31 (25 July 1996).

[40] Ibid.

[41] For a full list of all NGOs, visit www.un.org/esa/coordination/ngo.

[42] Art 10 of the International Covenant on Economic, Social and Cultural Rights 1966 (ICESCR), 993 UNTS 3; Art 19 of the Convention on the Rights of the Child 1989 (CRC), 1577 UNTS 3; Art 17 of the ACHR.

[43] Arts 5 and 14 of the CRC; Art 32 of the ACHR.

[44] Art 17 of the CRC; Art 14(3) of the ACHR.

[45] Art 22 of the CRC.

[46] Art 29 of the CRC.

Convention has a number of provisions on this and it is the first comprehensive multilateral treaty on organised crime to establish obligations for states. Article 24 provides that states shall take measures to protect witnesses, their relatives and others close to them from intimidation or retaliation in criminal proceedings.[47] These measures include, but are not limited to, relocation, anonymity, and provision of testimony through video links and other means.[48] Article 23 further obliges states to prosecute and punish those who intimidate or bribe witnesses in an attempt to obstruct the course of justice.

The treatment of witnesses is also provided for in the context of mutual legal assistance. Inclusion of such is perhaps inevitable as it is not always the case that witnesses reside in the same state where a crime is committed. Article 18 on mutual legal assistance provides some guidance to ensure that evidence can be transferred to a requesting state. This may be facilitated by transferring witnesses to a requested state (Article 18(3)(h)) or, if this is not possible, through a videoconference (Article 18(18)). In addition, states are to refrain from prosecuting, detaining, punishing or restricting personal liberty of witnesses in respect of acts/omissions prior to their departure (Article 18(27)). This is somewhat similar to the principle of speciality in the context of extradition, as explained in Chapter 3.

Further, it should also be recognised that those suspected or convicted of crime may serve as useful witnesses in other states, and their co-operation may become necessary. In addition to provisions relating to witness protection, other obligations are established under the Organised Crime Convention. For instance, the transfer of a suspect or defendant must be conducted with the consent of the person concerned.[49] Article 18(12) also prevents a state to which a suspect/convict is transferred from prosecuting or punishing him/her in respect of acts prior to his or her departure. Finally, mitigation of punishment or immunity might be granted if both sending and receiving states agree that such actions are appropriate in return for substantial co-operation.[50] In summary, it may be concluded that TCL as represented by the Organised Crime Convention establishes a decent international standard in relation to protection of witnesses and therefore marks an important step forward.

Examination shows that variation exists between states in how they approach witness protection. Some states do not currently have a system of witness protection in their domestic legal systems.[51] In states such as Egypt, Panama, Peru and the Republic of Korea, while they do have witness protection schemes, these do

---

[47] Art 24(1).
[48] Art 24(2).
[49] Art 18(10)(a).
[50] Art 26(5).
[51] They include Afghanistan, Burundi, Cameroon, Central African Republic, Chad, China (Macao SAR), Comoros, Congo, Côte d'Ivoire, Democratic Republic of the Congo, Gabon, Jordan, Monaco, Morocco, Myanmar, Sierra Leone and Sweden. Implementation Report 2008 No 2, above ch 3 n 113, para 60.

not extend beyond actual witnesses.[52] In addition, the adjustment of evidentiary rules to ensure protection of witnesses, such as the use of screens, video/teleconferencing and witness anonymity, is not recognised in Colombia, Indonesia, Trinidad & Tobago and Uruguay.[53] In these states, witnesses of organised crime are less likely to co-operate due to fear of reprisal, and this can have a negative impact on effective prosecution and punishment.

The second category is the victims of organised crime. In addition sometimes serving as witnesses in criminal proceedings, it was shown earlier that the principle of participation under global governance is wide enough to include those affected by rules and decisions. At first glance, it might be argued that the victims of organised crime are not directly affected by decisions or rules relating thereto (eg national criminal law) as they are victimised by criminals and criminal groups. Nevertheless, implementation and enforcement of relevant decisions are also part of governance, as noted above, and it is obvious that people are victimised because relevant law enforcement authorities are unwilling (through corruption or obstruction of justice) or unable (eg because of lack of adequate resources) to enforce these decisions in practice. Furthermore, it is important to create opportunities for victims to express their views, which may also be used to shape future policy on organised crime. Therefore the victims of organised crime are an important part of governance over transnational organised crime.

The Organised Crime Convention has a number of provisions on victims. The most pertinent provision is Article 25, and there are three key obligations imposed upon states. First, states must take appropriate measures to protect victims from the threat of, or actual, retaliation or intimidation. Secondly, Article 25 obliges them to provide access to compensation. Finally, states must, subject to their domestic law, enable the views and concerns of victims to be presented during criminal proceedings. While the recognition of these obligations is a significant step forward for an international instrument dealing primarily with criminal justice issues, they are simultaneously very general without detailed guidance on the types of measures to be taken. It is also problematic that the Organised Crime Convention does not take the special needs of particular victims, such as women and children, into consideration. These groups are often more vulnerable and require additional/special assistance, yet the Convention does not recognise this. Further, Article 25 does not make any reference to the rights of victims during criminal proceedings. It should be stressed here that states do not have to reflect the voices of victims during the proceedings if that conflicts with their domestic law. A lack of due regard to the victims of organised crime is problematic, particularly when the offences in question raise a wide variety of human rights concerns. This also strengthens the point made in Chapter 3 that TCL lacks a human rights approach.

---

[52] Ibid, para 61.
[53] Ibid, para 63.

Consequently, TCL on its own is not sufficient in this context, and therefore must be supplemented by IHRL in the same way as it is in the context of the rights of defendants. An obligation to protect victims of organised crime can be inferred from a general duty to secure, ensure or restore rights and provide remedies,[54] and is stipulated in instruments including the ICCPR,[55] the ECHR,[56] the ACHR[57] and the African Charter of Human and Peoples' Rights 1981.[58] It is important to note, however, that this obligation under IHRL arises when the crime in question violates one's human rights and states fail to provide protection. It is easy to establish such an obligation for crimes such as sexual/labour exploitation and child pornography because of their obvious human rights implications.[59] Arguably the same is not true for other crimes, including money laundering and computer fraud, which do not necessarily raise serious human rights concerns. However, even under such circumstances, norms have been developed to ensure that states provide access to justice, compensation, restitution and other assistance for victims of crime generally.[60]

Another aspect is the provision of compensation. This is an important measure, as prosecution and punishment of criminals alone do not necessarily alleviate the physical, psychological and other harms done to the victims. While compensation alone might not be enough to restore what victims enjoyed prior to the commission of a crime, it can nevertheless assist them to start their life again.[61] Provision of compensation is established under IHRL,[62] and this supplements TCL. However, given the potential scale of profits they can make, criminals are likely to engage in criminal activities repeatedly. In order to prevent them from doing so, the best approach is to use their criminal proceeds to compensate victims, thereby depriving criminals of a gain incentive. All of these mean that the obligations in relation to freezing and confiscation of criminal proceeds/assets as well as money laundering must be adhered to more rigorously, and this demonstrates that many obligations under TCL and other branches of international law, such as IHRL, are closely interlinked.

Moreover, the right of victims to participate in criminal proceedings is recognised in IHRL. Participation of victims in criminal proceedings is beneficial from a criminal justice point of view as testimony and evidence provided can expedite investigation, prosecution and punishment. However, it is more important from

---

[54] J Moor, 'From Nation State to Failed State: International Protection from Human Rights Abuses by Non-state Actors' (1999) 31 *Columbia Human Rights Law Review* 81, 92, 93 and 96.

[55] Art 2.

[56] Arts 1 and 13.

[57] Arts 1 and 2.

[58] Art 2, 1520 UNTS 217.

[59] See, eg Council of Europe Convention against Trafficking in Human Beings 2005, ETS No 197; Optional Protocol to the CRC; Migrant Workers' Convention.

[60] See, eg 'United Nations Basic Principles of Justice for Victims of Crime and Abuse of Power', A/RES/40/34 (29 November 1985).

[61] D Shelton, *Remedies in International Human Rights Law*, 2nd edn (Oxford, Oxford University Press, 2005) 291.

[62] Ibid, Chapter 9.

a human rights perspective, as it would allow victims to have their voice heard and to handle their anger and trauma in a constructive way.[63] Therefore, participation can lead to the restoration of their dignity and sense of self-worth.[64] In order to facilitate this process, Article 24 of the Organised Crime Convention should be interpreted in a way that encourages states to facilitate their active participation where appropriate and with their consent.

It should be borne in mind that many victims of organised crime, such as human trafficking, are foreign nationals, and IHRL imposes an obligation on states to provide them with the same degree of protection as their own nationals.[65] While states are entitled to take action against foreigners who do not have residency entitlements, a norm is being developed so that even this category of person should be entitled to protection when they are victims of serious human rights violations.[66] Like other vulnerable groups, such as women and children, foreign victims require specialised services. One example is consular assistance. This is guaranteed in Article 36 of the Vienna Convention on Consular Relations 1963,[67] and the ICJ has noted in the past that this Article created individual rights.[68] The Inter-American Court of Human Rights went further and stated that consular assistance, as part of the minimum due process guarantees, is recognised under Article 14 of the ICCPR.[69] Furthermore, the principle of *non-refoulement* becomes relevant if victims fear persecution both by states and non-state actors, as noted in Chapter 3. In order to allow them to stay at least temporarily, states should consider issuing them with appropriate visas. This has been facilitated in relation to human trafficking,[70] and states should consider extending it to victims of other crimes.

Finally, when criminal conduct crosses the threshold of international crime, ICL becomes pertinent. It is worth noting here that the Rome Statute provides

---

[63] N Roht-Arriaza, 'Punishment, Redress and Pardon: Theoretical and Psychological Approaches' in N Roht-Arriaza (ed), *Impunity and Human Rights in International Law and Practice* (Oxford, Oxford University Press, 1995) 19–21.

[64] Ibid.

[65] General Comment No 15, above ch 3 n 105.

[66] See, eg Migrant Workers' Convention; Chapter III of the Council of Europe Convention on Trafficking, above n 59.

[67] 596 UNTS 261.

[68] *LaGrand Case* (2001) ICJ Reports 466, para 77. See also *Avena and Other Mexican Nationals*, where the ICJ stated that the remedy for violating Art 36 of the Vienna Convention included review and reconsideration cases with a view to ascertaining whether the violation caused prejudice to the defendant in the process of administration of criminal justice. (2004) ICJ Reports 12, para 121.

[69] *The Right to Information on Consular Assistance in the Framework of the Guarantees of the Due Process of Law*, Advisory Opinion OC16/99, Ser A, No 16 (1999), paras 80, 83, 84, 87 and 122–24. See also Arts 16 and 23 of the Migrant Workers Convention.

[70] Council of Europe Convention on Trafficking; Directive 2004/EC/81 on the residence permit issued to Non-EU Member Country nationals who are victims of trafficking in human beings or who have been the subject of an action to facilitate illegal immigration, who cooperate with the competent authorities, OJ L261/19 (6 August 2004). The victims of trafficking may also be recognised as refugees under the 1951 Convention. United Nations High Commissioner for Refugees, 'Guideline on International Protection: Gender-Related Persecution in the Context of Art 1A(2) of the 1951 Convention and/or Its 1967 Protocol Relating to the Status of Refugees', HRC/GIP/02/01 (7 May 2002).

good guidance on how to treat victims and witnesses of international crime. Article 68 is a key provision and provides detailed guidance on protecting victims. To begin with, the ICC is to take appropriate measures to protect the safety, physical and psychological well-being, dignity and privacy of victims and witnesses. In so doing, it is obliged to take into account all factors, such as the age and gender of victims and witnesses, so as to provide tailor-made assistance. In order to protect witnesses and victims during criminal proceedings, the ICC can also conduct part of the proceedings *in camera* or facilitate or allow presentation of evidence through electronic and other means. In addition, provided that it is not prejudicial to the rights of the accused, the ICC can permit the views of victims and witnesses to be presented and considered. These and other measures are provided in more detail under ICL, and this again highlights the comparative weakness of TCL, which is influenced more by national interests of states.

Once again, actual state practice is inconsistent in the area of victim protection. In Burundi, the Central African Republic, Comoros, Monaco and Romania, for example, assistance to and protection of victims are not provided for under their domestic legal systems.[71] It is also the case that some states do not have procedures to provide access to compensation and restitution.[72] In addition, the views of the victims are not adequately reflected during criminal proceedings in states such as Afghanistan, Mauritius, Portugal and Trinidad & Tobago.[73] All of these examples demonstrate that the standards set by TCL and IHRL are not rigorously observed or implemented in practice.

4.2.2.2 Accountability

In the context of transnational organised crime, accountability arises primarily when individuals, criminal groups and other entities commit or become part of various forms of organised crimes, such as human trafficking and money laundering, because they would be in breach of rules prohibiting organised crime under such circumstances. As these rules are embodied mainly in domestic criminal law, a legal recourse is the primary means through which individuals and entities are held accountable. However, it will be shown that other forms of accountability are also appropriate and are applied in practice in relation to transnational organised crime.

4.2.2.2.1 Individual Criminal Responsibility

It was made clear in the previous chapter that the key aim of TCL is to prevent

---

[71] Implementation Report 2008 No 2, above ch 3 n 113, para 64.
[72] Ibid, para 65. They include Afghanistan, the Central African Republic, Chad, Chile, Comoros, Guatemala, Indonesia and Ireland.
[73] Ibid, para 66.

individuals committing organised crime. Does this mean that TCL imposes a direct obligation on them not to commit it? A starting point in understanding the nature of the obligation is the principle of 'individual criminal responsibility', which has been firmly established in the realm of international crime and ICL. Put simply, individual criminal responsibility means subjection to criminal sanctions. The modern example of this principle comes from the Charter of the International Military Tribunal (IMT), annexed to the Agreement for the Prosecution and Punishment of the Major War Criminals of the European Axis 1945.[74] Article 6 of the Charter provided that crimes over which the Tribunal had jurisdiction entailed individual responsibility.[75] This was later affirmed through the Principles of International Law Recognised in the Charter of the Nuremberg Tribunal and in the Judgement of the Tribunal adopted by the UN International Law Commission in 1950.[76] Principle I states that 'any person who commits an act which constitutes a crime under international law is responsible therefore and liable to punishment'. This constituted official recognition that any person can be held liable for committing a crime under international law.[77] The principle of individual criminal responsibility has been affirmed more recently in the Statutes of the ICTY and ICTR, as well as the Rome Statute of the ICC.[78]

A correlative aspect of criminal responsibility is the duty placed upon individuals not to commit these crimes. This has been elaborated by, among others, the IMT, which tried Nazi war criminals. It stated:

> That international law imposes duties and liabilities upon individuals as well as upon states has long been recognized . . . Individuals can be punished for violation of international law. Crimes against international law are committed by men, not by abstract entities, and only by punishing individuals who commit such crimes can the provisions of international law be enforced...[79]

It further stated that '[T]he very essence of the Charter is that individuals have international duties which transcend the national obligations of obedience imposed by individual states'.[80] Commentators also seem to be in agreement that ICL imposes an obligation on individuals in this regard.[81]

---

[74] 82 UNTS 279.

[75] Those crimes were crimes again peace, violations of laws and customs of war, and crimes against humanity. See also Art 5 of the Charter of the International Military Tribunal for the Far East ITAS No 1589; Art II.2 of the Control Council Law No 10, (1946) 3 Official Gazette Control Council for Germany 50–55. For a historical overview, see MC Bassiouni, *Crime Against Humanity in International Criminal Law*, 2nd edn (The Hague, Kluwer Law International, 1999) ch 1.

[76] Report of the International Law Commission Covering its Second Session, 5 June–29 July 1950, Document A/1316. The Principles of the London Charter were previously affirmed by the UN General Assembly in 1946 in its Resolution 95(I), UNDoc A/234 (1946).

[77] E Greppi, 'The Evolution of Individual Criminal Responsibility under International Law' (1999) 835 *International Review of the Red Cross* 531.

[78] Art 7 of the ICTY Statute; Art 6 of the ICTR Statute; Art 25 of the Rome Statute.

[79] International Military Tribunal, *Trials of the Major War Criminals* (14 November 1945–1 October 1946), Volume I (1947) 223.

[80] Ibid.

[81] Y Dinstein, 'International Criminal Law' (1985) 20 *Israel Law Review* 206, 207; A Clapham, *Human Rights Obligations of Non-state Actors* (Oxford, Oxford University Press, 2006) 29–30; R Cryer,

For the principle of individual criminal responsibility to be applied, it is generally accepted that conduct must constitute 'a crime under international law'. A crime under international law is a concern of the international community and is something for which the international community intends to hold the individual directly accountable.[82] In other words, the crime in question must be sufficiently serious to shock the conscience of the international community. While the term 'crimes under international law' was interpreted to mean crimes covered under the London Charter[83] in the first instance, this has been expanded to include crimes such as genocide,[84] war crimes[85] and apartheid.[86] The core crimes were once again affirmed in the Rome Statute. These crimes are to be punished directly by international law whether or not they are recognised as such under the domestic jurisdiction of states.[87] In other words, individuals are bound directly by international law, which creates scope for individual criminal responsibility in international law. There are two possibilities resulting from the principle of individual criminal responsibility. First, every state is entitled to exercise universal jurisdiction to punish criminals.[88] Second, criminals can be tried before an international tribunal such as the ICC. In relation to the latter, it has been noted that 'the critical factor in the progressive development of international criminal law is the existence of institutional structures that spur such growth and development'.[89]

In looking at this brief synopsis of the principle of individual criminal responsibility under ICL, a question may be asked whether the same also applies to transnational organised crime. There is no mention in TCL that organised crime is a 'crime under international law'. In addition, TCL does not stipulate that organised crime should be punished regardless of whether it is punished under domestic law. On the contrary, states must implement various legislative and others measures 'in accordance with domestic law' or 'consistent with

---

Prosecuting International Crimes: Selectivity and International Criminal Law Regime (Cambridge, Cambridge University Press, 2005) 118.

[82] S Ratner and J Abrams, *Accountability for Human Rights Atrocities in International Law*, 2nd edn (Oxford, Oxford University Press, 2001) 11.

[83] Greppi, above n 77. See also the 1996 'Draft Code of Crimes Against the Peace and Security of Mankind', in which the ILC uses the term 'crime under international law' to entail individual criminal responsibility.

[84] Convention on the Prevention and Punishment of the Crime of Genocide 1948, 78 UNTS 277.

[85] See, among others, Convention for the Amelioration of the Condition of the Wounded and Sick in Armed Forces in the Field 1949, 75 UNTS 31; Convention for the Amelioration of the Condition of Wounded, Sick and Shipwrecked Members of Armed Forces at Sea 1949, 75 UNTS 85; Convention Relative to the Treatment of Prisoners of War 1949, 75 UNTS 135; Convention Relative to the Protection of Civilian Persons in Time of War 1949, 75 UNTS 287.

[86] International Convention on the Suppression of the Crime of Apartheid 1973, 1015 UNTS 243.

[87] Art 6(c) of the London Charter. See also Bassiouni (1999), *Crime Against Humanity*, above n 75, 526.

[88] *Prosecutor v Furundija*, IT-95–17/1, Trial Judgment (10 December 1998), para 156. See also *Eichmann*, above ch 3 n 148; *In the Matter of the Extradition of John Demjanjuk*, 612 F Supp 544, 558 (N.D. Ohio 1985).

[89] Bassiouni, above ch 3 n 82, 32.

its legal principles' for prosecution and punishment or organised crime.[90] Also, individuals cannot be tried before the international tribunals such as the ICC for commission of transnational organised crime because TCL establishes 'an indirect system of interstate obligations generating national penal laws'.[91] This regime of indirect control over organised crime was promoted as a result of a lack of political will on the part of states to create a mechanism for direct control in the past.[92] An important element of indirect control is international co-operation, and it has been argued that transnational organised crimes are outlawed because they require international co-operation, not direct suppression by international law.[93] Therefore it seems apparent that TCL does not impose a direct obligation on individuals and that individual criminal responsibility cannot be established for transnational organised crime.

While it is important to acknowledge this current legal status, the distinction between TCL and ICL on individual criminal responsibility is not as clear as one might think. For instance, 'direct prohibition' through international law can arguably be applied to crimes other than international crimes in the strict sense. Lauterpacht once wrote that:

> Individuals are the real subjects of international duties not only when they act on behalf of the state. They are the subjects of international duties in all cases in which international law regulates directly the conduct of individuals as such. This applies, for instance, with regard to piracy. Individuals engaged in piracy break the rule of international law prohibiting piracy . . . The position is analogous in cases in which in numerous anti-slavery and similar treaties the injunction is addressed directly to individuals or in which the contracting parties grant one another the right to punish offenders who are nationals of the other party.[94]

It is worth noting here that the law on piracy does not directly regulate or prohibit the conduct of individuals. The United Nations on the Law of the Sea 1982, which is the key instrument on piracy, simply defines piracy and does not explicitly declare it to be a crime under international law.[95] The fact that piracy was not a crime under international law was supported by the Harvard Research Group, which undertook the draft of the law on piracy.[96] In addition the Convention does not provide for punishment of piracy before an international penal tribunal and an injunction is not directly addressed to individuals. If the law on piracy was nevertheless regarded as imposing an obligation on individuals, the same reasoning could apply to organised crime because, in addition

---

[90] See, eg Arts 6 (Money Laundering), 10 (Liability of Legal Persons) and 11 (Prosecution, Adjudication, Punishment) of the Organised Crime Convention.

[91] Boister, above ch 1 n 68, 962.

[92] Bassiouni, above ch 3 n 82, 34.

[93] Schabas, above ch 2 n 137, 269.

[94] H Lauterpacht, 'General Rules of the Law of Peace' in E Lauterpacht (ed), *International Law: Being the Collected Papers of Hersch Lauterpacht,* Vol 1 (Cambridge, Cambridge University Press, 1970) 284.

[95] Art 101.

[96] Bingham, above ch 3, n 71.

to national criminal law, criminals are in effect breaching the rules of international law prohibiting organised crime in the same way as pirates are breaching the Law of the Sea Convention. It should also be noted that the Organised Crime Convention grants states a right to punish nationals of the other parties under the principle of *aut dedere aut judicare*, as noted in Chapter 3.

In addition, the statement that a crime under international law is directly punishable under international law irrespective of the existence of domestic law requires clarification. There are two dimensions to this statement. First, the statement suggests that international law is directly enforceable in domestic courts and tribunals. This may be true for monist states such as the US, in which international law automatically becomes part of domestic law. Even if this is the case, it has been recognised that the legislature still has to pass laws to define and punish international crimes.[97] A significance of this is that even customary international law, which prohibits international crimes, may not be directly enforceable domestically. In dualist states, international law is regarded as different from national law. In these states, international norms and principles have to be incorporated through domestic legislation for them to have legal effect. Therefore, in practice, the nature of ICL and TCL are not too different in this respect, as both branches of law require states to enact legislation to prohibit criminal activities.

Another meaning of the above statement, following from the discussions throughout this book, is that crimes are punishable directly at the international level before an international penal tribunal such as the ICC. It is true that the ICC has competence or jurisdiction over core international crimes stipulated under the Rome Statute. That said, the power of the ICC is constrained by the principle of complementarity, as noted earlier in the book. This principle dictates that states have the primary obligation to prosecute and punish international crime within their domestic jurisdiction in the first instance.[98] Other treaties, such as the Geneva Conventions and the Genocide Convention, also provide that the primary obligation is on states to punish offenders.[99] This is the same for TCL, as the primary obligation to prosecute and punish is imposed upon states. The only key difference is that the ICC is available as a medium of last resort to try international crime whereas the same is not true for organised crime.

The question, then, is whether the existence of an international tribunal should be a necessary condition for establishing international criminal responsibility. If the answer is in the positive, then individual criminal responsibility would have no meaning without it. In looking at the historical development of ICL, however, it becomes apparent that this is not the case. The principle was

---

[97] Restatement, above ch 3 n 63, §404.

[98] The preamble of the Rome Statues provides 'it is the duty of every state to exercise criminal jurisdiction over those responsible for international crimes'. Further, Art 1 states that the ICC is complementary to national criminal jurisdictions'. For more on this topic, see J Kleffner, *Complementarity in the Rome Statute and National Criminal Jurisdictions* (Oxford, Oxford University Press, 2008).

[99] Dinstein, above n 81, 222.

affirmed even before the establishment of the ICTY, the ICTR and the ICC, as noted above, and the statutes establishing these institutions make no reference to the international penal tribunals in establishing the principle of individual criminal responsibility. It has been noted in this regard that individual criminal responsibility was recognised for crimes such as piracy and certain violations of the law of armed conflicts in the pre-World War I era.[100] It is submitted, therefore, that what matters is not where one is prosecuted for the commission of a crime, but how the relevant law (national or international) attaches responsibility to individuals. While a trial before an international penal tribunal underscores the seriousness of a crime, that should not negate the validity of individual criminal responsibility being enforced at other levels. What may be argued, then, is that the existence of an international tribunal is a sufficient, but not a necessary, condition for the principle of individual criminal responsibility. If one is to accept this position, TCL can be regarded as an important branch of international law which promotes this principle as the key aim or the end result is the same as ICL: prosecution and punishment of offenders.

It is by no means accurate to state that a notion of 'crime under international law' is set in stone. Although some instruments relating to international crime[101] make such a declaration, many other agreements on international crimes, including the Rome Statute, simply provide for the definitions of criminal conducts and oblige states to enact legislation to prosecute and punish, and/or stipulate the competence of an international penal tribunal to try these crimes. If all of these are the clear indications of conduct being 'a crime under international law', organised crime can be regarded as such, as the Organised Crime Convention provides definitions of various crimes and obliges states to prosecute and punish in the same way as the Rome Statute. Commentators such as Bassiouni also adopt this expansive notion of international crime and crime under international law.[102] In summary, international law does not exist in a vacuum. Its norms and principles evolve in line with the changing nature of international affairs and issues. While it is important to acknowledge the current legal position on individual criminal responsibility, there may be a time in the near future when the international community recognises the importance of this principle for other types of criminality, such as transnational organised crime. One advantage of such recognition is that it would exert stronger pressure on states to take action against the practice and that it would become more difficult for them to hide behind the rubric of state sovereignty.

One obstacle in establishing criminal responsibility at the national and international levels is the granting of immunity from prosecution and mitigation of punishment. In order to secure effective prosecution and punishment of serious criminals or leaders of criminal groups, for example, these measures are imple-

---

[100] Bassiouni (1999), *Crime against Humanity*, above n 75, 514.

[101] Art I of the Genocide Convention; Art I of the Apartheid Convention.

[102] MC Bassiouni, *International Criminal Law Conventions and Their Penal Provisions* (New York, Transnational Publishers, 1997).

mented in many jurisdictions.[103] States are also encouraged to consider these measures under Article 26 of the Organised Crime Convention, and the reduction of sentences is also stipulated for under Article 110 of the Rome Statute. In addition, states might consider other measures, such as amnesty and pardon.[104] These are appropriate particularly when criminals receive harsh punishments, such as the death penalty.[105] Nevertheless, these measures can have a detrimental effect upon the proper administration of justice, as justice might not be seen to be done from the point of view of the general public. Such measures can also make it difficult for victims to recover, especially when the crimes in question have serious human rights implications, such as sexual and labour exploitation. Further, this can hamper effective international co-operation as some states do not initiate extradition if a criminal has received a pardon or amnesty. Therefore, states must carefully weigh all competing interests in implementing these measures.

While establishing criminal responsibility is an important first step in prosecution and punishment, it is not sufficient to achieve long-term prevention and suppression of transnational organised crime. Given the profits generated by organised crime, criminals are likely to reoffend upon release from prison. Therefore, legal accountability alone might not be effective, so other measures against reoffending must be incorporated into any framework addressing organised crime. These might include, but are not limited to, education, rehabilitation and social integration during or after imprisonment. Particular attention must also be given to juveniles, who require additional guidance and support. Through these processes, criminals may recognise the wrongfulness of their conduct, and this can have a desirable deterrence effect. From the point of view of global governance over transnational organised crime, all of these measures may be regarded as non-legal ways to hold individuals accountable.

Unfortunately, TCL as represented by the Organised Crime Convention does not provide adequate guidance on the non-legal forms of accountability. It should be noted that Article 31 touches upon reintegration of convicted criminals. However, it simply obliges states to 'endeavour' to promote reintegration—the actual implementation of such measures is not required. Therefore, TCL must be supported by other branches of international law, in particular

---

[103] Implementation Report 2008 No 2, above ch 3 n 113, paras 31–35.

[104] See, eg Chapter VII of the Albanian Criminal Code, Law No 7895 (1995); Chapter 13 of the Russian Criminal Code, NO. 63-FZ (1996); Chapter 12 of the Penal Code of Slovenia; Chapter VI of the Criminal Code of Latvia (1998); Chapter 7 of the Penal Law of Laos People's Democratic Republic, No 4/PO (1990); Chapter 7 of the Bulgarian Penal Code as amended in 2005; Chapter 11 of the Serbian Criminal Code, Official Gazette of the Republic of Serbia, No 85/2005.

[105] It is worth noting in this respect that Art 6 of the ICCPR provides that 'anyone sentenced to death shall have the right to seek pardon or commutation of the sentence'.

IHRL. The key instruments in this regard include the ICCPR,[106] the CRC[107] and the Migrant Workers' Convention.[108] There are also non-binding instruments, such as the Standard Minimum Rules for the Treatment of Offenders 1955[109] and the Basic Principles for the Treatment of Prisoners 1990[110] adopted by the UN General Assembly.

4.2.2.2.2   Criminal Organisations

In addition to holding individuals accountable for the commission of organised crime, the responsibility of criminal groups such as the Yakuza and the Triads should also be established in order to promote effective responses to the practice. This is important because criminal organisations or networks continue to exist even when their members are prosecuted and punished. In other words, as long as these entities exist they will recruit new members and therefore organised crime itself will not disappear. There is also the problem of mafia bosses and other members of criminal groups not being properly prosecuted where they do not directly commit serious crimes if the authorities only focus on those who actually commit them.[111] Any legal framework therefore should be able to deal with this type of situation.

In the past, the liability of organisations was examined in the context of international crime and ICL. Article 9 of the London Charter provided that:

> At the trial of any individual member of any group or organization the Tribunal may declare (in connection with any act of which the individual may be convicted) that the group or organization of which the individual was a member was a criminal organisation.[112]

Article 10 continued:

> In cases where a group or organization is declared criminal by the Tribunal, the competent national authority of any Signatory shall have the right to bring individuals to trial for membership therein before national, military or occupation courts. In any such case the criminal nature of group or organisation is considered proved and shall not be questioned.[113]

---

[106] Art 10(3), which provides: 'The penitentiary system shall comprise treatment of prisoners the essential aim of which shall be their reformation and social rehabilitation'. See also General Comment No 21 (Art 10) (1992) of the Human Rights Committee. Compilation of General Comments, above ch 3 n 105.

[107] Art 40.

[108] Art 17.

[109] Adopted by the First United Nations Congress on the Prevention of Crime and the Treatment of Offenders, held at Geneva in 1955, and approved by ECOSOC in its Resolutions 663 C (XXIV) (31 July 1957) and 2076 (LXII) (13 May 1977).

[110] A/RES/45/111 (14 December 1990).

[111] H Van der Wilt, 'Joint Criminal Enterprises: Possibilities and Limitations' (2007) 5 *Journal of International Criminal Justice* 91, 93.

[112] Above n 74.

[113] Ibid.

In accordance with these provisions, four out of seven accused organisations (the SS, the SD, the Gestapo and the Leadership Corps of the Nazi Party) were declared criminal.[114] However, as these organisations could not be imprisoned, the IMT did not pursue group responsibility,[115] and the pronouncement of an organisation as criminal was merely declaratory and without any legal effect.

What happened instead was that the IMT prosecuted and punished individuals who participated in the activities of criminal organisations. In the case of the Leadership Corps of the Nazi Party, the IMT made a link between 'criminal organisation' and the Anglo-Saxon concept of 'criminal conspiracy' because the essence of both was said to be co-operation for criminal purposes.[116] A note of caution is that 'conspiracy' bears somewhat different meanings in domestic and international law. As noted previously, conspiracy is recognised as an inchoate offence in common law jurisdictions and generally refers to agreement to commit a crime.[117] Under this heading, one can be punished even if one does not physically commit the crime in question. In international law, however, this notion of conspiracy also included a form of participation.[118] It was later recognised that the term 'joint criminal enterprise' was more appropriate to describe this participation.[119] However, if a member of an organisation had no knowledge of criminal purposes before participating, then he/she would not be prosecuted and punished.[120] This means that mere membership of a criminal organisation should not form a basis for prosecution.[121] Recent jurisprudence before the ICTY has expanded this concept of 'joint criminal enterprise' to include cases where the risk of this crime was 'a predictable consequence of the execution of the common design and the accused was either reckless or indifferent to that risk'.[122] The doctrine of joint criminal enterprise is also recognised in Article 25(d) of the Rome Statute for ICC.

One question that should be asked for the purpose of this book is whether the same principle applies to organised crime. The answer seems to be yes, in accordance with Article 5 of the Organised Crime Convention. As noted in the previous chapter, this Article obliges states to criminalise participation in an organised criminal group. Similar to ICL, the focus is placed upon prosecution and punishment of individuals rather than criminal groups. The Convention also links 'participation in an organised criminal group' with 'conspiracy' in the sense of inchoate offence under Article 5(1)(a)(i) and joint enterprise under Article

---

[114] Above n 79, 261, 267–68 and 273.

[115] Cassese, above ch 2 n 131, 138.

[116] IMT, above n 79, 256. See also NH Jørgensen, *The Responsibility of States for International Crimes* (Oxford, Oxford University Press, 2000) 65.

[117] See further D Ormerod, *Smith and Hogan Criminal Law*, 12th edn (Oxford, Oxford University Press, 2008) 399.

[118] Cryer et al, above ch 3 n 176, 305; Bantekas and Nash, above ch 3 n 212, 35.

[119] *Prosecutor v Milutinovic*, above ch 3, n 12, para 26.

[120] IMT, above n 79, 256.

[121] Ibid.

[122] *Prosecutor v Tadic*, above ch 3 n 11, para 204; *Prosecutor v Kristic*, IT-98-33-T, Trial Judgment (2 August 2001), paras 615–16.

5(1)(ii). It is worth noting here that 'criminal conspiracy' under TCL has both national law and international law connotations. A further point to note is that Article 5 makes it clear that individuals will be punished where they intend to commit a crime with the knowledge of the criminal purposes. This means that mere membership of an organised criminal group might not serve as a basis for prosecution and punishment. Further, the Organised Crime Convention does not oblige states to declare an organisation criminal, unlike the Charter of the IMT.

An examination of national legislation reveals that state practice varies in dealing with criminal organisations. Under the Racketeer Influenced and Corrupt Organisations Act (RICO)[123] of the US, for example, mere membership of a criminal organisation can be prosecuted.[124] It is interesting to note that while a 'person' under the RICO includes any individual or entity capable of holding a legal or beneficial interest in property, it excludes criminal organisations such as La Cosa Nostra.[125] Canada, a neighbour of the US, takes a different approach, as mere membership does not create a liability. In order for one to be convicted, the individual has to have knowledge of the organisation and its purposes and/ or must knowingly participate in its activities in order to enhance its capability to commit criminal offences.[126] In Europe, membership[127] and establishment[128] of criminal organisations are proscribed. Whatever the stances states take, one common aspect of domestic legislation is that it is the individuals, not the organisations, who are held liable.

This being so, one may wonder whether there are any types of sanctions which can be imposed upon organisations themselves in addition to prosecuting and punishing their members. State practice demonstrates that the answer is in the affirmative. One of the key measures is the imposition of fines. This is stipulated under the RICO in the US, for example.[129] Another example is forfeiture of criminal proceeds. In addition to pecuniary gain, the proceeds can include other tangible and intangible personal property, including rights, privileges, interests, claims and securities.[130] Some states adopt a system of proscription or designation of organisations as criminal groups. In Japan, the Public Safety Commission is authorised to designate a group as *boryokudan* (criminal group).[131] Once this

---

[123] 8 USC §§1961–68. Enacted by §901(a) of the Organized Crime Control Act 1970, PubL 91-452, 84 Stat 992.

[124] EM Wise, 'RICO and Its Analogues: Some Comparative Considerations' (2000) 27 *Syracuse Journal of International Law and Commerce* 303, 311–12. See also *Pinkerton v United States* 328 US 440 (1949), which ruled that all parties to the conspiracy could be held liable for all crimes committed by their confederates.

[125] *United States v Bonanno Organized Crime Family of La Cosa Nostra* 879 F 2d 20 (2d Cir 1989).

[126] S 467.11 of the Canadian Criminal Code 1985, RSC 1985, c C-46.

[127] Art 450-1 of the French Penal Code. See also Art 416 of the Italian Penal Code as amended in 1982.

[128] S 129(1) of the Penal Code of Germany.

[129] §1963(a).

[130] §1963(b).

[131] Art 3 of the Law Concerning Prevention of Unjust Acts by Boryokudan Members 1991.

designation is confirmed, its members are forbidden to carry out a number of activities for financial gain.[132] A similar arrangement is found in South Australia, where control orders can be imposed against members who belong to declared criminal organisations.[133] Finally, in some states, criminal organisations can be ordered to be dissolved or reorganised.[134] These measures are necessary to deter organisations from committing crimes as prosecution and punishment of individual members are not sufficient.

One danger in targeting particular groups is its impact on the right to freedom of association as enshrined in appropriate human rights instruments. A similar argument has been made in relation to terrorist organisations,[135] and it equally applies to organised criminal groups. It should be said from the outset that there should be no right to join a criminal organisation. It is widely established that the freedom of association can be curtailed in the interest of national security, public safety, and prevention of crime and disorder.[136] Like terrorist organisations, there is no doubt that organised criminal groups will fall under this category and therefore any restriction placed upon them is justified. The power to proscribe an organisation or association can be used as a tool by states to suppress political opponents, pressure groups and others which are normally regarded as legitimate in domestic jurisdiction. Entities such as anti-abortion groups were regarded as falling under the organised crime legislation in the past.[137] This could also apply to others, such as animal rights or environmental groups.[138] While it is right that people and organisations are punished if they engage in criminal activities, such as criminal damage, intimidation and violence, it is questionable whether such specialised legislation on organised crime or terrorism can be justifiably used to curtail activities of organisations which are not traditionally regarded as criminal groups. Designation of an entity as 'a criminal organisation' will attach a certain degree of stigma, possibly resulting in an array of responses ranging from isolation to outright discrimination by the general public and the authorities.

---

[132] Hill, above ch 1 n 21, 159.

[133] Serious and Organised Crime (Control) Act 2008 of South Australia. See also the Crimes (Criminal Organisations Control) Act 2009 of New South Wales.

[134] §1964(a) of RICO.

[135] B Dickson, 'Law Versus Terrorism: Can Law Win?' (2005) *European Human Rights Law Review* 11; JC Tham, 'Possible Constitutional Objections to the Powers to Ban Terrorist Organisations' (2004) 27 *University of New South Wales Law Journal* 482.

[136] See, eg Art 22(2) of the ICCPR; Art 11(2) of the ECHR; Art 16(2) of the ACHR.

[137] *National Organization for Women, Inc v Scheidler* 510 US 249 (1994), in which the US Supreme Court held that prosecution under the RICO did not require economic motive. However, in *National Organization for Women, Inc v Scheidler* 537 US 393 (2003), the Supreme Court eventually held that the RICO did not apply to anti-abortion groups as 'coercion' was not the same as extortion and therefore not covered by the RICO. See B Dempsey, 'Racketeer Influenced and Corrupt Organization Act: Proscription of Illegitimate and Criminal Enterprises' (1979) 10 *University of Memphis Law Review* 633.

[138] It can also be applied to public/governmental department, as has been the case in the US under the RICO.

4.2.2.2.3 Legal Persons

A legal person is an entity recognised under domestic law as having legal rights and duties. It generally refers to corporate entities. In English law, a legal person is distinct from a natural person and therefore a separate liability can be imposed upon the former.[139] A legal person is also to be distinguished from a criminal organisation as domestic law does not grant legal rights upon the latter. There are two main ways in which the liability of legal persons becomes relevant. First, entities such as banks and other financial institutions may become part of criminal activities conducted by organised criminal groups, such as money laundering and fraud. In such circumstances these entities are more likely to be regarded as the secondary actors, and therefore establishing liability on the basis of secondary participation (aiding/abetting) would be appropriate when they take part in criminal activities with full knowledge and intention. Secondly, these legal persons might commit various crimes without the involvement of organised criminal groups. Such crimes may be more appropriately termed as white-collar crimes. This term was coined by Sutherland, and generally refers to crimes committed by business and professional people, including such conduct as commercial and public bribery, manipulation of stock markets, fraud and embezzlement.[140] In any event, when legal persons commit crimes, they can also be regarded as organised criminal groups themselves, as they fit into the definitions under the Organised Crime Convention, provided that a crime is committed for financial of other material benefits.

While it would not cause much difficulty in prosecuting and punishing individuals who commit these crimes, a question again may be raised as to whether or not legal persons can be directly held accountable. The principles relating to corporate criminal liability can help us understand this better. In general, corporate criminal liability is governed by the principle of *respondeat superior*, which provides that a corporation is liable for criminal acts of its employees or agents performed within the course of their employment.[141] In order for this to be established, however, an employee must have acted illegally to benefit his corporation.[142] This is a principle recognised in common law jurisdictions such as the UK and the US as vicarious liability, as well as in some civil law jurisdictions, including France and the Netherlands.[143]

The liability of legal persons is recognised under Article 10 of the Organised Crime Convention. This is an important step forward as the Convention is the first multilateral treaty on crime and criminal justice to touch upon this issue, and it can be distinguished from ICL, which does not establish liability

---

[139] Ormerod, above n 117, 245.

[140] EH Sutherland, 'White-Collar Criminality' (1940) 5 *American Sociological Review* 1, 1–3.

[141] J Arlen, 'The Potentially Perverse Effect of Corporate Criminal Liability' (1994) 23 *Journal of Legal Studies* 833, 838.

[142] VS Khanna, 'Corporate Criminal Liability: What Purpose Does it Serve?' (1996) 109 *Harvard Law Review* 1477, 1490.

[143] Ibid.

for corporate entities.[144] Article 10 was originally entitled 'Corporate Liability' and is based on the proposals put forward by the US and Uruguay.[145] It obliges states to establish liability for 'participation in serious crimes involving an organised criminal group and for offences established in accordance with articles 5, 6, 8, and 23 of this Convention'. The first part of this sentence (and also Article 5) suggests that Article 10 applies to the first scenario mentioned above (secondary participation). However, in relation to money laundering, corruption and obstruction of justice, legal persons can be punished even without the involvement of organised criminal groups. It should also be noted that the liability of legal persons ensues without prejudice to the criminal liability of the natural persons who have committed the offences. This means that it should be established in addition to prosecuting and punishing individual criminals. In addition, liability can take the form of criminal, civil or administrative sanctions. Article 31(2)(d) of the Convention in this regards provides for, among others, the prevention of convicted people from acting as directors/managers of legal persons, and the establishment of public records on those who establish or manage legal persons.

The principle of corporate criminal liability is recognised at the national level,[146] and states have adopted different forms of sanction. The most common form of sanctions is financial penalty. In the US, criminal fines can be imposed under the Criminal Fine Improvement Act 1987.[147] Denmark also imposes a fine for money laundering.[148] There are other forms of sanctions that can be imposed. In the UK a serious crime prevention order, which provides for prohibitions, restrictions and requirements in areas such as access and use of premises, financial or business dealings and the provisions of goods and services, can be imposed.[149] In Serbia a sentence of 'termination of the status of legal entity' can be imposed.[150] This has various legal consequences, such as termination or prohibition of certain activities and business operations, and forfeiture of permissions, concessions and subsidies granted by the authorities.[151] Dissolution of legal persons can also be imposed in states such as Angola, Belgium, Morocco and Peru.[152] However, in some jurisdictions, such as Belarus, Finland, Latvia, Mexico and Ukraine, the liability of legal persons has not yet been established.[153]

---

[144] Art 25 of the Rome Statute provides that the ICC has jurisdiction over 'natural persons' but not 'legal persons'.

[145] Above ch 2 n 108, 14. The wording was change to 'Liability of Legal Persons' from the fourth draft. Above ch 3 n 32, 14.

[146] See, eg Part 2.5 of the Australian Criminal Code; Art 30 of the Chinese Criminal Code; Art 121-2 of the French Penal Code.

[147] Pub. L. 100–85, 101 Stat 1279.

[148] UNODC, Legislative Guide, above ch 3 n 53, 123. See also Chapter 9 of the Finnish Criminal Code as amended in 2008 (940/2008).

[149] Serious Crime Act 2007, ss 1–5.

[150] Art 18 of the Law on the Liability of Legal Entities for Criminal Offences, Official Gazette of the Republic of Serbia, No 97/2008.

[151] Art 28.

[152] Implementation Report 2008 No 1, above ch 3 n 38, para 43.

[153] Ibid, para 40.

There are other non-legal forms of accountability for legal persons. Accountability for MNCs is a case in point. They sometimes become part of organised crime by employing child or exploitative labour, for instance, and there are ways to hold them accountable. To begin with, they are accountable to shareholders, who have the power to change the rules applicable to them and the behaviour of these entities,[154] and to fire/hire decision-makers at the top if they do not behave in an ethical manner. Members of civil society have also developed standards and certification mechanisms for internationally traded products, such as fair trade. This, together with measures such as consumer boycotts and voluntary codes of conduct,[155] including the Global Compact noted above, put enormous pressure on MNCs to modify their behaviour if they become part of organised crime in some way. Unlike organised criminal groups, which operate outside of the law, legal persons are sensitive to these pressures primarily because they operate in legal markets. Failure to act can result in massive loss of profits. Once again, all of these are in conformity with the concept of global governance explored above.

4.2.2.2.4 International Organisations

An examination into the position of international organisations is important for the discussion of transnational organised crime because there have been instances where their personnel have engaged in crimes such as human trafficking.[156] An important question, then, is the liability of these organisations under national and international law. States have traditionally been the key subjects of international law because they were regarded as 'international persons' bound by international law governing the relationship of states with one another.[157] However, it has been widely accepted that international organisations are also the subjects of international law and therefore that they possess rights and duties. One of the key cases which elaborated upon this was *Reparations for Injuries Suffered in the Service of the United Nations*[158] before the ICJ. The key issue in this case was whether or not the United Nations had the capacity to bring an international claim against a state. The ICJ concluded that the United Nations was an international person and 'a subject of international law and capable of possessing international rights and duties'.[159] That international organisations are bound by the general rule of international law was upheld in a subsequent decision by

---

[154] Above n 2, 146.

[155] Art 31(2) of the Organised Crime Convention encourages states to promote codes of conduct both in the public and private sectors.

[156] See Chapter 5 for the case study of Kosovo.

[157] RF Roxbrugh (ed), *Oppenheim's International Law: A Treatise*, 3rd edn (London, Longman, 1920) 125.

[158] (1949) ICJ Reports 174.

[159] Ibid, 179. On the discussion of international personality of international organisations, see J Klabbers, *An Introduction to International Institutional Law* (Cambridge, Cambridge University Press, 2002) 5; Clapham, above n 81, 80.

the ICJ[160] and supported by others.[161] All of this suggests that responsibility in relation to transnational organised crime might be attributed to international organisations. It is important to note, however, that international organisations do not possess the same degree of rights and duties as states. The ICJ in this respect stated that '[t]he subjects of law in any legal system are not necessarily identical in their nature or in the extent of their rights, and their nature depends upon the needs of the community'.[162]

There are several sources for the obligations of international organisations. To begin with, treaties establishing particular international organisations are pertinent.[163] For the United Nations, the relevant instrument is its Charter. In examining this, it becomes apparent that there is no mention of transnational organised crime. Nevertheless, one of the purposes of the United Nations is promoting international co-operation in solving international problems of, among others, economic and social characters.[164] Without doubt, transnational organised crime fits under this banner, and this is also recognised in the Preambles of the Organised Crime Convention.[165] Another pertinent part of the Charter is Chapter X on ECOSOC. Article 68 authorises ECOSOC to establish a functional commission to deal with economic and social matters. ECOSOC accordingly established the Commissions on Narcotic Drugs[166] and on Crime Prevention and Criminal Justice,[167] the latter of which has the mandate to deal with organised crime. Finally, some instances of organised crime can be regarded as a threat to international peace and security, as noted elsewhere in this book, and their maintenance is another key objective of the United Nations. Therefore, it can be concluded that the UN Charter implicitly recognises the obligations of the United Nations to address transnational organised crime. The same is true for other organisations, including the International Organisation for Migration (IOM) and the International Labour Organisation (ILO), which deal with human trafficking, labour exploitation and other aspects of organised crime.

This obligation of international organisations to address transnational organised crime is supplemented by IHRL and ICL. In relation to IHRL, it has been advanced by commentators that international organisations have the duty to protect 'customary international human rights'.[168] The customary norms of

---

[160] *Interpretation of the Agreement of 25 March 1951 between the WHO and Egypt* (1980) ICJ Reports 73.

[161] International Law Commission, 'Draft Articles on the Responsibilities of International Organisations', A/58/10 (May–August 2003), 33.

[162] Above n 158, 178.

[163] K Wellens, *Remedies against International Organisations* (Cambridge, Cambridge University Press, 2002) 13–14.

[164] Art 1 of the United Nations Charter.

[165] '*Deeply concerned* by the negative economic and social implications related to organized criminal activities, and convinced of the urgent need to strengthen cooperation to prevent and combat such activities more effectively at the national, regional and international level'.

[166] ECOSOC Resolution 9(1) (16 February 1946).

[167] ECOSOC Resolution 1992/1 (6 February 1992).

[168] F Hoffman and F Megret, 'The UN as a Human Rights Violator? Some Reflections on the United Nations' Changing Human Rights Responsibilities' (2003) 25 *Human Rights Quarterly* 314,

human rights which have relevance to organised crime include prohibition of inhuman or degrading treatment and forced labour and slavery.[169] If a particular form of organised crime crosses the threshold of international crime, then international organisations are additionally obliged to address it as it has been argued that international organisations are bound by norms of *jus cogens*.[170]

In addition, the rules relating to privileges and immunities are relevant sources for articulating obligations of international organisations. Similar to immunity granted to diplomats, as explored in Chapter 3, the immunity for international organisations and their personnel prevent them from being subjected to legal processes. Primarily, the rules of immunity are formulated by national law.[171] The International Organisations Immunities Act 1945 of the US and the International Organisations Act 1968 of the UK are good examples. These and other laws provide detailed rules on the treatment of international organisations at the domestic level. At the international level applicable rules on immunity are derived from treaties or customary international law. Most instruments establishing international organisations contain some provisions on immunity.[172] In addition to these are multilateral instruments specifically related to immunities and privileges. The two key instruments in this regard are the Convention on the Privileges and Immunities of the United Nations 1946[173] (General Convention) and the Convention on the Privileges and Immunities of the Specialized Agencies 1947[174] (Special Convention). They are regarded as codifying customary norms on the immunity of international organisations.[175] Various bilateral agreements made between states and international organisations (such as the Headquarter Agreement between the US and the UN of 1947) supplement these multilateral treaties.[176]

A key question that should be asked here is whether these rules on immunity prevent international organisations and their personnel from being prosecuted if they engage in transnational organised crime. This may become clear in looking at the nature of their immunity. To begin with, personnel of international organisations are said to enjoy functional immunity, a concept explained in Chapter 3.

317; CF Amerasinghe, *Principles of the Institutional Law of International Organisations* (Cambridge, Cambridge University Press, 1996) 247; R Wilde, '*Quis Custodiet Ipso Custodes?*: Why and How UNHCR Governance of 'Development' Refugee Camps Should be Subject to International Human Rights Law' (1998) 1 *Yale Human Rights and Development Law Journal* 107, 121.

[169] Restatement, above ch 3, n 63, §404.

[170] Clapham, above n 81, 67. See also *Yearbook of the ILC (1982)*, vol II, pt 2, 56, which contains ILC's commentary on the Vienna Convention on the Law of Treaties between states and international organisations or between international organisations.

[171] Reinisch, above ch 3 n 207, 134.

[172] See Art 105 of the UN Charter; Art 40 of the Constitution of International Labour Organisation 1919; Art 28 of the Constitution of the International Organisation for Migration 1953; Arts 133–35 of the Charter of the Organisation of American States 1948.

[173] 1 UNTS 14.

[174] 33 UNTS 261.

[175] M Singer, 'Jurisdictional Immunity of International Organisations: Human Rights and Functional Necessity Concern' (1995–96) 36 *Virginia Journal of International Law* 53, 98.

[176] Reinisch, above ch 3 n 207, 145.

This is evident in Article 105 of the Charter, which reads that the 'Organisation shall enjoy in the territory of each of its Member such privileges and immunities as are necessary for the fulfilment of its purposes'. The use of the term 'necessary' and the avoidance of a direct invocation of diplomat-type immunity in Article 105 mean that UN staff members were never intended to receive the level of protection accorded to diplomats.[177] Functional immunity was also affirmed by the ICJ[178] and adopted by other international organisations, including the World Health Organization[179] and the International Atomic Energy Agency.[180] It is also recognised in the General Convention.[181] As noted above, suppression of organised crime is implicitly recognised as one of the purposes of the United Nations. Therefore its commission will never be regarded as an official function of the United Nations itself and the same should go for other relevant international organisations.[182]

All of these mean that the immunity of the personnel of international organisations should be waived when they commit organised crime. In the case of the United Nations, this is entrusted to the Secretary-General, who has the right and duty to waive the immunity in any case where, in his opinion, the immunity would impede the course of justice.[183] A similar provision is found in the Special Convention.[184] The former Secretary-General Trygve Lie once stated in this regard that the 'United Nations personnel do not enjoy immunity from arrest or interrogation for alleged acts unrelated to their official duties which are unlawful in the Member States where they are committed or alleged to have been committed'.[185]

Once the immunity is lifted, these individuals can be tried before national courts and tribunals like any other criminals. While such instances are rare, there are some recent examples of staff members abusing their position to acquire financial or material benefits illegally. In June and August 2005, for instance, the Secretary-General waived the immunities of Alexander Yakovlev (a UN procurement officer) and Benon Sevan (Under-Secretary General in charge of Iraq's

---

[177] Rawski, above ch 3 n 207, 107.

[178] *Reparation Case*, above n 158. See also Case 2/88 *JJ Zwartveld and Others* [1990] ECR I-4405 before the European Court of Justice; Restatement, above ch 3 n 63, §467.

[179] Art 67(a) of the WHO Constitution.

[180] Art XV of the Statute of the International Atomic Energy Agency.

[181] S 18(a), Art V provides that officials of the UN shall be immune from legal process in respect of words spoken or written and all acts performed by them in their official capacity. This is strengthened by s 20, which makes it clear that privileges and immunities are granted to officials in the interests of the United Nations and not for the personal benefit of the individuals themselves.

[182] Generally, a decision on what constitutes 'official function' is to be determined by the Secretary-General, and not by national courts and tribunals. *Difference Relating to Immunity from Legal Process of a Special Rapporteur of the Commission on Human Rights* (1999) ICJ Reports 62, para 60.

[183] S 20.

[184] S 22.

[185] The Practice of the United Nations, the Specialized Agencies and the International Atomic Energy Agency Concerning Their Status, Privileges and Immunities: A Study Prepared by the Secretariat, UNDoc A/CN.4/L.118 Add 1 and 2 (1967), reprinted in the *Yearbook of International Law Commission* (1967) vol II, 265, para 249.

Oil-for-Food Programme), who were accused of taking more than $950,000 in bribes from contractors.[186] In September of the same year, Vladimir Kuznetsov, a Russian Chairman of UN Budgetary Advisory Committee, was also stripped of his immunity and arrested by the US FBI on a charge of money laundering.[187] These examples at least show that the UN Secretary-General is prepared to act when his staff commit serious and organised crime.

While immunity for international organisations is relatively straightforward, some difficulties have arisen in relation to the immunities of peacekeeping missions. Some participants in the past have been found to have engaged in organised criminal activities, such as trafficking of human beings or sexual exploitation of people.[188] Generally speaking, there are three components to a peacekeeping mission: (i) a civilian component; (ii) a civilian police; and (iii) a military component.[189] The personnel belonging to the first category, such as the civilian personnel recruited by the UN Department of Peacekeeping Operations, are regarded as 'officials of the United Nations' under Section 18 of the General Convention, and therefore the same rules on immunity and its waivers noted above apply to them. Those in the second category, such as members of the International Police Task Force or Civilian Police (UNCIVPOL), are treated as the 'Experts in Mission' under Section 22 of the General Convention.[190] They also enjoy functional immunity in the same way as staff members of the United Nations, and the UN Secretary-General has the right and the duty to waive immunity.[191]

A difficulty arises in relation to the third category. The conduct of the military personnel is commonly governed by the Status of Force Agreements (SOFAs). Under such an agreement, the military forces generally come under the criminal jurisdiction of the sending state, which retains the sole authority to waive immunity.[192] Therefore, if a soldier engages in sexual exploitation of

---

[186] news.bbc.co.uk/1/hi/world/middle_east/4131602.stm

[187] www.rferl.org/featuresArt/2005/09/18738683-f838–4b09-992b-a264c3f475be.html

[188] Investigation into Sexual Exploitation of Refugees by Aid Workers in West Africa: Note by the Secretary-General, A/57/465 (11 October 2002); Amnesty International, 'So Does It Mean That We Have the Rights?: Protecting the Human Rights of Women and Girls Trafficked for Forced Prostitution in Kosovo' (May 2004); A Comprehensive Strategy to Eliminate Future Sexual Exploitation and Abuse in United Nations Peacekeeping Operations: Report of the Secretary-General's Special Adviser, A/59/110 (2005); Refugee International, 'RI Bulletin: A Powerful Voice for Humanitarian Action' (March 2005); Report of the Group of Legal Experts on ensuring the accountability of United Nations Staff and Experts on Mission with Respect to Criminal Acts Committed in Peacekeeping Operations, A/60/980 (2006); Special Measures for Protection from Sexual Exploitation and Sexual Abuse: Report of the Secretary-General, A/61/957 (2007); Save the Children UK, 'No One to Turn: The Under-Reporting of Child Sexual Exploitation and Abuse by Aid-Workers and Peacekeepers' (2008).

[189] Speech by Kuniko Ozaki, Director of the Division of Treaty Affairs (UNODC), delivered at the International Congress of Social Defence (20–22 September 2007), available at www.defensesociale.org/xvcongreso/ponencias/KunikoOzaki.pdf.

[190] Model Status of Forces Agreement for Peacekeeping Operations: Report of the Secretary-General, A/45/594 (9 October 1990); Rawski, above ch 3 n 207, 107–08.

[191] S 23 of the General Convention.

[192] Rawski, above ch 3 n 207, 108. Bantekas and Nash argue that this is an established customary

a minor, for instance, the host state is excluded from exercising criminal jurisdiction over him. This rule is reflected, for instance, in the administration of Kosovo. Regulation No 2000/47 on the Status, Privileges and Immunities of the Kosovo Force (KFOR) and UNMIK and Their Personnel in Kosovo[193] has granted the KFOR personnel of the North Atlantic Treaty Organization (NATO) stationed in Kosovo immunity from local jurisdiction and exclusive jurisdiction by peacekeepers' respective nations.[194] Indeed, it has been a standard practice for the UN to leave all the investigations into misconduct by military personnel to the national contingent command.[195] This is an area of concern as there have been instances of soldiers not being properly prosecuted and punished by their own governments.

Another difficulty arises in relation to the immunity of international organisations themselves. International organisations have traditionally enjoyed absolute immunity. This is so because they have served a political function and been treated as collective entities representing states.[196] As a result, it was thought that the same rule as the diplomatic and other immunities relevant to states would apply to international organisations.[197] International organisations themselves also claimed absolute immunity in the past.[198] This seems to be confirmed by Section 2 of the General Convention, which provides that 'the United Nations . . . shall enjoy immunity from every form of legal process except insofar as in any particular case it has expressly waived its immunity'. The US also takes this position.[199] All of this suggests that, while individuals working for international organisations who commit organised crime can be punished, their conduct cannot be attributed to the organisations themselves.

Nevertheless, others maintain that such an argument is misguided as international organisations do not have the same rights and duties as states and

law, above ch 3 n 212, 43.

[193] UNMIK/REG/2000/47, 18 August 2000. It should be noted, however, that this instrument itself is not SOFA.

[194] It should be noted, however, that both the international and local UNMIK personnel were granted functional immunity under the same regulation.

[195] Report of the Special Committee on Peacekeeping Operations on Comprehensive Review of the Whole Question of Peacekeeping Operations in All Their Aspects, A/54/839 (20 March 2000), paras 65–66; Model SOFA, above n 190, para 47(b); Rawski, above ch 3 n 207, 115.

[196] Maginnis, above ch 3 n 227, 1010; Reinisch, above ch 3 n 207, 258–59 and 333.

[197] International Organizations Immunities Act 1945 (IOIA) of the US in this regard provides that 'international organizations . . . shall enjoy the same immunity from suit and every form of judicial process as is enjoyed by foreign governments'. See also *Boimah v United Nations General Assembly*, 664 F Supp 69, 71 (EDNY 1987); *FAO v Colagrossi* (Corte di Cassazione, 18 May 1992) of Italy.

[198] See, eg *Broadbent v Organization of American States* 628 F 2d 27 (DC Cir 1980) (where not only the OAS, but also others including the United Nations and Inter-American Development Bank submitted briefs in support of this assertion); *Food and Agriculture Organization of the United Nations (FAO) v Instituto Nationale di Previdenze per I Dirigenti di Aziende Industriali*, Supreme Court of Cassation, Judgement No 5399 of 18 October 1982, reported in 1982 UN Jurid YB 234, ST/LEG/SER.C/20. See further The Practice of the United Nations, the Specialized Agencies and the International Atomic Energy Agency Concerning Their Status, Privileges and Immunities: A Study Prepared by the Secretariat, UNDoc A/CN.4/L.118 Add 1and 2 (1967), reprinted in the *Yearbook of International Law Commission* (1967), vol II, 223.

[199] *Atkinson v Inter-American Development Bank* 156 F 3d 1335 (DC Cir 1998).

therefore cannot exert sovereign authority. Although international organisations are also subjects of international law and enjoy international legal personality, they do not have rights and duties to the same degree. Therefore, it has been argued that the principles relating to states should not be applied to international organisations and that 'absolute immunity' is not appropriate for international organisations.[200] The functional immunity approach was also affirmed by the ICJ in the *Reparations Case*[201] and by the European Court of Justice in *JJ Zwartveld and Others*.[202]

If one accepts this position, the legal liability of international organisations might be established. Does this mean that international organisations can be treated in the same way as a legal person at the domestic level? This depends on whether the legal personality of international organisations is recognised at the national level. The possession of domestic legal personality is essential for entering into legal relationships with others and also for becoming a party to legal proceedings before national courts.[203] This is generally conferred through national legislation. In the US it was held in *Balfour, Guthrie & Co Ltd et al v United States*[204] that the United Nations had a capacity to institute legal proceedings in the US by virtue of Article 104 of the UN Charter, which provides for domestic legal personality, as the Charter was already part of the US law. A similar approach has been adopted in other states, including Belgium and the Netherlands.[205] The UK, in contrast, is a dualist state, and therefore the International Organisations Act 1968 was necessary to recognise the legal personality of international organisations. Such a dualist system has also been adopted in Australia, Canada and New Zealand.[206] If the legal personality of international organisations is recognised, then the same measures as for other legal persons can be instituted. In practice, however, it is inconceivable that states will declare international organisations criminal or take any criminal action against them because of political expediency and the need to maintain good relations with them. It should also be noted that international organisations lack *locus standi* before international tribunals such as the ICJ. Article 34 of the ICJ Statute in this regard provides that only states may appear before the ICJ, although some recognise that there is a need to amend the appropriate Statute to include international organisations as parties.[207]

This means that types of accountability other than the legal one might be appropriate for international organisations when they are implicated in the

---

[200] Reinisch, above ch 3 n 207, 363 and Klabbers, above n 159, 165.
[201] Above n 158, 174.
[202] Above n 178.
[203] Reinisch, above ch 3 n 207, 37–38.
[204] 90 F Supp 831 (ND Val 1950).
[205] Reinisch, above ch 3 n 207, 47.
[206] Ibid, 49.
[207] International Law Association (ILA), 'Final Report on Accountability of International Organisations' (2004) 53. Reinisch points to the exception of the European Community, where cases can be brought against their organs such as the European Commission. Above ch 3 n 207, 39.

commission of organised crime. It has been noted that managers and high-ranking officials of the United Nations can be held liable for not doing enough to prevent and suppress organised crime. Under the 'Secretary-General's Bulletin on Special Measures for Protection from Sexual Exploitation and Sexual Abuse',[208] the heads of departments, offices or missions are responsible for creating and maintaining an environment that prevents sexual exploitation and sexual abuse.[209] They also have to take action if there is good ground to believe that their staff have engaged in the sexual exploitation of vulnerable people.[210] A failure to discharge these duties can be addressed through the existing managerial performance appraisal mechanisms for the purpose of promotion, for example.[211]

In more serious cases of misconduct, states can withhold or reject the appointment or reappointment of high-ranking officials such as the UN Secretary-General and the head of the Department of Peacekeeping Operations. They can also limit the scope of power to be exercised by them by modifying constitutive instruments. Reinisch notes that international organisations in general are highly dependent on states and therefore the political accountability of their organs serve as an effective restraint and internal control mechanisms.[212] In addition, NGOs and other members of civil society can hold international organisations accountable by exposing violations of human rights and other pertinent norms in relation to organised crime.[213] States can also refuse to pay voluntary contributions to the organisations, thereby hampering the functioning of international organisations.[214] Similar to the case of legal persons, these measures can be more effective compared to legal accountability. In summary, the concept of global governance is helpful in understanding the nature and the extent of the role to be played by non-state actors in preventing and suppressing transnational organised crime.

4.3   Towards an Inclusive Notion of the 'International Community'

Before concluding this chapter, it is worth exploring the notion of 'international community' in light of the earlier discussions on global governance and the role

---

[208] ST/SGB/2003/13 (9 October 2003).

[209] Para 4.1.

[210] Para 4.2.

[211] A Comprehensive Strategy to Eliminate Future Sexual Exploitation and Abuse in United Nations Peacekeeping Operations, A/59/710 (24 March 2005), paras 58–59.

[212] Above ch 3 n 207, 133.

[213] Clapham, above n 81, 132. He gives an example of the involvement of UNMIK in human trafficking.

[214] ILA Report, above n 207, 32; Reinisch, above ch 3 n 207, 134.

of non-state actors. The term is often used rhetorically by states and international organisations alike to consolidate or justify all efforts to deal with issues of international importance, such as terrorism. However, it has been difficult to come to an agreement on what it means precisely, due to the wide variety of views that have been advanced. A starting point in understanding this vague concept perhaps is to explore the idea of 'community'. It has been said that a community is a legal entity, with a constitution that strengthens the unity of the members it governs.[215] A constitution, as it is generally understood, sets out rules through which law is created and developed.[216] It establishes various organs which would implement laws, policies and decisions, and defines the limit of their powers. In addition, members of any legal community are said to have legal personality. At the municipal level, natural persons as well as legal persons are such examples. Finally, all members of a community have certain common interests, values and principles shared by them.[217]

In applying this notion of community at the international level, it has been argued that the United Nations best represents the international community. The United Nations Charter can be regarded as a constitution as it defines the powers and limitations of principal organs such as the General Assembly and the Security Council, and provides for various procedures for decision-making. It has been argued by some that the Charter reflects the constitutional principles of the international community.[218] Simma and Paulus also observe that 'what the Charter undoubtedly did achieve was the translation of the concept of the "international community" from an abstract notion to something approaching institutional reality'.[219] In addition, the members of the United Nations—states— have legal personality, as does the organisation itself, as noted earlier. Finally, there is no doubt that the United Nations and its members share common interests and values, which include, but are not limited to, protection of international peace and security, suppression of transnational organised crime and terrorism, and promotion of human rights.[220]

While this may be a fair description of the international community, others have argued that the membership of the international community should not be restricted to states and international organisations. There is no doubt that states are still the key members of the international community and this is recognised, for instance, in Article 53 of the Vienna Convention on the Law of Treaties 1969. This provides that *jus cogens* is a norm accepted and recognised

---

[215] B Fassbender, 'United Nations Charter as the Constitution of the International Community' (1998) 36 *Columbia Journal of Transnational law* 529, 566.

[216] H Mosler, *International Society as a Legal Community* (The Hague, Kluwer Law International, 1980) 16.

[217] K Annan, 'Problems Without Passports' (2002) *Foreign Policy* 30; B Simma and AL Paulus, 'The "International Community": Facing the Challenge of Globalisation' (1998) 9 *European Journal of International Law* 266, 268.

[218] GM Danilenko, *Law-Making in the International Community* (Dordrecht, Martinus Nijhoff Publishers, 1993) 11.

[219] Simma and Paulus, above n 217, 274.

[220] Art 1 of the UN Charter.

by 'the international community of states as a whole'. The Declaration on Principles of International Law concerning Friendly Relations and Co-operation among States in accordance with the Charter of the United Nations 1970[221] also provides that all states are equal members of the international community. This state-centric conception of the international community has been termed a 'positivist' [222] or realist understanding of 'community'[223] as it focuses on international law as the autonomous rules created and applied by states as the main subjects of law.

Many do not agree with this realist conception of the international community and argue that states are not the only members. The Kantian or universalist conception supports such an idea. In emphasising the importance of civil society, this view supports the inclusion of other key actors, such as MNCs and NGOs.[224] In between these realist and Kantian conceptions is the Grotian or internationalist conception. Under this notion, the international community is said to reflect the common interests of states as well as of mankind, and the role to be played by international organisations is regarded as important.[225] Whichever view one takes, the inclusive notion of the international community has gained strong support in modern times. The United Nations General Assembly, for instance, stated explicitly that the concerned actors of the international community include 'non-governmental organisations, multilateral financial institutions, regional organisations and all actors of civil society'.[226] Contemporary scholars also support the inclusion of relevant actors in this community.[227]

The analysis of governance over transnational organised crime suggests that perhaps a combination of these three concepts, which include all the relevant actors, might be more appropriate to describe the international community in the era of globalisation. If this position is to be accepted, then legally binding international law would not be the only form of decisions to be made by the international community, and this is in conformity with the concept of global governance explored above. While decisions without legal force might lead to instances of non-compliance, one definite advantage is that it allows participation by all relevant actors. Consensus is arrived at more easily compared to legally binding instruments, the conclusion of which requires an enormous amount of time and energy. Such flexibility is probably necessary for issues

---

[221] A/RES/25/2625 (24 October 1970). See also Draft Articles on Responsibility of States for Internationally Wrongful Acts with Commentaries, A/56/10 (April–August 2001), 35

[222] MS McDougal, WM Reisman and AR Willard, 'The World Community: A Planetary Social Process' (1988) 21 *U. C. Davis Law Review* 807, 812.

[223] Simma and Paulus, above n 217, 269.

[224] Ibid, 270. See also AM Slaughter, 'International Law in a World of Liberal States' (1995) 6 *European Journal of International Law* 503; FR Tesón, 'The Kantian Theory of International Law'(1992) 92 *Columbia Law Review* 53.

[225] Ibid, 270–71.

[226] A/RES/50/6 (24 October 1995), para 17.

[227] T Franck, *Fairness in International Law and Institutions* (Oxford, Oxford University Press, 1995) 477; J Crawford, 'Responsibility to the International Community as a Whole' (2001) 8 *Indiana Journal of Global Legal Studies* 303, 313–14.

such as transnational organised crime because of its constantly evolving nature and the need for rapid responses. Following from this, it may be argued that the possession of international legal personality would not be a prerequisite for membership to the international community. In this regard, it has been noted that the formulation of 'international community as a whole' does not imply that there is a legal person.[228] The concept of the international community is controversial and therefore will require further discussions. What is clear is that any description of the international community should reflect the reality of how international affairs are governed in modern times, and it is hoped that this chapter has shed some light in this regard.

4.4   Conclusions

This chapter examined the role of non-state actors in suppression and prevention of organised crime with particular reference to the concept of global governance and its key principles of participation and accountability. The main conclusion reached is that the concept is useful in promoting better understanding of their role and position in relation to transnational organised crime. Acceptance of global governance over transnational organised crime does not mean rejecting or ignoring the importance of international law or the principle of state sovereignty. It was acknowledged above that states continue to play a key role, and pertinent branches of international law—TCL, IHRL and ICL—provide good guidance on issues such as criminal liability, the protection of victims and witnesses, and the immunity of international organisations. It is submitted instead that global governance supplements the existing arrangement by recognising the additional contributions made by those other than states. It also helps one realise that the law is not the only answer to the development of effective action and govern-ance over transnational organised crime.

Following from the analysis on the nature of states' obligations in Chapter 3, what becomes evident from the international legal framework to address tran-snational organised crime is the inherent tension between the responses against the practice and state sovereignty. While states remain the key actors for preven-tion and suppression of transnational organised crime, and the principle of state sovereignty has been explicitly acknowledged and preserved under TCL, an analysis of non-state actors demonstrates that the preservation of this principle will not lead to effective action against this criminality. This argument becomes more compelling when a conduct is regarded an international crime or a gross violation of human rights as these are now regarded as the concerns of the international community as a whole. The key to the success of any framework

---

[228] J Crawford, *The International Law Commission's Arts on state Responsibility: Introduction, Text and Commentaries* (Cambridge, Cambridge University Press, 2002) 40–41.

against transnational organised crime is to acknowledge this and facilitate active co-operation and co-ordination among all of those concerned. This is one of the key areas to be examined in Part II, which present case studies of national, regional and international responses to transnational organised crime.

Part II

Enforcement of Norms
and Principles

5

National Case Studies of Thailand, Serbia, Kosovo and the UK

5.1 Introduction

This chapter presents national case studies of Thailand, Serbia, Kosovo and the UK. Its main purpose is to analyse how the international norms and principles explored in Chapters 3 and 4 are incorporated or implemented in practice at the national level. These states have been chosen as they can be classified roughly as a developing state (Thailand), states/territories in transition (Serbia and Kosovo) and a developed state (UK), respectively. This chapter will analyse how these states in various stages of development deal with organised crime and the extent to which the legislative and law enforcement frameworks display similarities as well as differences. Kosovo is included in this study because, although it declared independence in July 2008, and this has been recognised by some states,[1] others[2] have not been so quick to do so. As a result, its status remains unclear. It also provides a case study of the personnel of international organisations and peacekeeping missions engaging in aspects of organised crime. The four jurisdictions can also be regarded as major supplier (Thailand), transit (Serbia and Kosovo) and consumer states (UK) for illicit goods and services, and this chapter will examine how these states address the supply and demand dynamics. The main conclusion reached is that, while the legislative frameworks in these jurisdictions are broadly in line with international standards as set by the Organised Crime Convention and other instruments, a wide variety of problems have prevented their effective enforcement in practice.

---

[1] They include France, Germany, the US and the UK.
[2] They are China, Russia and Serbia.

5.2 Thailand[3]

5.2.1 Legal Framework to Address Organised Crime

5.2.1.1 Legislation on Substantive Offences

Thailand lacks comprehensive legislation that applies to all types of organised crime. Rather, it is dealt with in a piecemeal fashion through legislation which prohibits substantive crimes. To begin with, the key criminal law in Thailand is the Thai Penal Code 1956.[4] While prohibiting offences such as corruption,[5] criminal association,[6] counterfeiting currencies[7] and extortion,[8] the Penal Code does not contain a definition of the 'organised criminal group'. This was adopted only recently, under the Anti-Trafficking in Persons Act 2008.[9] Section 4 provides:

> 'Organized Criminal Group' means a structured group of three or more persons, notwithstanding being formed permanently or existing for a period of time, and no need to have formally defined roles for its members, continuity of its membership or a developed structure, acting in concert with the aim of committing one or more offences punishable by a maximum imprisonment of four years upwards or committing any offence stipulated in this Act, with the aim to unlawfully obtain, directly or indirectly, property or any other benefit.

It is evident here that the definition reflects that of the Organised Crime Convention, and this indicates Thailand's willingness to abide by international standards. However, this definition applies within the context of human trafficking only and therefore the usefulness of this definition can be limited for other offences.

Another pertinent piece of legislation is the Order of the Office of the Prime Minister No139/2546 on the Suppression of Persons of Influence 2003, which defines a 'person of influence' as:

> a person, acting independently or in a group, who either commits offences themselves, or orders other people to commit offences or things above the law; and when such behaviour is a criminal offence, with the virulent results affecting all sectors of society and inciting annoyance, loss or fear. They also construct networks to spread these effects, which are economically, socially and politically destructive in addition to eroding the peace, order and morality of the people.[10]

---

[3] Thailand has signed the Organised Crime Convention in December 2000, but had not ratified it as of January 2010.

[4] BE 2499.

[5] Title II, Chapters 1 (Offences against Officials) and 2 (Malfeasance in Office), and Title III, Chapters 1 (Offences against Judicial Officials) and 2 (Malfeasance in Judicial Office).

[6] S 210.

[7] Title VII, Chapter 1 (Offences Relating to Currencies).

[8] Title XII, Chapter 1 (Extortion, Blackmail, Robbery and Gang-Robbery).

[9] BE 2551.

[10] Order of the Office of the Prime Minister No 139/2546 on the Suppression of Persons of Influence, 8 July 2003.

The core activities listed in the Order are dealing in narcotics, bid-rigging, extortion from public transport, factories and shops, tax evasion, illegal gambling, trafficking for sexual exploitation, smuggling of migrants, arms trade and assassination.[11] A clear link with organised crime is thus recognised. In particular, it is clear that the Order is designed to target the bosses of criminal groups. The only problem is that the list of offences is exhaustive and therefore the Order does not apply to other types of organised crime.[12]

Other laws touch upon a variety or offences which may be classified as organised crime. They include the Anti-Money Laundering Act 1999,[13] the Act on Measures for the Suppression of Offenders in an Offence Relating to Narcotics 1991,[14] the Prevention and Suppression of Prostitution Act 1996[15] and the Anti-Trafficking in Persons Act 2008. It is also important to note that these statutes also cover inchoate offences, such as conspiracy.[16] Furthermore, under Thai criminal law, criminal liability can also be imposed upon legal persons with punishment in a form of a fine.[17] It should be noted that periods of limitation are recognised under the Thai Penal Code.[18] If a conduct carries imprisonment of between one and seven years, the period of limitation is 10 years, after which prosecution cannot occur.[19] In comparing this provision with others noted in Chapter 3, it might be argued that the limitation period in Thailand is relatively longer, making it difficult for criminals to evade responsibility. Also, the Thai Criminal Procedure Code provides for pardon granted by the king.[20] In looking at substantive criminal laws in Thailand, then, it may be concluded that while the key statute (the Penal Code) does not provide the definitions of serious crime or organised criminal groups stipulated under the Organised Crime Convention, other laws do cover major forms of organised crime.

It is worth noting that the Office of the Attorney General has taken a lead in preparing draft legislation to incorporate the Organised Crime Convention.[21] Thailand is a dualist state and therefore requires domestic legislation to incorporate any international standards.[22] While draft legislation has been in existence for some time, since the government signed the Convention in 2000, there is no sign of enactment as yet. Perhaps this demonstrates a lack of political will to incorporate international standards fully. Thailand has long experienced polit-

---

[11] Ibid.
[12] W Roujanavong, *Organised Crime in Thailand* (Bangkok, Rumthai Press, 2006) 13.
[13] BE 2542.
[14] BE 2534, as amended in 2000.
[15] BE 2539.
[16] S 9 of the Anti-Money Laundering Act; s 8 of the Act on Measures for the Suppression of Offenders in an Offence Relating to Narcotics; s 7 of the Measures in Prevention and Suppression of Trafficking in Women and Children Act 1997, BE 2540.
[17] Roujanavong, above n 12, 152.
[18] Chapter 9.
[19] Art 95.
[20] Division VII, above n 4.
[21] Interview with Mr Uthai Arthivech, Office of Attorney General (2 November 2009).
[22] Ibid.

ical instability, which intensified after the military coup against the government of Thaksin Shinawatra in 2006.[23] It is therefore quite possible that this might have changed the political priorities of the current government. From a practical point of view, it has been difficult to define the powers to be given to key law enforcement agencies, such as the police and the public prosecutor.[24] This perhaps illustrates a degree of tension between the politicians on the one hand and the law enforcement agencies on the other, or between law enforcement agencies.

5.2.1.2   Legislation on Criminal Procedure and International Co-operation

5.2.1.2.1   Criminal Jurisdiction and Investigative Powers

To begin with, the Thai Penal Code and the Criminal Procedure Code[25] and other statutes provide for the exercise of criminal jurisdiction over organised crime. The territorial and flag principles[26] as well as the protective principle[27] are explicitly recognised in these statutes. Its criminal jurisdiction also extends to individuals who commit offences abroad and are found in the territory of Thailand.[28] The nationality[29] and passive personality principles[30] are recognised for organised crimes, such as extortion, sexual offences and fraud. Finally, the universality principle can be applied to offences such as counterfeiting of currencies and documents.[31] It is therefore apparent that, while the Organised Crime Convention has not been incorporated fully into domestic legal system, Thai laws do reflect international standards on criminal jurisdiction.

Investigative powers, such as arrest, search and seizure, are defined under Title V of the Criminal Procedure Code. The key agency in Thailand dealing with organised crime is the Royal Thai Police, which is the primary agency for leading criminal investigations in Thailand.[32] Currently there are approximately 250,000 police officers working in Thailand.[33] There are 24 bureaus under the police, the relevant ones for organised crime including the Central Investigation Bureau, the Narcotics Suppression Bureau and the Immigration Bureau.[34] There are Transnational Crime Co-ordination Centres within the police and the Immi-

---

[23] Human Rights Watch, 'World Report 2009', 315.

[24] Ibid, and interview with the Major General Krerkphong Pukprayura of the Royal Thai Police (3 November 2009).

[25] BE 2477 (1928).

[26] S 4 of the Penal Code; s 18 of the Thai Criminal Procedure Code.

[27] S 5.

[28] S 20 of the Criminal Procedure Code.

[29] S 8 of Penal Code; s 6 of the Money Laundering Act 1999.

[30] Ibid.

[31] S 7.

[32] S 17 of the Criminal Procedure Code confers the power of investigation on the Police.

[33] The Police is said to have more officers than armed forced combined. Interview with the Major General Pukprayura, above n 24.

[34] Ibid.

gration Bureau which engage in intelligence analysis.[35] To complement the Royal Thai Police, the Department of Special Investigation was established within the Ministry of Justice by the Special Cases Investigation Act 2004.[36] The Department is headed by a civil servant known as the Special Case Inquiry Official, who is assisted by the Special Case Inquiry Officer.[37] The Department has the power to investigate and enforce laws on special cases, including transnational organised crime, in conjunction with the Office of the Attorney General.[38] Once an investigation is completed, a case will be put forward to the Public Prosecutor, who will file an indictment. Unlike other jurisdictions, the power of the Public Prosecutor to investigate is restricted as the police take the lead in this area.[39]

Given the complex and transnational nature of organised crime, some special measures are necessary in order to facilitate effective prosecution and punishment. In Thailand, while these special measures are not stipulated under the Criminal Procedure Code, they are recognised in other laws. For instance, under the Anti-Money Laundering Act 1999 the authorities can issue an order prohibiting financial transaction if there is a reasonable ground for suspecting that money laundering is taking place.[40] The authorities can also confiscate criminal assets and proceeds upon receipt of an order issued by a court.[41] In addition, the Narcotics Control Act 1976[42] provides for the power to enter premises suspected of hiding criminals and narcotics without a search warrant[43] and allows the authorities to intercept communications when authorised by the judiciary.[44] However, these powers are limited to money laundering and drug-related offences and do not apply to other forms and aspects of organised crime. This was remedied recently by the Special Case Investigation Act 2004 noted above. Similar to statutes on money laundering and drug offences, this Act gives extended powers to enter, search and seize evidence, and to intercept communication.[45] The Thai government acknowledges that the legislation does not apply to violent crimes and other conduct stipulated under the Organised Crime Convention.[46] In addition, other special techniques stipulated under the Convention, such as joint investigations, surveillance and controlled delivery, are not

---

[35] Ibid.

[36] BE 2547.

[37] Ss 14–16.

[38] S 21.

[39] Interview with the Major General Pukprayura, above n 24. See also the Criminal Procedure Code; the Regulation of Public Prosecutor Officers Act 1978, BE2521.

[40] Ss 35 and 36.

[41] Ss 48 and 49.

[42] BE 2519 as amended several times.

[43] S 13.

[44] S 14.

[45] Ss 24 and 25.

[46] Office of the Prime Minister, 'Thai Country Report, submitted to the Eleventh United Nations Congress on Crime Prevention and Criminal Justice held in Bangkok' (April 2005), 25 (Thai Country Report).

explicitly provided for under the 2004 Act.[47] Therefore Thailand still has much to do to enhance its special investigative techniques.

5.2.1.2.2   The Rights of Suspects/Defendants, Victims and Witnesses

The rights of those involved in the criminal justice process in Thailand are recognised mainly under the Criminal Procedure Code. First, Sections 7bis and 8 of the Code state that the accused has the rights to legal counsel, examination of evidence put before him and medical assistance. If a suspect is a foreign national, he/she is also entitled to an interpreter.[48] The principle of *nullum crimen sine lege* and public hearing in the presence of the accused are also guaranteed.[49] Therefore the Criminal Procedure Code is broadly in conformity with the established norms stipulated under IHRL, such as the ICCPR.[50] There are, however, some concerns in the area of pre-trial detention. Under normal circumstances detention of a suspect is limited to 48 hours.[51] While any further detention must be authorised by a court,[52] a major concern is that a longer period of detention can be imposed for serious crimes. For an offence carrying imprisonment of six months to 10 years, for instance, one can be detained up to 48 days, while a suspect may be held up to 84 days if the offence committed attracts a longer penalty.[53] While it is understandable that it may take time to obtain evidence for complex cases such as organised crime, a period of 84 days is an excessive amount to time to spend in detention and raises serious human rights concerns.

The Thai legislation also provides for protection of witnesses. The Act for the Protection of Witnesses in Criminal Cases 2003[54] is the key legislation in this respect. Protection is afforded to witnesses of organised crime and others which carry the imprisonment of 10 years or longer.[55] It stipulates measures including testifying through TV and video, anonymity of witnesses, modification of personal records, including names and addresses, and provision of accommodation.[56] These measures can also be extended to the families of witnesses.[57] The Act also establishes an offence of obstruction of justice (intimidation and violence against witnesses) in line with Article 23 of the Organised Crime Convention. Finally, the Act established the Witness Protection Bureau within

---

[47] Ibid, 25–26. However, controlled delivery is stipulated for narcotics offences.
[48] S 13.
[49] Ss 161 and 172.
[50] Thailand acceded to it in 1996.
[51] S 87 of the Criminal Procedure Code.
[52] Ibid.
[53] Ibid.
[54] BE 2546.
[55] S 8.
[56] S 10.
[57] S 11.

the Ministry of Justice, which initiates or co-ordinates all activities in relation to protection of witnesses.[58]

In addition, the rights of victims of organised crime are recognised. It is worth noting from the outset that injured persons or victims have a right to institute criminal prosecution in Thailand, along with the Public Prosecutor.[59] This right reflects the norms relating to the human rights of victims, as noted in Chapter 4. The victims can also bring civil proceedings against the defendants at the same time as the criminal proceedings. Specifically, they can seek restitution in cases of theft, robbery, gang robbery, piracy, extortion, cheating and fraud, criminal misappropriation and receiving stolen property,[60] many of which are aspects of organised crime. Other legislation also touches upon victim protection. The Anti-Trafficking in Persons Act 2008 is a good example. Under Chapter 4 of this statute, the Ministry of Social Development and Human Security is responsible for providing victims of trafficking with food, shelter, medical assistance, education and training, and legal aid. It is worth noting in this regard that the number of shelters for trafficked victims recently increased from 99 to 138, providing protection for over 600 victims in 2008.[61] It should also be noted that, while the government is responsible for providing protection under the legislation, it works closely with NGOs that have expertise in this area,[62] and therefore it recognises the important role to be played by members of civil society in Thailand.

5.2.1.2.3 *Mutual Legal Assistance in Criminal Matters*

Thailand does have a legal framework to facilitate mutual legal assistance in criminal matters, despite its non-ratification of the Organised Crime Convention. For instance, the current procedure of extradition is governed by the Extradition Act 2008.[63] The key principles, such as double criminality, are recognised under Section 7. A request for extradition is communicated to the Attorney General's Office, the designated central authority, if a bilateral treaty exists.[64] Previously it had to go through a diplomatic channel (eg Ministry of Foreign Affairs), which was communicated to the Ministry of Interior and then to the Department of Public Prosecution.[65] This process was regarded as time-consuming and cumbersome,[66] and the new Act rectifies this by allowing a communication to be sent to the law enforcement agency directly. If there is no bilateral treaty, the

---

[58] S 13.
[59] S 28 of the Criminal Procedure Code. If prosecution is instituted by the Public Prosecutor, a victim also has a right to associate himself/herself as a prosecutor at any time during criminal proceedings (s 30).
[60] S 43.
[61] Trafficking in Persons Report 2009, above ch 2 n 145.
[62] Ibid.
[63] BE 2551 (2008). It was previously governed by the Extradition Act 1929, BE 2472.
[64] S 8.
[65] Ss 6–8 of the 1929 Act.
[66] Thai Country Report, above n 46, 40–41.

request still has to go through a diplomatic channel.[67] It is also worth noting that Thai nationals could not be extradited under the old legislation.[68] Instead, the government used to prosecute and punish criminals in its territory.[69] This complied with the principle of *aut dedere aut judicare* noted elsewhere in this book and therefore non-extradition of Thai nationals per se is not in breach of an international obligation. However, this rule has been relaxed over the course of time under bilateral treaties,[70] and Section 12 of the 2008 Act puts this on a legislative footing.

One difficulty which should be highlighted in relation to extradition in Thailand is continued application of the death penalty. It was noted in Chapter 3 that the norm against extradition of individuals to states which retain the death penalty is developing. This puts Thailand in a difficult position as other states refrain from extraditing criminals to Thailand because of the death penalty, meaning the principle of reciprocity is not respected.[71] In response, Thailand has concluded bilateral agreements to restrict the imposition of the death penalty.[72] However, such an arrangement has facilitated another problem of criminals in Thailand escaping to states which do not extradite due to the existence of the death penalty.[73] This inevitably results in different treatments of criminals who have committed the same crime when some evade capital punishment by fleeing abroad. One option which Thailand might consider is abolition of the death penalty in line with the international trend.

Other types of mutual legal assistance are governed by the Act on Mutual Assistance in Criminal Matters 1992.[74] The Attorney General's Office is the designated central authority for this purpose,[75] and it receives and responds to the request for assistance and determines whether or not to render such assistance.[76] The decision made by the central authority is final unless altered by the prime minister.[77] It is to be noted here that the law enforcement authority, as opposed to the diplomatic channel through the Ministry of Foreign Affairs, plays the key role in facilitating mutual assistance in Thailand. This is desirable, as those working on the ground have expertise and are therefore in a position to decide the best course of action to be taken. This stands in comparison to diplomats, who are constrained more by political considerations at a higher level.[78] The types of assistance which can be provided under this Act include the taking of

---

[67] S 8 of the 2008 Act.
[68] S 16 of the 1929 Act.
[69] Thai Country Report, above n 46, 40.
[70] Ibid.
[71] Interview with Mr Arthivech, above n 21.
[72] Ibid.
[73] Ibid.; interviews with Major General Pukprayura, above n 24.
[74] BE 2535.
[75] S 6.
[76] S 7.
[77] S 11.
[78] It should be acknowledged that under s 10 of the Act, the direct contact with the Central Authority is allowed for states with which Thailand has bilateral agreements.

statements, search and seizure of evidence, transmission of intelligence available within the Thai government, serving of legal documents and transfer of individuals in custody for testimonial purposes.[79] In looking at substantive and procedural laws dealing with organised crime in Thailand, it may be concluded that they are broadly in line with international standards set by the Organised Crime Convention.

5.2.2 Assessment of Law Enforcement in Thailand

There are some examples of good practices in relation to law enforcement against organised crime. For instance, the government has toughened its stance on child sexual exploitation. In 2008, two Thai women were convicted and sentenced to 34 and 50 years' imprisonment respectively for forcing children into prostitution.[80] Without a doubt these are harsh punishments and can therefore serve as strong deterrence. In the area of asset recovery, the Anti-Money Laundering Office[81] in 2007 initiated 83 civil asset forfeiture cases, resulting in confiscation of 134 million Baht ($3.9 million).[82] It also received over 47,000 reports of suspicious financial transactions from financial institutions in 2008.[83] This latter point illustrates that non-governmental entities do co-operate with the authorities to combat money laundering and organised crime. Further, the government seized 2,370 kilograms of opium and 11 million tablets of methamphetamine (commonly known as crystal meth) in 2008.[84]

Thai law enforcement agencies also actively co-operate with foreign governments and international organisations to address organised crime. The government established the Foreign Anti-Narcotics and Crime Community, which consists of law enforcement authorities from 19 states.[85] The law enforcement agencies from these states work closely with the Royal Thai Police for the prevention and suppression of organised crime. Another good initiative is the International Law Enforcement Academy (ILEA), which was established in 1998 with the assistance of the US government.[86] The Academy is open to law enforcement agencies in South East Asia, and conducts training, seminars and other events every month.[87] The transnational nature of organised crime makes

---

[79] Chapter 2 of the 1992 Act.
[80] Trafficking in Persons Report 2009, above ch 2 n 145.
[81] Established by the Anti-Money Laundering Act 1999.
[82] International Narcotics Control Strategy Report 2009, above ch 2 n 168.
[83] Ibid.
[84] Ibid.
[85] Interview with the Major General Pukprayura, above n 24. They are Australia, Belgium, Canada, China, France, Germany, Indonesia, Israel, Italy, Japan, South Korea, the Netherlands, New Zealand, Norway, Spain, Sri Lanka, Switzerland, the US and the UK.
[86] Visit www.ileabangkok.com for more information.
[87] Interview with the Major General Pukprayura, above n 24.

it essential to facilitate effective co-operation, and Thailand has a long tradition in his regard.[88]

While these examples of good practice should be recognised, a variety of problems have been identified in relation to law enforcement. For instance, the government has not made sufficient financial commitment to enhance the capability of law enforcement. As in many other states, salaries of police officers are not as high as those of other professions in Thailand.[89] While increasing remuneration would help maintain the morale among those working in the field, this is difficult in practice as the government would also have to take the same measure for other public and law enforcement officials to ensure fairness.[90] Low pay can lead to problems such as corruption and inability to recruit enough law enforcement officers. High turnover of personnel[91] is an additional problem as the government must expend more resources training new people. The end result of all of this is the limited manpower and expertise to conduct effective investigations into organised crime. The government recognises this problem and is seeking assistance from foreign states and international organisations in this regard.[92]

Corruption is another key problem. It has widely been acknowledged that organised criminal groups and networks have strong connections with local and national politicians, government and law enforcement officials, and other sectors, enabling them to carry out their operations.[93] In the area of human trafficking, for example, the police actively protect brothels and other venues for sexual services, as well as sweatshops, from raids.[94] In addition to low salaries among the law enforcement and public authorities, one of the important factors facilitating corruption in Thailand is said to be the disregard for the rule of law. This has been facilitated through the military control over many of political institutions.[95] While the Thai Penal Code punishes corruption, as noted above, its endemic nature suggests that the current legislative framework is an inadequate remedy. This means that it will have to move beyond merely criminalising corruption and address its root causes such as low pay and other economic hardships.

A lack of co-ordination among concerned agencies is also recognised. It has been noted that various agencies mistrust and are jealous of each other, hampering active co-operation to tackle organised crime.[96] This, unfortunately, is said to be a common feature of the Thai criminal justice system, which is

---

[88] Ibid.
[89] Ibid.
[90] Ibid.
[91] Trafficking in Persons Report 2009, above ch 2 n 145.
[92] Interview with the Major General Pukprayura, above n 24.
[93] Roujanavong, above n 12, 21.
[94] Trafficking in Persons Report 2009, above ch 2 n 145.
[95] M Raghu, 'Sex Trafficking of Thai Women and the United Sates Asylum Law Response' (1997) 12 *Georgetown Immigration Law Journal* 145, 148–49.
[96] Roujanavong, above n 12, 24.

based on the hunger for power and resistance to change.[97] An inability of the government to come up with comprehensive legislation on organised crime, as explained earlier, should be analysed in this context as well because one of the difficulties has been the division of power among concerned law enforcement agencies such as the Royal Thai Police and the Public Prosecutor. The practical implication of this is the duplication of efforts, which places further burdens on the scarce resources available to address organised crime.

In addition to some of the issues already explored, various aspects of law enforcement raise a set of human rights concerns. This has been particularly evident in the 'war on drugs' declared by the former prime minister Thaksin Shinawatra in 2003.[98] Like the war on drugs declared by the US, the campaign in Thailand has been characterised by violence and the militarisation of law enforcement against drug production and trafficking.[99] In the first three months of this campaign, for instance, there were over 2,800 cases of extrajudicial killings.[100] More than half of these cases were said to have nothing to do with drug production or trafficking.[101] These serious violations of human rights were accompanied by a lack of due process and effective/independent investigation.[102] Systematic police brutality, corruption and abuse of power in anti-drugs operation has also been reported recently,[103] and the government in 2008 announced that a new 'war on drugs', similar to the one carried out in 2003, would be launched shortly.[104] This is a concerning development as it demonstrates that Thailand has not learned much from the past and is willing to engage in further violations of human rights. It was also noted in Chapter 3 that any action which disregards human rights is counterproductive as it can incite much hatred and animosity towards law enforcement agencies. Therefore, if Thailand seeks to promote an effective strategy, the war on drugs must not be repeated.

Finally, Thailand needs to take further steps to address the supply of illicit goods and services. While opium production is declining, it has been reported that production of some drugs such as methamphetamine has increased.[105] What is needed is not forcible eradication, as represented by the war on drugs noted above, but a sound alternative development strategy where producers can find

[97] Ibid.
[98] 'Thailand's War on Drugs', a Briefing Paper by International Harm Reduction Association and Human Rights Watch (2009).
[99] Human Rights Watch, 'Not Enough Graves: The War on Drugs, HIV/AIDS, and Violations of Human Rights' (2004), 6–19.
[100] Ibid.
[101] Ibid. See also Concluding Observations of Human Rights Committee: Thailand, CCPR/CO/84/THA (8 July 2005), para 10; Report of the Special Rapporteur on Extrajudicial, Summary and Arbitrary Executions: Summary of Cases Transmitted to Governments and Replies Received, E/CN.4/2004/7/Add.1 (24 March 2004), paras 557 and 558; written statement submitted by the Asian Legal Resource Centre (ALRC), A/HRC/12/NGO/24 (7 September 2009).
[102] Human Rights Watch, above n 99, 20–26.
[103] Amnesty International, 'State of the World's Human Rights 2009', 322.
[104] Human Rights Watch, above n 23, 315. The Minister of Interior was quoted as saying 'if this will lead to 3,000–4,000 deaths of those who break the law, then so be it'.
[105] International Narcotics Control Strategy Report 2009, above ch 2 n 168.

other means of income. It should be noted here that Thailand, in conjunction with international organisations and other states, has instituted alternative development measures. This has led to a massive reduction in opium production.[106] The same should be implemented for the production of other drugs. Thailand is also used as a transit point for drug trafficking and, while the government has intensified its effort to strengthen border control, it has been noted that there is scope for improvement.[107] Also, while such strict penalties as the death penalty and long imprisonments are available for the production and importation of drugs such as heroin,[108] the systematic nature of corruption in Thailand means that criminals do not always receive penalties heavy enough to serve as a deterrent. Therefore, more needs to be done to eliminate instances of corruption.

Some concerns are also expressed in relation to human trafficking and sexual exploitation of women and children. The Prostitution Prevention and Suppression Act 1996[109] makes all forms of prostitution illegal in Thailand. Yet the sex industry in Bangkok, Pattaya and other key areas continues to flourish, because it serves as a reliable source of income for women and others engaging in the business, and as such the authorities do not necessarily implement harsh measures against them.[110] This is exacerbated by Thailand's position as a developing state where poverty, economic hardship and other problems are very much alive. The current legislative framework therefore should be strengthened by other measures, including education and vocational training, alternative employment and gender mainstreaming. The ample supply of women and children for sexual exploitation in Thailand means that there is a strong demand for them as well. In addition to domestic markets, Thailand is a major destination for sex tourism.[111] It has been noted that sex tourists are simply deported instead of receiving harsh penalties for deterrence.[112] While states including the US[113] and Australia[114] punish their nationals for engaging in sexual offences abroad, this must be accompanied by stricter law enforcement against sex tourists in Thailand to deter them from engaging in sexual exploitation.

---

[106] UNODC, 'Alternative Development: A Global Thematic Evaluation' (2005), 4.

[107] International Narcotics Control Strategy Report 2009, above ch 2 n 168.

[108] S 65 and 67 of the Narcotics Act 1979, BE 2552, as amended.

[109] BE 2539. This replaced the previous legislation, the Prostitution Prevention and Suppression Act 1960.

[110] Interview with the Major General Pukprayura, above n 24.

[111] See, eg ECPAT International, 'Global Monitoring Report on the Status of Action against Commercial Sexual Exploitation of Children (Thailand)' (2006).

[112] Obokata, above ch 2 n 51, 52; interview with the Major General Pukprayura, above n 24.

[113] The PROTECT (Prosecutorial Remedies and Other Tools to end the Exploitation of Children Today) Act 2003, 18 USC. § 2252(B) (b).

[114] Part III A of the Commonwealth Crimes Act 1914.

5.3 Serbia[115]

5.3.1 Legal Framework to Address Organised Crime

5.3.1.1 *Legislation on Substantive Offences*

Similar to Thailand, organised crime in Serbia is addressed in a number of statutes. The most appropriate one is the Act on Organisation and Competences of State Authorities in Combating Organised Crime 2002, which has been amended several times.[116] According to Article 3, an organised criminal group is defined as:

> a group of three or more persons, which exists for a certain period of time, acts consensually in order to commit one or more criminal offences for which the prescribed sentence is four years of imprisonment or more, in order to directly or indirectly gain financial or other pecuniary gain.

As this law was initially passed after Serbia's ratification of the Organised Crime Convention, it is no surprise that the definition of a criminal group resembles the one given under the Convention.

What is confusing is that the above legislation is not the only one providing the definition of a criminal group. Article 21 of the Criminal Procedure Code 2006[117] in this regard stipulates that:

> The term 'organized crime' in the present Code pertains to cases where reasonable suspicions exist that a criminal offense for which four years of imprisonment or a more severe sentence is envisaged, is a result of actions performed by three or more persons associated in a criminal organization, ie criminal group, with the aim of committing grave criminal offenses in order to gain proceeds or power.

This definition is a consolidated version of the definitions which appeared previously in various statutes[118] and therefore reflects the one given under the 2002 Act. There are a number of conditions attached to this definition. Article 21 further provides that at least three of the following conditions must also be met:

1) that each member of the criminal organization, ie criminal group, had previously determined, ie, obviously determinable task or role;

---

[115] Serbia ratified the Organised Crime Convention in September 2001. See the Act on Confirmation of the UN Convention Against Transnational Organised Crime and Additional Protocols, Official Gazette of the Republic of Serbia, No 6/2001.

[116] Official Gazette of the Republic of Serbia, Nos 42/2002, 27/2003, 39/2003, 67/2003, 29/2004, 58/2004, 45/2005, 61/2005.

[117] Official Gazette of the Republic of Serbia, No 46/2006. This legislation will come into force shortly.

[118] United Nations Interregional Crime and Justice Research Institute (UNICRI), 'The Fight against Organized Crime in Serbia: From the Existing Legislation to a Comprehensive Reform Proposal' (2008) 121.

2) that the activity of the criminal organization was planned for an extensive or indefinite period of time;

3) that the activities of the organization are based on implementing certain rules of inner control and discipline of members;

4) that the activities of the organization are planned and implemented internationally;

5) that the activities include applying violence or intimidation or that there is readiness to apply them;

6) that economic or business structures are used in the activities;

7) that money laundering or illicit proceeds are used;

8) that there exist influence of the organization, or part of the organization, on political structures, the media, legislative, executive or judicial authorities or other important social or economic factors. [119]

These conditions certainly limit the scope of the definition of a criminal group, making it narrower than the one given under the Organised Crime Convention. It is important to further note that these two pieces of legislation are concerned with the special powers conferred upon law enforcement authorities, and that organised crime or a serious crime committed by a criminal group is not established as a substantive offence. In practice, this means that, while the definitions can be used as guidance among concerned authorities to identify the practice, they cannot be used as a legal basis to prosecute and punish organised crime generally. This also means that organised and ordinary crimes are treated as more or less the same as there are no special provisions or penalties attached to the former which reflect their complexity and seriousness.[120]

The Serbian Criminal Code[121] adds another complexity to organised crime. This consolidated many of the criminal law statutes which existed previously.[122] Article 112(22), for instance, provides that 'organised group is a group comprising minimum three persons acting in conspiracy to commit criminal offences'. While the number of people is the same as above, it does not say anything about the severity of a criminal offence to be committed. There is also no link with financial or material benefits. There is another provision on 'criminal alliance' (Article 346) which provides that: 'Whoever organises a group or other alliance whose purpose is committing criminal offences punishable by imprisonment of three or more years, shall be punished by imprisonment of three months to five years'. The same article also criminalises membership of such an association and the organisers of such an association if the offence committed carries imprisonment of 20 years or longer. In any event, this Article does not reflect the definition of 'criminal group' stipulated in other statutes noted above. What is evident, then, is that multiple definitions of organised crime or criminal groups exist in the legal framework in Serbia, and this serves as a source of confusion among

---

[119] Official Gazette of the Republic of Serbia, 46/2006.

[120] UNICRI, above n 118, 55.

[121] Official Gazette of the Republic of Serbia, No 85/2005.

[122] F István, 'The Evolution of the Serbian Criminal Legislation: From the Beginning of the Transition until the New Criminal Code' (2008) 16 *European Journal of Crime, Criminal Law and Criminal Justice* 283, 284.

those concerned. This not only undermines their effectiveness,[123] but also affects the principle of legality, which dictates that a criminal offence must be defined clearly.

Other substantive offences are covered in the Criminal Code. It prohibits offences such as child pornography (Article 185), copyright breaches (Article 198), credit card fraud (209), extortion (Article 214), blackmail (Article 215), counterfeiting of currencies (Article 223), money laundering (Article 231), drug trafficking (Article 246), facilitation of illegal border crossing (Article 350), human trafficking (Article 388) and corruption (Articles 359 to 369). The Criminal Code is supplemented by other laws, such as the Act on Organisation and Competences of State Authorities in Fighting Cyber Crime 2005[124] and the Act on Money Laundering 2005.[125] Serbia also enacted law to criminalise legal persons in October 2008.[126] While prohibition of these core offences complies with international standards, the Criminal Code simultaneously recognises periods of limitation under Chapter 10 and amnesty/pardon under Chapter 11. In summary, while Serbia's willingness to conform to international standards as set by the Organised Crime Convention can be recognised to some extent, the current legislative framework is confusing to say the least due to the existence of multiple definitions of criminal groups.

5.3.1.2   Legislation on Criminal Procedure and International Co-operation

5.3.1.2.1   Criminal Jurisdiction and Investigative Powers

In Serbia both the Criminal Code and the Criminal Procedure Code provide for the exercise of criminal jurisdiction over organised crime. First, the territoriality principle is recognised as the primary basis for criminal jurisdiction in the same way as Thailand and other jurisdictions.[127] However, other parts of the Code establish different types of jurisdiction. Article 26, for instance, permits the exercise of the flag principle where offences are committed on ships or aircrafts.[128] The Criminal Code also provides for the nationality,[129] passive personality and protective[130] principles. Finally, a Serbian court can exercise jurisdiction over foreigners present in its territory even when an offence is committed abroad under Article 9 of the Criminal Code. This reflects a form of

---

[123] UNICRI, above n 118, 120.

[124] Official Gazette of the Republic of Serbia, No 61/2005. See also Arts 298–304 of the Criminal Code on offences against security of computer data.

[125] Official Gazette of the Republic of Serbia, No 107/2005, 117/2005.

[126] Law on the Liability of Legal Entities for Criminal Offences, Official Gazette of the Republic of Serbia, No 97/2008.

[127] See, eg Arts 25, 28, 29 and 30 of the Criminal Procedure Code; Art 6 of the Criminal Code.

[128] See also Art 6 of the Criminal Code, ibid.

[129] Art 8. See also Art 28 of the Criminal Procedure Code.

[130] Art 9.

the universality principle noted elsewhere. In summary, the grounds of criminal jurisdiction stipulated under the Organised Crime Convention are recognised in Serbia, enabling the concerned authorities to address the transnational nature of organised crime.

Several agencies are charged with the suppression of organised crime. The first is the police. They come under the control of the Ministry of Interior and are divided into 26 districts.[131] The normal investigatory powers to be exercised by the law enforcement authorities are set out in Chapter VII of the Criminal Procedure Code, and relate to search of persons and premises and seizure of evidence. It is worth noting here that in Serbia it is the Public Prosecutor who is authorised to conduct preliminary investigation into crime.[132] In this regard, he/she is in a position to direct or guide the police and other concerned agencies to conduct investigation.[133] A hierarchical relationship between the Public Prosecutor and other agencies is therefore established under the Criminal Procedure Code. This can be contrasted with Thailand, where the police are the key agency that conducts initial investigations, as noted above.

The second agency is the Office of the Special Prosecutor for Organised Crime, which has the competence to deal with cases of organised crime in Serbia. This office was established by the Act on Organisation and Competences of State Authorities for Combating Organised Crime 2002, and he/she is appointed by the Chief Public Prosecutor for a fixed term of two years with a possibility of reappointment.[134] The Chief Prosecutor also appoints deputy special prosecutors upon recommendation from the Special Prosecutor.[135] Upon encountering a case on organised crime, the Special Prosecutor requests the Chief Prosecutor to confer upon him/her jurisdiction to deal with it.[136] The Chief Prosecutor therefore enjoys certain discretion in granting jurisdiction without specific rules imposed upon him/her. A further change has been made with the establishment of the new Office of the Prosecutor for Organised Crime, which will start its operation in 2010.[137]

In addition, in order to strengthen the capacity of the police, the 2002 Act established a Special Service for the Suppression of Organised Crime and Corruption within the Ministry of Interior.[138] Approximately 300 officers, who have to have at least five years of experience of criminal investigation, are employed in this section.[139] Its main function is to assist the Special Prosecutor for Organised Crime to deal with cases involving organised crime and corruption.[140] Within

---

[131] Group of States against Corruption (GRECO), 'Evaluation Report on the Republic of Serbia' (Strasbourg, Council of Europe, 2006), 8 (GRECO Report).

[132] Art 45.

[133] Ibid, and Art 46.

[134] Art 5.

[135] Art 8.

[136] Art 6.

[137] OSCE, 'Special Prosecutor's Office for Organised Crime: The First Six Years' (2009) 14.

[138] Art 10.

[139] GRECO Report, above n 131, 8.

[140] Art 10 of the 2002 Act.

the Service are units dealing with specific crimes such as cyber crime, drugs and human trafficking.[141] The 2002 Act also established the Special Department for Organised Crime within the Belgrade District Court.[142] The judges within the Department are appointed by the President of the Belgrade District Court and serve for a period of two years, which is the same duration as the Special Prosecutor.[143] While these judges did not have much experience in organised crime when they were first appointed, they were said to have acquired expertise through a series of national, regional and international workshops and training, which followed after the creation of the Department.[144]

The creation of specialised agencies and departments for organised crime in Serbia illustrates a few important points. First, the government seems to have recognised that effective law enforcement against organised crime requires personnel with sufficient expertise and training, and agencies with special powers. These specialised agencies are able to focus specifically on organised crime, and this can reduce the instances of backlog of pending cases. All of this shows Serbia's commitment to abide by international standards and promote concerted action as a member of the international community. It should be noted, however, that the effort of Serbia to comply with international standards is facilitated mainly by its desire to join the EU in the near future.[145] In April 2008 Serbia signed the Stabilisation and Association Agreement, which established a framework of co-operation between Serbia and the EU.[146] If Serbia wishes to join the EU, it is required to improve in a variety of areas, including protection and promotion of human rights, justice and home affairs.

In order to promote effective law enforcement, Chapter VIII of the Criminal Procedure Code provides for special investigative techniques. These are authorised by the judiciary upon the request of the Public Prosecutor,[147] adding another layer of procedural safeguards and in conformity with the human rights principles noted in Chapter 3. Under this chapter, measures including the use of audio/visual surveillance and phone tapping,[148] rendering of simulated business

[141] Interview with Mladen Spacic, Adviser on Organised Crime to the Minister of Interior (26 December 2008).

[142] Art 12.

[143] Art 13.

[144] UNICRI, above n 118, 156.

[145] Interview with Drazen Maravic, Director of the Bureau for International Co-operation and European Integration, Ministry of Interior (26 December 2008). Serbia is regarded as a 'potential' candidate, not a candidate state. Currently Croatia, the Former Yugoslav Republic of Macedonia and Turkey are officially regarded as candidate states.

[146] European Commission, 'Serbia Progress Report 2009', SEC(2009) 1339/2 (14 October 2009), 4–5. However, the implementation of the Agreement on the part of the EU depends on, among other things, Serbia's co-operation with the ICTY.

[147] Art 146.

[148] Arts 146–47. Tapping is allowed if there is a reasonable ground to suspect that one belongs to a criminal group and commits money laundering, counterfeiting, production and holding of narcotics, possession of weapons and explosives, blackmail, extortion and kidnapping. This is to be conducted by the police or the Security Information Agency.

services to and conclusion of simulated legal affairs,[149] undercover operation[150] and controlled delivery[151] can be resorted to. The Criminal Procedure Code also touches upon confiscation of proceeds of crimes. Upon conviction, the court may order the confiscation of pecuniary benefits obtained through commission of crime.[152] This is augmented by Chapter VII of the Criminal Code, which sets out the rules in relation to confiscation of material gains.[153] Finally, the Criminal Procedure Code provides for a reduction of sentences for those who co-operated with the law enforcement authorities to provide evidence or testimony.[154] In looking at these provisions, it can be concluded that the Serbian legislation on criminal procedure is in conformity with international standards established by the Organised Crime Convention, particularly in the areas of criminal jurisdiction, exercise of special powers over organised crime and other means to facilitate law enforcement co-operation.

5.3.1.2.2   The Rights of Suspects/Defendants, Victims and Witnesses

In relation to the treatment of suspects or defendants, there are extensive provisions on their rights under the Criminal Procedure Code. Article 3, for instance, provides for the presumption of innocence until proven guilty and imposes an obligation on the public authorities, media and others to respect this rule, and a fine can be imposed in case of breaches. Rights during a trial, such as to be informed of criminal charges, trial within a reasonable time, sufficient time to prepare for the case, not to incriminate oneself and rights to communicate with consular/diplomatic staff and an interpretation service, are also stipulated under Articles 5, 7, 8 and 12.[155] These are broadly in conformity with international standards on the rights of suspects/defendants established under human rights treaties, including the ICCPR.[156] Serbia is additionally bound by the ECHR,[157] which is probably more significant for the government.

There are also provisions to protect witnesses in criminal proceedings under the Criminal Procedure Code. Article 116 imposes a general obligation on the law enforcement authority to protect witnesses from threat and intimidation, and, for these purposes, measures such as examination *in camera*, protection of witnesses' identity (such as concealing names and faces during a trial) and

---

[149] Arts 148–50. This measure is available for counterfeiting, money laundering, unauthorised production and trade in narcotics, unlicensed holding of weapons and explosives, human trafficking, trafficking in children for the purpose of adoption, giving and receiving bribe and abuse of office.

[150] Arts 151–53.

[151] Art 154.

[152] Arts 491–97.

[153] See also Art 87, which provides for confiscation of pecuniary gain and objects used to commission of crime. These objects include buildings used for crime (plant for production of drugs, brothels, etc). UNICRI, above n 118, 170.

[154] Art 163.

[155] See also Arts 67 and 71.

[156] Arts 9 and 14. The former Yugoslavia ratified it in 1971 and Serbia succeeded it in 2001.

[157] Arts 5 and 6. Serbia ratified it in 2004.

the use of video links are provided for.[158] It is important to note, however, that these measures apply only to offences carrying imprisonment of 10 years or longer.[159] This raises a serious concern, as many forms of organised crime are not as serious as this, as noted throughout this book. Article 117(2) provides that protective measures can be taken for less serious offences attracting imprisonment of between four and 10 years under 'special circumstances'. There is no clear guidance as to what constitutes such circumstances. Further, while there is an offence of subornation of perjury,[160] which prohibits bribery of witnesses, it does not cover other acts, such as the use of threat of violence against them. While these individuals may be prosecuted for assault and other offences against the person, given the importance attached to the proper administration of justice, a separate offence with severe penalties should be established, in accordance with Article 23 of the Organised Crime Convention.

Some improvements, however, were made when the Act on the Programme for the Protection of Participants in Criminal Procedure 2005[161] entered into force in January 2006. This was passed to fulfil Serbia's obligation under the Organised Crime Convention to provide effective protection for witnesses.[162] One benefit of this Act is that it extends protection to people close to participants in criminal proceedings, without being limited to immediate family and relatives.[163] This actually goes beyond what is required by the Organised Crime Convention and can therefore be regarded as an example of good practice. A commission was established for the programme to oversee the implementation of the various measures afforded to witnesses.[164] The protection programme can start before, during or after completion of criminal proceedings, and measures to be afforded under the programme include physical protection, relocation of residence and change of identity.[165]

In relation to victims, they are permitted to initiate criminal prosecution independently of the Public Prosecutor in Serbia. This is known as private prosecution and is provided for under the Criminal Procedure Code.[166] These victims can also continue prosecution even when the Public Prosecutor drops charges against particular defendants.[167] Once a victim becomes a private prosecutor, he/she is entitled to all the rights enjoyed by the Public Prosecutor in facilitating a criminal proceeding.[168] If one is a minor—where he/she is a victim of sexual exploitation, for instance—a legal representative can act on his/her behalf.[169]

---

[158] Art 117.
[159] Ibid.
[160] Art 336 of the Criminal Code.
[161] Official Gazette of the Republic of Serbia, 85/2005.
[162] UNICRI, above n 118, 143.
[163] Ibid, 144.
[164] Ibid, 145.
[165] Ibid, 144.
[166] Chapter V.
[167] Arts 60 and 61.
[168] Art 63.
[169] Art 64.

However, a prosecution must be brought within three months of the date the authorised person becomes aware of the criminal offence,[170] and in the case of discontinuance by the Public Prosecutor, within six days after his/her decision.[171] The provisions on private prosecution are thus more extensive in Serbia than in Thailand. However, unlike the legal framework in Thailand, the Criminal Procedure Code does not provide any guidance on civil action alongside the criminal proceedings.

5.3.1.2.3 *Mutual Legal Assistance in Criminal Matters*

Mutual assistance in criminal matters and extradition are provided for under Chapters IV and V of the Criminal Procedure Code respectively. In relation to the former, assistance can be facilitated in areas such as execution of certain evidentiary and other procedural actions, such as interrogation of the defendant, witnesses or expert witnesses, crime scene investigation, search of dwellings or persons and seizure of objects, as well as handing over of files, documents and other objects in connection with preliminary criminal proceedings in the requesting state.[172] Article 511 also touches upon enforcement of foreign court judgments. While Serbian courts cannot enforce criminal judgments of foreign courts, a sanction imposed by them can be enforced provided that it is allowed under international treaties or based upon the principle of reciprocity. This is significant as measures such as this reflect the principle of mutual recognition, as noted in Chapter 3. A movement towards mutual recognition is going to continue as it is the principle being recognised within the framework of the EU.[173] Further, transfer of criminal cases (foreign nationals committing a crime in Serbia) can also be facilitated under Article 513. On this issue, Serbian legislation goes further than international standards set by the Organised Crime Convention. It is rather ironic that Serbia has not exactly been co-operative in relation to the handing over of Ratko Mladic, who is wanted for his alleged involvement in international crimes such as genocide and is believed to be hiding in the territory of Serbia.

The extradition procedure in Serbia also broadly complies with international standards. A request for extradition is transmitted to the Public Prosecutor, which will forward it to an investigative judge.[174] After examining each case, including preconditions for extradition, the investigative judge will forward his/her opinion to a trial chamber, which will make a determination on the existence of the preconditions.[175] The decision of a trial chamber will then be referred

---

[170] Art 52.
[171] Arts 60 and 61.
[172] Art 508.
[173] See Chapter 6 for more detail.
[174] Art 519 of the Criminal Procedure Code.
[175] Arts 521 and 522.

back to the Public Prosecutor for final decision.[176] What is evident in looking at the extradition procedure is that good judicial safeguards are in place to protect the rights of suspects/defendants. However, a few points should be noted. Like Thailand, Serbia does not extradite its own nationals.[177] Also, an offence in question must not be committed in Serbia or against its nationals.[178] This means that territoriality and passive personality will take precedence and that extradition is limited to foreigners who commit crimes abroad. Double criminality, the statute of limitations and pardon/amnesty also prevent Serbia from extraditing.[179] Finally, an extradition to an international court, such as the ICC, is permitted provided that Serbia has previously ratified the appropriate instruments.[180]

At a political level, the Ministry of Interior, Bureau of International Co-operation, facilitates international co-operation. Operational co-operation is facilitated formally with agreements or informally on an ad hoc basis with entities such as Interpol, the the Organization for Security and Co-operation in Europe (OSCE) and the IOM, as well as with states including the US, the UK, Germany and Italy.[181] As it aims to join the EU, Serbia has increased co-operation with relevant organisations, such as Europol. It concluded an agreement with it in 2008 and Serbia has established a special unit for Europol.[182] As a state in transition, it is inevitable that Serbia will seek technical, financial and other assistance from regional and international organisations, as well as from developed states. These co-operative arrangements seem to demonstrate Serbia's determination to improve its fight against organised crime. In addition, Serbia is part of the Regional Cooperation Council, a regional co-operative framework for South East Europe (formerly known as the Stability Pact),[183] and facilitates co-operation in areas including justice and home affairs with other states in transition, such as Albania, Bosnia Herzegovina and Croatia.[184]

5.3.2 Assessment of Law Enforcement in Serbia

The recent statistics demonstrate that Serbia's effort is paying off to some extent. Soon after the establishment of the special departments/sections in 2003, for instance, 13 indictments against 156 suspects were instituted.[185] This had increased to 21 indictments involving 256 suspects in 2006.[186] In 2007, a total

---

[176] Arts 524 and 525.
[177] Art 517.
[178] Ibid.
[179] Ibid.
[180] Ibid.
[181] Interview with Mr Maravic, above n 145.
[182] Ibid.
[183] Ibid. It was established in 1999.
[184] For more information, see www.rcc.int.
[185] UNICRI, above n 118, 156.
[186] Ibid, 159.

of 450 cases relating to organised crime were prosecuted.[187] The fruits of effort can also be seen in the area of enforcement against drug trafficking. Between January and August 2009, 580 kilograms of drugs were seized and 3,450 indictments were filed.[188] There is also evidence of financial institutions co-operating with the authorities to prevent money laundering. It is worth noting in this regard that the Administration for the Prevention of Money Laundering received 2,087 reports of suspicious transactions in 2008 alone.[189]

While the willingness and endeavours of Serbia to implement effective action against organised crime should be recognised, there are various issues hampering effective enforcement of pertinent legislation. One problem is the different interpretations of organised crime and criminal groups adopted by law enforcement agencies in Serbia. It has been noted in this regard that police, prosecutors and judges interpret laws differently, making it difficult to seek uniformity of application.[190] This reflects the problem of multiple definitions adopted under several statutes, as noted above. An additional problem arising from multiple definitions is that it is difficult to seek inter-agency co-operation or co-ordination, as conduct might be regarded as organised crime by one agency but not by another. While the government acknowledges this problem, no attempt to harmonise definitions has been implemented to date.[191]

It should also be noted that law enforcement agencies suffer from a lack of sufficient resources and the capability to address organised crime effectively.[192] Decision-making within the Police is said to be highly centralised, resulting in insufficient management of human resources.[193] The Public Prosecutor also lacks adequate infrastructure and training to lead criminal investigations into organised crime.[194] In addition, a good system of intelligence analysis, including establishment of a common database to be used by all law enforcement agencies, does not exist in Serbia as yet.[195] All of these mean that Serbia has to actively seek assistance from regional or international organisations as well as other states.[196]

As in Thailand, corruption is a deep-rooted problem, and has been aggravated by prolonged political instability.[197] Poor remuneration for law enforcement officials also serves as an incentive for them to engage in corrupt behaviour.[198] In addition to the assassination of the prime minister in 2003, where those accused

---

[187] Interview with Mr Spacic, above n 141.

[188] European Commission, above n 146, 53.

[189] International Narcotics Control Strategy Report 2009, above ch 2 n 168.

[190] Ibid.

[191] Interview with Mr Spacic, above n 141.

[192] Ibid; interview with Mr Tomo Zoric, Office of the Public Prosecutor (26 December 2008).

[193] European Commission, above n 146, 54.

[194] Ibid.

[195] Ibid.

[196] Interview with Maravic, above n 145.

[197] Chr Michelsen Institute, 'Corruption in Serbia 2007: An Overview of Problems and Status of Reforms' (Bergen, 2007) 14.

[198] Ibid, 25.

were members of the Special Operation Unit under the Ministry of Interior and the State Security Service,[199] a recent style of corruption is 'bankruptcy mafia'. In 2007, a total of 36 defendants, including Goran Kljajevic (former president of the Belgrade Commercial Court) and Delinka Djurdjevic (a commercial court judge), faced charges of bribery, abuse of office and illegal bankruptcy.[200] In a more recent case, a judge of the Supreme Court of Serbia was indicted for exercising influence over a case involving organised crime.[201] The unfortunate situation is that those prosecuted for corruption do not receive sufficiently heavy penalties to deter them or others from committing crimes in the future. In a high-profile case of human trafficking in Novi Pazar in August 2008, the government prosecuted and convicted 12 trafficking offenders, including the Deputy Public Prosecutor and two police officers. While the principal trafficker in this case received an 8 year sentence, the two police officers received suspended sentences and the prosecutor was given a suspended sentence of three years and was released after one year.[202]

The existence of corruption is recognised by the Serbian authorities[203] and some attempts have been made to counter the problem. The government, for instance, has established mechanisms to deal with corruption. Within the Ministry of Interior, the office of Inspector General was established in 2003. The Inspector General has the competence to investigate cases of corruption committed by members of the Ministry of Interior, including the police.[204] In 2008, a special department to deal with corruption was also established within the Public Prosecutors' Office and a new agency to fight corruption will be established in 2010.[205] This has become all the more important as the reduction of corruption is necessary in order for Serbia to join the EU.[206] Whether such arrangements will work is open to question, as it has been noted in the past that the Serbian government has been reluctant to enforce the law in practice.[207]

Another technical problem is the terms of offices of the Special Prosecutor and judges in the Special Department. While the creation of Special Prosecutor is a positive step forward for the effective fight against organised crime, a period of two years might be regarded as relatively short.[208] Given that many cases of organised crime take a long time to be concluded before the judiciary, a longer period is desirable. Frequent changes of personnel, a problem

---

[199] UNICRI, above n 118, 158.
[200] US Department of State, 'Human Rights Report 2007', available at www.state.gov/g/drl/rls/hrrpt/2007/index.htm. The government accused the defendants of operating a lucrative scam in which the commercial court would declare enterprises bankrupt and the Postal Savings Bank would provide cheap loans to favoured businessmen to buy the enterprise's assets at a below-market price.
[201] UNICRI, above n 118, 159.
[202] Trafficking in Persons Report 2009, above ch 2 n 145.
[203] GRECO Report, above n 131, 4.
[204] Ibid, 8.
[205] Interview with Mr Zoric, above n 192.
[206] Ibid.
[207] Above n 200.
[208] Interview with Mr Zoric, above n 192.

also noted in Thailand, has a negative impact on the continuation of various cases. The Group of States against Corruption (GRECO) within the Council of Europe recommends in this regard that the term of office should be extended.[209] As regards judges, the possibility of an extension to their time in office is not stipulated in the Act. This means that after two years new judges will hear the cases, causing major delays as they familiarise themselves afresh.[210] There is an additional problem of various resources invested in training being wasted if personnel turnover is very quick. In recognition of these problems, a reform of the Criminal Procedure Code is under way in order to enhance the law enforcement responses to organised crime, although the exact timeframe is not yet clear.[211]

Problems relating to co-operation have also been identified. At some level, it has been noted that there is a lack of trust and understanding between the police and the prosecutors.[212] Some members of the police have been reported to have raised complaints that there is a lack of specialisation on organised crime and other complex cases among prosecutors and investigative judges on organised crime, and therefore that they have found it difficult to process these cases and secure indictments.[213] In return, some prosecutors have stated that police sometimes withhold essential information from them, and this has had an impact upon investigation, prosecution and punishment.[214] While the division of tasks is clearly set out in the Criminal Procedure Code, as noted above, this lack of co-operation and co-ordination can be interpreted as indicating that a power struggle between the concerned agencies also exists in Serbia. In addition, the lack of specialisation noted by the police is quite important, as it suggests that the specialised departments and sections established by the 2002 Act might not be functioning in practice as well as was hoped.

Finally, although Serbia serves as a transit point for illicit goods and services, such as drugs and people, little has been done to address this.[215] Its southwestern Sandzak region, located between Montenegro and Kosovo and on the heroin smuggling route connecting Afghanistan to Western Europe, is the key area for narcotics trafficking.[216] Traffickers are said to use Serbia's highways running southeast to north from Bulgaria and Macedonia to Croatia and Hungary.[217] Serbia requires effective immigration and border control to limit the flow of illicit goods and illegal migration. Yet border management is said to be still weak, and this has been exploited by organised criminal groups.[218] This is

---

[209] GRECO Report, above n 131, 14.

[210] UNICRI, above n 118, 185.

[211] Interview with Mr Spacic, above n 141.

[212] GRECO Report, above n 131, 4.

[213] Ibid.

[214] Ibid, 15.

[215] US Department of State, 'International Narcotics Control Strategy Report 2008', available at www.state.gov/p/inl/rls/nrcrpt/2008/index.htm; Trafficking in Persons Report 2009, above ch 2 n 145.

[216] Ibid. The major route for illicit goods and services is known as the Balkan Route.

[217] Ibid.

[218] Ibid.

particularly evident at the Kosovo–Serbia border.[219] Improvements are gradually being made, with the introduction of a new law in November 2008 and the conclusion of bilateral agreements with neighbouring states such as Montenegro and the Former Yugoslav Republic of Macedonia.[220] The problem is intensified by the fact that the Serbian judiciary does not impose severe penalties for trafficking. In 2007, for instance, of 8,658 people convicted for drug trafficking, 6,141 individuals received suspended sentences.[221] A similar trend can be seen in relation to human trafficking.[222] These patterns do little to deter trafficking through Serbia. What has become apparent, then, is that, although the legislative framework against organised crime in Serbia generally conforms to international standards, its enforcement has been problematic.

5.4 Kosovo

5.4.1 Legal Framework to Address Organised Crime

5.4.1.1 Legislation on Substantive Offences

The unique political and legal status of Kosovo should be explained before examining its legislative response to transnational organised crime. After the Kosovo war and the NATO bombing of then Yugoslavia, international administration of Kosovo began in 1999 when the United Nations Security Council passed a Resolution establishing the United Nations Interim Administration Mission in Kosovo (UNMIK).[223] Under Regulation 1999/1,[224] the very first legal instrument adopted, the Special Representative had the power to exercise legislative and executive authority on behalf of UNMIK.[225] However, a move towards self-governance was gradually promoted since the establishment of UNMIK. In 2001 it passed Regulation 2001/9, which established a constitutional framework for provisional self-government in Kosovo and created the Provisional Institutions of Self-Government (PISG).[226] It is worth noting here that the PISG did not have competence over justice and home affairs, which was reserved to UNMIK. In this respect, Regulation 2001/9 stated that that the Special Representative

---

[219] European Commission, above n 146, 53.
[220] Ibid, 51.
[221] International Narcotics Control Strategy Report 2008, above n 215.
[222] Trafficking in Persons Report 2009, above ch 2 n 145.
[223] Established by the Security Council Resolution 1244 (10 June 1999).
[224] UNMIK/REG/1999/1 (25 July 1999).
[225] In relation to the legislative function, he has approved and promulgated UMNIK Regulations which touched upon all aspects of life in Kosovo. It should be noted, however, that the previous laws applicable in the territory of Kosovo continue to apply in so far as they do not conflict with the Security Council Resolution or UNMIK Regulations.
[226] They are Assembly, Presidency, Government (Prime Minister) and Courts.

exercises control over law enforcement institutions in Kosovo and retains powers and responsibilities of an international nature in the legal field.

Further political development occurred in 2005, when former Finnish President Martti Ahitsaair was appointed by the UN Secretary-General as a special envoy to prepare a proposal for the future status of Kosovo.[227] After a series of negotiations, he recommended supervised independence of Kosovo in 2007.[228] On 17 February 2008 Kosovo declared independence, and the Constitution of the Republic of Kosovo was passed in June of the same year. The matter has been complicated by the various international responses. A number of states, including the US, Australia and European states such as France, Italy and the UK, have recognised its independence.[229] Others, including Serbia[230] and Russia, still have not. The Security Council Resolution establishing UNMIK remains in force, rendering Kosovo technically still under international administration. Nevertheless, devolution of various functions from UNMIK has been taking place to promote self-governance.[231] In the meantime, the EU has increased its presence in Kosovo by establishing the European Union Rule of Law Mission (EULEX).[232] On 8 October 2008 the United Nations General Assembly adopted a resolution submitted by Serbia requesting the ICJ to issue an advisory opinion on the following question: 'Is the unilateral declaration of independence by the Provisional Institutions of Self-Government in Kosovo in accordance with international law?'

Having briefly examined the current political situation, it is now useful to explore the legislative framework tackling organised crime. The key legislation which addresses organised crime is the Criminal Code of Kosovo 2008.[233] Article 274 on organised crime provides the following definitions:

The term 'organized crime' means a serious crime committed by a structured group in order to obtain, directly or indirectly, a financial or other material benefit.

The term 'organized criminal group' means a structured group existing for a period of time and acting in concert with the aim of committing one or more serious crimes in order to obtain, directly or indirectly, a financial or other material benefit.

[227] European Commission, 'Kosovo 2007 Progress Report', SEC (2007) 1433, 5.
[228] Ibid.
[229] 63 UN states have recognised its independence.
[230] Statement made by Ambassador Miroslava Beham, in Response to the Addresses of Ambassador Lamberto Zannier, Special Representative of the Secretary-General of the United Nations and the Head of the United Nations Interim Administration in Kosovo/Serbia, PC/DEL/734/08 (4 September 2008).
[231] The size of the UNMIK personnel has been reduced to just over 500 in July 2009. Report of the Secretary-General on the United Nations Interim Administration Mission in Kosovo, S/2009/497 (30 September 2009), para 2
[232] Joint Action 2008/124/CFSP on 4 February 2008 on the creation of a European Union Rule of Law Mission in Kosovo (EULEX), OJ L42/92 (16 February 2008).
[233] It was originally known as the Provisional Criminal Code passed by UNMIK in its Regulation 2003/25 (UNMIK/REG/2003/25). In 2008, the Kosovo Assembly passed Law No 03/L-002, changing the name to 'Criminal Code of Kosovo'.

The term 'serious crime' means an offence punishable by imprisonment of at least four years.

The term 'structured group' means a group of three or more persons that is not randomly formed for the immediate commission of an offence and does not need to have formally defined roles for its members, continuity of its membership or a developed structure.[234]

These definitions are in line with those given by the Organised Crime Convention and thus international standards. There is no surprise here as the Criminal Code was passed by UNMIK, which was in the position to respect and promote such.

The Criminal Code further criminalises other substantive offences, such as trafficking and smuggling of migrants,[235] facilitation of prostitution,[236] child pornography,[237] production, possession and trafficking of narcotics,[238] counterfeiting currencies,[239] trafficking of prohibited items,[240] computer fraud[241] and corruption.[242] The Criminal Code does not contain an offence of money laundering, but this was rectified by Regulation 2004/2.[243] What is evident, then, is that the Criminal Code is comprehensive enough to cover a variety of activities associated with organised crime and is therefore in line with the Organised Crime Convention. It should be noted that the Kosovo Criminal Code recognises a period of limitation for all crimes under Chapter IX. Although the period for commission of serious crime is long,[244] this might be exploited by criminals. Further, the same Code provides for amnesty and pardon.[245]

---

[234] These definitions were originally given in the Regulation 2001/22 on Measures against Organised Crime, UNMIK/REG/2001/22 (20 September 2001).

[235] Arts 138 and 139. The involvement of organised criminal groups is regarded as an aggravating circumstance.

[236] Art 201.

[237] Art 202.

[238] Arts 229 and 230. The involvement of organised criminal groups is regarded as an aggravating circumstance.

[239] Art 244.

[240] Art 246.

[241] Art 264.

[242] Art 343. For corruption, see also Suppression of Corruption Law (Law No 2004/34) (22 April 2005) adopted by the Kosovo Assembly. This law was promulgated by Regulation 2005/25, UNMIK/REG/2005/26 (12 May 2004). This Law also established Anti-Corruption Agency.

[243] UNMIK/REG/2004/2 (2 February 2004) on the Deterrence of Money Laundering and Related Criminal Offences. This was amended by Regulation 2005/42.

[244] For example, 10 years for a crime which carries imprisonment of five years.

[245] Chapter X.

5.4.1.2 Legislation on Criminal Procedure and International Co-operation

5.4.1.2.1 Criminal Jurisdiction and Investigative Powers

The Criminal Code provides for various grounds for exercising criminal jurisdiction. Article 99 recognises the territorial and flag principles as the primary ground of criminal jurisdiction. It is worth noting that the flag principle applies only to civil aircrafts but not vessels. This is understandable as Kosovo is landlocked. The nationality and passive personality principles are also recognised under Article 101 and 102, respectively.[246] Finally, Article 100 of the Code also provides for universal jurisdiction over a limited number of crimes such as international crime,[247] aircraft hijacking,[248] piracy,[249] slavery and forced labour,[250] human trafficking,[251] hostage-taking[252] and counterfeiting of currency.[253] In summary, the Criminal Code is in line with the Organised Crime Convention, which obliges states to exercise criminal jurisdiction.

The Kosovo Republic Police (KRP) currently has general powers to conduct preliminary investigations, search and retain evidence, and make arrests in relation to all crimes committed in Kosovo.[254] When UNMIK took over the administration of Kosovo in 1999, the UNMIK Police was established to maintain law and order on a temporary basis.[255] One of its mandates was to create a new police force in Kosovo,[256] and the Kosovo Police Service was soon established under the authority of the UN Special Representative and the UNMIK Police. With the development of the constitutional framework, as noted above, the functions relating to criminal justices have gradually been transferred to the Kosovo Police Service.[257] The name was changed to the KRP in 2008.[258] The General Police Directorate is the central headquarters in charge of all of Kosovo,[259] under which are the Regional Police Directorates and the Border Police.[260] Within the

---

[246] However, the passive personality principle applies only when a perpetrator is found in Kosovo. The question of Kosovo citizenship and nationality was addressed in Law on Citizenship of Kosova (Law No 03/34) passed by the Assembly in 2008.

[247] Genocide under Art 116, Crime against Humanity under Art 117, and War Crimes under Arts 118–21.

[248] Art 132.

[249] Art 136.

[250] Art 137.

[251] Art 139.

[252] Art 143.

[253] Art 244.

[254] Arts 200–06; Chapter XXIV, 240–53 of the Criminal Procedure Code.

[255] Security Council Resolution 1244 (1999), para 11.

[256] Ibid.

[257] Interview with Mr Fatos Haziri, Director, Directorate against Organised Crime, the Kosovo Republic Police (23 December 2008).

[258] Law on Police (2008), Law No 03/L-035.

[259] Art 31.

[260] Ibid.

KRP, there is a department dealing with organised crime. This was established in 2001 and, as of 2008, there were 140 full-time police officers working within this department.[261]

In any event, when the KRP concludes its preliminary investigations it is obliged to compile reports to be submitted to the Public Prosecutor,[262] who conducts official investigations into all crimes in Kosovo.[263] It should be noted here that the KRP must obey any order or direction issued by the Public Prosecutor.[264] This suggests that the KRP comes under the supervision of the Public Prosecutor, and therefore the latter is ranked higher in the criminal justice system in Kosovo. The Public Prosecutor then decides whether or not to proceed with further investigation.[265] In so doing, he/she can gather more information or direct the judicial police for this purpose.[266] When the Public Prosecutor is satisfied that he/she has enough evidence to support indictment, he/she files it before a court.[267] The power of the Public Prosecutor to deal with organised crime was augmented by Law No 03/L-052,[268] which endorsed the Office of Special Prosecutor previously established by UNMIK.[269] The prosecutors working for this Office have attained expertise through special training and retain exclusive competence to investigate and prosecute terrorism, international crime and organised crime.[270] All law enforcement agencies in Kosovo are required to render assistance.[271] The establishment of the Office demonstrates Kosovo's commitment to tackle organised crime more effectively.

The special measures for law enforcement are provided for under various laws in Kosovo. The Criminal Procedure Code, for instance, authorises undercover investigations, surveillance with the use of electronic and other devices, interception of communication and controlled delivery.[272] The Public Prosecutor can issue orders for video/photographic surveillance and monitoring of conversations in public places and undercover operations, while surveillance measures in private sphere, controlled delivery and interception of communication must be ordered by the judiciary.[273] It should be noted that the authorisation of undercover operations by the Public Prosecutor rather than by the judiciary could raise issues of human rights, as explained in Chapter 3. This can be contrasted with the Serbian Criminal Procedure Code, which requires an order from an

---

[261] Interview with Mr Haziri, above n 257.

[262] Art 207 of the Criminal Procedure Code; Art 6 of the Law on Police.

[263] Art 46.

[264] Art 6 of the Law on Police.

[265] Art 221 of the Criminal Procedure Code.

[266] Art 209. This includes the examination of the defendants and witnesses. See Chapter XXVIII of the Criminal Procedure Code.

[267] Art 304.

[268] Law on Special Prosecution Office of the Republic of Kosovo.

[269] UNMIK Administrative Direction 2006/15, UNMIK/DIR/2006/15 (30 September 2006).

[270] Art 5 of the Law on Special Prosecution Office.

[271] Art 4.

[272] Art 256.

[273] Art 258.

investigative judge.[274] The Kosovo Criminal Code also allows a court to confiscate criminal proceeds after one is found guilty.[275] This is strengthened by the Money Laundering Regulation noted above.[276] Despite the fact that the PISG has not been in existence for long, the above analysis shows that the legislative framework to address organised crime meets international standards stipulated by TCL and IHRL. This undoubtedly is the result of the involvement of the United Nations and other intergovernmental organisations whose main function has been to promote such standards.

5.4.1.2.2 *The Rights of Suspects/Defendants, Victims and Witnesses*

The rights of defendants and suspects are recognised in various parts of the Criminal Procedure Code. In relation to those arrested, the rights to be informed of the reasons of arrest, to remain silent and to have access to an interpreter, legal counsel, medical treatment and consular assistance are recognised, among others.[277] During criminal proceedings, equality of arms is guaranteed,[278] and a defendant enjoys other rights, such as the right to be informed of the charges against him and not to incriminate himself, adequate time and facility to prepare his case, legal assistance and interpretation.[279] These are broadly in conformity with the human rights norms and principles established by relevant instruments noted above. An added benefit for Kosovo perhaps is the international territorial administration, through which relevant regional and international organisations are to take an active part in promoting the established human rights norms and principles. In this regard, Security Council Resolution 1244, which established UNMIK, clearly states that the main responsibilities of the international civil presence (UNMIK) include protecting and promoting human rights.[280]

Witnesses and victims are covered by various measures set out in Chapter XXI of the Criminal Procedure Code. If there is a serious risk to witnesses, victims and their family members, then a court can grant protective measure or anonymity.[281] Such measures include, but are not limited to, protection and non-disclosure of their identity and addresses, the use of shields, voice-altering devices and video links during proceedings, and proceedings *in camera*.[282] In line with the Organised Crime Convention, the Criminal Code provides for an offence of obstruction of justice, through which those who use threats or violence or bribe witnesses are punished with imprisonment of up to five years.[283]

---

[274] Art 151 of the Serbian Criminal Code.
[275] Chapter VII.
[276] Arts 11 and 12.
[277] Arts 213–14.
[278] Art 10.
[279] Arts 11, 12 and 15.
[280] Para 11(j).
[281] Art 169.
[282] Art 170.
[283] Arts 309 and 310.

Finally, victims of organised crime are afforded various rights in Kosovo. For instance, they have a right to file a property claim in civil proceedings at the same time as the criminal proceedings,[284] which may be awarded by a court. They can also propose and examine evidence, put questions to the defendants and witnesses, and issue statements during criminal proceedings.[285] In addition, if the Public Prosecutor decides not to proceed with a case, victims are entitled to continue prosecution.[286] The legislative framework in Kosovo, like those in Thailand and Serbia, allows victims a chance to have their voice heard and pursue justice.

5.4.1.2.3 *Mutual Legal Assistance in Criminal Matters*

Mutual assistance in criminal matters is provided for under Chapter XLVII of the Criminal Procedure Code and has gradually been facilitated with states which have recognised Kosovo's independence.[287] If the Kosovan authorities wish to obtain assistance from foreign states, a request is transmitted by a court through diplomatic channels in the first instance.[288] The request is then passed on to the central authority, which in turn directs it to appropriate judicial authorities.[289] A request can be transmitted directly to agencies responsible for law enforcement on the basis of reciprocity in urgent cases or cases involving money laundering.[290] Direct co-operation between agencies which institute criminal proceedings (eg Public Prosecution) is also possible, but only on the basis of reciprocity and international agreements.[291] In comparison to other states, it can therefore take more time to facilitate co-operation in Kosovo. The use of diplomatic channels also means that any decision to render assistance might be influenced by political interests.

In terms of the substance of co-operation, extradition is provided for under Chapter XLVIII of the Criminal Procedure Code. First, Kosovo does not extradite its own nationals.[292] The territorial and passive personality principles also take precedence, and Kosovo will prosecute those who commit crimes in Kosovo or against its nationals.[293] Other issues, such as double criminality, statutory limitation, double jeopardy and the political offence exception, place limitations on extradition.[294] It should further be noted that the refusal of extradition under

---

[284] Arts 80 and 108 of the Criminal Procedure Code.
[285] Art 80.
[286] Arts 62–68.
[287] Report of the Secretary-General, above n 231, para 28. International co-operation with other states are facilitated through UNMIK.
[288] Art 507.
[289] Art 508.
[290] Arts 507(2).
[291] Art 507(3).
[292] Art 517.
[293] Ibid.
[294] Ibid.

the Criminal Procedure Codes is more human rights compliant compared to Thailand and Serbia as the grounds for refusal include the existence of the death penalty, *non-refoulement* on account of persecution and torture, inhuman or degrading treatment, and recognition as a refugee.[295] As in many other jurisdictions, a request for extradition is transmitted through a diplomatic channel to the pre-trial judge, who makes a determination as to whether there are grounds to allow it.[296] The pre-trial judge then sends a file for a final decision to be made by a panel of three judges.[297] The decision is then transmitted to the central authority, which executes the decision.[298]

As for other measures for mutual assistance, the Criminal Procedure Code authorises the arrest and detention of convicted criminals (by foreign courts) who are found in Kosovo,[299] and execution of a judgment on conviction and sanction passed by a foreign court.[300] These decisions are to be decided by a panel of three judges as opposed to a single judge to add a layer of procedural safeguards.[301] As noted elsewhere, such provisions are designed to facilitate mutual recognition of judicial decisions. Article 512 allows foreign criminals convicted in Kosovo to serve their sentences in their states of nationality. Another notable provision is Article 513, which obliges the judicial authorities to transmit data to the central authority in connection with the commission of organised crime such as money laundering, drug trafficking, child pornography and human trafficking, when such transmission is required by international agreements. In this regard, Kosovo is more advanced than Serbia, which has yet to establish a comprehensive database, as noted above. Finally, the Public Prosecutor can prosecute Kosovo residents who commit crimes abroad, if requested by foreign authorities under Article 515. In analysing the legislative framework of Kosovo, it seems reasonable to argue that it more or less reflects international standards set by the Organised Crime Convention and other instruments.

5.4.2 Assessment of Law Enforcement in Kosovo

Despite the fact that the Kosovo criminal law and justice system broadly meets the criteria set by the Organised Crime Convention and other relevant instruments, a wide variety of problems have been identified. For instance, organised crime is not regarded as a priority in Kosovo[302] and the country does not have a solid crime control strategy.[303] This has unfortunately resulted in a lack of

---

[295] Ibid.

[296] Arts 518–21.

[297] Arts 522–23.

[298] Art 525.

[299] Art 510. This is conditional upon satisfaction of the rule of double criminality.

[300] Art 509.

[301] Art 511.

[302] Interview with Mr Haziri, above n 257; International Narcotics Control Strategy Report 2009, above ch 2 n 168.

[303] European Commission, 'Kosovo 2009 Progress Report', SEC(2009) 1340 (11 October 2009) 47.

adequate resources to enhance the capacity of law enforcement agencies and the judiciary.[304] It was noted in this regard that, while the KRP is good at dealing with minor crimes, it still does not have adequate knowledge and skills to combat serious crimes such as drug trafficking.[305] As in Thailand and Serbia, the low salaries for police officers have made recruitment difficult.[306] A lack of co-ordination among various law enforcement authorities has also been identified as a problem.[307] A number of initiatives have been undertaken to improve this situation. For instance, US$8 million has been invested in equipment and police vehicles, and over 1,000 training courses have been implemented in the past few years.[308] The KRP and donor agencies/states such as the OSCE and the US government regularly meet to discuss improvements to various aspects of criminal justice.[309]

While the presence of international organisations has undoubtedly benefited Kosovo in many ways, it has simultaneously created confusion over the territorial administration of Kosovo. After the declaration of independence, although the Special Representative of the United Nations still retains the executive authority under Security Council Resolution 1244, he has found it difficult to exercise his legal authority because Kosovo now treats its Constitution as the main legal authority.[310] While UNMIK still retains international responsibilities for rule of law functions throughout Kosovo for the time being, EULEX has started to exercise similar functions.[311] What is evident, then, is a duplication of work among the authorities of Kosovo and regional and international organisations. This inevitably leads to a waste of human, financial and other resources without effective co-operation. It should also be noted that the personnel of these organisations, including the Special Representative himself, receive a high salary compared to their domestic counterparts.[312] If they do not have many jobs to do, it does not make much sense to keep paying these international staff.

To ameliorate this problem, the UN Secretary-General decided to downsize UNMIK. In his report of November 2008 he stated that EULEX would assume more responsibilities in the areas of policing, justice and customs under the overall authority of the United Nations.[313] On the basis of an operational arrangement on access to and disclosure of materials concerning certain criminal

---

[304] Interview with Haziri, above n 257; European Commission, 'Kosovo 2008 Progress Report', SEC(2008) 2697 final (5 November 2008) 47 and 54.

[305] European Commission, ibid, 53.

[306] Ibid.

[307] European Commission, above n 303, 46.

[308] Interview with Mr Haziri, above n 257.

[309] Ibid.

[310] Special Representative of the Secretary General's Address to the OSCE Permanent Council, 4 September 2008, available from www.osce.org/documents/pc/2008/09/32822_en.pdf.

[311] Ibid.

[312] An average salary for judges and prosecutors is approximately €450 per month. Organization for Democracy, 'Anticorruption and Dignity "Çohu"', Report on the Situation of the Justice System in Kosova (January 2009) 6.

[313] Report of the Secretary-General on the United Nations Interim Mission in Kosovo, S/2008/692 (24 November 2008), para 23.

investigations and related judicial proceedings, UNMIK has began to facilitate access by EULEX prosecutors to the case files handled by international prosecutors and special prosecutors.[314] Access to police material concerning certain criminal investigations is also granted to the EULEX police component on the basis of a similar arrangement agreed upon in September 2008.[315] While this transition has been welcomed by the Kosovo authorities,[316] this is not the case for some members of the general public. In 2008, approximately 1,000 people staged a demonstration calling for a withdrawal of EULEX from Kosovo.[317]

An added problem is the tension between Serbia and Kosovo, and this has hampered effective co-operation to tackle organised crime to some extent. Many Kosovo Serbs refuse to co-operate with the Kosovan authorities but are willing to co-operate with UNMIK.[318] This has affected the fight against organised crime as a large number of Kosovo-Serb police officers refuse to work within the KRP and remain suspended from service.[319] The municipal courts in the Kosovan Serb-dominated areas are also not functioning properly.[320] In the north, four municipal structures function on the basis of the law on local self-governance of Serbia.[321] In addition to a lack of co-operation, what is at issue here is that the pertinent laws on organised crime explored above are not uniformly applied and enforced throughout Kosovo. This provides ample opportunities for criminal groups to promote their business as they tend to operate where law enforcement is lax.

Following the discussions in Chapter 4 on the accountability of international organisations, another problem in Kosovo has been the involvement of the international personnel of UNMIK and KFOR in organised crime. Trafficking of women is a case in point. International military and civilian personnel are said to be the major clients of the sex industry in Kosovo, where many trafficked women are exploited.[322] UNMIK claims to deal with any of its personnel who purchase sex or become involved in trafficking. For instance, it publishes a list of 'off-limits' establishments suspected of prostitution and trafficking on a monthly basis, and disciplinary actions are taken against those who are found in these premises.[323] Between 2002 and 2004, UNMIK found 52 KFOR soldiers, three international police and eight international civilians from various agencies in

---

[314] Ibid, para 24.

[315] Ibid.

[316] Ibid, para 25.

[317] Report of the Secretary-General, above n 231, para 27.

[318] Ibid, para 8

[319] Ibid.

[320] Ibid.

[321] Ibid, para 4.

[322] T Roopnaraine, 'Child Trafficking in Kosovo' (Kosovo, Save the Children in Kosovo, 2002) 20; Amnesty International, 'Kosovo (Serbia and Montenegro): "So Does It Mean that We Have the Rights?"' Protecting the Human Rights of Women and Girls Trafficked for Forced Prostitution in Kosovo (2004) 47.

[323] UNMIK, 'Combating Human Trafficking in Kosovo: Strategy & Commitment' (May 2004) 17.

these off-limits establishments.[324] Such discovery, however, must be accompanied by effective and appropriate disciplinary sanction to deter future occurrence. Unfortunately, this has been an area of concern for some time. Of those discovered in off-limits establishments, the KFOR soldiers were handed back to their sending states, while the international personnel were returned to their home states.[325] What happened afterwards, however, remains uncertain. This is problematic because justice is not seen to be done in the eyes of the victims in Kosovo.

What is desirable, then, is initiation of criminal prosecutions against these international officers in Kosovo. One difficulty in bringing criminal prosecution is the officers' immunity, as noted elsewhere in this book. In Kosovo the pertinent instrument is Law No 03/L-33, passed by the Kosovo Assembly in March 2008.[326] This sets out the types of offices or individuals entitled to immunity from criminal proceedings. They include the International Civilian Representative,[327] the United Nations and its specialised agencies, the OSCE, and diplomatic and consular missions. Section 2 provides that the personnel of KFOR (excluding locally recruited ones) are immune from the criminal jurisdiction of Kosovo courts and tribunals, as they come under the exclusive jurisdiction of the sending states. In relation to UNMIK, high-ranking officials such as the Special Representative of the Secretary-General, the Principal Deputy and the four Deputy Special Representatives of the Secretary-General, as well as the Police Commissioner, are immune from local criminal jurisdiction in accordance with Section 3. Other officials, however, are not immune from criminal jurisdiction as they are obliged to respect the laws applicable in the territory of Kosovo and regulations issued by the Special Representative of the Secretary-General, and this includes those relating to organised crime.

UNMIK states that the waiver of immunity of those who commit crimes is always requested to the UN Secretary-General so that these people can be properly prosecuted.[328] There are some examples of this. In November 2005 an official of the United Nations High Commissioner for Refugees was sentenced to three years' imprisonment for exploitation of a minor.[329] The waivers were also requested and granted in one case in 2002 and another in 2003, enabling prosecutions of two officers to take place.[330] However, it has been noted that such instances of waiver are rare.[331] Instead, these personnel were simply sent

---

[324] Ibid.

[325] Ibid.

[326] Previously Regulation 2000/47, UNMIK/REG/2000/47 (18 August 2000) was in force.

[327] Appointed in February 2008 to oversee the Comprehensive Proposal for the Kosovo Status Settlement submitted by the UN Special Envoy Martti Ahtisaari. The ICP also holds a mandate as the European Union Special Representative.

[328] UNMIK, Combating Trafficking, above n 323, 18.

[329] US Department of State, 'Trafficking in Persons Report 2006', available at www.state.gov/g/tip/rls/tiprpt/2006/65990.htm.

[330] Amnesty International, above n 322, 52.

[331] Ibid, 47, 49–50 and 52; interview with Mr Haziri, above n 257.

home,[332] and a question remained as to whether they were ever prosecuted.[333] As noted in Chapter 3, some states can exercise extraterritorial jurisdiction based on the nationality principle for crimes such as human trafficking. However, if there is no such legislation, then those responsible for facilitating crimes are not properly punished. An added problem is the international military presence, such as KFOR. While locally recruited KFOR personnel do not enjoy immunity if they commit crimes, international personnel enjoy complete immunity from the criminal jurisdiction of the local courts and are instead subject to the exclusive jurisdiction of the sending states.[334] Not much can be done in Kosovo except to send them back to their home states. There are examples of the UK Royal Marine Commandos and French KFOR personnel being sent home for becoming part of trafficking or being found in off-limits places such as lap-dancing bars.[335] Many of them were said to have escaped any criminal proceedings in their home countries.[336]

A related problem is corruption among public authorities in Kosovo. UNMIK alleges that widespread corruption exists within the KRP due to traffickers' greater resources and willingness to use threats.[337] While there is no evidence of systematic corruption in Kosovo to support such a claim in recent times, sporadic instances of corruption are reported every year. For instance, there are reported cases of some enforcement officers accepting bribes and allowing narcotics to pass through borders, due to the officers' low salaries and lack of benefits.[338] It has also been reported that UNMIK has turned a blind eye to corruption that was widespread in the KRP.[339] This last point casts doubt on the ability of UNMIK and other relevant agencies such as EULEX to promote the rule of law in Kosovo, and such instances can further fuel feelings of resentment among the general public.

Finally, as is the case for Serbia, Kosovo is a major transit route for illicit goods and services such as narcotics,[340] and the government needs to do more to stem such and respond effectively to supply and demand dynamics. Like Serbia, Kosovo has a border control problem. It has recently been noted by the European Commission that the Border Police lack good communication systems to collect and exchange data on exit and entry, and cannot access the criminal records of people seeking to enter/exist Kosovo.[341] Staffing is also a problem, with

---

[332] Ibid, 52. Between 2002 and 2003, for instance, approximately 100 UNMIK police officers were dismissed and repatriated for prostitution and trafficking.

[333] Ibid, 52–53.

[334] Art 10 of Regulation 2000/47.

[335] Amnesty International, above n 322, 51.

[336] Ibid, 54.

[337] International Narcotics Control Strategy Report 2009, above ch 2 n 168.

[338] Ibid.

[339] E Giatzidis, 'The Challenge of Organized Crime in the Balkans and the Political and Economic Implications' (2007) 23 *Journal of Communist Studies and Transition Politics* 327, 339.

[340] Kosovo, like Serbia, is located on the Balkan route that is used for drug and human trafficking. European Commission, above n 304, 52.

[341] Ibid. 51.

the number of officers, including senior officials who are in a position to supervise, being inadequate in some regions, and there is a consistent need for better training in intelligence gathering and other areas.[342] In addition, formal border management agreements have not been signed with neighbouring states,[343] and this makes it difficult to seek active co-operation. In this regard, it has been shown above that the concentration of drug activities on the Kosovo–Serbia border is a serious problem. Despite recent improvements, border management is far from adequate.[344] These problems, coupled with the general lack of capability on the part of law enforcement agencies noted above, have made it difficult for Kosovo to deal with the situation.

5.5   The UK[345]

5.5.1   Legal Framework to Address Organised Crime

5.5.1.1   *Legislation on Substantive Offences*

Unlike the other jurisdictions examined in this chapter, the UK does not have a single criminal code that covers a variety of offences. Criminal offences, including organised crime, are dealt with in a piecemeal fashion through numerous Acts of Parliament and secondary legislation known as statutory instruments. It should also be noted that the UK legislation does not provide for a legal definition of organised crime. Instead, the law enforcement agencies have adopted a working definition of organised criminals or groups as 'those involved, normally working with others, in continuing serious criminal activities for substantial profit, whether based in the UK or elsewhere'.[346] The government argues that this definition captures the essence of organised crime.[347] Indeed, this working definition is somewhat broader than the ones given by the Organised Crime Convention. The phrase 'normally working with others' recognises that criminals may sometimes work alone: for example, individual drug dealers or pimps, who do not necessarily belong to criminal groups. In addition, unlike the Organised Crime Convention, which only applies to 'transnational' crimes, the definition used by the UK law enforcement agencies applies also to cases where crimes are purely local. However, the broad definition can also create a danger of it being

---

[342] EULEX, Programme Report 2009, 53–66.
[343] Ibid.
[344] European Commission, above n 303, 44.
[345] The UK has ratified the Organised Crime Convention on 9 February 2006.
[346] The definition was originally adopted by the National Criminal Intelligence Services (now part of the Serious and Organised Crime Agency), and reappears in the government's White Paper entitled 'One Step Ahead', above ch 1 n 57.
[347] Ibid, 7.

applied to a variety of groups or criminal activities which have not much to do with organised crime. For instance, burglary committed on several occasions by a single person can come under the working definition. While the authorities are not likely to designate such an act as organised crime, they still have discretion to rely on legislation which gives them special powers to prosecute and punish.

There is something to be said about the UK's commitment to fulfil international obligations. The government has already ratified the Organised Crime Convention and therefore should incorporate the definitions stipulated under it in order to facilitate more effective co-operation with other states. Furthermore, with the passage of the Framework Decision on Organised Crime adopted by the EU, the government must also incorporate the definitions stipulated there in accordance with the principle of European Law.[348] Nevertheless, unlike Thailand, Serbia and Kosovo, this has not been done as yet. This casts some doubts on the extent to which the UK seriously regards international obligations to prevent and suppress organised crime. It also highlights the impact of the principle of state sovereignty on implementing measures against the practice.

As noted above, various statutes criminalise aspects of organised crime in the UK. They touch upon narcotics-related offences,[349] human trafficking,[350] arms trafficking,[351] fraud,[352] corruption/bribery,[353] money laundering,[354] child pornography[355] and internet grooming,[356] currency counterfeiting and forgery,[357] and various other offences. Many of these crimes are now regarded as 'serious offences' under Schedule 1 of the Serious Crime Act 2007. Finally, inchoate offences such as conspiracy are provided for under the Criminal Law Act 1977 and the Criminal Attempt Act 1981. In summary, while the UK legislation does not recognise the definitions of organised crime or criminal groups as yet, the prohibition of substantive offences is in place. Two more points should be noted. First, unlike other jurisdictions, the UK legislation establishes a period of limitation only for summary offences punishable by imprisonment of six months or less.[358] This is important as there is no scope for criminals who commit serious offences to escape from the reach of law. Second is the power of the sovereign known as the royal prerogative of mercy, which is a form of pardon.[359] A highly

---

[348] See Chapter 6 for more detail.

[349] Misuse of Drugs Act 1971; Drug Trafficking Act 1994; Drugs Act 2005.

[350] Sexual Offences Act 2003; Asylum and Immigration (Treatment of Claimants, etc) Act 2004.

[351] Firearms Act 1968; Customs and Excise Management Act 1979.

[352] Fraud Act 2006.

[353] Public Bodies Corrupt Practices Act 1889; Prevention of Corruption Act 1906.

[354] Proceeds of Crime Act 2002. See also secondary legislation: SI 2003/3075 and SI 2007/2157 implementing the EU Money Laundering Directive.

[355] Protection of Children Act 1978; Criminal Justice Act 1988; Criminal Justice and Immigration Act 2008.

[356] Sexual Offences Act 2003.

[357] Forgery and Counterfeiting Act 1981.

[358] S 127 of Magistrates Court Act 1980.

[359] In England and Wales, the Secretary of State for Justice recommends the exercise of this power, and in Scotland the power is devolved to the First Minister by virtue of the Scotland Act 1998. In Northern Ireland, the Secretary of State for Northern Ireland recommends it. For more

publicised example of this is the reduction of sentences for the drug traffickers John Haase and Paul Bennett granted by the then Secretary of State for Home Department Michael Howard.[360]

5.5.1.2 Legislation on Criminal Procedure and International Co-operation

5.5.1.2.1 Criminal Jurisdiction and Investigative Powers

Some of the key principles of criminal jurisdiction are also found in legislation. While the territorial principle remains the key form of jurisdiction,[361] other principles, such as the flag,[362] nationality,[363] passive personality[364] and effect principles,[365] are recognised in various statutes. As noted elsewhere, the UK can exercise universal jurisdiction for some offences. This applies, for instance, to drug trafficking that is carried out at sea.[366] More recently, under the Criminal Justice and Immigration Act 2008, the UK can exercise jurisdiction over foreign nationals residing in its territory who commit sexual offences abroad.[367] This is in line with international standards set by the Organised Crime Convention.

As in other jurisdictions, the police are the primary agency responsible for investigation. Their powers are governed by the Police and Criminal Evidence Act 1984 (PACE), as amended.[368] There are 43 forces and in England and Wales, eight regional forces in Scotland and one in Northern Ireland, known as the Police Service of Northern Ireland.[369] The Act governs the powers of the police in relation to stop and search, entry, search of premises, seizure, arrest and detention. PACE also established Codes of Practice to be adopted by police officers. Currently there are eight Codes of Practice[370] relating to stop and search of a

information, see Ministry of Justice, 'Review of the Executive Royal Prerogative Powers: Final Report' (October 2009), 15–18.

[360] See http://news.bbc.co.uk/1/hi/uk/7671946.stm.

[361] JDM Lew, 'The Extra-Territorial Criminal Jurisdiction of English Courts' (1978) 27 *International and Comparative Law Quarterly* 168, 168–69.

[362] S 281 of the Merchant Shipping Act 1995.

[363] S 4 of the Asylum and Immigration (Treatment of Claimants, etc) Act 2004; s 72 of the Sexual Offences Act 2003.

[364] Terrorist Act 2002 as amended by the Crime (International Co-operation) Act 2003. This is pertinent where there is a nexus between organised crime and terrorism.

[365] This applies, for instance, to forgery and handling stolen goods, as well as conspiracy, attempt or incitement to commit defraud under the Criminal Justice Act 1993. See also s 4 of the Computer Misuse Act 1990, which criminalises offences of unauthorised access to a computer.

[366] Ss 19–21 of the Criminal Justice (International Co-operation) Act 1990.

[367] S 72.

[368] The legislation in Northern Ireland is the Police and Criminal Evidence (Northern Ireland) Order 1989, and the one in Scotland is the Criminal Procedure (Scotland) Act 1995.

[369] M Davies et al, *Criminal Justice*, 4th edn (London, Pearson, 2010), 165.

[370] Available from http://police.homeoffice.gov.uk/operational-policing/powers-pace-codes/pace-code-intro/.

person or vehicle without arrest,[371] entry and search of premises and seizure of property,[372] detention, treatment and questioning of suspects,[373] identification of people,[374] recording of interviews,[375] video-recording of interviews,[376] arrest without warrant,[377] and detention, treatment and questioning of terror suspects.[378] Breach of these Codes does not constitute a criminal offence but can be a basis of complaint against the police.[379] It used to be the case that the police in the UK also prosecuted criminal offences and therefore had wider power in the criminal justice system.[380] This changed with the creation of the Crown Prosecution Service (CPS) in 1985,[381] which now initiates indictments for most criminal cases.[382]

In order to deal effectively with serious and organised crime, the legislation bestows special powers to law enforcement authorities. The Serious Organised Crime Agency (SOCA) should be mentioned at this point. This was established by the Serious Organised Crime and Police Act 2005 and its overall objectives are the prevention and detection of serious organised crime.[383] The agency was created in response to the government's concerns over overlapping activities and unclear division of responsibilities among various bodies.[384] SOCA merged the National Criminal Intelligence Service and the National Crime Squad,[385] as well as investigative, intelligence and immigration crime aspects of the Customs and Excise Service and organised immigration crime aspects of the Immigration Services.[386] Many of these organisations were charged with the collection of intelligence, and it is clear that SOCA aims to promote intelligence-led investigations into serious organised crime. The Director General of SOCA can designate its members as officers having the powers of a police constable, a customs officer or an immigration officer.[387] The Serious Crime Act 2007 further merged the Asset Recovery Agency into SOCA.[388] As such, SOCA performs multiple functions normally entrusted to other agencies. SOCA also has the powers to institute

---

[371] Code A as amended in January 2009.

[372] Code B.

[373] Code C.

[374] Code D.

[375] Code E.

[376] Code F.

[377] Code G.

[378] Code H.

[379] Davies et al, above n 369, 174.

[380] Ibid, 214.

[381] Prosecution of Offences Act 1985.

[382] Other regulatory agencies do have some power to prosecute. Davies et al, above n 369, 213. In Scotland, the Procurator Fiscal Service is in charge of prosecuting offences in that jurisdiction.

[383] S 2. Scotland additionally has the Scottish Crime and Drug Enforcement Agency established by the Police, Public Order and Criminal Justice (Scotland) Act 2006. In Northern Ireland, the Organised Crime Taskforce was established in 2000. See www.octf.gov.uk/.

[384] Home Office (2004), above ch 1 n 57, 22.

[385] Both of these were created by the Police Act 1997.

[386] Home Office (2004), ch1 n 57, 22.

[387] S 43.

[388] Chapter 2.

criminal proceedings and assist law enforcement agencies within and outside of the UK to deal with organised crime.[389] In turn, the police and others have a general duty to pass on information and assist SOCA to deal with organised crime.[390] The budget for 2008–09 was set at £494 million,[391] so it can be said that SOCA is generally well-funded compared to the other jurisdictions explored in this chapter.

Special powers to deal with organised crime are given by other statutes. The Regulation of Investigatory Powers Act 2000 (RIPA)[392] is a good example. This legislation grants the power to intercept postal and other communication with the consent of those involved or with a warrant issued by the Secretary of State.[393] Such a warrant is to be issued when it is necessary in the interests of national security or for the purposes of detecting and preventing serious crime.[394] It is therefore obvious that this power can be exercised against organised crime. The same legislation also provides for lawful (authorised) directed or intrusive surveillance in the UK and abroad.[395] Further, RIPA also allows the authorities to rely on 'covert human intelligence sources',[396] who might be officials working as undercover agents or moles who are not part of any agency. The Proceeds of Crime Act 2002 is also important as it gives the authorities the power to freeze and confiscate criminal assets and proceeds, and also imposes an obligation on financial and other related institutions to disclose suspicious transactions.[397] Finally, the Serious Crime Act 2007 created a regime of 'serious crime prevention orders'.[398] Such orders can be issued against people or legal persons who have been involved in serious crimes, and can impose prohibitions, restrictions or requirements in relation to their financial or business dealings, provision of goods and services, the use of premises, association with other individuals/organisations, and travel.[399] It seems evident here that the UK is in line with international standards on special investigative techniques under the Organised Crime Convention.

---

[389] S 5. In Scotland, the SOCA operates with consent from the Lord Advocate, the chief legal office of the Scottish government and also the chief prosecutor.

[390] Ss 36 and 37.

[391] SOCA, Annual Report 2008/09, 9.

[392] Previously stipulated in statutes including the Interception of Communications Act 1985 and Police Act 1997. The Scottish equivalent is the Regulation of Investigatory Powers (Scotland) Act 2000.

[393] Ss 3and 5. This power was previously granted to MI5 (HM Security Service) and MI6 (HM Secret Intelligence Services) by the Security Services Acts 1989/1996 and the Intelligence Services Act 1994.

[394] S 5.

[395] Ss 27, 29 and 32. Intrusive surveillance may be carried out in private residences or vehicle.

[396] S 29.

[397] Ss 330–32.

[398] This applies to England, Wales and Northern Ireland.

[399] S 5.

5.5.1.2.2   The Rights of Suspects/Defendants, Victims and Witnesses

A relevant statute which protects the rights of defendants or suspects is the Human Rights Act 1998 (HRA). This effectively incorporates the ECHR into UK law and imposes an obligation on public authorities to act in accordance with the European Convention.[400] Persons whose Convention rights have been breached can thus bring a case before a national court.[401] Pertinent provisions under the ECHR are Article 5 on the right to liberty and security, which is relevant to the arrest and detention of suspects, and Article 6, which lays down detailed rules on the right to a fair trial, including the rights to be informed, to have adequate time and facility to prepare, to have legal assistance, to examine witnesses and evidence, and to have free assistance of interpreters. As in the case of Serbia, which is a party to the ECHR, these human rights norms are an important part of UK domestic law. Consequently, it can be argued that the UK legislative framework meets the international standards set by IHRL and other laws. Some of the Codes adopted under PACE noted above, such as Codes C and G, are also pertinent to uphold human rights.

Several statutes are relevant in relation to witnesses. The Youth Justice and Criminal Evidence Act 1999, for instance, provides for measures to be applied in relation to those under 17 years of age and/or suffering from mental disorder or fearing reprisals. These measures include use of screens, provision of evidence through a video-link, giving of evidence in private and video-recorded evidence.[402] Those accused of sexual offences are excluded from cross-examining witnesses who claim to be the victims of such.[403] The court may also order the media not to publish information relating to witnesses.[404] At common law, a trial *in camera* can also be instituted if the interest of justice so requires,[405] and recent legislation authorises the court to order witness anonymity.[406] Finally, disclosure of information about witness protection regimes[407] and the intimidation of and violence against witnesses[408] are established as separate offences.

A variety of rights are recognised for victims of organised crime, including that of initiating private prosecutions under the Prosecution of Offences Act 1985.[409] However, the Public Prosecutor has a right to take over such criminal prosecution.[410] In doing so, the Public Prosecutor applies the Full Code test to see whether

---

[400] S 6.

[401] S 7.

[402] Ss 16–18 and 23–27.

[403] S 34.

[404] S 46. See also s 11 of the Contempt of Court Act 1981.

[405] *Scott v Scott* [1913] AC 417. See also Criminal Procedure Rules 2005 as amended by SI 2005/384.

[406] Criminal Evidence (Witness Anonymity) Act 2008.

[407] Serious Organised Crime and Police Act 2005.

[408] S 51 of the Criminal Justice and Public Order Act 1994; ss 39 and 40 of the Criminal Justice and Police Act 2001.

[409] S 6.

[410] S 6(2).

(i) there is enough evidence and (ii) it is in the public interest to prosecute.[411] The second point raises a concern, because while the prosecutor should use the objective criteria in determining the existence of public interest,[412] a degree of subjectively can come in, or his/her opinion might be influenced by political and other factors. Further, the Public Prosecutor can also discontinue private prosecution when it interferes with the investigation and prosecution of another criminal offence.[413] What may be concluded here is that the right of victims in relation to criminal prosecution is limited compared to the other jurisdictions explored in this chapter. Other rights of victims are set out in the Code for Victims of Crime,[414] launched by the UK government in 2006. Under this Code, services such as access to information on the progress of criminal investigation and prosecution and referral to victim support may be provided. Unlike other jurisdictions, the Code is not enforceable, and therefore its breach will not entail any legal consequence for public authorities.[415] Victims suffering from injuries caused by criminal conduct may apply for compensation provided by the Criminal Injury Compensation Authority or compensation orders issued by the court as part of the sentence.[416] Here, there is also a good evidence of the government working with charities such as Victim Support[417] to assist the victims of crime.

5.5.1.2.3 Mutual Legal Assistance in Criminal Matters

A modern system of extradition in the UK is governed by the Extradition Act 2003. The procedure varies depending on the status of foreign states requesting extradition. Category 1 states are those without the death penalty, and include all Member States of the EU.[418] The procedure for these states was created as a result of the European Arrest Warrant (EAW) adopted by the EU,[419] which aims to simplify extradition among the EU Member States. To begin with, if one consents to extradition, then one is to be returned within 20 days.[420] If consent is not forthcoming, a request for extradition is transmitted to the competent authority, which in the UK is SOCA.[421] When a warrant of arrest for a wanted

---

[411] Available at www.cps.gov.uk/publications/code_for_crown_prosecutors/codetest.html.

[412] Ibid.

[413] Ibid.

[414] Issued under s 32 of the Domestic Violence, Crime and Victims Act 2004. It applies to England and Wales. A similar document, National Standards of Victims of Crime (2005), is available in Scotland.

[415] Instead, they can approach the Parliamentary Ombudsman under the Parliamentary Commissioner Act 1967, as amended by Schedule 7 of the Domestic Violence, Crime and Victims Act 2004.

[416] Davies et al, above n 369, 79–80.

[417] Available at www.victimsupport.org.uk/.

[418] Extradition Act 2003 (Specification of Category 1 Territories) Order 2009, SI 2009/2768.

[419] Framework Decision 2002/584/JHA on the European arrest warrant and the surrender procedures between Member States, OJ L190/1 (18 July 2002).

[420] Ss 45, 46 and 47 of the Extradition Act 2003. After one consents, a judge has 10 days to issue an extradition order. He/she then has to be returned within 10 days starting with from date on which the order is made.

[421] Crown Office and Procurator Fiscal in Scotland.

person is issued by the judiciary of a requesting state, it is then executed by a police constable or customs officer.[422] The arrested person is then brought before a judge,[423] who will determine whether the offence in question is an extraditable one.[424] If it is, the judge will then consider whether any grounds for refusal apply. [425] The judge will also determine whether extradition would be in breach of the UK's obligation under the ECHR.[426] The principle of double criminality is relaxed for 32 crimes under the EAW, most of which are classified as organised crime.[427] Once an order is made, extradition must occur within 10 days.[428] A highly publicised example of the execution of the EAW is that of Hussain Osman. Found guilty of placing an explosive at a London underground station on 21 July 2005,[429] he fled to Italy, where he was arrested, then returned to the UK two months later.[430]

The process is slightly different for Category 2 states. If one consents to extradition, then an extradition hearing does not have to be conducted as under the Category 1 procedure.[431] If this is not the case, then an initial request for extradition is made to the Secretary of State, not SOCA.[432] If the request is valid, the Secretary of State transmits it to the court. While the rest of the procedure resembles that of the Category 1 procedure, there are some differences. For instance, the rule of double criminality must be satisfied for extradition to/ from a Category 2 state.[433] Decisions by the court are transmitted to the Secretary of State, who then makes a final decision.[434] In addition, the defence has four weeks to make representations,[435] and the Secretary of State has up to two months to execute the order of extradition.[436] Finally, once an extradition order is issued, it must be fulfilled within 28 days.[437] The key differences between the Category 1 and 2 procedures, then, are that the latter procedure can be influenced by political considerations and takes longer to implement. Even then, the

---

[422] Ss 2 and 3.

[423] S 4.

[424] S 10.

[425] Ss 12–19. They are rules on double jeopardy, extraneous consideration (eg persecution and no guarantee of a fair trial), the passage of time, the person's age, hostage taking consideration, speciality and the person's earlier extradition to the UK from another state.

[426] S 21.

[427] The relevant crimes listed include participation in criminal organisation, terrorism, human and organ trafficking, sexual exploitation of children and child pornography, drug trafficking, corruption, fraud, money laundering, counterfeiting, computer-related crime, trafficking of endangered species and cultural goods, facilitation of unauthorised entry, extortion, forgery/trafficking of documents, and trafficking of nuclear materials.

[428] S 35.

[429] M Mackarel, 'Surrendering the Fugitive: The European Arrest Warrant and the United Kingdom' (2006–2007) 71 *Journal of Criminal Law* 362, 376.

[430] Ibid.

[431] Ss 127 and 128 of the Extradition Act 2003.

[432] S 70.

[433] S 137.

[434] S 92.

[435] S 93(6) as amended by Schedule 13 of the Police and Justice Act 2006.

[436] S 99(3).

[437] Ss 117 and 118.

systems implemented under the Extradition Act 2003 are more simplified and less time-consuming than the old arrangement under the Extradition Act 1989, which could take over five years to implement.[438]

The provision of other types of mutual assistance is governed by, among other legislation, the Criminal Justice (International Co-operation) Act 1990. This empowers the authorities to facilitate co-operation in criminal proceedings and investigations abroad. They can request overseas authorities to obtain evidence to be used before the UK courts and tribunals.[439] In return, the UK courts and tribunals assist overseas authorities to obtain evidence on the basis of reciprocity.[440] The legislation also facilitates a transfer of prisoners from the UK abroad or from abroad to the UK to give evidence.[441] Further, the law enforcement authorities can conduct investigations in the UK on behalf of the overseas authorities.[442] The 1990 Act has been strengthened by the Crime (International Co-operation) Act 2003. This adds additional measures, such as the execution of an overseas freezing order,[443] obtaining evidence through television link or telephone,[444] exchange of information on banking transactions[445] and surveillance conducted by foreign authorities.[446] Other statutes, including the Serious Organised Crime and Police Act 2005[447] and the Criminal Justice and Immigration Act 2008,[448] provide for other measures of international co-operation. In summary, it may be stated that the legislative framework in the UK to prevent and suppress organised crime are broadly in line with the Organised Crime Convention.

5.5.2   Assessment of Law Enforcement in the UK

As with the other jurisdictions examined in this chapter, the UK's effort to address organised crime should be recognised. The key strategy of UK law enforcement is to create an environment hostile to criminal activity and to reduce the overall harm caused to the state.[449] Some of the measures necessary to achieve these aims are reducing profit incentives, disrupting criminal activi-

---

[438] A Sambei and JRWD Jones, *Extradition Law Handbook* (Oxford, Oxford University Press, 2005) 8.

[439] S 3.

[440] S 4.

[441] Ss 5 and 6.

[442] S 7.

[443] Ss 20–25.

[444] Ss 29–31.

[445] Ss 32–36.

[446] S 83.

[447] Ss 95 and 96 on enforcement of overseas forfeiture orders and mutual assistance in freezing of property.

[448] Part 6 on mutual recognition of financial penalties and assistance in revenue matters.

[449] Home Office, 'Extending Our Reach: A Comprehensive Approach to Tackling Serious Organised Crime' (July 2009), 15.

ties and increasing the risk of them by effective prosecution and punishment.[450] It is important to recognise that these aims have been achieved to some extent, particularly after the establishment of SOCA. Since 2006, SOCA has arrested over 5,000 criminals, with a conviction rate of 94%.[451] A total of £460 million of criminal proceeds have been frozen or confiscated, and 266 tons of Class A drugs have been seized.[452] There is no doubt that all of these efforts will hinder criminal activities.

In terms of mutual assistance, the UK has facilitated extradition with foreign states. In 2008 alone 351 people were extradited from the UK, and 78 people were surrendered to the UK from the EU Member States.[453] Between 2004 and 2008, a total of 16,142 EAWs were issued to and by the UK authority.[454] This large traffic in EAWs shows that the UK actively co-operates with other EU Member States. The UK also conducts joint investigations with foreign authorities. Under Operation Hobart, UK law enforcement agencies, in conjunction with other agencies in the US and Colombia, led investigations into a North London criminal group responsible for trafficking Class A drugs into the UK. During the investigation, illegal drugs with an estimated street value of £3.7 million, $6 billion in counterfeit bonds and letters of credit with a face value of over £3 billion were seized. The three principals implicated were sentenced to a total of 74 years' imprisonment and their seven associates a total of 70 years' imprisonment.[455] SOCA also assisted Somalian police in seizing 600 kilograms of cocaine trafficked from Colombia.[456]

Despite these examples of good practice, the UK has also experienced some difficulties in enforcing the appropriate legislation on organised crime. One problem identified is the lack of reliable data, which is caused by the lack of legal definitions of organised crime and criminal groups. While the government claims that it uses the working definition noted above, one senior minister was quoted as conceding that there was no single agreed-upon definition of organised crime.[457] A practical consequence of this lack of official definition is that organised crime is understood to cover a wide range of criminal conduct, and this has made it difficult to produce reliable data to facilitate intelligence-led investigations.[458] The need to improve intelligence gathering has also been noted in the recent report published by the government's Inspectorate of Constabulary.[459]

---

[450] Ibid.
[451] Ibid, 2.
[452] Ibid.
[453] Hansard, Vol 487, Part No 21 (House of Commons Written Answer 28 January 2009)
[454] Ibid.
[455] SOCA, Annual Report 2007/2008, 22.
[456] Home Office (2009), above n 449, 31.
[457] This was Tony McNulty, who was the Minister for the Home Office in 2006. Quoted in PA Sproat, 'An Evaluation of the UK's Anti-Money Laundering and Asset Recovery Regime' (2007) 47 *Crime Law and Social Change* 169, 179.
[458] Ibid, 180.
[459] Her Majesty's Inspectorate of Constabulary, 'Getting Organised: A Thematic Report on the

Another issue is the existence of multiple organisational mandates among law enforcement agencies and duplication of various activities. The establishment of SOCA is an important step forward in the fight against organised crime, as it performs multiple functions as a lead agency to address the practice. However, the government still concedes that arrangements for interagency activities need to be clearer.[460] One good example is the investigation and prosecution of fraud, which can be carried out by a number of agencies, such as SOCA, the CPS and the Serious Fraud Office.[461] In order to use the resources effectively and reduce duplication, the government is looking into the establishment of 'a new strategic centre' to combat serious organised crime.[462] The extent to which such a centre will improve the current situation is not at all clear. SOCA was established mainly for this purpose,[463] yet the government's recognition of the need for better co-ordination demonstrates that SOCA has not yet been able to address this problem effectively. It is still a relatively young agency, established only in 2006, and more time is needed to judge its effectiveness. It may, however, be argued that the government is wasting its energy and resources in establishing another centre when it can devote them to improving the efficiency of SOCA.

It should also be noted that the extent to which some of the measures adopted have the desired effect is not clear. The asset recovery regime (confiscation/ freezing of criminal proceeds/assets) is a case in point. Between 2008 and 2009, a total of £46.4 million was confiscated through confiscation orders and civil recovery.[464] Given that criminals are said to make a profit of £15 billion annually through the provision of goods and services in the UK,[465] the amount seized may not be regarded as significant enough to deter criminals from operating there. While this does not necessarily illustrate a consistent failure by UK law enforcement authorities in relation to confiscation of criminal proceeds, it does highlight the sophisticated methods which criminals use to launder and conceal their profits. Likewise the practical difficulty of gathering reliable intelligence to prosecute and punish criminals exists, even for the UK agencies, which have better capability and more resources to deal with organised crime. Further, the asset recovery regime must be accompanied by the imposition of severe penalties for the commission of organised crime. While various reports published by the government often list the amount of money seized to highlight its success, little space is devoted to the extent of punishments imposed upon criminals. Any solid evidence should be publicised by the government to send a clear message to the criminals. As in the case of Serbia, the efficacy of law enforcement should be questioned if many do not receive appropriate penalties. This is so because, given the level of profits they can make, criminals are likely to

Police Service's Response to Serious and Organised Crime' (April 2009) 16.
   [460] Home Office (2009), above n 449, 21.
   [461] Ibid.
   [462] Ibid, 21.
   [463] Home Office (2004), above ch 1 n 57, 22
   [464] SOCA, above n 391, 32
   [465] SOCA, 'The United Kingdom Threat Assessment of Organised Crime 2009/10', 8.

reoffend, particularly if they know that they will not receive heavy penalties. A similar argument has been made in relation to drug trafficking[466] and surely applies to other forms of organised crime.

A variety of human rights concerns have been raised in relation to UK law enforcement, which have relevance to action against organised crime. In *S and Marper v United Kingdom*[467] before the European Court of Human Rights, the key issue was the indefinite retention of fingerprints and DNA samples[468] obtained from people subsequently not convicted. The European Court ruled that this breached Article 8 on the right to privacy.[469] As a result of this decision, the UK government passed the Crime and Security Act 2010, under which fingerprints and samples of innocent people are to be destroyed within six years.[470] In *R v Moon*,[471] the Court of Appeal found that there had been entrapment when the defendant was lured into committing a crime (possession of Class A drugs) while there was a lack of proper authorisation of the undercover operation against her. Further, in *Lisowski v Poland*[472] the High Court reversed a decision of a lower court and accepted that there was a serious risk that a fair trial would not be conducted for the appellant, who was accused of fraud, due to the passage of time (over 10 years).[473] On the positive side, these and other cases also demonstrate that the UK courts do consider human rights implications arising from law enforcement and rectify the situation where necessary.

The government also needs to do more to address the demand for illicit goods and services. This is not to state that it has not done anything at all. In relation to illicit consumption of narcotics, for instance, the government has long utilised the classification system (Classes A, B and C) with varying degrees of punishment to deter people from trafficking and using illicit drugs.[474] In order to reduce the demand for illegal workers, the government also established the Gangmasters Licensing Authority. This body operates a licensing scheme to ensure, among other things, that employers do not employ illegal workers and subject workers to forced labour and slavery.[475] In addition, the government

---

[466] Sproat, above n 457, 183–84.

[467] Applications nos 30562/04 and 30566/04 (2008).

[468] Authorised by s 64 of PACE.

[469] *S and Marper*, above n 467, paras 125 and 126.

[470] Ss 14–23.

[471] [2004] EWCA Crim 2872. See also the case of *Loosely* noted in Chapter 3.

[472] [2006] EWHC 3227.

[473] A similar reasoning applied to *Kociukow v District Court of Bialystok III Penal Division* [2006] EWHC 56. In *R (on the application of Pillar) v Bow Street Magistrates Court* [2006] EWHC 1886, the High Court accepted the argument by the appellant that the European Arrest Warrant issued by Austria was vague and did not satisfy the requirement set by Extradition Act 2003, and that the district judge could not order his extradition. The same reasoning applied to *Hall v Germany* [2006] EWHC 462 (drug trafficking); *Hunt v Court of First Instance, Antwerp, Belgium* [2006] EWHC 165 (money laundering); *Palar v Court of First Instance of Brussels* [2005] EWHC 915 (credit card fraud). In *R (on the application of Nikonovs) v Governer of Brixton Prison* [2005] EWHC 2405, a writ of habeas corpus was granted as the claimant was not brought before the relevant court promptly.

[474] Misuse of Drugs Act 1971.

[475] Gangmasters (Licensing) Act 2004.

claims to have run public awareness and educational campaigns targeted at the general public to reduce the demand for illicit goods and services.[476]

However, it is difficult to say whether the government's effort has been successful in actually reducing the demand for illicit goods and services. In relation to drug use and misuse, it should be recognised that the number of reported offences relating to possession and use of drugs has been on a decline.[477] Nevertheless, it has been noted that the use of Class A drugs has increased over the past few years.[478] The number of drug-induced deaths has also increased from 1,314 in 1995 to 2,025 in 2006,[479] and many more people entered into drug treatment in 2006 (49,625) than in 2003 (28,087).[480] This suggests that, despite the official endeavours, the demand for drugs remains strong, and drug use and abuse are still serious problems in the UK. In addition, even though the Gangmasters Licensing Authority has conducted successful inspections on numerous occasions and revoked licences,[481] there is evidence of some employers shifting to unregulated activities and exploiting workers.[482] Severe penalties, such as hefty fines or imprisonment, are necessary to deter employers from exploitative practices. Such arrangements already exist,[483] but proper enforcement is required to achieve the desired effect. It should also be noted that prostitution itself is not illegal in the UK, whereas associated acts, such as exploitation of prostitutes or keeping of brothels, are.[484] As a result, the sex industry in the UK still thrives and the demand for sexual services has increasingly been fuelled by adverts placed in local newspapers.[485] A positive development in relation to this is the recent enactment of the Policing and Crime Act 2009, which criminalises purchase of sex from trafficked victims. Only time will tell whether this will lead to a reduction in demand or drive the practice further underground.

Finally, more needs to be done to educate the general public. A recent survey conducted by the Home Office on attitudes towards organised crime reveals that criminal conduct such as smuggling of tobacco and purchasing counterfeit goods such as DVDs elicited a low level of concern among the general public, because they think that such activities only harm the relevant industries and

---

[476] Home Office (2009), above n 449, 61.

[477] 105,308 cases in 2003 and 86,528 in 2006. EMCDDA (European Monitoring Centre for Drugs and Drug Addiction) Statistical Bulletin, available from www.emcdda.europa.eu/stats09.

[478] Home Office Statistical Bulletin, 'Drug Misuse Declared: Findings from the 2008/2009 British Crime Survey', 8.

[479] EMCDDA Statistical Bulletin, above n 477.

[480] Ibid.

[481] Gangmasters Licensing Authority, 'Annual Report and Accounts' (1 April 2008 to 31 March 2009) 11–12.

[482] Parliamentary Home Affairs Committee, above ch 3 n 189, 22.

[483] This is provided for in s 12 of the Gangmasters (Licensing) Act 2004; s 15 of the Immigration, Asylum and Nationality Act 2006.

[484] See, eg s 33 of the Sexual Offences Act 2003 (keeping of brothels); s 1 of the Sexual Offences Act 1985 (kerb crawling).

[485] Parliamentary Home Affairs Committee, above ch 3 n 189, 27–28.

not themselves.[486] They even think that these activities are beneficial to them,[487] showing a degree of tolerance for these activities. While many think human trafficking is a serious crime, it also elicited a low level of concern as people believe the practice does not affect them personally.[488] The mentality of the UK general public seems to be that they are willing to turn a blind eye to instances of organised crime as long as these have no negative impact on them personally. The key task of the government, then, is to reverse this mentality and make the public aware that their actions are fuelling the demand for illicit goods and services, which often result in undesirable consequences such as sexual/labour exploitation and violations of human rights.

5.6 Comparative Analysis

A variety of observations can be made in comparing the four jurisdictions explored in this chapter. To begin with, the case studies demonstrate the importance of having uniform definitions of organised crime or criminal groups to facilitate effective law enforcement. The limited applicability to certain crimes (Thailand), the existence of multiple definitions (Serbia) and the lack of formal definition (UK) have made it difficult for law enforcement authorities to effectively identify the practice, and/or promote inter-agency co-operation. A lack of appropriate definitions also affects the principle of legality. In the context of criminal law and justice, this means, among other things, that a particular offence must be defined in a clear manner and that no punishment can be imposed without a law.[489] In addition, a lack of uniform definition at the international level will make it more difficult to promote mutual assistance in criminal matters, because a criminal conduct in one state may not be regarded as such in another. All of these show that there is some merit in adopting common definitions in relation to organised crime and criminal groups. At the same time, it is evident that the principle of state sovereignty has made it difficult to achieve this.

Aside from the definitional issue, it seems reasonable to conclude that the legislative frameworks to address organised crime in all jurisdictions are broadly in line with the Organised Crime Convention as they criminalise a wide variety of conduct associated with organised crime. While many laws or statutes had been adopted before the Organised Crime Convention, the movements to modify the legal framework in accordance with international standards are more evident in Thailand, Serbia and Kosovo. In the case of the UK, steps have been taken to modify its domestic legal framework in accordance with European law, as can

---

[486] Home Office, 'Public Concern about Organised Crime', Research Report No 16 (2009), 5.
[487] Ibid.
[488] Ibid.
[489] The latter is known by the Latin maxim *nullum crimen sine lege*.

be seen in, among others, the Extradition Act 2003.[490] This is understandable because, as will be shown in Chapter 6, the UK is legally obliged to implement EU measures. Nevertheless, the extent to which the UK government pays attention to the Organised Crime Convention is not clear. While a 2004 White Paper mentions the Convention once in relation to international co-operation,[491] a recent 2009 White Paper[492] does not refer to it at all. As noted above, there is still no sign of adopting the definitions under the Convention. All of these cast some doubt on the UK's commitment to promote international standards in relation to organised crime.

The case studies also show that some of the difficulties noted in Chapter 3 are real problems in the four jurisdictions. In all jurisdictions there are provisions for the grant of amnesty or pardon to convicted criminals. Although such cases might be rare, an example of such in the UK noted above does illustrate that such a measure can be granted against criminals who commit serious organised crime. While the then Home Secretary granted this in exchange for useful information, one of the two pardoned was a career criminal who was a major figure of drug trafficking in the UK. It might be asked whether the Home Secretary was right to rely on the royal prerogative of mercy. It is also the case that all jurisdictions recognise periods of limitation, although this is restricted to minor offences in the UK. Further, the grant of immunities to personnel of international organisations and peacekeeping force has been problematic in Kosovo. Although instances are rare, some cases of diplomats being involved in organised crime have also been reported in Thailand,[493] Serbia[494] and the UK.[495] All of these examples illustrate the practical difficulty in balancing the political interests of the governments against proper administration of justice. Diplomatic immunity provides an added layer of difficulty as states are acting in accordance with domestic and international law.

It is also evident that the legal frameworks adopted in the four jurisdictions are not properly enforced. This means that international standards are not currently implemented effectively in practice. It has been noted that politically weak states are likely to be affected by organised crime more than others as the capability of law enforcement authorities is not adequate to prevent and suppress the practice.[496] Corruption also makes it easier for criminals to operate with impunity. The analysis of case studies shows that this has been so in Thailand

---

[490] See also Chapter 6 of the Serious Organised Crime and Police Act 2005, which mentions the Council Framework Decision on the Execution in the European Union of Orders Freezing Property or Evidence.

[491] Home Office (2004), above ch 1 n 57, 18.

[492] Home Office (2009), above n 449.

[493] 'Smuggling Wildlife: From Eggs in a Bra to Geckos in Underwear,' www.physorg.com/news168697589.html.

[494] 'Guinea Ambassador to Serbia—Mohammad Isiga Kuruma—Cigarette Smuggling,' available at http://accountability-international.blogspot.com/2009/04/guinea-ambassador-to-serbia-mohammad.html.

[495] Hansard, Col 29WS (19 June 2009).

[496] Williams and Godson, above ch 2 n 19, 316.

and Serbia, which are regarded as a developing state and a state in transition respectively. While Kosovo is also a territory in transition, instances of corruption have not been as systematic as in the other two states. This is perhaps because of the international administration, which has been instrumental in rebuilding Kosovo's infrastructure. This underscores the point raised elsewhere in the book that organised crime cannot be addressed effectively by governments alone, and this is particularly true for the less developed states explored in this chapter.

This is not to say that developed states are immune from organised crime. The UK is a developed state and has adequate financial and human resources to invest in the fight against organised crime, as noted above. Compared to others, it is also regarded as a democratic state which respects the rule of law, legality and respect for human rights. Because of this, states such as the UK are said to inhibit the growth of organised crime.[497] Even so, the UK is deeply affected by organised crime. The main reason, it is submitted, is that the UK government has not been very proactive in addressing the demand for illicit goods and services, with a result that criminals continue to supply them to meet this demand. The existence of lucrative markets continues to serve as a strong pull factor attracting organised crime and organised criminal groups, and it seems reasonable to conclude that this applies to the UK.

The difficulty in enforcing legislation experienced in all jurisdictions also illustrates the sophisticated and complex nature of operations conducted by criminals and criminal groups. As explained in Chapter 2, they engage in a variety of risk management tactics to avoid law enforcement and accumulate their wealth by providing goods and services. Given that the four jurisdictions are deeply affected by organised crime, the conclusion must be that criminals have outperformed the law enforcement authorities. In order to get ahead of these criminals, implementation of intelligence-led law enforcement becomes all the more important. Unfortunately, the case studies do not indicate that this has been done. In addition, Thailand, Serbia and Kosovo are affected by a lack of resources and capability on the part of law enforcement agencies. States must also impose tougher sentences for criminals and strengthen the asset recovery regime to strip them of their criminal proceeds, as all of these can help create a hostile environment for them to operate.

In addition, it can be concluded that all jurisdictions explored in this chapter are not doing enough to address the supply and demand dynamics for illicit goods and services. The economic model explored in Chapter 2 tells us that organised criminals keep supplying illicit goods and services because of strong demand. However, simply cutting the supply, and therefore targeting supplier states such as Thailand, is not enough. Criminals will always shift their operation to other states or regions, or start supplying goods and services which are less regulated. Therefore, any supply reduction strategy should be accompanied by

---

[497] Ibid, 320–21.

measures to cut the flow of these goods and services en route (or in transit), and also to reduce the demand. Further, other measures, such as a poverty reduction and employment strategies, particularly in economically and politically unstable states, should be facilitated to reduce the incentives for involvement in organised crime. In summary, the case studies of four jurisdictions underscores the need to move beyond simply criminalising and punishing organised crime to adopting a comprehensive strategy to address multi-faceted aspects of organised crime.

It is also the case that a wide variety of human rights concerns exist in relation to law enforcement against organised crime in all jurisdictions. While the protection and promotion of human rights are recognised in domestic law, the authorities sometimes have gone too far in restricting or violating the rights of freedoms not only of criminals, but also of innocent citizens who have nothing to do with organised crime. This highlights the inadequacy of TCL as represented by the Organised Crime Convention and the need to promote human rights through IHRL. In relation to the extent of human rights violations, Thailand displays more serious disregard for human rights, particularly in the area of drug law enforcement. While violations of human rights exist in other jurisdictions, they are not as extreme as in Thailand.[498] This perhaps supports an argument that it is difficult to seek effective protection and promotion of human rights in states which are experiencing many political, economic and other problems. While Serbia and Kosovo as not well developed as yet and are still experiencing various problems, the former is bound by the ECHR and the latter has been placed under international administration. The UK is also bound by the ECHR, the effect of which has been strengthened by the HRA, as noted above. Therefore there are better systems of scrutiny and accountability in these jurisdictions. Additional political pressures exist for Serbia and Kosovo as both seek recognition as legitimate members of the community of states regionally and internationally.

In relation to facilitation of international co-operation, one of the driving forces in the Organised Crime Convention, all jurisdictions have legislative and other frameworks in place. Many of them were implemented prior to the adoption of the Organised Crime Convention, and therefore the extent to which it has played a part in this field is not clear. While Thailand, Serbia and Kosovo are more willing to conform to international standards, this is not clear for the UK for the reasons stated above. One thing which is clear, however, is that the UK is bound by European law and therefore is more likely to pay attention to the EU arrangements than the international ones. It is also clear that Thailand, Serbia and Kosovo require active intervention of international organisations and developed states in facilitating mutual legal assistance. The UK is in the position to assist these and other states, and continues to do so. In any event, the case studies show that, while all of them do not have the exact same procedures,

---

[498] This is obviously different for measures against terror suspects as various allegations of gross violations of human rights have been made in the UK.

and therefore the principle of state sovereignty is evident, various co-operative arrangements are in place and states do generally co-operate with one another and with other non-state actors to prevent and suppress organised crime.

5.7 Conclusions

In this chapter, national case studies of Thailand, Serbia, Kosovo and the UK were presented. It was shown that, although the legislative frameworks in all the jurisdictions are broadly in line with international standards and therefore can be used to prosecute and punish organised crime, a series of problems exist in relation to their law enforcement. In particular, intelligence-led law enforcement, while being promoted with assistance from other states and international organisations, has much room for improvement. The general conclusion reached is that, although the efforts of the states examined in this chapter should be recognised, and things are gradually improving, there is a long way to go to fully implement international standards set by the Organised Crime Convention.

The analysis shows that organised crime affects all states regardless of their status as developing states, states in transition or developed states. While less developed states are affected by the practice more due to a lack of capacity and resources, organised crime is also prevalent in developed states. In comparing the four jurisdictions, there are no major differences in the ways in which they deal with organised crime; a criminal justice response through prosecution and punishment has been the major mechanism for all. However, the case studies clearly demonstrate that a criminal justice response alone is not adequate. It must be accompanied by measures to address wider issues, such as the causes of organised crime and the supply and demand dynamics. In this regard, the case studies also support the conclusion reached previously that the Organised Crime Convention alone is not capable of addressing organised crime. It is also evident that states on their own are not capable of preventing and suppressing organised crime. The transnational nature of organised crime makes it inevitable that the practice is addressed simultaneously at the regional and international levels. The role of organisations such as the EU and the United Nations becomes particularly important. The next two chapters focus on these organisations and examine how they work closely with states and others to prevent and suppress organised crime.

6

The EU and Transnational Organised Crime

6.1 Introduction

This chapter examines the action against organised crime implemented by the EU as an example of a regional response. Western Europe has been regarded by organised criminal groups as good 'hunting grounds'[1] because its economic power and wealth facilitate the purchase of illicit goods and services. This somewhat mirrors the case study of the UK in Chapter 5. Free movement of goods, people and capital throughout the EU have made some criminal activities easier to perform. The break-up of the Soviet Union in the late 1980s/early 1990s also created an abundance of opportunities for criminals. The proximity of the successor states to the EU was a further impetus for criminals to get involved. The resulting concern of European governments with control of transnational criminal activities[2] led to progressive legal and institutional development within the EU to prevent and suppress them.

What follows is an examination of the past, present and future action against transnational organised crime. It will start by highlighting the measures adopted by the Treaty on European Union (TEU). It then moves on to examine the current action against the practice, with particular references to the approximation of national laws, mutual recognition and the principle of availability. Finally, with the Lisbon Treaty having come into force on 1 December 2009, the measures stipulated under the revised treaties have become pertinent. This chapter will highlight the key legal and institutional changes and their potential role for effective prevention and suppression of organised crime. The main conclusion reached is that, while the EU has been instrumental in adopting various measures against organised crime, a variety of problems, such as the principle of state sovereignty, the protection of human rights and the practical difficulty of promoting the key principles, are affecting its ability to effectively prevent and suppress the practice.

---

[1] C Harding, 'European Regimes of Crime Control: Objectives, Legal Bases and Accountability' (2000) 7 *Maastricht Journal of European and Comparative Law* 224, 229.

[2] Ibid.

6.2 Law, Policies and Measures under the TEU

6.2.1 Overview

The TEU[3] came into force in 1 November 1993 and provided for co-operation in criminal matters among Member States under the so-called 'Third Pillar'.[4] The relevant part was Title VI, on provisions on police and judicial co-operation in judicial and criminal matters, also known as the justice and home affairs provisions. It should be noted that some co-operation on justice and home affairs existed prior to this Treaty. For instance, the Directive 1/308/EEC on money laundering[5] obliged Member States to criminalise the practice. The development of a single market also led to tightening of EU's external borders,[6] some of which had relevance for organised crime. Nevertheless, it was the TEU which established a formal intergovernmental system of co-operation in criminal matters.[7] Under the TEU the key themes in relation to measures against organised crime were the promotion of functional co-operation among Member States and the approximation/harmonisation of national laws and systems. This becomes clear when looking at some of the measures implemented.

One of the early attempts to deal with organised crime at the EU level was the adoption of the European Union Action Plan to Combat Organised Crime in 1997,[8] a result of political pressure to strengthen the measures against the practice.[9] The Action Plan recognised the need to promote a coherent and co-ordinated approach to organised crime through co-operation and harmonisation. It contained a list of measures to be taken, including adopting common definitions/standards for analysis, judicial co-operation, active involvement of Europol and mutual evaluation of domestic measures among Member States.[10] The need for a co-ordinated response was also recognised by the European Parliament, which called for the adoption of a common definition of organised crime.[11]

Some of the measures described in the Action Plan were subsequently

---

[3] OJ C191/1 (29 July 1992).

[4] The first pillar was the Community pillar and the second pillar related to common foreign and security policy.

[5] Directive 1/308/EEC on prevention of the use of the financial system for the purpose of money laundering, OJ L166/77 (28 June 1991).

[6] Harding, above n 1, 231.

[7] S Peers, *EU Justice and Home Affairs Law*, 2nd edn (Oxford, Oxford University Press, 2006) 6.

[8] OJ C251/1 (15 August 1997).

[9] Mitsilegas, above ch 3 n 14, 566.

[10] L Paoli and C Fijnaut, 'The Initiatives of the European Union and the Council of Europe' in Paoli and Fijnaut, above ch 1 n 3, 635.

[11] Doc 5858/98 LIMITE, CRIMORG 17(February 18 1998), quoted in Mitsilegas, above ch 3 n 14, 568.

implemented. For instance, the Council adopted a Joint Action 'on making it a criminal offence to participate in a criminal organization in the European Union.'[12] This Joint Action can be seen as the first step towards a common EU approach to organised crime. It provided a definition of a criminal group[13] that was used as a model for the definition under the Organised Crime Convention. The offences covered as part of this Joint Action included drug trafficking, trafficking in nuclear materials, trafficking/smuggling of human beings, and others listed in Article 2 and Annex of the Europol Convention.[14] Under this Joint Action, Member States had to 'undertake' to punish these offences committed by criminal groups with effective penalties.[15] Beyond this, the Joint Action did not oblige Member States to take effective action against organised crime except to co-ordinate the establishment of criminal jurisdictions.[16] Other Joint Actions covered some of the aspects of organised crime, including ones on money laundering,[17] trafficking of human beings,[18] drug trafficking[19] and corruption.[20] Yet other Joint Actions related to promoting co-operation among Member States. For instance, Joint Action 96/748/JHA extended the mandate of the Europol Drug Unit to deal with issues such as people trafficking.[21] Joint Action 98/428/JHA[22] established the European Judicial Network (EJN). There were also Joint Actions on mutual legal assistance[23] and on co-operation among judiciary and magistrates.[24]

Another notable development under the TEU was the establishment of the specialised agencies tasked to deal with organised crime. The European Drug Unit (EDU) is a good example. It was established in 1993 as a predecessor to Europol. While the main focus of its activity was drug trafficking, as the name

---

[12] Above ch 2 n 97. It ceased to exist with the adoption of the Framework Decision 2008/841/JHA of 24 October 2008 on the fight against organised crime, OJ L300/42 (11 November 2008) (Framework Decision on Organised Crime).

[13] Art 1.

[14] Ibid.

[15] Arts 2 and 3.

[16] Art 4.

[17] Joint Action 98/699/JHA on money laundering, the identification, tracing, freezing, seizing and confiscation of instrumentalities and the proceeds of crime, OJ L333/1 (9 December 1998).

[18] Joint Action 97/154/JHA concerning action to combat trafficking in human beings and sexual exploitation of children, OJ L63/2 (4 March 1997); Joint Action 96/700/JHA establishing an incentive and exchange programme for persons responsible for combating trade in human beings and sexual exploitation of children, OJ L322/7 (12 December 1996).

[19] Joint Action 96/699/JHA concerning the exchange of information on the chemical profiling of drugs to facilitate improved cooperation between Member States in combating illicit drug trafficking, OJ L322/5 (12 December 1996); Joint Action 96/698/JHA on cooperation between customs authorities and business organizations in combating drug trafficking, OJ L322/3 (12 December 1996).

[20] Joint Action 98/742/JHA on corruption in the private sector, OJ L358/2 (31 December 1998).

[21] OJ L342/4 (31 December 1996).

[22] OJ L191/4 (7 July 1998).

[23] Joint Action 98/427/JHA on good practice in mutual legal assistance in criminal matters, OJ L191/1 (7 July1998).

[24] Joint Action 96/277/JHA concerning a framework for the exchange of liaison magistrates to improve judicial cooperation between the Member States of the European Union, OJ L105/1 (27 April 1996).

suggests, its mandate was later expanded to deal with other forms of organised crime, including trafficking of radioactive/nuclear materials, clandestine immigration networks and money laundering, as noted above. The key task of the EDU was, however, limited to collection/analysis of intelligence. This is provided for in Article 2(2), which provided that the 'Unit shall act as a non-operational team for the exchange and analysis of information and intelligence'.

This changed somewhat with the establishment of Europol as provided by the Convention on the Establishment of the European Police Office (Europol Convention)[25] in 1995. In accordance with the provisions of the Europol Convention, Europol began its operation on 1 July 1999 and was envisaged to have an important role to play in relation to organised crime. In this regard, Article 1 of the Europol Convention provides:

> The objective of Europol shall be . . . to improve, by means of the measures referred to in this Convention, the effectiveness and cooperation of the competent authorities in the Member States in preventing and combating terrorism, unlawful drug trafficking and other serious forms of international crime where there are factual indications that an organized criminal structure is involved and two or more Member States are affected by the forms of crime in question in such a way as to require a common approach by the Member States owing to the scale, significance and consequences of the offences concerned.

It is worth noting here that Article 1 uses phrases such as 'cooperation of the competent authorities in the Member States'. It is clear from this wording that, unlike the EDU, Europol was mandated to go beyond gathering and analysing intelligence on organised crime. In this regard, the Convention mandates Europol to provide, among other things, technical assistance and training to national authorities.[26] Another key term is 'a common approach'. The EU made clear its view that a unified, EU-wide and integrated response to organised crime was essential.

In line with the Europol Convention, Europol has engaged in a wide variety of activities to combat organised crime. For instance, Europol has facilitated joint investigation among Member States. In February 2007, Operation Baltico was carried out by Europol in conjunction with the Italian Arma dei Carabinieri in Milan, against a criminal group suspected of committing many robberies against well-known jewellery shops there and in other cities.[27] Thirty-five EAWs were executed in Estonia, Lithuania, Finland, Spain, France and Germany on charges of criminal association.[28] The proceeds of the robberies were estimated to be as high as €40 million and were believed to have been reinvested to finance a drug trafficking ring.[29] In June 2007, Europol also supported the authorities from Spain, Colombia and the US in initiating a joint police action against a

---

[25] OJ C316/2 (27 November 1995). It came into force in 1 October 1998.
[26] Art 3.
[27] Europol, Annual Report 2007, 22.
[28] Ibid.
[29] Ibid.

Colombian criminal network producing counterfeit euro and USD banknotes.[30] This operation involved 113 investigators and resulted in nine arrests and confiscation of counterfeit tender, including €400,000 and $1,000,000 in forgeries.[31]

The EJN has played an important role in prevention and suppression of organised crime.[32] This body consists of national authorities of Member States who have competence in international co-operation and judicial authorities (so called 'contact points'). These contact points act as intermediaries to facilitate judicial co-operation[33] by providing legal and practical information domestically and across Member States. As will be shown below, the role of the EJN has become particularly important in facilitating EAWs and other recent mechanisms to deal with organised crime. The EU has also established a funding mechanism to support functional co-operation among competent authorities of Member States. An example of such is the FALCONE Programme,[34] which was operational between 1998 and 2002, and funded activities such as training, meetings and seminars, research, and dissemination of information on the issues of organised crime. What has become apparent is that the initial EU action against organised crime was to a large extent limited to the gathering of intelligence through specialised bodies, although co-ordination among Member States was also envisaged.

6.2.2 Analysis of the TEU Measures

A number of issues and problems were identified in relation to the measures adopted by the TEU. To begin with, the legal nature of Joint Actions, the major instruments adopted for tackling organised crime, lacked clarity and definition under the TEU. This can be contrasted with measures taken under the first, or Community, pillar, such as Regulations, which have a direct effect on national legal systems of Member States. Some argue that Joint Actions also have some legal effect. The Advocate-General in *Commission v Council*[35] noted that a Joint Action was binding. Most Member States at that time also considered that Joint Actions were obligatory in law and that the extent of the obligation on the Member States depended on the content and the terms of each Joint Action, although the UK and Portugal denied such an effect.[36]

Despite these views, the available evidence suggests that Member States did not necessarily implement measures in practice. The aforementioned Joint Action on criminal organisation is a good example. In a survey conducted three years

---

[30] Ibid, 24.
[31] Ibid.
[32] Its establishment was envisaged in Recommendation 21 of the 1997 Action Plan.
[33] Art 4 of the Joint Action.
[34] Joint Action 98/245/JHA establishing a programme of exchanges, training and cooperation for persons responsible for action to combat organised crime, OJ L99/8 (31 March 1998).
[35] C-170/96 [1998] ECR I-2763.
[36] Peers, above n 7, 17.

after its adoption, only seven of the 15 Member States stated that they had incorporated the definition of 'criminal organisation' into their domestic law.[37] The reasons given for not incorporating the definition were that some states already had similar definitions under their domestic law and that domestic rules relating to evidence and other matters prevented incorporation.[38] Another example is the measures against trafficking of human beings. The Joint Action mentioned above obliged Member States to provide protection to victims of such, but only a few did so.[39] This failure on the part of Member States to implement Joint Actions has been exacerbated by the lack of an effective follow-up/enforcement mechanism to ensure implementation. The European Commission itself noted the necessity to adopt a stronger instrument on organised crime,[40] implicitly recognising that the pre-existing Joint Actions were not entirely effective.

One of the reasons why these Joint Actions were not followed was the principle of state sovereignty. At the time the TEU entered into force Member States were reluctant to seek active co-operation in the area of justice and home affairs (JHA). This was particularly because the area entailed national security implications and was therefore regarded as a matter of domestic concern.[41] Consequently, by the late 1990s only a limited number of measures for criminal law harmonisation and for judicial/police co-operation had been adopted,[42] despite the fact that these were regarded as important from an early stage. This meant that it was extremely difficult, if not impossible, for the EU to promote a comprehensive Union-wide approach to organised crime as envisaged in the 1997 Action Plan. This was acknowledged in the Tampere Conclusions adopted by the European Council in 1999.[43]

From the point of view of the institutional arrangement, there were a number of imbalances in the decision-making process. Under Article K3(2) of the TEU, the Council had the power to adopt JHA measures. While Member States and the Commission had a shared power of initiative on asylum, immigration and co-operation in civil matters, the Commission did not have the right of initiative

---

[37] Questionnaire on the implementation of the joint action of 21 December 1998 on making it a criminal offence to participate in a criminal organisation in the Member States of the European Union, 13151/01, LIMITE CRIMORG 112 (26 October 2001).

[38] Ibid. In France, for instance, it was noted by lawmakers and others that the offence of 'criminal conspiracy' was wide enough to cover participation in a criminal group. T Godefroy, 'The Control of Organised Crime in France: A Fuzzy Concept but a Handy Reference' in Paoli and Fijnaut, above ch 1 n 3, 773.

[39] Obokata, above ch 2 n 51, 98.

[40] Proposal for a Council Framework Decision on the fight against organised crime, COM(2005) 6 final (19 January 2005).

[41] D McGuinness and E Barrington, 'Immigration, Visa and Border Controls in the European Union' in G Barrett (ed), *Justice Cooperation in the European Union: The Creation of a European Legal Space* (Dublin, Institute of European Affairs, 1997) 157. See also P Turnbull, 'The Fusion of Immigration and Crime in the European Union: Problems of Cooperation and the Fight against Trafficking in Women' in P Williams (ed), *Illegal Migration and Commercial Sex* (London, Frank Cass, 1999) 195.

[42] V Mitsilegas, 'The Constitutional Implications of Mutual Recognition in Criminal Matters in the EU' (2006) 43 *Common Market Law Review* 1277, 1278.

[43] Available from www.europarl.europa.eu/summits/tam_en.htm.

in relation to police and judicial co-operation in criminal matters and customs co-operation.[44] In accordance with Article K6, the European Parliament only had the right to be informed of discussions and to be consulted by Member States. In addition, the European Court of Justice (ECJ) had virtually no role. Article K3(2) gave the Court jurisdiction to interpret Conventions, but this did not extend to other instruments. All of these mean that any decision made in relation to JHA lacked transparency[45] and political interference was inevitable. Finally, specialised mechanisms dealing with organised crime are also said to be political. Europol's governing body, the Management Board, consists of one representative from each of the Member States, and political differences between them result in varied perceptions on the functions of Europol. Some envisage minor roles, such as monitoring performance and setting strategic direction, while others advocate a more hands-on approach for the organisation.[46] This has affected the effective functioning of Europol.

In summary, the measures adopted under the TEU were not as effective in terms of promoting functional co-operation and harmonisation of national criminal law and criminal justice systems. The EU acknowledged that more had to be done to implement effective common EU action against organised crime. Prior to the coming into force of the Treaty of Amsterdam, the Council of European Union and the Commission adopted the Action Plan on How Best to Implement the Provisions of the Treaty of Amsterdam on an Area of Freedom, Security and Justice.[47] Some of the priorities identified were: improvement/ empowerment of Europol, effective implementation of the EJN and minimum rules on organised crime (harmonisation). The commitment to combat transnational organised crime was further affirmed by the European Council (a meeting of heads of states and governments) in October 1999, when it adopted the European Council Conclusions.[48] In the Conclusions, the European Council called for, among other things, the strengthening of Europol, the establishment of Eurojust, harmonisation of national criminal laws for key organised crimes such as drug and human trafficking and money laundering, and mutual recognition of judicial decisions. This was followed by the Prevention and Control of Organised Crime: A European Union Strategy for the Beginning of the New Millennium,[49] which reiterated the EU's commitment to implement effective measures against organised crime. The next section examines the extent to which these plans and proposals have been implemented in practice.

---

[44] Art K3.2.
[45] Peers, above n 7, 20.
[46] SD Brown, 'The EU Solution' in SD Brown (ed), *Combating International Crime: The Longer Arm of the Law* (Oxon, Routledge-Cavendish, 2008) 65–66.
[47] Also known as the Vienna Action Plan. OJ C19/1 (23 January 1999).
[48] Above n 43.
[49] OJ C124/1 (3 May 2000).

6.3 Law, Policies and Measures under the TEU as Revised by the Treaty of Amsterdam

6.3.1 Overview

The Treaty of Amsterdam[50] made some structural changes to the third pillar of the TEU. Provisions on immigration, asylum and civil law were incorporated into the first pillar. As will be shown below, some measures against organised crime were taken under this pillar. This strengthens the argument that the existing pillar structure and resultant differentiation of powers is no longer tenable to deal effectively with organised crime. Some changes were also made in relation to the powers of the European institutions. For instance, the Commission has gained a shared initiative with Member States to make proposals in matters relating to organised crime.[51] The ECJ can exercise jurisdiction to over criminal and police matters.[52] In addition, the Council acts unanimously on the initiative of the Commission or a Member State after consulting the European Parliament.[53] What is apparent here is that the EU is moving toward a more democratic decision-making, with more power entrusted to bodies other than the Council.

After a transitional period of the Treaty of Amsterdam, the European Council adopted the Hague Programme in 2004.[54] Similar to the Tampere Conclusions, this provides for achieving an Area of Freedom, Security and Justice[55] and sets out a framework for attaining such over five years.[56] The Hague Programme establishes 10 priorities, one of which is the fight against organised crime. To be specific, the EU is to develop and implement a strategic concept on tackling organised crime at the EU level and make full use of and further develop Europol and Eurojust.[57] The development of the strategic concept includes improving knowledge of the phenomenon and investigation of and co-operation on organised crime within and outside of the EU with other partners.[58] In relation to the role of Europol and Eurojust, the European Council urged Member States to enable these organisations to take an active role in the fight against organised crime, and these two organisations were to co-operate closely in such measures

---

[50] OJ C325/5 (24 December 2002).

[51] Art 34(2).

[52] Art 46.

[53] Arts 34 and 39.

[54] OJ C53/1 (3 March 2005).

[55] Formerly 'Justice and Home Affairs'.

[56] M Fletcher, 'Extending "Indirect Effect" to the Third Pillar: The Significance of *Pupino*' (2005) 30 *European Law Review* 862, 869.

[57] Communication from the Commission to the Council and the European Parliament on The Hague Programme: Ten Priorities for the Next Five Years, COM(2005) 184 final (10 May 2005) 6.

[58] Ibid, 10.

as the joint investigation teams.[59] These and other measures stipulated in the Hague Programmes have been implemented under the three broad areas of harmonisation or approximation of national law, mutual recognition of judicial decisions and the principle of availability. Detailed examination of these concepts now follows.

6.3.2 Approximation of National Laws

Approximation or harmonisation of criminal laws among Member States has been one of the important developments under the Treaty of Amsterdam. The growth of transnational organised crime undoubtedly facilitated this process as it can no longer be dealt with adequately by domestic criminal law alone.[60] Criminals have exploited the heterogeneity of national criminal laws and identified the safe havens.[61] In order to counter this, approximation has been regarded as necessary not only by academics, but also by practitioners.[62] The European Council was less enthusiastic and careful not to state that approximation should be sought for every single crime within the Member States. As a result, it was decided that approximation should be focused on a limited number of crimes, such as 'financial crime (money laundering, corruption, Euro counterfeiting), drugs trafficking, trafficking in human beings, particularly exploitation of women, sexual exploitation of children, high tech crime and environmental crime'.[63] Approximation may be distinguished from 'unification', through which more systematic changes of internal laws are sought.[64]

The legal basis for approximation is Article 31(e) of the TEU as revised by the Treaty of Amsterdam. This provides for the progressive adoption of 'measures establishing minimum rules relating to the constituent elements of criminal acts and to penalties in the fields of organised crime, terrorism and illicit drug trafficking'. Framework decisions are adopted under Article 34 in order to achieve this.[65] These are binding upon the Member States as to the result to be achieved but do not entail direct effect. This generally means that, although they are legally binding on Member States, they cannot be directly enforced before the national courts and tribunals. In *Pupino*,[66] however, the ECJ held that national

---

[59] Hague Programme, above n 54, 9–10.

[60] K Ambos, 'Is the Development of a Common Substantive Criminal Law for Europe Possible? Some Preliminary Reflections' (2005) 12 *Maastricht Journal of European and Comparative Law* 173, 174; A Weyembergh, 'The Functions of Approximation of Penal Legislation within the European Union' (2005) 12 *Maastricht Journal of European and Comparative Law* 149, 164.

[61] Weyembergh, ibid, 164.

[62] Ibid.

[63] Tampere Conclusions, above n 43, para 48.

[64] A Weyembergh, 'Approximation of Criminal Laws, the Constitutional Treaty and the Hague Programme' 42 (2005) *Common Market Law Review* 1567, 1567.

[65] 'Decisions' under the same part are adopted for the purposes other than approximation of national laws.

[66] Case C-105/03 *Criminal Proceedings against Maria Pupino* [2005] ECR I-5285.

courts must give indirect effect to framework decisions because the legal nature of framework decisions are similar to directives adopted under the EC Treaty, and therefore courts should interpret national law in conformity with them.[67] This derives from the binding nature of framework decisions and the principle of loyal co-operation, which imposes an obligation on Member States to ensure the effectiveness of Community law.[68] Another point to note in relation to framework decisions is that Member States can choose the form and methods of implementation, which allows them a degree of flexibility. As such, it is much easier to adopt framework decisions compared to other instruments such as Conventions, where all Member States have to agree on each and every provision. Consequently, the EU has made use of framework decisions more than others.[69]

Since the coming into force of the Treaty of Amsterdam, a wide variety of framework decisions in the area of organised crime have been adopted. The most important is the Framework Decision on Organised Crime. To begin with, this instrument adopted a definition of a 'criminal organisation':

'criminal organisation' means a structured association, established over a period of time, of more than two persons acting in concert with a view to committing offences which are punishable by deprivation of liberty or a detention order of a maximum of at least four years or a more serious penalty, to obtain, directly or indirectly, a financial or other material benefit.

'structured association' means an association that is not randomly formed for the immediate commission of an offence, nor does it need to have formally defined roles for its members, continuity of its membership, or a developed structure.[70]

It is apparent that this definition is broadly in conformity with the Organised Crime Convention.[71] It is worth noting here that the Council, on behalf of the European Community, signed the Organised Crime Convention and its Protocols on Trafficking and Smuggling.[72] Therefore the intention of the EU to abide by international standards is clear. As the Framework Decision on Organised Crime is a legally binding instrument, all Member States must adopt this definition in their domestic law.[73] This is particularly relevant for states that currently lack legal definitions of organised crime and criminal groups, such as the UK.

The Framework Decision on Organised Crime also establishes various other

---

[67] Para 34.

[68] Fletcher, above n 56, 867.

[69] Peers, above n 7, 384.

[70] Art 1.

[71] The key difference is the number of people to constitute a criminal organisation (two people). Under the Organised Crime Convention, it is listed as three people.

[72] Under Art 36 of the Organised Crime Convention, regional economic integration organisations can sign the Convention and its Protocols. Decision 2001/87/EC on the signing, on behalf of the European Community, of the United Nations Convention against transnational organised crime and its Protocols on combating trafficking in persons, especially women and children, and the smuggling of migrants by land, air and sea, OJ L30/44 (1 February 2001).

[73] The initial deadline for implementation was set as 11 May 2010.

obligations. For instance, Member States are to establish criminal jurisdiction on the basis of territoriality[74] and nationality[75] principles. Furthermore, a state can exercise jurisdiction over offences committed for the benefit of a legal person established in its territory. If the offence in question takes place abroad, this will be a form of effect principle. States can also exercise jurisdiction in accordance with their domestic law and therefore the possibility of universal jurisdiction is not excluded. In addition, Member States are obliged to establish liability of legal persons if they become part of organised crime.[76] It also enshrines the principle of *aut dedere aut judicare* if a Member States does not extradite its nationals.[77] In summary, it is evident that the Framework Decision on Organised Crime is broadly in line with the standards set by the Organised Crime Convention.

There are other framework decisions which touch upon different forms of organised crime. They include those on human trafficking,[78] drug trafficking,[79] counterfeiting of euro,[80] sexual exploitation of children,[81] corruption,[82] terrorism,[83] attacks against information systems[84] and facilitation of unauthorised entry and residence.[85] In addition to substantive offences, there are various framework decisions which aim to promote harmonisation of criminal justice processes across Member States. This goes beyond what is provided under Article 31(3) of the TEU, as noted above, and therefore may be regarded as innovative. They include confiscation of criminal proceeds,[86] orders freezing

---

[74] Art 7(a).

[75] Art 7(b).

[76] Arts 5 and 6.

[77] Art 7(3).

[78] Framework Decision 2002/626/JHA on combating trafficking in human beings, OJ L203/1 (1 August 2002). See also a Proposal for a Council Framework Decision on preventing and combating trafficking in human beings, and protecting victims, repealing Framework Decision 2002/629/JHA, COM(2009) 316 final.

[79] Framework Decision 2004/757/JHA laying down minimum provisions on the constituent elements of criminal acts and penalties in the field of illicit drug trafficking, OJ L335/8 (11 November 2004).

[80] Framework Decision 2000/383/JHA on increasing protection by criminal penalties and other sanctions against counterfeiting in connection with the introduction of euro, OJ L140/1 (14 June 2000).

[81] Framework Decision 2004/68/JHA on combating the sexual exploitation of children and child pornography, OJ L13/44 (20 January 2004). See also Proposal for a Council Framework Decision on combating the sexual abuse, sexual exploitation of children and child pornography, repealing Framework Decision 2004/68/JHA, COM(2009) 315 final.

[82] Framework Decision 2003/568/JHA on combating corruption in the private sector, OJ L192/54 (31 July 2003).

[83] Framework Decision 2002/475/JHA on combating terrorism, OJ L164/3 (22 June 2002).

[84] Framework Decision 2005/222/JHA on the attacks against information systems, OJ L69/67 (13 March 2005). For its implementation report, see COM(2008) 448 final.

[85] Framework Decision 2002/946/JHA on the strengthening of the penal framework to prevent the facilitation of unauthorised entry, transit and residence, OJ L328/1 (5 December 2002).

[86] Framework Decision 2005/212/JHA on confiscation of crime-related proceeds, instrumentalities and property, OJ L68/40 (15 March 2005). For its implementation report, see COM(2007) 805 final. See further Communication from the Commission to the Council and the European Parliament on Proceeds of Crimes, COM(2008) 766 final (20 November 2008).

property and evidence,[87] the EAW,[88] the European Evidence Warrant (EEW)[89] and the standing of victims in criminal proceedings.[90] A proposal to harmonise the rights of defendants throughout the Member States is currently being considered.[91] Finally, there are framework decisions establishing mechanisms to facilitate co-operation in criminal matters. They relate to, among other things, joint investigation[92] and exchange of intelligence.[93] In summary, it is evident that the EU has been proactive in promoting the principle of approximation after the coming into force of the Treaty of Amsterdam. The approximation of national laws and procedures is also in line with the Organised Crime Convention.

6.3.3　Mutual Recognition of Judicial Decisions

The basic premise of mutual recognition is that a judicial decision made by one Member State takes effect in the legal system of another Member State. This principle was introduced by the UK during its presidency of the EU in 1998 to promote judicial co-operation in criminal matters throughout Member States.[94] It was also recognised in the following year as evidenced in the Tampere Conclusions, where the principle of mutual recognition of judicial decision was regarded as the cornerstone of criminal judicial co-operation.[95] In 2000 the European Commission transmitted its communication on this matter to the Council and the European Parliament,[96] and in the following year the Commission launched a programme to promote this principle.[97] Finally, the Hague

---

[87] Framework Decision 2003/577/JHA on the execution in the European Union of orders freezing property or evidence, OJ L196/45 (2 August 2003). For its implementation report, see COM(2008) 885 final.

[88] Above ch 5 n 419.

[89] Framework Decision 2008/978/JHA on the European evidence warrant for the purpose of obtaining objects, document and data for use in proceedings in criminal matters, OJ L350/72 (30 December 2008).

[90] Framework Decision 2001/220/JHA on the standing of victims in criminal proceedings, OJ L82/1 (22 March 2001).

[91] COM(2004) 328 final, OL C 324/5 (30 December 2004).

[92] Framework Decision 2002/465/JHA on joint investigation teams, OJ L162/1 (20 June 2002). This Framework Decision will cease to exist when the Convention on Mutual Assistance in Criminal Matters enters into force in all Member States. Council Act of 29 May 2000 establishing the Convention by the Council in accordance with Article 34 of the Treaty on the European Union, on Mutual Assistance in Criminal Matters between the Member States of the European Union, OJ C197/3 (12 July 2000) .

[93] Framework Decision 2006/960/JHA on simplifying the exchange of information and intelligence between law enforcement authorities of the Member States of the European Union, OJ L386/89 (29 December 2006).

[94] Mitsilegas, above n 42, 1278.

[95] Above n 43, para 33.

[96] Communication from the Commission to the Council and the European Parliament, Mutual Recognition of Final Decisions in Criminal Matters, COM(2000) 495 final (26 July 2000).

[97] Programme of measures to implement the principle of mutual recognition of decisions in criminal matters, OJ C12/10 (15 January 2001).

Programme reaffirms this principle as an important measure to prevent and suppress serious crimes.[98]

The principles of mutual recognition and approximation of national laws display similarities as well as differences. Similar to approximation of national laws, the main motivation for mutual recognition was that existing divergence among national legal systems hindered effective co-operation.[99] If harmonisation can be achieved, it will undoubtedly make it easier for states to recognise each other's decision. In this sense, approximation can be regarded as a tool to promote mutual recognition.[100] However, mutual recognition does not necessarily require approximation of national laws. It has been noted in this regard that the aim of harmonisation is to eliminate differences, while these differences are recognised under the principle of mutual recognition.[101] The ECJ also noted that nothing in Title VI of the TEU has made the application of the principle of mutual recognition conditional upon harmonisation of criminal laws of Member States.[102] For this reason, the principle of mutual recognition has been regarded as a good alternative to harmonisation of national laws as it does not require substantial alteration of national legislation and systems.[103]

The very first measure to be adopted to promote mutual recognition was that dealing with the EAW.[104] This has replaced the traditional extradition processes among Member States with a view to promoting faster and smoother transfer of suspects and criminals. The quick adoption of this measure came after the September 11 attack in New York in 2001, and the Framework Decision entered into force in August 2002. The EAW is

> a judicial decision issued by a Member State with a view to the arrest and surrender by another Member State of a requested person, for the purposes of conducting a criminal prosecution or executing a custodial sentence or detention order.[105]

As this is adopted through a framework decision, it can be used to facilitate approximation of surrender procedures among Member States.

Some provisions of the EAW should be noted. Article 2(1) provides that

> a European arrest warrant may be issued for acts punishable by the law of the issuing Member State by a custodial sentence or a detention order for a maximum period of at least 12 months or, where a sentence has been passed or a detention order has been made, for sentences of at least four months.

---

[98] Above n 54, 12.

[99] Mitsilegas, above n 42, 1278.

[100] M Fichera, 'The European Arrest Warrant and the Sovereign State: A Marriage of Convenience?' (2009) 15 *European Law Journal* 70, 77.

[101] Ibid, 74.

[102] Case C-303/05 *Advocaten voor de Wereld v Leden van de Ministerraad* [2007] ECR I-3633 para 59.

[103] Mitsilegas, above n 42, 1280.

[104] This instrument replaced the pre-existing instruments on extradition. For a general overview of this instrument, see R Blekxtoon and W van Ballegooij (eds), *Handbook on the European Arrest Warrant* (The Hague, TMC Asser Press, 2005).

[105] Art 1.

The scope of the EAW therefore is wide, and most of the acts which may be termed as organised crime will come under this. Furthermore, a wide range of organised criminal activities give rise to the surrender without verification of the rule of double criminality. They include terrorism, participation in a criminal organisation, drug/human trafficking, money laundering and computer-related crimes.[106] In addition, the EAW sets a general time limit on the surrender of suspects to the maximum of 90 days,[107] which has substantially decreased the amount of time required for surrender. As the simplified procedure is provided for under the Organised Crime Convention, the surrender system in place within the EU is generally in conformity with international standards. The statistical information illustrates the importance of the EAW in facilitating quicker surrender of fugitives. In 2007 a total of 11,000 EAWs were issued by all Member States, up from 6,750 in 2006.[108] The number of persons traced or arrested as a result of the EAW amounted to 4,200 in the same year, compared to 2,040 in 2006.[109]

Another important instrument intended to promote the principle of mutual recognition is the EEW. Similar to the EAW, the EEW simplifies the procedure for gathering and transferring evidence used in criminal proceedings. The EEW is a judicial decision issued by a competent authority of a Member State with a view to obtaining objects, documents and data which are already available in another Member State.[110] Consequently it cannot be issued to obtain new evidence through interviews and bodily examination for the purpose of extracting DNA samples and fingerprints.[111] Nor is it to be used to obtain information through surveillance or interception of communication.[112] Finally, the EEW may be issued only when obtaining evidence necessary to facilitate criminal proceedings or other judicial and administrative proceedings associated directly with criminal proceedings. Therefore it is not designed to facilitate preliminary investigations.[113]

Other instruments on mutual recognition include the Framework Decisions on the Application of the Principle of Mutual Recognition to Financial Penalties,[114] on the Execution in the EU of Orders Freezing Property or Evidence, on the Application of the Principle of Mutual Recognition to Judgments in Criminal Matters Imposing Custodial Sentences or Measures Involving Deprivation of Liberty for the Purpose of their Enforcement in the EU, [115] and on

---

[106] Art 2(2).

[107] Art 17. If one consents to extradition, then that must be carried out within ten days.

[108] European Commission, 'An Extended Report on the Evaluation of the Hague Programme', SEC(2009) 766 final (10 June 2009), 89.

[109] Ibid.

[110] Art 1.

[111] Art 4.

[112] Ibid.

[113] Art 6.

[114] 2005/214/JHA, OJ L76/16 (22 March 2005).

[115] 2008/909/JHA, OJ L327/27 (5 December 2008).

Confiscation of Crime-Related Proceeds, Instrumentalities and Properties.[116] It is therefore evident that the principle of mutual recognition is gradually finding its place in the EU legal order.

The role of specialised bodies becomes crucial in promoting this principle of mutual recognition. As noted in the Tampere Conclusions, these bodies were set up to simplify mutual assistance in criminal matters by allowing law enforcement authorities to contact each other directly instead of going through diplomatic channels.[117] One example is Eurojust. It is specifically mentioned in Article 31 of the TEU as revised by the Treaty of Amsterdam and was finally established with a Council Decision in 2002.[118] It consists of judges, prosecutors or police officers of Member States who jointly form the College of Eurojust,[119] and who are aided by assistants and deputies. Its primary purpose is to co-ordinate mutual legal assistance, including investigation, prosecution and extradition.[120] The Hague Programme noted above has envisaged a bigger role for Eurojust in fighting organised crime.[121] This materialised when the Council adopted another Decision to strengthen its mandate in 2009.[122] This Decision gave it more power[123] and established the On-Call Co-ordination, which operates 24 hours a day, 7 days a week to deal with urgent cases.[124]

Another relevant organisation, as noted above, is the EJN. The 1998 Joint Action which established the EJN was replaced by a Council Decision 2008/976/JHA in 2008.[125] The initial task of the EJN was to facilitate judicial co-operation for serious offences such as organised crime by allowing the competent authorities in charge of international judicial co-operation to provide legal and practical information for the purpose of preparing effective judicial co-operation.[126] The national contact points were also to meet on a regular basis to exchange information.[127] Similar to Eurojust, the 2008 Council Decision expanded the

---

[116] For a discussion on further development of this principle, see Communication from the Commission to the Council and the European Parliament Communication on the mutual recognition of judicial decisions in criminal matters and the strengthening of mutual trust between Member States, Com (2005) 195 final (19 May 2005).

[117] Above n 43, para 46.

[118] Decision 2002/187/JHA on setting up Eurojust with a view to reinforcing the fight against serious crimes, OJ L63/1 (28 February 2002).

[119] As of December 2009, there were 24 career prosecutors and one judge as National Members.

[120] Arts 1 and 2. In accordance with Art 4, Eurojust is competent to deal with the following crimes: computer crime, fraud/corruption, crime against financial interests of the EC, money laundering and participation in criminal organisation. This has been expanded to all crimes which Europol is competent to deal with.

[121] Above n 54, 12–13.

[122] Decision 2009/426/JHA on the strengthening of Eurojust and amending Decision 2002/187/JHA, OJ L138/14 (4 June 2009).

[123] Examples include the powers to receive, transmit and facilitate decisions on judicial co-operation, execute requests for judicial co-operation, authorise controlled delivery in urgent cases, and participate in joint investigation teams. These powers were not previously defined.

[124] Ibid.

[125] Decision 2008/976/JHA on the European Judicial Network, OJ L348/130 (24 December 2008).

[126] Art 4 of the 1998 Joint Action.

[127] Arts 5 and 6.

role of EJN. For instance, the national contact points are to organise training sessions on judicial co-operation in their Member States.[128] The experience gained through the EJN is also to be communicated to the Commission and Council for further discussion and possible legislative changes.[129] This point is important as it demonstrates that the EJN has gained a degree of legitimacy whereas previously its status was not clear.

The EAW provides a more concrete example of how these two bodies may be involved in combating organised crime. The issuing authority can transmit the EAW through the EJN if they so wish,[130] although, as of 2009, this has been relied upon only by Poland.[131] When more than two Member States issue EAWs for the same person, they can seek advice from Eurojust to determine which state should execute it.[132] Finally, Member States are to inform Eurojust if they cannot observe the time limit specified in the EAW.[133] It is worth noting that Eurojust has been instrumental in assisting Member States to execute EAWs. There are examples of Eurojust resolving jurisdictional conflicts between Member States, co-ordinating criminal investigations and the execution of the EAW, and establishing a team dedicated to the execution of the EAW.[134] Similar functions are to be performed in relation to the EEW. Once again, mutual recognition is stipulated in the Organised Crime Convention, and it seems reasonable to conclude that the EU has taken active steps to promote this principle.

It is worth noting that the Council Decisions setting up Eurojust and the EJN touch upon the relationship between these two. The need to maintain a good working relationship based on consultation and complementarity is recognised[135] and some measures are adopted to facilitate this. For instance, the secretariat for the EJN also forms part of the Eurojust secretariat.[136] Article 10 of the Council Decision on the EJN obliges it to provide information on national legislation/legal systems to Eurojust and allow the members from Eurojust to attend meetings. What is evident here is the EU's effort to reduce the instance of duplication of work among various bodies in order to seek effective co-operation and co-ordination against organised crime.

---

[128] Art 4(3) of the 2008 Decision.

[129] Art 5(2).

[130] Art 10.

[131] N Long, 'Implementation of the European Arrest Warrant and Joint Investigation Teams At EU and National Level' (Brussels, European Parliament, 2009) 27.

[132] Art 16.

[133] Art 17. In 2007, 9 Member States reported the breaches of the time limits in accordance with this Art. Eurojust Annual Report 2007.

[134] Long, above n 131, 25–26.

[135] Arts 26 and 10 of the Decisions on Eurojust and the EJN respectively.

[136] Art 26 of the Decision on Eurojust.

6.3.4 The Principle of Availability—Intelligence Exchange

The principle of availability is a new concept and was identified recently in the Hague Programme as a way of facilitating exchange of information and intelligence among law enforcement authorities of Member States.[137] In other words, it may be said that this principle is a vital component of the intelligence-led law enforcement against serious organised crime as reflected in international standards noted in Chapter 3. This principle means that

> a law enforcement officer from one Member State can obtain information in the course of his duties from another Member State, and that a law enforcement agency in another Member State will make that information available for the stated purpose.[138]

Where mutual recognition is mainly concerned with judicial decisions, the principle of availability is more relevant for police co-operation in criminal matters. However, some rightly point out that the principle of availability is interconnected with mutual recognition from a practical point of view because the use of intelligence obtained from a Member State by another means that the latter has to trust or recognise the reliability of such intelligence.[139] What is evident, then, is that mutual recognition is spilling over to other areas of co-operation in criminal matters.

Various instruments have been adopted to promote this principle. In 2006 the Council adopted a Framework Decision on the Exchange of Information.[140] Under this, intelligence can be requested for the purpose of detection, prevention and investigation of an offence,[141] and exchange of intelligence is conducted directly by the law enforcement authorities of Member States. Two years later, on the initiative of the parties to the Convention on the Stepping Up of Cross-Border Cooperation, Particularly in Combating Terrorism, Cross-Border Crime and Illegal Migration 2005,[142] the Council adopted a decision to incorporate this treaty into the EU legal framework.[143] This has enabled law enforcement

---

[137] Above n 54, 6.

[138] Ibid, 7; Extended Report, above n 108, 40.

[139] M Fletcher, R. Lööf and B Gilmore, *EU Criminal Law and Justice* (Cheltenham, Edward Elgar Publishing, 2008) 94.

[140] Framework Decision 2006/960/JHA of 18 December 2006 on simplifying the exchange of information and intelligence between law enforcement authorities of the Member States of the European Union, OJ L386/89 (29 December 2006). This was proposed by Sweden. See Initiative of the Kingdom of Sweden with a view to adopting a Framework Decision on simplifying the exchange of information and intelligence between law enforcement authorities of the Member States of the European Union, in particular as regards serious offences including terrorist acts, OJ C281/5 (18 November 2004).

[141] Art 5.

[142] Council of European Union, CRIMORG 65, ENFOPOL 85, MIGR 30 (7 July 2005). They were Austria, Belgium, France, Germany, Luxemburg, the Netherlands and Spain.

[143] Decision 2008/615/JHA on the stepping up of cross-border cooperation, particularly in combating terrorism and cross-border crime, OJ L210/1 (6 August 2008); Decision 2008/616/JHA on the implementation of Decision 2008/615/JHA on the stepping up of cross-border cooperation, particularly in combating terrorism and cross-border, OJ L210/12 (8 August 2008). In 2008, a total of €7.8 million was allocated for this. Extended Report, above n 108, 57.

authorities to gain access to decentralised DNA, fingerprint and vehicle registration databases. In relation to fingerprints, the Commission drew up a proposal for a common centralised database known as the Criminal Automated Fingerprint Identification System.[144] This measure has been accompanied by a Decision to allow enforcement authorities to access the Visa Information System,[145] a Directive for retention of data[146] and a Framework Decision on Exchange of Information from Criminal Records.[147] It has been noted that the EU is moving towards an integration of intelligence/information systems to allow access to more law enforcement agencies across the EU territories.[148]

In addition to bodies such as Eurojust and the EJN, Europol has long played an important role in facilitating information exchange. This is done, among others, through the Europol Information System, the European Knowledge Management Centre and the Schengen Information System. According to recent statistics, over 260,000 information exchange activities were conducted in 2007.[149] This may be contrasted with the 35,366 information exchanges that took place in 2000.[150] Some of the intelligence gathered is also made available to the public, as Europol publishes an EU Organised Crime Threat Assessment on an annual basis. Europol has seen some transformations in recent times in line with the institutional development of other relevant bodies, such as Eurojust and the EJN. Numerous amendments have been made to the original Europol Convention, and the length of ratification process generally means that it has taken some time for these amendments to come into force.[151] In order to simplify the legal framework, the Council adopted its Decision in April 2009.[152] Additional tasks stipulated under the Decision include requesting Member States to initiate or co-ordinate investigations, providing intelligence and analytical support to Member States,[153] and participation in joint investigation teams.[154] Europol may also establish co-operative relations with other EU bodies, including Eurojust,

---

[144] Ibid, 4.

[145] Regulation (EC) No 380/2008 of 18 April 2008 amending Regulation (EC) No 1030/2002 laying down a uniform format for residence permits for third-country nationals, OJ L115/1 29 (April 2008).

[146] Directive 2006/24/EC on the retention of data generated or processed in connection with the provision of publicly available electronic communications services or of public communications networks and amending Directive 2002/58/EC, OJ L105/54 (13 April 2006).

[147] Framework Decision 2009/315/JHA on the organisation and content of the exchange of information extracted from the criminal record between Member States, OJ L93/23 (7 April 2009).

[148] T Mathieson, 'Lex Vigilatoria—Towards a Control System without a State?' in S Armstrong and L McAra (eds), *Perspectives on Punishment: The Contours of Control* (Oxford, Oxford University Press, 2006) 119–31.

[149] Above n 27, 32.

[150] Ibid, 33.

[151] Proposal for a Council Decision establishing the European Police Office (Europol), COM(2006) 817 final (20 December 2006).

[152] Decision 2009/371/JHA establishing the European Police Office (Europol), OJ L121/37 (15 May 2009).

[153] Art 5.

[154] Art 6.

the European Anti-Fraud Office and the European Central Bank,[155] and conclude agreements on co-operation with non-Member States and third-party organisations such as Interpol.[156] It should be emphasised that Europol is a co-ordinating body and therefore is prevented from taking coercive measures on its own initiatives.

6.3.5 Analysis of Measures under the TEU as Revised by the Treaty of Amsterdam

6.3.5.1 Application of Approximation, Mutual Recognition and the Principle of Availability

It should be recognised that the EU has come a long way in promoting effective action against organised crime. The measures adopted since the Treaty of Amsterdam have improved the problems encountered by the original TEU, as the legal nature of the instruments is clearer. States have become more willing to adopt framework decisions to seek a degree of harmonisation of substantive and procedural criminal law and to recognise each other's decisions to facilitate cross-border co-operation. The principle of availability, while being a new concept which requires further development for an in-depth analysis, is also advantageous for intelligence-led law enforcement. This has become a necessary response in line with the level of sophistication displayed by organised criminal groups. All of this means that measures under the TEU as revised by the Treaty of Amsterdam generally meet the standards set by the Organised Crime Convention.

It is also evident that implementation of approximation, mutual recognition and the principle of availability is difficult in practice, and state sovereignty has much to do with this problem. In relation to approximation, the Framework Decision on Child Pornography provides for the definition of this offence.[157] Nevertheless, it was reported that Czech Republic, Estonia, Latvia, Lithuania, Luxembourg, Poland, Spain and Sweden have not incorporated it into their domestic legislation.[158] Another related point is that Member States do not always comply with deadlines for implementation and reporting. In relation to corruption, the relevant Framework Decision set an implementation deadline of 22 July 2005,[159] but only Finland and the Netherlands met this.[160] Implemen-

---

[155] Art 22. However, the EJN is no specifically mentioned under this Art.

[156] Art 23.

[157] Art 1.

[158] Report from the Commission Based on Art 12 of the Council Framework Decision of 22 December 2003 on combating the sexual exploitation of children and child pornography, COM(2007) 716 final (16 November 2007).

[159] Art 9.

[160] Report from the Commission to the Council based on Article 9 of the Council Framework Decision 2003/568/JHA of 22 July 2003 on combating corruption in the private sector, COM(2007)

tation of obligations is clearly a first step towards approximation and therefore non-implementation prevents the EU from achieving this aim. Unfortunately there is no strong enforcement mechanism against non-compliance under the third pillar, unlike the first pillar, where there is a procedure to address infringement.[161] Given this track record of Member States, it is likely that the Framework Decision on Organised Crime will experience delays in implementation or even non-implementation.

Some inconsistencies can also be recognised in relation to imposition of penalties against organised crime. The wording of some framework decisions on penalties is vague in that they use the phrase 'effective, proportionate and dissuasive criminal penalties' and do not provided for the minimum or maximum penalties to be imposed, except for aggravating circumstances.[162] Other framework decisions stipulate the minimum/maximum sentences but still allow some leeway. In this regard, the Framework Decision on Organised Crime provides for a maximum of at least 2–5 years' imprisonment, while 1–3 years' imprisonment is listed under the one on drug trafficking.[163] In addition to the possible variations which can result from these instruments, a question may be raised whether or not some of these penalties are proportionate or dissuasive enough. It is worth noting that the Framework Decision on Sexual Exploitation of Children and Child Pornography provides for a maximum of at least 1–3 years' imprisonment.[164] Given that these offences raise serious human rights concerns, many would rightly argue that these penalties are not appropriate.

State practice reflects these confusions created by the various framework decisions. In Austria, drug trafficking attracts a maximum of five years' imprisonment,[165] whereas five years is regarded as the minimum for the same offence in Germany.[166] Sales and distribution of child pornography carries a maximum of two years' imprisonment in Finland,[167] while the Child Trafficking and Pornography Act 1998 of the Republic of Ireland provides for one year's imprisonment for the same offence.[168] An added complication in relation to child sex offences is the age of sexual consent. This is regarded as 13 in Spain, whereas it is 16 for states including Belgium, Finland, Germany, Latvia and

---

328 final (18 June 2007). The same is true for the Framework Decision on Trafficking, where only four states (France, Finland, Cyprus and Austria) responded. Report from the Commission to the Council and the European Parliament Based on Article 10 of the Council Framework Decision of 19 July 2002 on combating trafficking in human beings, COM(2006) 187 final (2 May 2006). As to the Framework Decision on Sexual Exploitation of Sexual Exploitation of Children and Child Pornography, only Austria and Belgium observed the deadline. Above n 158.

[161] L Marin, 'The European Arrest Warrant in the Italian Republic' (2008) 4 *European Constitutional Law Review* 251, 257.

[162] They include the Framework Decisions on Human Trafficking, Euro Counterfeiting, and Facilitation Unauthorised Entry and Residence.

[163] Art 3 and Art 4 respectively.

[164] Art 5.

[165] S 12 of Narcotic Drugs Act 1951 as amended.

[166] S 30a of the Act to Regulate the Traffic in Narcotics 1981 as amended.

[167] S 18 of the Finnish Criminal Code.

[168] S 5.

Luxembourg.[169] This poses a problem for offences such as child pornography as the Framework Decision provides for the exclusion of criminal liability for child pornography involving children who have reached the age of sexual consent.[170] All of these examples vividly illustrate the difficulty posed by the principle of state sovereignty, even in the context of the EU, where Member States are more willing to facilitate active co-operation and co-ordination.

Some difficulties are also indentified with mutual recognition. The EAW is a case in point. The number of EAWs issued since the coming into force of the Framework Decision demonstrates that Member States are increasingly willing to recognise the decisions made by other Member States. However, it is not entirely accurate to say that judicial authorities trust the judgments of their counterparts in other Member States. Although the EAW abolishes the rule of double criminality for offences stipulated under Article 2(2) of the Framework Decision, various states, including Belgium, Germany, Italy, Poland, Slovenia and the UK, still rely on this principle in making their decisions under certain circumstances.[171] This means, first, that it is difficult to achieve harmonisation or approximation among Member States. Second, the refusal of extradition on the ground of double criminality, or on other grounds for that matter, effectively prevents the courts of some Member States from recognising the judicial decisions made by others.

This can be illustrated more clearly by looking at the protection of human right as the ground for refusal to execute the EAW. The Extradition Act 2003 of the UK, as noted in Chapter 5, requires judges to consider whether extradition to Member States breaches the Convention rights by virtue of the Human Rights Act 1998. A provision such as this is important as it serves as an additional safeguard. It goes further than the Framework Decision as the protection of human rights is not included in the mandatory or optional grounds for refusal under the EAW. A similar arrangement also exists in Italy.[172] From the point of view of mutual recognition, this creates situations where courts in requested states are sometimes forced to analyse whether or not the requesting states are in conformity with the human rights obligations, rather than accepting that they are in compliance. It might be recalled in this regard that in *Lisowski v Poland* the High Court of the UK held that the appellant would not receive a fair trial if returned to Poland.[173] Italy and Germany also support the 'counter-limits doctrine', which provides that 'Community acts that infringe fundamental rights or other fundamental values are not applicable in the domestic legal order and the Constitutional Court can sanction the violation of such constitutional

---

[169] Above n 158.

[170] Art 3.

[171] Long, above n 131, 21.

[172] Act No 69 Implementing the Framework Decision, *Gazzetta Officiale* [2005] No 98, 29 April 2005. For an analysis of this Act, see Marin, above n 161.

[173] Above ch 5 n 472. For other issues making the execution of EAW difficult in the UK, see N Padfield, 'The Implementation of European Arrest Warrant in England and Wales' (2007) 3 *European Constitutional Law Review* 253

limits'.[174] All of these can make it difficult to promote mutual recognition. It was noted above that mutual recognition is not conditional upon approximation of national laws and systems. However, these examples show that mutual recognition is difficult to achieve in practice precisely because of the constitutional and other differences in Member States. Therefore, arguably the effective implementation of mutual recognition depends upon the degree to which approximation of national criminal laws and procedures can be achieved.

As to the principle of availability, the reluctance of Member States to share intelligence is problematic. It was noted that not all Member States pass on information to specialised bodies such as Eurojust.[175] Non-implementation of relevant instruments has also been recognised. This applies to the Directive on data retention under which certain data can be made available to police and judicial authorities for the purpose of the prevention, investigation, detection and prosecution of serious crime. As of 2009, four Member States have not implemented this Directive and 18 Member States have decided to delay implementation in relation to internet access, internet telephony and e-mail.[176] Such unwillingness of Member States is understandable given the sensitive nature of intelligence relating to serious and organised crime, including terrorism. It also shows that sufficient mutual trust has not been developed as yet in this area. This is further complicated by a lack of ability for effective intelligence gathering and transmission in some Member States. In the area of Passenger Name Records (PNR), for instance, only a handful of Member States are said to have the fully functioning system.[177]

Another serious issue arising from the principle of availability is data protection and human rights of individuals. This can be seen in the regime of PNR. In the aftermath of the September 11 attack, the US government required airlines to pass on information on passengers prior to their arrival.[178] This prompted the EC/EU to negotiate and conclude various agreements with the US government, and eventually led to the adoption of a Council Decision[179] and a Commission Decision.[180] In response, the European Parliament brought the Commission and

---

[174] Marin, above n 161, 257. The constitutionality and legitimacy of the EAW were also questioned previously in states such as Cyprus, Germany and Poland, and this forced the respective governments to implement constitutional changes. Long, above n 131, 16–19.

[175] Communication from the Commission to the Council and the European Parliament on the role of Eurojust and the European Judicial Network in the fight against organised crime and terrorism in the European Union, COM(2007) 644 final (23 October 2007) 3.

[176] Extended Report, above n 108, 43

[177] House of Lords European Union Committee, 'The Passenger Name Record Framework Decision' (15th Report of Session 2007–08), paras 2–3. The Commission drafted a proposal on this, but has not been adopted as yet. Proposal for a Council Framework Decision on the use of Passenger Name Record (PNR) for law enforcement purposes, COM(2007) 654 final (6 November 2007).

[178] V Mitsilegas, *EU Criminal Law* (Oxford, Hart Publishing, 2009) 269.

[179] Decision 2004/496/EC on the conclusion of an Agreement between the European Community and the United States of America on the processing and transfer of PNR data by Air Carriers to the United States Department of Homeland Security, Bureau of Customs and Border Protection, OJ L183/83 (20 May 2004).

[180] Decision 2004/535/EC on the adequate protection of personal data contained in the Passenger

the Council before the ECJ on the grounds, among others, that such measures breach Article 8 of the ECHR and asked for annulment of these decisions.[181] While the ECJ annulled these decisions on grounds other than human rights, the opinion of the Advocate-General on these cases shed some light on the position of the EU. In analysing the PNR's purpose, the Advocate-General noted that the Council and the Commission had a wide margin of appreciation.[182] In weighing the protection of right to privacy on the one hand and the fight against terrorism and serious crimes on the other, the Advocate-General concluded that the PNR did not breach the right to privacy as there were enough safeguards on data protection in place.[183] It is submitted here that the Advocate-General put too much faith in the safeguards without considering the extent to which such measures would actually be observed and implemented. The track record of the US on torture, degrading treatments and extraordinary rendition arguably cast some doubt on its willingness to observe them. In any event, after the annulment of the Decisions, the EU decided to negotiate an interim agreement. This became applicable in October 2006 and expired at the end of July 2007.[184] A long-term PNR agreement[185] was later signed with the US in July 2007.

Another issue in relation to intelligence collection and storage is discrimination. In *Huber v Federal Republic of Germany*,[186] an Austrian national argued that entry of his personal data in the German centralised register for the purpose of fighting crime was discriminatory as this was not done for German nationals. In examining the compatibility of the German measure with Article 12 of the Treaty on European Community, which prohibits discrimination on grounds of nationality, the ECJ held that:

> [A]s regards a Member State, the situation of its nationals cannot, as regards the objective of fighting crime, be different from that of Union citizens who are not nationals of that Member State and who are resident in its territory . . . Therefore, the difference in treatment between those nationals and those Union citizens which arises by virtue of the systematic processing of personal data relating only to Union

Name Record of air passengers transferred to the United States' Bureau of Customs and Border Protection, OJ L235/11 (6 July 2004).

[181] Cases C-317/04 and C-318/04 *European Parliament v Council of the European Union and Commission of the European Community* [2006] ECR I-4721.

[182] Opinion of the Advocate-General, para 231.

[183] Ibid, para 243.

[184] Agreement between the European Union and the United States of America on the processing and transfer of Passenger Name Record (PNR) data by air carriers to the United States Department of Homeland Security, OJ L298/29 (27 October 2006).

[185] Agreement between the European Union and the United States of America on the processing and transfer of Passenger Name Record (PNR) data by air carriers to the United States Department of Homeland Security (DHS) (2007 PNR Agreement), OJ L204/18 (4 August 2007). This will last until 2014. Similar agreements have been concluded with Canada and Australia. See Agreement between the European Community and the Government of Canada on the processing of Advance Passenger Information and Passenger Name Record data, OJ L82/15 (21 March 2006); Agreement between the European Union and Australia on the processing and transfer of European Union-sourced Passenger Name Record (PNR) data by air carriers to the Australian customs service, OJ L213/49 (8 August 2008).

[186] Case C-524/06 [2008] ECR I-0000.

citizens who are not nationals of the Member State concerned for the purposes of fighting crime constitutes discrimination.[187]

While this decision should be welcomed, it only relates to EU citizens (ie citizens of Member States) and does not apply to third-country nationals. The ECJ previously considered that different treatment of non-EU citizens is permissible.[188] None of the Member States have signed or ratified the Migrant Workers' Convention as yet, suggesting that they will continue to apply different treatment to aliens.[189] This might be regarded as a violation of human rights under certain circumstances. While states can impose conditions in areas of entry, movement and employment, for instance, aliens are entitled to the same rights as citizens, including the rights to privacy, once they are allowed entry.[190] Therefore, while taking information from aliens upon entry might be justified, it might not be for those who are lawfully residing in a Member State.

Finally, a question may be raised on the use of data obtained in breach of a right to privacy in criminal proceedings. The current jurisprudence under the ECHR applicable to all Member States of the EU points to a conclusion that the use of such evidence does not necessarily lead to a breach of the right to a fair trial[191] and that the issue of admissibility of evidence should be left to national authorities.[192] An added complication is the data obtained by private individuals. In terms of its use in criminal proceedings, the European Court held that Article 8 is relevant if there is a degree of involvement by the public authorities.[193] As such, most acts of intelligence gathering done by private individuals may be regarded as a breach of Article 8, because it is likely that they are assisted or instructed by the law enforcement authorities. Yet there are cases where the data is obtained without the involvement of public authorities. The information obtained by airline staff at a check-in counter acting on their own initiative is one example. Under such circumstances the extent to which Article 8 can be engaged remains unclear.

It is important to recognise that the Council recently adopted a Framework Decision on Protection of Personal Data in the Framework of Police and Judicial Co-operation in Criminal Matters.[194] It sets out a list of measures to be taken to

---

[187] Paras 79 and 80.

[188] See, eg Case C-230/97 *Criminal Proceedings against Ibiyinka Awoyemi* [1998] ECR I-6781, para 29.

[189] For an analysis of the Migrant Workers' Convention, see E MacDonald and R Cholewinski, *The Migrant Workers' Convention in Europe* (Paris, UNESCO, 2007).

[190] General Comment No 15, above ch 3 n 105, paras 6 and 7.

[191] See, eg *Schenk v Switzerland* (1988) 13 *EHRR* 242. A violation of Art 6 depends on 'whether the evidence could be contradicted in trial, whether it was the only evidence on which a conviction was based, or whether, because of the way the evidence was collected, it should be considered to violate the right not to contribute to one's own incrimination'. The EU Network of Independent Experts on Fundamental Rights, 'Opinion on the Status of Illegally Obtained Evidence in Criminal Procedures in the Member States of the European Union' (30 November 2003), 6.

[192] Ibid, para 45.

[193] *MM v The Netherlands*, Application No 39339/98 (2003).

[194] 2008/977/JHA, OJ L350/60 (30 December 2008).

protect the human rights of those concerned. For instance, Member States are to observe the principles of lawfulness, proportionality and purpose.[195] The Framework Decision also obliges them to inform a person from whom personal data is extracted and to grant them access to such data.[196] The person concerned also has a right to compensation and judicial remedies in case of unlawful processing.[197] However, there are a number of problems with this system. To begin with, the Framework Decision is without prejudice to the 'essential national security interests and specific intelligence activities in the field of national security'.[198] On this basis, the access to personal data by the person concerned can be restricted.[199] The Framework Decision also may not apply to commitments or obligations previously established under bilateral or multilateral agreements.[200] Therefore various guaranteed rights may not be relied upon for arrangements such as the PNR with the US. Furthermore, the vague concept of 'effective, proportionate and dissuasive' penalties in the case of breach is once again also provided for.[201] It is worth noting in this regard that under the Data Protection Act 1998 of the UK an offence of illegally obtaining information is punished with a fine. The question may be asked whether this punishment is effective or dissuasive. Finally, given the track record of Member States for delay and non-implementation noted earlier, there is no guarantee that the Framework Decision will be implemented properly and promptly.

6.3.5.2   Other Issues

In addition to various difficulties relating to approximation, mutual recognition and the principle of availability, there are other, wider issues of concern applicable to the EU action against organised crime in general. For instance, there is a lack of due regard to the rights of suspects and defendants. Promoting a common European rule on the rights of suspects is important, because otherwise their treatment can vary depending on where they are arrested, prosecuted and punished. Further, heterogeneity in criminal laws and procedures 'leads to a lack of transparency, reduces access to justice and affects legal certainty'.[202] The European Commission noted in this regard that it was 'desirable for the Member States to confirm a standard set of procedural safeguards for suspects and defendants'.[203] As a result, it proposed a framework decision on this issue in

---

[195] Art 3.
[196] Arts 16 and 17.
[197] Arts 19 and 20.
[198] Art 1(4).
[199] Art 17.
[200] Art 26.
[201] Art 24.
[202] Weyembergh, above n 60, 167.
[203] Green Paper from the Commission: Procedural Safeguards for Suspects and Defendants in Criminal Proceedings Throughout the European Union, COM(2003) 75 final (19 February 2003), 9.

2004.[204] Aside from protection and promotion of human rights, the framework decision was regarded as necessary in order to further promote the principle of mutual recognition. As the Commission succinctly puts it:

> Mutual recognition can only operate effectively in a spirit of confidence, whereby not only the judicial authorities, but all actors in the criminal process see decisions of the judicial authorities of other Member States as equivalent to their own and do not call in question their judicial capacity and respect for fair trial rights.

No actual framework decision has been accepted to date and various instruments adopted under the TEU as revised by the Treaty of Amsterdam do not make reference to the rights of suspects or defendants.[205] In *Pupino*, noted above, it was held that the third-pillar measures had to be interpreted in light of human rights principles, including the jurisprudence of the European Court of Human Rights.[206] However, the lack of a legally binding instrument gives the impression that the rights of the defendants are secondary to their prosecution and punishment. As such, it can be concluded that the EU approach mirrors the Organised Crime Convention, which also lacks due regard to the rights of defendants, as noted elsewhere in this book.

An additional challenged is posed by enlargement. The growth of criminal activities accelerated after the fall of the Soviet Union as criminals took advantage of the weak economic, political and criminal justice systems of the newly independent states.[207] This was exacerbated by the opening of borders, and the resultant increased flow of people, goods and capital. This poses a particular challenge for the EU and its Member States, because accession states such as Poland, the Czech Republic and Hungary serve as transit points for a wide variety of criminal activities, such as drug and human trafficking, originating beyond EU territory. As more states join the EU in the future, the expansion of EU borders will exacerbate the problem. As noted in Chapter 5, candidate states[208] as well as potential candidates[209] have to undergo a series of transformations to ensure that their standards and capabilities are adequate to deal with freedom, security and justice. Nevertheless, variations in legal and political developments among these states mean that their capabilities to deal with organised crime are bound to be different. Therefore the EU must be able to address this sufficiently so that these new states are suitably equipped and trained.

Finally, Member States of the EU are key destinations for illicit goods and services, and the demand for them is high. As noted throughout this book, a

---

[204] Proposal for a Council Framework Decision on certain procedural rights in criminal proceedings throughout the European Union, COM(2004) 328 final (28 April 2004).

[205] They include the Framework Decisions on Drug Trafficking, Human Trafficking, Counterfeiting of Euro, and Sexual Exploitation of Children and Child Pornography.

[206] Above n 66, paras 58–60.

[207] M Nozina, 'Organized Crime in the New EU states of East Central Europe' in K Henderson (ed), *The Area of Freedom, Security and Justice in the Enlarged Europe* (Basingstoke, Palgrave McMillan, 2005) 29.

[208] Croatia, the former Yugoslav Republic of Macedonia and Turkey.

[209] Albania, Bosnia Herzegovina, Kosovo, Montenegro, Serbia and Iceland.

comprehensive strategy to prevent and suppress organised crime must include measures to address the dynamics of supply and demand. The EU has not been instrumental in this regard. In relation to drug problems, the Tampere Conclusions highlighted the need for a comprehensive strategy.[210] In line with this, the EU Drug Strategy 2000–2004 adopted by the Council recognised the need to address the demand for drugs.[211] The EU subsequently adopted a number of measures to address this.[212] While the Commission noted that the EU and Member States have made some progress on this front, particularly through information campaigns,[213] the efficacy of these measures is not corroborated by solid evidence.[214] Nor has the EU implemented effective measures regarding demand for other goods and services. The Framework Decisions on Trafficking of Human Beings, on Sexual Exploitation of Children and Child Pornography, and on Organised Crime, noted above, fail to consider this.[215] While the Hague Programme touches upon crime prevention,[216] there is no mention of the demand reduction within this. Nor does the latest evaluation by the Commission on the Hague Programme[217] refer to the supply and demand dynamics. In conclusion, the criminal justice response has been the main drive behind the current EU action against organised crime under the TEU as revised by the Treaty of Amsterdam, and the EU and Member States have so far failed to address wider issues, such as the rights of defendants and the demand for illicit goods and services.

---

[210] Above n 43, para 50.

[211] 12555/2/99 CORDROGUE 64 REV 2 (1 December 1999). This was followed by the EU Drug Strategy 2005–2012, 15074/04 CORDROGUE 77 (22 November 2004).

[212] See, eg New Public Health Programme (2003–2008) which funded drug prevention projects, OJ L271/1 (9 October 2002). The EU also established the European Monitoring Centre for Drugs and Drug Addiction (EMCDDA), whose main task is to provide information to the EU and its Member States.

[213] Communication from the Commission to the Council and the European Parliament on the results of the final evaluation of the EU Drugs Strategy and Action Plan on Drugs (2000–2004), COM(2004) 707 final (22 October 2004).

[214] EMCDDA, 'The State of the Drugs Problem in Europe: Annual Report 2009', 26.

[215] Proposals to replace the Framework Decisions on Trafficking and on Sexual Exploitation of Children are currently under consideration, and they do provide for provisions to reduce the demand. This in itself is a clear recognition that the current legal frameworks are not sufficient.

[216] Above n 54, point 2.6.

[217] Communication from the Commission to the Council, the European Parliament, the European Economic and Social Committee, and the Committee of the Regions, Justice, Security and Freedom in Europe since 2005: An Evaluation of the Hague Programme and Action Plan, COM(2009) 263 final (10 June 2009).

6.4 The Future of the EU Action against Organised Crime in Light of the Lisbon Treaty

The Treaty of Lisbon entered into force on 1 December 2009. It was drafted in response to the rejection of the European Constitution in 2007. It amends the TEU and the Treaty establishing the European Community. Specifically, the European Community was replaced by the EU, thereby maintaining a single legal personality.[218] This means that the EU has taken over all the competence entrusted to the Community previously, effectively abolishing the three-pillar structure. This is significant because previously the competence of the EU differed between the three pillars, the second and the third being the weaker. The result is that legal instruments to be adopted are the same in all areas. They include Regulations, with direct effect; Directives, which are similar to the Framework Decisions under the previous TEU; Decisions; and Recommendations, without legal effect.[219] However, the legal effects of the instruments adopted before the coming into force of the Lisbon Treaty will be preserved until they are repealed, annulled or amended.[220]

The TFEU made some institutional changes. It has created an 'ordinary legislative procedure' under which instruments are adopted jointly by the European Parliament and the Council, on proposal from the Commission.[221] There is also a special procedure which only requires participation by either the European Parliament or the Council.[222] Another key procedural change is that decisions relating to judicial co-operation in criminal matters, Eurojust, Europol and non-operational police co-operation are to be adopted by qualifying majority votes as opposed to the previous requirement for unanimous voting.[223] This undoubtedly makes it easier to adopt measures in relation to the area of freedom, security and justice, including organised crime, as the consent of every single Member States is no longer required. Finally, the role of the ECJ is strengthened as it has competence to rule on infringement proceedings,[224] a power not recognised previously. All of these institutional changes have the potential to promote effective and comprehensive action against organised crime.

The relevant part of the TFEU is Title V (Area of Freedom, Security and Justice). Both mutual recognition and approximation have a more defined status. Article 82, for instance, makes it clear that judicial co-operation in criminal

---

[218] With this, the Treaty establishing the European Community became the Treaty on the Functioning of the European Union (TFEU), while the TEU keeps its name. OJ C115/1 (9 May 2008).

[219] Art 288 of the TFEU.

[220] Art 9 of the Protocol No 36 on Transitional Provisions.

[221] Art 289.

[222] Ibid.

[223] Art 16(4) of the TEU. It is defined as 'at least 55 % of the members of the Council, comprising at least fifteen of them and representing Member States comprising at least 65 % of the population of the Union'. This will take effect from 1st November 2014.

[224] Arts 258–60 of the TFEU.

matters 'shall be based on the principle of mutual recognition of judgments and judicial decisions'.[225] Articles 82 and 83 further provide that mutual admissibility of evidence, the rights of individuals in criminal procedure, the rights of victims, the definitions of criminal offences and sanctions (which include organised crime), and the approximation of nationals laws shall be implemented by means of directives in order to establish minimum rules. Here the Treaty recognises that a degree of approximation may be necessary in implementing the principle of mutual recognition, contrary to what others have argued previously. It is also important to note that the rights of defendants and victims are specifically mentioned, allowing the EU to move beyond the criminal justice approach. This is further strengthened by the incorporation of the Charter of Fundamental Rights of the EU into the EU legal framework.[226] This means that Member States and the EU institutions are bound by it, and the ECJ can force them to modify their behaviour when the Charter's provisions are violated.[227] Finally, in the area of police co-operation, the Council is to establish measures for operational co-operation among Member States under a special procedure.[228]

The importance of specialised bodies to facilitate co-operation is also recognised. The European Parliament and the Council may, by means of regulations, confer a power on Eurojust to initiate criminal investigations or propose the initiation of prosecutions to be conducted by national authorities.[229] These two institutions are also to define the functions of Europol through regulations, which include co-ordination of investigative or operational actions conducted by Member States.[230] What is notable here is that the involvement of national parliaments is provided for in evaluating the activities of Eurojust and Europol. This is a positive feature as it promotes transparency. Another significant development is the establishment of the European Public Prosecutor to combat crimes affecting the financial interests of the EU.[231] Organised crime undoubtedly comes under this. The Public Prosecutor will perform the functions of a prosecutor in the competent courts of Member States and will be responsible for investigating, prosecuting and bringing to justice perpetrators and accomplices.[232] This goes further than the previous arrangement and will contribute to the creation of a common European criminal procedure and system. However, the prospect of

---

[225] This wording is not found in Art 31 of the previous TEU.

[226] Art 6 of the TEU. It should be noted that the Czech Republic, Poland and the UK opted out of the various aspects of this Charter. See Protocol No 30 on the Application of the Charter of Fundamental Rights of the European Union to Poland and to the United Kingdom, and Declaration made by the Czech Republic on the Charter of Fundamental Rights of the European Union.

[227] The relevant provisions for the purpose of this book include Art 4 (prohibition of torture), Art 6 (right to liberty and security) and Chapter VI, which touches upon the rights of defendants.

[228] Art 87 of the TFEU.

[229] Art 85.

[230] Art 88.

[231] Art 86. This is done through a special procedure with the unanimous act of the Council with the consent from the European Parliament. The original proposal was submitted by the Commission in 2000. Communication from the Commission: The criminal protection of the Community's financial interests: a European Prosecutor, COM(2000) 608 final (29 September 2000).

[232] Art 86(2).

the actual establishment of the office is not clear. As the wording 'may establish' suggests, it is an option rather than a legally binding obligation, and, given that the European Public Prosecutor can take away many powers from the competent authorities of Member States, opposition to the measure is likely to be very strong.

On the face of it, all of these changes are generally positive. The ability to adopt instruments with direct effect means that they can be enforced or challenged directly before national courts and tribunals. The active role of the European Parliament in decision-making means that it can not only promote transparency, but also reflect the voices of the EU citizens who elect Members of the European Parliament on a regular basis. The increased power of the ECJ, particularly in relation to infringement proceedings, can ensure that non-compliance will be dealt with more rigorously than before. Consequently it can be argued that democratic accountability is enhanced. This improves the current problem of democratic deficit in the decision-making process on the action against transnational organised crime.[233]

However, the extent to which the new arrangements will lead to the adoption of effective and comprehensive response to organised crime is not yet clear, mainly because of the preservation of the principle of state sovereignty. Article 72 of the TFEU in this regards provides that '[t]his Title shall not affect the exercise of the responsibilities incumbent upon Member States with regard to the maintenance of law and order and the safeguarding of internal security'. It should also be noted that both the EU and Member States have shared competence in this area.[234] This is different for the areas such as customs union, competition, and common commercial policy,[235] where the EU has 'exclusive competence'.[236] To give a more concrete example, Article 76 provides that instruments relating to judicial and police co-operation in criminal matters are proposed by the Commission or on the initiative of a quarter of Member States. Therefore, a degree of political interference by Member States will be inevitable. In addition, the key instruments, Regulations, are not provided for under judicial and police co-operation between Member States, although they may be adopted to define the mandates of specialised bodies. Furthermore, the infringement proceedings may become a double-edged sword in that Member States or the EU institutions may not adopt legal instruments with clear and detailed obligations in order to avoid unfavourable ruling by the ECJ. This can affect the development of effective action against organised crime. Finally, opt-outs have been secured by some Member States, including the UK, Ireland and Denmark,[237] in the

---

[233] F Calderoni, 'A Definition that Could not Work: the EU Framework Decision on the Fight against Organised Crime' (2008) 16 *European Journal of Crime, Criminal Law and Criminal Justice* 265, 268.

[234] Art 4 of the TFEU.

[235] Art 3.

[236] This means that only the EU may legislate and adopt legally binding acts.

[237] See, eg Protocol 19 on the Schengen Acquis Integrated into the Framework of the European Union and Protocol No 22 on the Position of Denmark.

area of freedom, security and justice. All of these features may hamper effective co-operation and co-ordination between Member States and the European institutions and bodies. In summary, the Lisbon Treaty has undoubtedly brought about positive change, particularly in relation to the institutional structure of the EU, but the principle of state sovereignty may continue to have a negative impact on the future of the EU action against organised crime.

6.5   Conclusions

This chapter examined EU action against organised crime as an example of a regional response. It explored the past, present and future action, and the main conclusion reached is that, although the EU and its Member States have been proactive in promoting a variety of measures against organised crime, there is still scope for improvement. It is also evident that the criminal justice response has been the main style of EU action against organised crime. It is therefore similar to the approach promoted by TCL as represented by the Organised Crime Convention. The EU case study also strengthens the argument made in relation to the national case studies in Chapter 5 that such an approach on its own does not lead to an effective and comprehensive action against organised crime. This will change to some extent thanks to the Lisbon Treaty, as issues such as the rights of defendants and victims are specifically provided for. Nevertheless, it is not clear whether the EU will be able to address other key issues, such as the demand for illicit goods and services, which serves as the pull factor for organised crime. Article 84 of the TFEU touches upon crime prevention and it will be interesting to see how it will be interpreted by the EU institutions and Member States to address wider issues.

It is also clear that even in the EU the principle of state sovereignty has hindered the implementation of effective action against organised crime. This mirrors the status of organised crime in international law explored earlier in the book, and the conclusion must be that it will take some time for organised crime to have a stronger place in the European legal order. Despite this, it is clear that the EU developments are far more progressive, as similar legal/institutional arrangements and political commitment do not exist in other regions of the world. While this perhaps has much to do with the EU's financial and political powers compared to other regional organisations, other regions still have much to learn from the EU in developing an effective strategy to tackle organised crime by identifying good practices as well as areas of concern.

The lack of similar arrangements in other regions also demonstrates the existence of regional variations in the responses to organised crime. One question that may be asked is whether it is preferable to promote a regional rather than an international response to transnational organised crime. The Organised Crime Convention undoubtedly aims to promote a concerted effort by the international community as a whole. However, the varied political, economic, social, cultural and legal traditions globally make this difficult to achieve in practice, as demonstrated throughout this book. An argument might then be made that it is preferable to promote regional approaches to organised crime. States are more likely to co-operate with each other when they share similar history, values and so on. The same point has been raised in relation to the protection and promotion of human rights. Some argue that co-operation and compliance might be achieved more easily at the regional level than at the universal or international level for this and other practical reasons, such as the smaller number of states involved and their geographical proximity.[238] However, it is also a fact that all regions of the world do not have the same capability to address organised crime, and this can lead to fragmentation of action. The task of the international community, then, is to ensure that all regions are able to enhance their capacity and communicate with each other to avoid fragmentation. The role of international organisations, bodies and initiatives becomes particularly crucial in this regard, and this will be the topic of the next and final chapter.

---

[238] On this, see the opinions of commentators contained in H Steiner, P Alston and R Goodman, *International Human Rights in Context: Law Politics and Morals*, 3rd edn (Oxford, Oxford University Press, 2008) 925–33.

7

International Responses to Transnational Organised Crime

7.1 Introduction

This chapter examines the international response to transnational organised crime. One of the themes running through this book is the need for effective co-ordination and co-operation. International organisations, bodies and initiatives are well placed to facilitate these because of their expertise, experience and resources. As in other branches of international law, such as IHRL and ICL, international organisations can also promote implementation of international standards. This chapter will explore the extent to which these objectives are achieved in relation to transnational organised crime. It provides analysis of the following key areas: monitoring implementation of the Organised Crime Convention; provision of technical assistance; and inter-state/inter-agency co-operation. In so doing, this chapter examines the role of the Conference of Parties (COP) established by the Organised Crime Convention, the United Nations Office of Drugs and Crime (UNODC), the UN Commissions on Narcotic Drugs (CND) and on Crime Prevention and Criminal Justice (CCPCJ), and the International Criminal Police Organisation (Interpol). As an example of inter-agency co-operation, the United Nations Inter-Agency Project on Trafficking of Human Beings in the Greater Mekong Sub-region (UNIAP) will also be analysed. The main conclusion reached is that, while international organisations, bodies and initiatives have been instrumental in promoting co-ordination and co-operation at various levels and therefore play an important part in prevention and suppression of transnational organised crime, their efforts are undermined by the principle of state sovereignty and political interference. Some recommendations for improvement are presented at the end of the chapter.

7.2 Monitoring Implementation of the Organised Crime Convention

The key mechanism tasked with monitoring implementation of the Organised Crime Convention is COP, which was established by Article 32 of the Convention. As the name suggests, it is a political body consisting of state parties, although UNODC serves as its secretariat.[1] Article 32(1) explicitly provides that one of the key tasks of COP is to review the implementation of the Organised Crime Convention—otherwise there is no separate independent body performing this task. This is different for IHRL, where there are several bodies consisting of independent experts, such as the Human Rights Committee, the Committee on Economic, Social and Cultural Rights and the Committee on the Rights of the Child. Article 32(3)(d) allows COP to establish a mechanism which monitors implementation of the Convention, and there were some discussions on this at the first session of COP in 2004. The Government of Mexico proposed that a peer-review system of monitoring, as used under the Convention on Nuclear Safety, should be adopted in order to strengthen mutual confidence, dialogue and co-operation among state parties.[2] However, other states thought that such a mechanism would not be appropriate for the Organised Crime Convention.[3] There was no substantive discussion on the possibility of creating an independent monitoring mechanism.

It is important to recognise that states are not uniformly opposed to the idea of establishing independent treaty-monitoring bodies. This can be seen in the area of human rights. The fact that this is yet to be done under the Organised Crime Convention suggests that states are not willing to subject themselves to scrutiny in relation to prevention and suppression of organised crime. In addition to factors such as national security implications arising from organised crime and the principle of state sovereignty, this is perhaps due to the fact that clear norms and principles on the subject have not yet been established. It is therefore difficult to promote solidarity among states in this instance, compared to prohibition of international crime. This once again highlights the weak position of TCL in the international legal order. The international community has the challenging task of changing the *status quo* for the future.

In any event, COP has so far issued a set of questionnaires relating to the Convention and its Protocols in order to gather information on implementation.[4] Based on information received, the secretariat prepares analytical reports which are presented to COP during its sessions. Although this promotes trans-

---

[1] A/RES/55/25 (8 January 2001).

[2] Report of the Conference of Parties to the United Nations Convention against Transnational Organised Crime on its first session, held in Vienna from 28 June to 8 July 2004, CTOC/COP/2004/6 (23 September 2004), paras 35 and 36.

[3] Ibid, para 35.

[4] Three questionnaires in the first session and four in the second.

parency and provides information on implementation, some problems remain. The analytical reports are rather descriptive and mainly list what states have said in their questionnaires. Unlike the treaty bodies under IHRL, the secretariat does not provide a detailed country-by-country analysis to highlight good practice and areas of concern, or recommendations for further improvement. This is understandable, given that UNODC is not mandated to do so. Even if it receives such a mandate in the future, a lack of resources (as will be shown below) is likely to prevent it from engaging in in-depth analysis. It should also be reiterated that COP is a political body and therefore is not likely to exert strong pressure on states in order not to breach the principle of state sovereignty. This is supported by the fact that Organised Crime Convention did not create an enforcement mechanism to secure compliance by states. Some state parties have openly admitted that they are not in compliance with some provisions,[5] and the only response from COP to date has been to urge compliance.

In addition to the institutional weakness regarding monitoring is a lack of co-operation from state parties. Their observance of reporting deadlines clearly illustrates this. At the end of the third session in 2006, only 49% of state parties had submitted replies to the questionnaires issued at the first session.[6] A failure by states to observe the reporting deadlines is not a new problem and is experienced by other branches of international law. In the area of transnational organised crime, a key reason for non-observance, as argued by a number of state parties, is their inability to implement the Convention due to a lack of capacity and infrastructure.[7] The national case studies presented in Chapter 5 support these claims to some extent. It was also noted that, because the questionnaires were rigorous and time-consuming, a degree of reporting fatigue was evident among states.[8]

From a technical point of view, there has been no systematic database to gather and store information received from states, making effective analysis by the secretariat difficult. Consequently the Working Group of Government Experts on Technical Assistance was established by COP in its decision 2/6 (2005), and it requested the secretariat to establish a tool for simple and effective information gathering.[9] This was completed in May 2008, and consequently those state parties which had not submitted reports in the past started doing so.[10]

The above analysis suggests that a more effective body is needed. In line with

---

[5] This amounted to 31 states at that time the report was written. Possible mechanisms to review implementation of the United Nations Convention against Transnational Organized Crime and the Protocols thereto, CTOC/COP/2008/3 (26 August 2008), para 8.

[6] Development of tools to gather information from states on the implementation of the United Nations Convention against Transnational Organized Crime and each of the Protocols thereto CTOC/COP/2008/2 (25 July 2008), para 3.

[7] Above ch 3, n 38, para 102.

[8] Above n 5, para 5.

[9] Report on the meeting of the Open-ended Interim Working Group of Government Experts on Technical Assistance held in Vienna from 3 to 5 October 2007, CTOC/COP/2008/7 (16 October 2007), para 2.

[10] Above n 6, paras 5 and 11.

treaty bodies established by other branches of international law, establishment of a non-political body which can provide an objective assessment might be desirable. While the sensitive nature of intelligence might deter states and COP from establishing such a body, there is no reason why this cannot be done. In the area of narcotics, a body of independent experts known as the International Narcotics Control Board (INCB) has been in operation since the adoption of the Single Convention on Narcotic Drugs in 1961. This body engages in monitoring the implementation of relevant instruments, facilitates dialogues among state parties and promotes transparency. However, the extent to which such a non-political body would be capable of promoting effective implementation of the Organised Crime Convention is not entirely clear. In the area of human rights, states do not necessarily accept views and recommendations issued by treaty bodies. Similar types of human rights violations are reported before these bodies and regional human rights courts year after year, and the attention paid by to these bodies may be doubted.[11] The same problems will probably arise for the Organised Crime Convention.

An alternative option would be a system of peer review, as proposed by the Government of Mexico, noted earlier. This arrangement could create a space for mutual learning and foster a sense of mutual confidence, as states will respect the principle of state sovereignty. States are more likely to co-operate with other states than with non-governmental bodies, which are often critical of their action or inaction. A peer-review mechanism has already been established in the area of money laundering by the Financial Action Task Force (FATF). Originally established by the G7 Summit in 1989, the FATF currently has 34 Member States.[12] The evaluation of its activities among Member States is based on mutual or peer observation,[13] which is said to have attained strong support from the states.[14] Nevertheless it is also possible that states might not engage in critical evaluation of counterparts in order to avoid unnecessary political confrontations and criticisms. The secretariat has been examining various options, and has recommended that COP adopt an effective mechanism.[15] It remains to be seen whether COP will be able to do so.

7.3   Provision of Technical Assistance

In addition to reviewing the implementation of the Organised Crime Convention, Article 32(1) provides that COP's task is to improve the capacity of state parties to prevent and suppress organised crime. A lack of capacity on the

---

[11] Steiner, Alston and Goodman, above ch 6 n 238, 913–914.
[12] see www.fatf-gafi.org/pages/0,2987,en_32250379_32235720_1_1_1_1_1,00.html.
[13] See FATF, 'Handbook for Countries and Assessors' (June 2006).
[14] Above n 5, para 14.
[15] Ibid.

part of states has been identified as a problem. In order to address this, COP established the Working Group on Technical Assistance, as noted above. The Working Group's mandate, however, is limited to making recommendations to the secretariat,[16] which is responsible in practice for implementing various measures on technical assistance. UNODC was established in 2002 and merged the United Nations International Drug Control Programme[17] and the Centre for International Crime Prevention.[18] Its headquarters are located in Vienna, and it operates 20 field offices as well as liaison offices in New York and Brussels.[19] Due to its long-established expertise and experience in assisting states in combating transnational organised crime, UNDOC had taken a leadership role in this field even before the adoption of the Organised Crime Convention.

A wide variety of activities and measures aimed at improve the capacity of states to combat transnational organised crime have been implemented over the course of time. For instance, UNODC provides individually tailored legislative assistance to states so as to bring their domestic law in line with the Organised Crime Convention and other relevant suppression conventions.[20] Its intervention occurs in three phases. In Phase I, UNODC undertakes preliminary analysis of documents and information received by states. It conducts legal advisory missions to provide guidance under Phase II.[21] There is a possibility of further missions and training under Phase III.[22] As of July 2006, legislative assistance had been provided to 59 states.[23] It is worth noting that the majority of states receiving such assistance are developing states or states in transition,[24] and this reflects the finding illustrated in Chapter 5. Similar assistance to facilitate implementation of treaty obligations is also encouraged in human rights[25] and the environment,[26] and therefore the regime for organised crime is in line with international trends.

UNODC has also implemented more hands-on activities in the field. The Global Programme against Money Laundering launched in 1997 is one example. As part of this programme, UNODC provides long-term in-country assistance to states in the areas of financial investigation, asset forfeiture and develop-

---

[16] Above n 9.

[17] Established by the General Assembly Resolution 45/179 (21 December 1990).

[18] Secretary-General's Bulletin on the Organisation of the UN Office of Drugs and Crime, ST/SGB/2004/6 (14 March 2004). It was formerly known as the UN Office for Drug Control and Crime Prevention. See A/50/950 (14 July 1997).

[19] UNODC, 'Making the World Safer from Crime, Drugs and Terrorism' (2007).

[20] Technical assistance activities: working paper prepared by the Secretariat, COTC/COP/2006/9 (14 August 2006), para 6.

[21] Ibid, paras 7 and 8.

[22] Ibid, para 9.

[23] Ibid, para 10.

[24] 28 African states, 10 Asian states, 11 East European states, 9 Latin American states, and 1 Western European and Other state.

[25] See, eg Report of the Chairpersons of the Human Rights Bodies on Their Sixteenth Meeting, A/59/254 (11 August 2004).

[26] Technical Assistance Activities, working paper prepared by the Secretariat, CTOC/COP/2005/6 (5 September 2005).

ment of financial intelligence units.[27] Mentors who liaise with governments to implement this programme are placed in a number of regions, including the Eastern Caribbean, the Pacific, Central Asia, Africa and the Middle East.[28] States such as Afghanistan, China, Fiji, Nigeria, Peru and Yemen have benefited from this.[29] In the area of international judicial co-operation, UNODC, with assistance from governmental and non-governmental experts, has developed manuals and model laws for states' guidance purposes. They include Model Laws on Extradition (2004) and on Mutual Legal Assistance in Criminal Matters (1998), and the Model Bilateral Agreement on Confiscation of Criminal Proceeds (2005).[30] Furthermore, UNODC provides technical assistance to law enforcement authorities. It has specialised training manuals, which covers such techniques as undercover operations, surveillance and controlled deliveries. Over 60 states across the globe have requested assistance from UNODC in this area.[31]

These activities of UNODC are monitored by two functional commissions established by ECOSOC. The first is CND. Established in 1946,[32] CND currently consists of 53 Member States of the United Nations.[33] The two key functions of CND are to assist ECOSOC in supervision of instruments related to narcotic drugs[34] and to advise the Council on matters relating to control of narcotics. In 1998 the UN General Assembly adopted a Political Declaration on Drugs and CND was further mandated to review biennial reports on implementation of this Declaration submitted by states.[35] Another pertinent body is CCPCJ. It was established in 1992[36] and consists of 40 Member States. Similar to CND, the main task of CCPCJ is to provide guidance on crime prevention and criminal justice to ECOSOC and other key organs.[37] CCPCJ also provides direction to the United Nations Congress on Crime Prevention and Criminal Justice, which takes place every five years. At the 11th Congress, which took place in Bangkok in 2005, the delegates spent some time exploring measures against transnational organised crime and agreed that an integrated strategy against the practice, including universal ratification of the Organised Crime Convention, was necessary.[38] However, unlike CND, CCPCJ does not have a treaty-monitoring role as it is not specifically mentioned in the Organised Crime Convention.

---

[27] Above n 20, para 19.
[28] Ibid, para 19.
[29] Ibid, para 28.
[30] Ibid, para 29.
[31] Ibid, para 46 and 53.
[32] ECOSOC Resolution 9(1) (16 February 1946).
[33] ECOSOC Resolution 1991/49 (21 June 1991).
[34] The role of Commission is stipulated under the relevant instruments. Art 8 of the Single Convention 1961; Art 17 of the Psychotropic Substances Convention 1971; Art 21 of the Drug Trafficking Convention 1988.
[35] A/S-20/4 (8–10 June 1998). The most recent report was published in 2008. See E/CN.7/2008/2 (21 February 2008).
[36] ECOSOC Resolution 1992/1 (6 February 1992).
[37] A/RES/46/152 (18 December 1991).
[38] Report of the Eleventh United Nations Congress on Crime Prevention and Criminal Justice, A/CONF.203/18 (17 May 2005), para 114.

Both CND and CCPCJ are regarded as the governing bodies of UNODC because the budgets of the United Nations International Drug Control Programme and the United Nations Crime Prevention and Criminal Justice Fund within UNODC are approved by CND[39] and CCPCJ[40] respectively. The Executive Director of UNODC submits his reports annually to these Commissions, which examine them and set policy directives for UNODC to follow.[41] As these two Commissions are represented by all regions of the world, they play an important role of facilitating international dialogues and co-operation among nations.

While the effort of UNODC and two Commissions in the prevention and suppression of organised crime should be recognised, a number of problems can be identified. For instance, a lack of funding to implement initiatives and measures against transnational organised crime has been a problem for UNODC.[42] This is not a new issue for international organisations, but UNODC has a complex funding structure which cannot be seen in other organisations. As noted above, the bulk of UNODC's funding is approved by CND and CCPCJ on the basis of voluntary contribution. UNODC also receives a regular budget as approved by the UN General Assembly.[43] The combined income can further be divided into two categories. The first is the earmarked special-purpose fund, where donor states have substantial influence in deciding how it should be spent. It amounts to 80% of the total budget allocated to UNODC.[44] The second is the unearmaked general-purpose fund, which UNODC can allocate as it sees fit. Recent trends have shown an increase in the special-purpose fund but a declining balance in the general-purpose fund.[45] In addition, there has been very little growth in the regular budget allocated by the General Assembly.[46] According to CND and CCPCJ, the main reason for this trend is that UNODC has failed to communicate or facilitate dialogue with states.[47] It seems that this affected mutual confidence and trust, and discouraged states from making voluntary contributions. As with other international organisations, this vividly demonstrates that UNODC cannot survive without the support of states.

A comparative analysis of funding allocated to various UN bodies provides further insight into the United Nations' priorities. For 2008 and 2009 UNODC

---

[39] A/RES/46/185 (20 December 1991).

[40] A/RES/61/252 (22 December 2006).

[41] See, eg Commission on Crime Prevention and Criminal Justice: Report on the Eighteenth Session, E/CN.15/2009/20 (16–24 April 2009); Commission on Narcotic Drugs: Report on the Fifty Second Session, E/CN.7/2009/12 (11–20 March 2009).

[42] Open-ended intergovernmental working group on improving the governance and financial situation of the United Nations Office on Drugs and Crime, E/CN.15/2009/21 (24 April 2009), para 9.

[43] E/CN.7/2008/11–E/CN.15/2008/15 (18 February 2008), para 2.

[44] Improving the governance and financial Situation of the United Nations Office of Drugs and Crime, E/CN.7/2009/CPR.7–E/CN.15/2009/CPR.7 (16 March 2009).

[45] Ibid.

[46] Ibid.

[47] Ibid.

received $37 million[48] as part of the UN regular budget. In contrast, the Office of the UN High Commissioner for Human Rights received $115 million.[49] The budgets allocated for trade and development and for protection of Palestinian refugees amounted to $123 million and $40 million respectively.[50] While it is important to recognise that the United Nations has to address a wide variety of global problems, it is evident that crime prevention and criminal justice, including action against transnational organised crime, are not high on its agenda. Needless to say, the shortage of funding makes it more difficult for UNODC to implement new initiatives, such as servicing a treaty-monitoring mechanism. This being so, it can be argued that the United Nations and its Member States have unrealistic expectations of UNODC's ability to implement effective action against organised crime. There is also an element of hypocrisy, in that the United Nations and Member States have repeatedly expressed their commitment to address this criminality, but this is not matched by adequate funding.

Dependence on states for funding sometimes politicises UNODC's activities. This is particularly evident in the area of harm reduction, which aims to address drug misuse and abuse. States such as the US, Japan, Russia and Sweden oppose harm reduction,[51] and such opposition has had ramifications for the functioning of CND and UNODC. CND currently operates by consensus, and therefore a single state can block a resolution or initiative.[52] It should be pointed out that the Political Declaration and the Plan of Action on International Co-operation towards an Integrated and Balanced Policy to Counter the World Drug Problem, adopted by CND in March 2009, do not make any reference to harm reduction. This is due to the oppositions of some states.[53] In the past, UNODC was also forced to remove references to harm reduction and needle/syringe exchange in documents, websites, publications and statements.[54] An added complexity is that, while UNODC has increasingly been supporting harm reduction despite strong opposition, INCB, a treaty-monitoring body, does not.[55] All of these demonstrate

[48] Above n 43, para 5.

[49] OHCHR, '2008 Report: Activities and Results', 172.

[50] Programme Budget for the Biennium 2008–2009, A/C.5/62/L.19 (24 December 2007).

[51] International Harm Reduction Association, available at www.ihra.net/March 2009#IHRAMakesstatementatUNCommissiononNarcoticDrugs.

[52] R Elliot et al, 'Harm Reduction, HIV/AIDS, and the Human Rights Challenge to Global Drug Control Policy' (2005) 8 *Health and Human Rights* 104, 112.

[53] Commission on Narcotic Drugs, Report on the Fifty-Second Session, E/CN.7/2009/12 (11–12 March 2009). The following states are said to support harm reduction: Germany, Australia, Bolivia, Bulgaria, Croatia, Cyprus, Estonia, Finland, Georgia, Greece, Hungary, Latvia, Liechtenstein, Lithuania, Luxembourg, Malta, the Netherlands, Norway, Poland, Portugal, Romania, Saint Lucia, Slovenia, Spain, Switzerland and the UK. However, Colombia, Cuba, the Russian Federation, Sri Lanka and the US oppose it.

[54] UK Harm Reduction Alliance, at www.ukhra.org/statements/US_UNODC.html.

[55] A Wodak and L McLeod, 'The Role of Harm Reduction in Controlling HIV among Injecting Drug Users' (2008) 22 *AIDS* 81, 86 and 88. It is important to note that INCB is not against all measures of harm reduction. While it does not support measures such as injection rooms, it is not against needle exchange, provided that it does not lead to drug abuse. Correspondence from Mr Saul Takahashi, former Drug Control Officer at the INCB Secretariat (2 January 2010).

that UN agencies are often subjected to political interference and because of this are sometimes not able to arrive at consensus and develop coherent strategies or policies on organised crime.

Aside from the politicisation of UNODC, some internal management problems within the Organisation have been identified. It has been noted by the United Nations Office of Internal Oversight Services that UNODC lacks a strategic direction. This has resulted in inconsistencies among policy/programme documents, and various initiatives implemented in the field were often regarded as uncoordinated and ad hoc without sufficient internal/external consultation.[56] There has also been no coherent funding strategy.[57] In addition, various divisions of UNODC, such as Treaty Affairs, Management and Operations, are competing with each other without effective co-ordination, and the terms of reference for some offices, such as the Deputy Executive Director, are not entirely clear.[58] Despite the fact that more than two-thirds of UNODC's staff are located in field offices around the world, the headquarters does not always consult with them before making important decisions.[59] An inevitable implication of all of this is a waste of financial and human resources, placing additional burden on already stretched funding. In response to these problems, UNODC has developed a strategic plan for 2008–2011 that aims to address these and other shortcomings identified by the UN Internal Oversight Services.[60] It remains to be seen if UNODC will be able to act in accordance with it and, in doing so, will placate its critics.

Another area of concern is participation of civil society. As noted in Chapter 4, NGOs with consultative status can participate in the meetings held by CND and CCPCJ in accordance with Article 71 of the UN Charter and the relevant ECOSOC resolutions. This has not been achieved sufficiently in practice. Participation in meetings held by CND provides a good example, where the chair of CND has the discretion to permit observation and submission of statements by NGOs. This has led to limited participation.[61] NGOs can also be excluded from informal negotiations and CND's sessions at the request of any Member State.[62] This makes transparency in decision-making difficult and may be contrasted with NGO participation in protecting and promoting of human rights. Participation of NGOs in meetings held by the Human Rights Council (formerly the Commission on Human Rights) is governed by the same rules as other functional commissions established by ECOSOC,[63] yet the willingness of states

---

[56] United Nations Office of Internal Oversight Services, 'Inspection of Programme Management and Administrative Practices in the Office of Drugs and Crime', MECD-2006-003 (19 March 2007), para 15.

[57] Ibid, para 18.

[58] Ibid, para 21.

[59] Ibid, para 25.

[60] E/CN.7/200714-E/CN.15/2007/5 (9 February 2007).

[61] UNODC, 'Independent Evaluation of Beyond 2008' (August 2009) 12. Beyond 2008 is an initiative by a consortium of NGOs to review the UN General Assembly's Special Sessions on Illicit Drugs.

[62] International Harm Reduction Association, 'Civil Society: A Silenced Partner?' (2009) 2.

[63] A/RES/60/251 (3 April 2006).

to allow active participation is more evident. This can be seen in the statements made by the representatives of governments at the first session of the Human Rights Council in 2006.[64] The Office of the UN High Commissioner for Human Rights has a dedicated civil society unit which facilitates the engagement of NGOs,[65] and they can participate in the Universal Periodic Review, which examines human rights situations in every Member State of the United Nations, by attending review sessions and submitting relevant information.[66] This comparison underscores the point expressed elsewhere that organised crime has yet to attain a degree of significance within the international legal system.

7.4   International Co-operation

7.4.1   Inter-state Co-operation

International organisations and bodies play an important role in facilitating inter-state co-operation. In addition to the activities conducted by UNODC noted above, COP under the Organised Crime Convention established an open-ended working group to examine various issues of international co-operation,[67] and requested its secretariat to develop and promote tools to facilitate it.[68] In particular, it requested the establishment of an online directory and a network of central authorities, as well as a catalogue of examples of cases on extradition, mutual legal assistance and international co-operation.[69] In response, UNODC consolidated the existing directory on central authorities used in relation to narcotics to cover the Organised Crime Convention and its Protocols. The upgraded directory was finalised in 2007.[70] This undoubtedly makes it easier for states to identify and contact appropriate authorities directly to facilitate mutual assistance in criminal matters. In relation to the catalogue, UNODC

---

[64] See in particular the statements made by Austria, Brazil, Canada, Finland, Germany, Greece, Malaysia, the Netherlands, available at www2.ohchr.org/english/bodies/hrcouncil/1session/190606.htm.

[65] www.ohchr.org/EN/AboutUs/Pages/CivilSociety.aspx.

[66] Human Rights Council Resolution 5/1, A/HRC/RES/5/1 (18 June 2007). See OHCHR, 'Information and Guidelines for Relevant Stakeholders on the Universal Periodic Review Mechanism' (June 2008).

[67] Decision 2/2.

[68] Relationship of the Conference of the Parties to the United Nations Convention against Transnational Organized Crime with the Commission on Crime Prevention and Criminal Justice and the future Conference of the state parties to the United Nations Convention against Corruption, CTOC/COP/2005/5 (12 August 2008), para 2.

[69] Decision 3/2.

[70] Work done by the United Nations Office on Drugs and Crime to promote the implementation of the provisions on international cooperation in the United Nations Convention against Transnational Organized Crime: regional workshops, CTOC/COP/2008/5 (12 August 2008), para 6.

has not yet developed one, mainly due to a lack of systematic information at the national level.[71]

In addition to the UN bodies, there is another key agency which has been instrumental in facilitating functional co-operation among national law enforcement agencies. That is the International Criminal Police Organization (Interpol), originally established in 1923.[72] Located in Lyon, France, it currently has 188 Member States, with seven regional offices globally and representative offices in New York (at the United Nations) and Brussels (engaging with the EU).[73] In accordance with Article 2 of the Constitution, the key aim of Interpol is to promote mutual assistance between the police authorities of Member States.[74] Interpol thus plays an important role in implementing international standards on mutual assistance under the Organised Crime Convention. Contrary to its popular image, Interpol does not have the authority or power to conduct investigations and engage in coercive actions in Member States on its own initiative.[75] Each Member State appoints a National Central Bureau (NCB), which liaises with Interpol and other NCBs.[76] Interpol maintains a global communication system which enables police forces in all of its Member States to request, submit and access vital police data.[77] Interpol also provides operational supports, such as a 24 hour contact point and expert assistance in the field.[78]

One of the main activities of Interpol is the distribution of notices on fugitives, suspected terrorists, dangerous criminals, missing persons and weapons threats.[79] Currently there are six colour-coded notices issued by Interpol: red (wanted persons), blue (individuals of interest in relation to particular crimes), green (warnings and intelligence about dangerous criminals), yellow (missing persons), black (unidentified body) and orange (dangerous materials, criminal acts or events that pose a potential threat to public safety).[80] Interpol also issues special notices in relation to individuals associated with Al-Qaeda and the Taleban, as agreed with the UN Security Council.[81] In 2008 alone Interpol

---

[71] Ibid, para 28.

[72] Formerly known as the International Criminal Police Commission. It changed its name to the International Criminal Police Organization in 1946 as it was thought that the word 'Organization' communicated a sense of permanence compared to 'Commission'. See M Fooner, *Interpol: Issues in World Crime and International Criminal Justice* (New York, Plenum Press, 1989) 67.

[73] Interpol, 'Interpol: An Overview', available at www.interpol.int/Public/ICPO/FactSheets/GI01.pdf. They are located in Argentina, Cameroon, Côte d'Ivoire, El Salvador, Kenya, Thailand and Zimbabwe.

[74] Interpol Constitution was adopted by its General Assembly in 1956.

[75] J Sheptycki, 'The Accountability of Transnational Policing Institution: The Strange Case of Interpol' (2004) *California Journal of Law and Society* 107, 114.

[76] Arts 31–33 of the Constitution.

[77] Above n 73. The database contains names and photographs of known criminals, wanted persons, fingerprints, DNA profiles, stolen or lost travel documents, stolen motor vehicles, child sex abuse images and stolen works of art.

[78] Interpol, 'Annual Report 2008', 9.

[79] Ibid, 13.

[80] Ibid.

[81] Ibid.

issued a total of 4,596 notices leading to 5,680 arrests.[82] This may be contrasted with 2,037 notices and 2,357 arrests in 2003,[83] and demonstrates the increasing importance and usefulness of the notice system in apprehending criminals operating transnationally.

Interpol regards organised crime as a priority issue and as such has been involved in various related endeavours with Member States. One of the most highly publicised examples is Operation Vico (2007), a global public appeal which led to the arrest of a Canadian paedophile by the name of Christopher Paul Neil. Known also as 'Mr Swirl' or 'Swirl Face' because of computer technology he used to disguise his face, Neil sexually abused young boys in Cambodia, Vietnam and Thailand.[84] Interpol also maintains Incidence Response Teams, which deliver emergency responses and investigative support. They have been involved in, among other operations, forensic investigation of computers seized from FARC in Colombia, drug seizures in Liberia and terrorist attacks in Mumbai.[85]

Compared to other international organisations, such as UNODC, Interpol is said to be less political. It was not established by a treaty, negotiation of which is a political activity conducted primarily by states. Its predecessor organisation, the International Criminal Police Commission (ICPC), was established by the International Criminal Police Congress in 1923 to allow police authorities across the globe to co-operate with each other and carry out activities without undue political interference.[86] This position was maintained in 1946 when the ICPC changed its name to Interpol.[87] However, in order to increase Interpol's resources, it was necessary to enhance the involvement of states and a new constitution was adopted in 1956.[88] Even so, the members of Interpol are police authorities[89] and not bureaucrats of states and governments such as diplomats or high-ranking officials. Article 3 of the Interpol Constitution also provides that Interpol is prohibited from engaging in activities of a political, military, religious or racial character. The historical development of Interpol suggests that it has been able to develop 'without sacrificing its organizational culture, reducing its autonomy, or compromising its mandate' and that its apolitical nature has been the secret of its success.[90]

However, Interpol is also a victim of political interference to some extent. A clear example is its change of stance over the course of time on terrorism. Despite pressure from states, Interpol initially regarded terrorism as political and

---

[82] Ibid. They are 3,216 red notices, 304 blue notices, 664 green notices, 385 yellow notices, 91 black notices, 7 orange notices and 26 special notices.

[83] Ibid.

[84] Ibid, 25.

[85] Ibid,11.

[86] M Barnett and L Coleman, 'Designing Police: Interpol and the Study of Change in International Organizations' (2005) 49 *International Studies Quarterly* 593, 603.

[87] Ibid, 607.

[88] Ibid.

[89] Art 4 of the Constitution.

[90] Barnett and Coleman, above n 86, 609.

maintained that it would not get involved in anti-terrorism activities.[91] When the German police requested Interpol to provide information after the killing of Israeli athletes during the Munich Olympics in 1972, Interpol refused on this ground.[92] This, however, had its costs. States responded by creating specific organisations which could deal with terrorism and their mandates began to resemble that of Interpol, resulting in an increased competition for resources.[93] This was significant, as Interpol depended upon states for funding. As such, terrorism was rendered 'criminal' rather than 'political'.[94] This raises a separate yet important point: states are not alone in manipulating interpretation of legal documents to their advantage. While it is understandable that international organisations must bow to political and other pressures for their own survival, this can have an impact upon effective action against transnational crime, as noted above.

Another problem in relation to Interpol is the difficulty of establishing accountability for its actions. It should be noted that there are various bodies within Interpol which can serve as checks against other bodies. The General Assembly is regarded as the Supreme Organ as it has the powers to adopt regulations, set a policy direction, examine and approve programmes prepared by the Secretary-General, and facilitate agreements with other organisations.[95] The Executive Committee supervises the decisions made by the General Assembly, plans Interpol's activities and oversees the work of the Secretary-General.[96] The Secretary-General (or the Secretariat) implements decisions made by the General Assembly and the Executive Committee, provides secretarial support to these bodies, liaises with other organisations and produces publications.[97] There is a degree of accountability as the General Assembly has the power to elect the President, Vice Presidents and Delegates of the Executive Committee. The Secretary-General is also appointed by the Assembly upon proposal by the Executive Committee.[98]

The key problem is that NCBs are not answerable to any organs of Interpol and, because of this, the principle of state sovereignty prevails in practice.[99] It has already been noted that whether Interpol can facilitate active co-operation depends on the capacity of NCBs appointed by their governments.[100] The technology which allows faster and more effective flow of intelligence is prevalent in North America and Western Europe, but not in developing regions such as Africa and the Middle East. This, coupled with other factors such as financial

---

[91] Ibid, 610.
[92] Ibid.
[93] Ibid, 611.
[94] Ibid, 612.
[95] Art 8 of the Constitution.
[96] Art 22.
[97] Art 26.
[98] Art 28.
[99] Sheptycki, above n 75, 123.
[100] Ibid, p. 124.

constraints and a lack of political will among some states, affects the ways in which NCBs can operate in practice.[101] This in turn has an impact upon the capability and credibility of Interpol to facilitate mutual co-operation. Despite these shortcomings, Interpol's long history has enabled it to gain significant expertise and experience in inter-state co-operation. In the era of globalisation and transnationality of organised crime, there is no doubt that it will continue to play an important role in facilitating law enforcement co-operation.

7.4.2   Inter-Agency Co-operation: UNIAP

In addition to inter-state co-operation, it is necessary to examine the extent to which international bodies and organisations are able to promote inter-agency co-operation. This is important as various organisations implement similar programmes on organised crime. Oftentimes these organisations do not have a clear picture of what other organisations are doing,[102] and this inevitably has resulted in duplication. This is more evident in action against human trafficking, as multiple organisations, including UNODC,[103] the United Nations Human Rights Council,[104] the IOM, the ILO[105] as well as regional bodies such as the OSCE[106] are involved in one way or another. In order to save limited resources available to these organisations, a high degree of co-operation and co-ordination is necessary.

To put this into a context, the UNIAP initiative will be examined. The Mekong Sub-region[107] is deeply affected by human trafficking. In order to consolidate efforts to prevent and suppress this crime, UNIAP was established by the Ted Turner Fund (UN Foundation) in 1999 as a pilot project to promote inter-agency co-operation.[108] It is an inter-agency project and, as such, various UN agencies, governments of the Mekong Sub-region and NGOs have become part of this initiative.[109] This underscores the point raised elsewhere that effective action against organised crime requires involvement of states and non-state actors. The funding for this project comes from sources other than the UN agencies, and

---

[101] Ibid, 125–27.

[102] Above n 9, para 64.

[103] It has developed, among other documents, a model law on trafficking (2009), a handbook for parliamentarians (2009) and a toolkit to combat trafficking (2008) to enhance the capability of law enforcement and other authorities, as well as members of civil society.

[104] It appointed special procedures, such as the Special Rapporteurs on Trafficking of Human Beings and on Contemporary Forms of Slavery.

[105] For the role of the IOM and ILO, see Obokata, above ch 2 n 51, Chapter 3.

[106] It has a dedicated Office of Special Representative and Special Co-ordinator for Combating Trafficking in Human Beings. Visit www.osce.org/cthb/.

[107] This area consists of Cambodia, China, Laos, Myanmar, Thailand and Vietnam.

[108] Obokata, above ch 2 n 51, 105.

[109] The relevant international organisations include ILO, IOM, UNAIDS, UNESCO, UNODC and UNFPA. The participating NGOs are Save the Children, ECPAT, World Vision. UNIAP, 'UNIAP Phase III Mid-Term Evaluation Report' (March 2009), 47.

therefore UNIAP is said to be able to maintain neutrality in facilitating inter-agency co-operation.[110]

There are three phases to UNIAP's activities. Phase I lasted until 2003, and focused on networking and running small projects.[111] The execution of these projects was carried out by three committees. The National Project Committees consisted of governments, UN agencies and NGOs, and implemented counter-trafficking projects.[112] Their activities were assisted by the Project Steering Committee and the Project Working Committee, which also had governmental and non-governmental representations.[113] These Committees performed a supervisory role and provided inputs and operational support to UNIAP. What becomes apparent immediately is UNIAP has actively facilitated the involvement of all actors in decision-making. One example of good practice is the provision of education and vocational training, with the assistance of Save the Children UK, to over 97,000 children in Myanmar who were at risk of being trafficked.[114] In Cambodia UNIAP funded an NGO initiative to improve protection of trafficked victims. It established a network of governmental and non-governmental agencies through a series of workshops and training sessions.[115]

Phase II began in December 2003 and ended in June 2006. During this period UNIAP developed a Memorandum of Understanding (MoU), which was signed by all states of the Mekong Sub-region.[116] The aim of this document was to improve individual and regional action against trafficking. While not a legally binding instrument and therefore not entailing any legal obligations, the signing of this MoU by all Mekong states demonstrates recognition that more is needed to be done to enhance their capacity for counter-trafficking. In any event, soon after the signing of the MoU, the COMMIT Process (Co-ordinated Mekong Ministerial Initiative against Trafficking) was formally established to facilitate inter-state co-ordination and co-operation, and UNIAP has served as its secretariat. Some of the achievements made as a result of the COMMIT Process include the establishment of regional and in-country training programmes for government and law enforcement authorities, enhancement of victim identification and protection at the national level, and development of national action plans among Mekong states.[117] The evaluation conducted at the end of the Phase II notes that UNIAP has been able to catalyse counter-trafficking policies and activities nationally and regionally.[118]

---

[110] Ibid.

[111] Obokata, above ch 2 n 51, 105.

[112] Project of the Mekong Sub-region: Project Revision, RAS/00/H01/C/JB/31 (1 October 2001), 7.

[113] Ibid.

[114] Save the Children UK, 'First Progress Report to UNIAP/UNOPS' (30 August 2002), 1–2.

[115] UNIAP, 'Semi-Annual Project Report for the United Nations Foundation and for United Nations Fund for International Partnership' (August 2002).

[116] Memorandum of Understanding on Co-operation against Trafficking in Persons in the Greater Mekong Sub-Region (24 October 2004).

[117] UNIAP, 'The COMMIT Sub-Regional Action Plan: Achievements in Combating Trafficking in the Greater Mekong Sub-Region' (December 2007).

[118] UNDP, 'Evaluation of UNDP's Second Regional Cooperation Framework for Asia and the

It might be recalled that a regional arrangement exists in the context of the EU where Member States and EU institutions have adopted legally binding instruments and mechanisms relevant to counter-trafficking. Nevertheless, it was also shown that Member States are generally reluctant to fulfil their legally binding obligations. The COMMIT Process was created purely on a voluntary basis without any legal ramifications, yet the Mekong states have been instrumental in facilitating regional co-operation. This perhaps shows the value of non-legal instruments or arrangements in tackling organised crime, as noted in Chapter 4. They are more flexible in that states can develop at their own pace without stringent reporting or implementation deadlines. The non-legal route is also more informal and this might make it easier for states to agree upon a solution, unlike with legally binding instruments, which can take a lot of time to conclude. In addition, non-legal arrangements encourage states to participate in regional or international initiatives more actively as they are not held legally accountable and therefore there is no stigma attached to non-compliance.

UNIAP is currently in Phase III, which will last until November 2010. This phase aims to consolidate and institutionalise various initiatives.[119] There are four objectives under Phrase III: (1) services to governments; (2) services to UN partners; (3) services to the anti-trafficking sector in general; and (4) special projects.[120] One of the important initiatives developed to date is the Strategic Information Response Network (SIREN). This aims to deliver high-quality, up-to-date information and data on human trafficking to all relevant actors and to facilitate dialogue and policy discussions on counter-trafficking.[121] In relation to objective 2, UNIAP organises inter-agency meetings at the national and regional levels as ways to exchange information and co-ordinate activities. In Cambodia, the UNIAP Country Office has formed an advisory group consisting of 10 major agencies, including the United Nations Development Programme (UNDP), the United Nations Children's Fund (UNICEF) and the ILO, as well as NGOs such as Childwise and World Vision.[122] It meets twice a year to develop and evaluate a plan of action on trafficking and communicates its decision to the COMMIT Process for further action.[123]

What is evident here is that UNIAP has been playing an important role in facilitating co-ordination and co-operation at various levels and enhancing their capacity to address trafficking of human beings. One reason why UNIAP has been able to achieve this is that it is a project, rather than an UN agency. This means that it is not constrained by a specific mandate, unlike other agencies whose tasks are defined and limited by their respective mandates.[124] Indeed, UNIAP does not focus on one particular aspect of human trafficking, such as

Pacific' (May 2007), 27
[119] Mid-Term Evaluation above n 109, 11.
[120] Ibid.
[121] UNIAP, 'Introduction to SIREN' (June 2007).
[122] Mid-Term Evaluation, above n 109, 32.
[123] Ibid.
[124] Ibid, 2.

migration (IOM), forced labour (ILO), organised crime (UNODC) or human rights (OHCHR), and is therefore able to promote a holistic approach. Due to its effort, UNIAP has gradually been able to reduce the instances of duplication of effort since it was established in 1999.[125]

However, some problems in inter-agency co-operation have also been reported. For instance, because of their mandates, the contributing agencies still treat trafficking only from certain angles[126] and occasionally compete with each other to advance their own agendas.[127] As noted above, international organisations rely heavily on voluntary contributions or donations from wealthy states, mainly in North America and Western Europe. This naturally increases the competition between relevant organisations as they have to fight for limited funding to implement their own projects. It has also been noted that collaborative work is often seen as additional work and co-ordination takes place mainly when it benefits particular organisations.[128] A lack of inter-agency co-ordination has also been identified in other regions. UNODC's involvement in counter-trafficking being promoted by the Southern African Development Community (SADC)[129] is a case in point.[130] It has been reported that communication and co-ordination between UNODC and the SADC was poor, as the former did not adequately consult with the latter.[131] This demonstrates that inter-agency co-operation is not an easy task in reality.

The funding for UNIAP itself is also limited, with the result that staff are often forced to spend time fund-raising instead of running or implementing counter-trafficking initiatives.[132] The bulk of money comes from 15 donor governments, who have increasingly been giving specific direction regarding the use of such money.[133] As a result, UNIAP is often not allowed to use available resources as it would prefer, and its decisions on resource allocation are influenced by political consideration. It is evident from this that the wealthy developed states shape important policies on organised crime in many cases. While states from around the world contributed to the drafting of the Organised Crime Convention and other relevant legal instruments of organised crime based on the principle of sovereign equality, wealthy developed states use funding as weapons to advance their own agendas. Weaker developing states often have no choice but to accept

---

[125] Obokata, above ch 2 n 51, 117.

[126] Mid-Term Evaluation, above n 109, 4.

[127] Obokata, above ch 2 n 51, 117.

[128] RJ Miller, 'Managing Human Trafficking in the Greater Mekong Sub-region: An Investigation into Organisational Culture Its Impact on International Co-operation', paper presented at the When Women Gain, So Does the World, IWPR's Eighth International Women's Policy Research Conference (June 2005), 5. Available at www.iwpr.org/PDF/05_Proceedings/Miller_Rebecca.pdf.

[129] Member States are Angola, Botswana, Democratic Republic of Congo, Lesotho, Madagascar, Malawi, Mauritius, Mozambique, Namibia, Seychelles, South Africa, Swaziland, Tanzania, Zambia and Zimbabwe.

[130] UNODC Regional Office for Southern Africa, 'Terminal Evaluation Report' (2008), 8.

[131] Ibid, 12.

[132] Mid-Term Evaluation, above n 109, 24.

[133] Ibid, 25.

this due to a lack of capacity and resources to deal with organised crime by themselves. To be more specific, regional and international initiatives such as UNIAP are funded by wealthy donor states in the hope of enhancing the capacity of developing states (such as those of the Mekong Sub-region) to cut the flow of illicit goods and services, such as people and drugs, which often originate from these weaker states. While this is an important step forward, it was noted elsewhere that wealthy states have failed to implement measures to curtail their own domestic demand for illicit goods and services. Such an unbalanced approach unfortunately will not lead to the elimination of organised crime.

7.5 Conclusions

In this chapter the role of international organisations, bodies and initiatives against organised crime was examined. In addition to the role of COP in monitoring implementation of international standards set by the Organised Crime Convention, the key players in the field, such as UNODC, CND, CCPCJ and Interpol, were analysed. The case study of UNIAP provided an example of how inter-agency co-operation was conducted in practice. While these international organisations, bodies and initiatives play an important role in bringing various actors together to implement action against organised crime, their activities are affected by the principle of state sovereignty and political interference on the part of states. Fijnaut argued in 2000 that international organisations such as the United Nations were best placed to promote international co-operation and co-ordination over transnational organised crime because of their resources and expertise in addressing the practice and assisting states to develop or maintain their capacity.[134] However, he also cautioned that the issue could become nothing more than a pawn in the conflict of interests between influential states if these organisations are not instrumental enough.[135] In looking at the case study of various international responses explored in this chapter, it becomes apparent that Fijnaut's analysis has been fairly accurate.

What can be done to improve the current situation? The nature of the current international legal system means that it is not possible to eliminate political interference entirely. However, it is possible to mitigate this situation so that international organisations and bodies can better fulfil their functions. This can be done by increasing the involvement of non-state actors. In relation to treaty monitoring, a body of independent experts would be able to conduct an objective analysis of compliance by states and also enhance transparency. This would reduce the burdens on the secretariat, allowing it to devote its time and resources to other issues, such as technical assistance. In line with the funding structure of

---

[134] Fijnaut, above ch 1 n 39, 125.
[135] Ibid.

INCB under narcotics conventions, financial assistance for such a body would come from the regular UN budget as opposed to voluntary contributions from states.[136] This would mean less political interference. As the Organised Crime Convention is a young instrument, with its norms and principles still developing, it might take some time for states to allow such a mechanism. However, the same has been accomplished under narcotics conventions (INCB), and it may only be a matter of time before COP establishes such a body.

There are also things which the UN bodies should do. UNODC could increase its effort to obtain funding from private donors. In 2008 it received contributions from entities including the Ford Foundation (a philanthropic organisation), ANTEL (a chemical producer), Drug Abuse Prevention Centre of Japan (an NGO) and Banco de Prevision Social (a financial institution).[137] By targeting industries that are more likely to be affected by organised crime, such as financial, pharmaceutical and retail corporations, UNODC can not only reduce the instances of political interference, but also facilitate dialogue and co-operation with these actors in preventing and suppressing organised crime. From the point of view of MNCs, financial contributions may be regarded as good publicity, and this might encourage them to co-operate more. In addition, similar to the regime under IHRL, participation of civil society in decision-making processes within CND and CCPCJ should be encouraged. All of this is in line with the concept of global governance as explored elsewhere in this book, and it is submitted that active participation of relevant non-state actors is essential for the international community to maintain legitimacy in its action against transnational organised crime. A lack of transparency and accountability has been the major problem for counter-terrorism measures implemented at the national, regional and international levels, and the international community has a valuable opportunity not to make the same mistake in relation to transnational organised crime.

---

[136] Correspondence Mr Takahashi, above n 55.
[137] UNODC, Annual Report 2009, 54.

8

Conclusion

The main focus of this book was the international legal framework addressing transnational organised crime. Part I examined the key norms, principles and concepts relating to transnational organised crime. It considered not only the legal development, but also other theoretical and conceptual frameworks to articulate the core obligations imposed upon states as well as the role of non-states actors. Part II in turn explored how relevant norms and principles on the prevention and suppression of transnational organised crime are implemented in practice at national, regional and international levels. There are several conclusions which can be made. First, although TCL as represented by the Organised Crime Convention provides a comprehensive framework to prevent and suppress this criminality, the principle of state sovereignty, the main drive behind this branch of international law, poses a major obstacle to promoting a concerted response. Therefore, seeking uniformity of action at the international level is difficult in practice at the moment. This may be contrasted with states' responses to terrorism. The counter-terrorism measures have gained wide support among states, particularly because terrorism has been recognised as a threat to international peace and security. While transnational organised crime also has implications for international peace and security, as argued throughout this book, it is far from being recognised as such. This suggests a lack of political will among states to take firmer action than they already have. This also means that it will take more time for TCL to mature under the international legal order.

Second, it is also clear that TCL on its own is not sufficient to prevent and suppress this criminality. TCL represents a criminal justice response, in that its main focus is the prosecution and punishment of criminals through prohibition and international co-operation. Although such a response is an important first step forward, it was shown that any effective action against transnational organised crime requires a holistic approach which takes into consideration wider issues, such as the causes and consequences of organised crime, the supply and demand dynamics and the rights of the victims, as well as those of the suspects and defendants. Unfortunately TCL is not well equipped to develop such an approach, and therefore must be assisted by other branches of international law, IHRL in particular. This would not necessarily lead to fragmentation of the international legal frameworks to address transnational organised crime, as obligations arising from these branches of international law are mutually reinforcing, rather than conflicting with each other. For instance, a lack of due regard to the rights of defendants under TCL can be strengthened by the relevant provisions of IHRL or ICL. In turn, TCL has extensive provisions on international co-operation, which are lacking under IHRL and ICL. As issues of international importance increasingly overlap with each other, so do the legal frameworks for addressing them.

Third, the current international legal framework does not fully support participation of the relevant non-state actors in decision-making processes. This is mainly due to the fact that international law generally creates rights and duties for states but not other actors, except for the principle of individual criminal responsibility for the commission of international crime. While TCL recognises the importance of non-state actors in the prevention and suppression of organised crime, an obligation to co-operate is still imposed upon states. It may be accepted that this is the nature of international law. However, it has been demonstrated that such a framework does not reflect the reality that the involvement of non-state actors has been increasingly evident in the matters of international importance, such as transnational organised crime, and therefore is not suited to address these issues. Consequently, it is submitted that the time is ripe for all concerned to reassess the nature and role of international law in the era of globalisation, and to seriously consider the extent to which it should regulate the conduct of non-state actors. Further consideration of the concept of the international community may be a step forward in this regard.

In terms of enforcement of norms and principles on transnational organised crime, it is difficult to state at this stage that they are properly implemented, particularly at the national level. In addition to the principle of state sovereignty, which has led to varied interpretations and implementation, this is partly due to the fact that states are still grappling with the notions of organised crime and criminal groups, as well as the core obligations established under the Organised Crime Convention, as the norms and principles are still developing. Further, these norms and principles will have to be incorporated into domestic legal systems for proper enforcement, and this can take a very long time—particularly in dualist states, where international law is not automatically regarded as part of domestic law. As a result, it will take more time to accurately assess the extent to which states have been able to observe and implement key obligations. In relation to regional and international organisations, their activities are hampered by political interference, and this highlights the reality that they cannot survive without support from the key members of the international community—states. However, they still play an important role in promoting international standards on transnational organised crime and assist other actors to implement measures against it. All in all, it is evident that relevant actors at the national, regional and international levels have started taking transnational organised crime more seriously than before.

Another important point to be raised is the value of non-legal instruments or arrangements in preventing and suppressing transnational organised. Generally speaking, it takes longer to conclude legal instruments, such as treaties, as their binding nature makes it difficult for states to reach consensus quickly. Further, states are likely to water down various obligations as they do not want to be frequently found in breach. To an extent, TCL is an example of this, as the principle of state sovereignty dominates. All of this suggests that the sole reliance on legally binding law and frameworks does not necessarily produce positive results. In this regard, one might recall the COMMIT Process established by an MoU in the Mekong Sub-region. This has proved to be successful in promoting domestic and regional actions against human trafficking. Such an arrangement can also be participated in by non-state actors in line with the concept of global governance, and therefore the significance of non-legal arrangements is likely to increase in the coming years.

Will the international community be able to promote and implement effective action against transnational organised crime in the future? This question is rather difficult to answer when looking at the current state of affairs. However, international community has taken an important step by adopting the Organised Crime Convention. This instrument should be regarded as an expression of a promise on the part of the international community to take firmer action, and the time has come for it to fulfil this promise by promoting a concerted, holistic response. In order for all concerned actors to work together to achieve this aim, however, more needs to be done to deepen understanding of this criminality and identify appropriate responses which reflect its complex, sophisticated, dangerous and constantly evolving nature. While this book focused primarily on the international legal framework to address this plague of modern society, it is hoped that it has been able to elucidate wider issues which might be used as points for further discussion and research.

Selected Bibliography

Books and Articles

Akande, D, 'International Law Immunities and the International Criminal Court' (2004) 98 *American Journal of International Law* 407

Allum, F and Sands, J, 'Explaining Organised Crime in Europe: Are Economists Always Right?' (2004) 41 *Crime, Law and Social Change* 133

Ambos, K, 'Is the Development of a Common Substantive Criminal Law for Europe Possible? Some Preliminary Reflections' (2005) 12 *Maastricht Journal of European and Comparative Law* 173

Amerasinghe, CF, *Principles of the Institutional Law of International Organisations* (Cambridge, Cambridge University Press, 1996)

Annan, K, 'Problems without Passports' (2002) *Foreign Policy* 30

Arlacchi, P, 'The Dynamics of Illegal Markets' in P Williams and D Vlassis (eds), *Combating Transnational Crime: Concepts, Activities and Responses* (London, Frank Cass, 2001)

Arlen, J, 'The Potentially Perverse Effect of Corporate Criminal Liability' (1994) 23 *Journal of Legal Studies* 833

Arquilla, J and Ronfeldt, D, *Networks and Netwars* (Santa Monica, RAND, 2001)

Bantekas, I and Nash, S, *International Criminal Law* (London, Routledge-Cavendish, 2007)

Barnett, M and Coleman, L, 'Designing Police: Interpol and the Study of Change in International Organizations' (2005) 49 *International Studies Quarterly* 593

Bassiouni, MC, 'The Penal Characteristics of Conventional International Criminal Law' (1983) 15 *Case Western Reserve Journal of International Law* 27

Bassiouni, MC, *International Extradition: United States Law and Practice*, 2nd edn (New York, Oceania Publications, 1987)

Bassiouni, MC and Wise, EM, *Aut Dedere, Aut Judicare: The Duty to Extradite or Prosecute in International Law* (Dordrecht, Matinus Nijhoff Publishers, 1995)

Bassiouni, MC and Vetere, E, (eds), *Organized Crime: A Compilation of UN Documents 1975–1998* (New York, Transnational Publishers, 1998)

Bassiouni, MC, *Crime Against Humanity in International Criminal Law*, 2nd edn (The Hague, Kluwer Law International, 1999)

Bassiouni, MC, 'Universal Jurisdiction for International Crimes: Historical Perspectives and Contemporary Practice' (2001) 42 *Virginia Journal of International Law* 81

Bibes, P, 'Transnational Organized Crime and Terrorism: Colombia, A Case Study' (2001) 17 *Journal of Contemporary Criminal Justice* 243

Bingham, JF, 'Codification of International Law: Part IV: Piracy' (1932) 26 *American Journal of International Law Supplement* 739

Blackmun, HA, 'The Supreme Court and the Law of Nations' (1994) 104 *Yale Law Journal* 39

Blakesley, CL, 'United States Jurisdiction over Extraterritorial Crime' (1982) 73 *Journal of Criminal Law and Criminology* 1109

Block, A and Chambliss, WJ, *Organizing Crime* (New York, Elsevier, 1981)

Block, A, *East Side–West Side: Organized Crime in New York City, 1930–1950*, 2nd edn (New Brunswick, Transaction Publishers, 1995)

Blok, A, *The Mafia of a Sicilian Village 1860–1960: A Study of Peasant Entrepreneurs* (Oxford, Basil Blackwell, 1974)

Boister, N, 'Transnational Criminal Law?' (2003) 14 *European Journal of International Law* 953

Bossard, A, *Transnational Crime and Criminal Law* (Chicago, University of Chicago Office of International Criminal Justice, 1990)

Brown, SD, 'The EU Solution' in SD Brown (ed), *Combating International Crime: The Longer Arm of the Law* (Abingdon, Routledge-Cavendish, 2008)

Brownlie, I, *Principles of Public International Law*, 6th edn (Oxford, Oxford University Press, 2003)

Bruinsma, G and Bernasco, W, 'Criminal Groups and Transnational Illegal Markets' (2004) 41 *Crime, Law and Social Change* 79

Calderoni, F, 'A Definition that Could Not Work: the EU Framework Decision on the Fight against Organised Crime' (2008) 16 *European Journal of Crime, Criminal Law and Criminal Justice* 265

Calica, A, 'Self-Help is the Best Kind: The Efficient Breach Justification for Forcible Abduction of Terrorists' (2004) 37 *Cornell International Law Journal* 389

Cameron, G, 'Multi-Track Microproliferation: Lessons from Aum Shinrikyo and Al Qaida' (1999) 22 *Studies in Conflict and Terrorism* 277

Carnegie, AR, 'Jurisdiction over Violations of the Laws and Customs of War' (1963) 39 *British Yearbook of International Law* 402

Cassese, A, 'Is the Bell Tolling for Universality? A Plea for a Sensible Notion of Universal Jurisdiction' (2003) 1 *Journal of International Criminal Justice* 589

Cassese, A, *International Criminal Law*, 2nd edn (Oxford, Oxford University Press, 2007)

Cohen, A 'The Concepts of Criminal Organisation' (1977) 17 *British Journal of Criminology* 97

Chu, YK, *The Triads as Business* (London, Routledge, 2000)

Clapham, A, *Human Rights Obligations of Non-State Actors* (Oxford, Oxford University Press, 2006)

Crawford, J, 'Responsibility to the International Community as a Whole' (2001) 8 *Indiana Journal of Global Legal Studies* 303

Crawford, *The International Law Commission's Articles on State Responsibility: Introduction, Text and Commentaries* (Cambridge, Cambridge University Press, 2002)

Cressey, D, *Theft of the Nation* (New York, Harper Collins, 1969)

Cryer, R, *Prosecuting International Crimes: Selectivity and International Criminal Law Regime* (Cambridge, Cambridge University Press, 2005)

Cryer, R, et al, *An Introduction to International Criminal Law and Procedure* (Cambridge, Cambridge University Press, 2008)

Currie, R, 'Human Rights and International Mutual Legal Assistance: Resolving the Tension' (2000) 11 *Criminal Law Forum* 143

Danilenko, GM, *Law-Making in the International Community* (Dordrecht, Martinus Nijhoff Publishers, 1993)

Danner, A and Martinez, J, 'Guilty Associations: Joint Criminal Enterprise, Command Responsibility and the Development of International Criminal Law' (2005) 93 *California Law Review* 75

Davies, M, et al, *Criminal Justice*, 4th edn (London, Pearson, 2010)

Denza, E, *Diplomatic Law: Commentary on the Vienna Convention on Diplomatic Relations* (Oxford, Oxford University Press, 1998)

Dickinson, ED, 'Codification of International Law: Part II: Jurisdiction with Respect to Crime' (1935) 29 *American Journal of International Law Supplement* 435

Dinstein, Y, 'Criminal Jurisdiction over Aircraft Hijacking' (1972) 7 *Israel Law Review* 195

Dinstein, Y, 'International Criminal Law' (1985) 20 *Israel Law Review* 206

Elliot, R, et al, 'Harm Reduction, HIV/AIDS, and the Human Rights Challenge to Global Drug Control Policy' (2005) 8 *Health and Human Rights* 104

Enache-Brown, C and Fried, A, 'Universal Crime, Jurisdiction and Duty: The Obligation of *Aut Dedere Aut Judicare* in International Law' (1997) 43 *McGill Law Journal* 613

Falk, R and Strauss, A, 'On the Creation of a Global Peoples Assembly: Legitimacy and the Power of Popular Sovereignty' (2000) 36 *Stanford Journal of International Law* 191

Fassbender, B, 'United Nations Charter as the Constitution of the International Community' (1998) 36 *Columbia Journal of Transnational law* 529

Fichera, M, 'The European Arrest Warrant and the Sovereign State: A Marriage of Convenience?' (2009) 15 *European Law Journal* 70

Fijnaut, C, 'Organized Crime: A Comparison Between the United States of America and Western Europe' (1990) 30 *British Journal of Criminology* 321

Fijnaut, C 'Transnational Crime and the Role of the United Nations, in Its Containment through International Cooperation: A Challenge for the 21st Century' (2000) 8 *European Journal of Crime, Criminal Law and Criminal Justice* 119

Findlay, M, *The Globalisation of Crime* (Cambridge, Cambridge University Press, 1999)

Finkelstein, L, 'What is Global Governance?' (1995) 1 *Global Governance* 367

Fletcher, M, 'Extending "Indirect Effect" to the Third Pillar: The Significance of *Pupino*' (2005) 30 *European Law Review* 862

Fletcher, M., Lööf, R and Gilmore, B, *EU Criminal Law and Justice* (Cheltenham, Edward Elgar Publishing, 2008)

Fooner, M, *Interpol: Issues in World Crime and International Criminal Justice* (New York, Plenum Press, 1989)

Fox, H, 'International Law and Restraints on the Exercise of Jurisdiction by National Courts of States' in M Evans (ed), *International Law*, 2nd edn (Oxford, Oxford University Press, 2006)

Franck, T, *Fairness in International Law and Institutions* (Oxford, Oxford University Press, 1995)

Fulvetti, G, 'The Mafia and the "Problem of the Mafia": Organised Crime in Italy 1820–1970' in L Paoli and C Fijnaut (eds), *Organised Crime in Europe: Concepts, Patterns and Control Policies in the European Union and Beyond* (Dordrecht, Springer, 2006)

Gambetta, D, *The Sicilian Mafia: The Business of Private Protection* (Cambridge, Harvard University Press, 1993)

Giatzidis, E, 'The Challenge of Organized Crime in the Balkans and the Political and Economic Implications' (2007) 23 *Journal of Communist Studies and Transition Politics* 327

Gilbert, G, *Aspects of Extradition Law* (Dordrecht, Martinus Nijhoff Publishers, 1991)

Gilinskiy, Y and Kostjukovsky, Y, 'From Thievish Artel to Criminal Corporation: The History of Organised Crime in Russia' in L Paoli and C Fijnaut (eds), *Organised Crime in Europe: Concepts, Patterns and Control Policies in the European Union and Beyond* (Dordrecht, Springer, 2006)

Gilmore, W, Warbrick, C and McGoldrick, D, 'Drug Trafficking at Sea: The Case of *R Charrington and Others*' (2000) 49 *International and Comparative Law Quarterly* 477

Gómez-Céspedes, A and Strangeland, P, 'Spain: The Flourishing Illegal Drug Haven in Europe' in L Paoli and C Fijnaut (eds), *Organised Crime in Europe: Concepts, Patterns and Control Policies in the European Union and Beyond* (Dordrecht, Springer, 2006)

Godefroy, T, 'The Control of Organised Crime in France: A Fuzzy Concept but a Handy Reference' in L Paoli and C Fijnaut (eds), *Organised Crime in Europe: Concepts, Patterns and Control Policies in the European Union and Beyond* (Dordrecht, Springer, 2006)

Goodwin, JM, 'Universal Jurisdiction and the Pirate: Time for an Old Couple to Part' (2006) 39 *Vanderbilt Journal of Transnational Law* 973

Greppi, E, 'The Evolution of Individual Criminal Responsibility under International Law' (1999) 835 *International Review of the Red Cross* 531

Halberstam, M, 'Terrorism on the High Seas: The Achille Lauro, Piracy and the IMO Convention on Maritime Safety' (1988) 82 *American Journal of International Law* 269

Harding, C, 'European Regimes of Crime Control: Objectives, Legal Bases and Accountability' (2000) 7 *Maastricht Journal of European and Comparative Law* 224

Harlow, C, 'Global Administrative Law: The Quest for Principles and Values' (2006) 17 *European Journal of International Law* 187

Held, D, *Democracy and the Global Order: From the Modern State to Cosmopolitan Governance* (Cambridge, Polity Press, 1995)

Held, D and McGrew, A, 'Introduction' in D Held and A McGrew (eds), *Governing Globalization: Power, Authority and Global Governance* (Cambridge, Polity Press, 2003)

Henkin, L, 'A Decent Respect to the Opinions of Mankind' (1992) 25 *John Marshall Law Review* 215

Higgins, R, *Problems and Process: International Law and How We Use It* (Oxford, Oxford University Press, 1995)

Hill, P, *The Japanese Mafia: Yakuza, Law and the State* (Oxford, Oxford University Press, 2003)

Hoffman, F and Megret, F, 'The UN as a Human Rights Violator? Some Reflections on the United Nations' Changing Human Rights Responsibilities' (2003) 25 *Human Rights Quarterly* 314

Holmes, JT, 'The Principle of Complementarity' in RS Lee (ed), *International Criminal Court: The Making of the Rome Statute* (The Hague, Martinus Nijhoff Publishers, 1999)

István, F, 'The Evolution of the Serbian Criminal Legislation: From the Beginning of the Transition until the New Criminal Code' (2008) 16 *European Journal of Crime, Criminal Law and Criminal Justice* 283

Jamieson, A, 'Transnational Organized Crime: A European Perspective' (2001) 24 *Studies in Conflict and Terrorism* 377

Jessup, PC, *Transnational Law* (New Haven, Yale University Press, 1956)

Jørgensen, NH, *The Responsibility of States for International Crimes* (Oxford, Oxford University Press, 2000)

Kaplan, D and Dubro, A, *Yakuza: Japan's Criminal Underworld* (Berkeley, University of California Press, 2003)

Keohane, R, 'Global Governance and Democratic Accountability' in D Held and M Koeing-Archibugi (eds), *Taming Globalization* (Cambridge, Polity Press, 2003)

Khanna, VS, 'Corporate Criminal Liability: What Purpose Does it Serve?' (1996) 109 *Harvard Law Review* 1477

Kingsbury, B, Krisch, N and Stewart, RB, 'The Emergence of Global Administrative Law' (2005) 68 *Law and Contemporary Problems* 15

Klabbers, J, *An Introduction to International Institutional Law* (Cambridge, Cambridge University Press, 2002)

Klerks, P 'The Network Paradigm Applied to Criminal Organisations: Theoretical Nitpicking or a Relevant Doctrine for Investigators? Recent Developments in the Netherlands' in A Edwards and P Gill (eds), Transnational Organised Crime: Perspectives on Global Security *(London,* Routledge, 2005)

Kontrovich, E, 'The Piracy Analogy: Modern Universal Jurisdiction's Hollow Foundation' (2004) 45 *Harvard International Law Journal* 183

Kraytman, YS, 'Universal Jurisdiction: Historical Roots and Modern Implications' (2005) 2 *BSIS Journal of International Studies* 94

Krisch, N, 'The Pluralism of Global Administrative Law' (2006) 17 *European Journal of International Law* 247

Lal, R, 'South Asian Organized Crime and Terrorist Networks,' (2005) 49 *Orbis: Journal of World Affairs* 293

Lange, K, '"Many a Lord is Guilty, Indeed for Many a Poor Man's Dishonest Deed": Gangs of Robbers in Early Modern Germany' in L Paoli and C Fijnaut (eds), *Organised Crime in Europe: Concepts, Patterns and Control Policies in the European Union and Beyond* (Dordrecht, Springer, 2006)

Lauterpacht, H, 'General Rules of the Law of Peace' in E Lautherpacht (ed), *International Law: Being the Collected Papers of Hersch Lauterpacht,* Vol 1 (Cambridge, Cambridge University Press, 1970)

Lee, GD, *Global Drug Enforcement: Practical Investigative Techniques* (Boca Raton, CRC Press, 2004)

Leong, A, *The Disruption of International Organised Crime: An Analysis of Legal and Non-Legal Strategies* (Aldershot, Ashgate, 2007)

Lew, JDM, 'The Extra-territorial Criminal Jurisdiction of English Courts' (1978) 27 *International and Comparative Law Quarterly* 168

Lillich, RB and Paxman, JM, 'State Responsibility for Injuries to Aliens Occasioned by Terrorist Activities' (1977) 26 *American University Law Review* 217

Lowe, V, 'Jurisdiction,' in M Evans (ed), *International Law,* 2nd edn (Oxford, Oxford University Press, 2006)

Mackarel, M, 'Surrendering the Fugitive: The European Arrest Warrant and the United Kingdom' (2006–07) 71 *Journal of Criminal Law* 362

Maginnis, VL, 'Limiting Diplomatic Immunity: Lessons learned from the 1946 Convention on the Privileges and Immunities of the United Nations' (2002–03) 28 *Brooklyn Journal of International Law* 989

Maguire, M, 'Policing by Risks and Targets: Some Dimensions and Implications of Intelligence-Led Crime Control' (2000) 9 *Policing and Society* 315

Marin, L, 'The European Arrest Warrant in the Italian Republic' (2008) 4 *European Constitutional Law Review* 251

Mathieson, T, 'Lex Vigilatoria – Towards a Control System without a State?' in S Armstrong and L McAra (eds), *Perspectives on Punishment: The Contours of Control* (Oxford, Oxford University Press, 2006)

McClanahan, G, *Diplomatic Immunity: Principles, Practice, Problems* (London, C. Hurt and Co, 1989)

McClean, D, *International Judicial Assistance* (Oxford, Clarendon Press, 1992)

McClean, D, *International Co-operation in Civil and Criminal Matters* (Oxford, Oxford University Press, 2002)

McClean, D, *Transnational Organized Crime: A Commentary on the UN Convention and Protocols* (Oxford, Oxford University Press, 2007)

McDougal, MS, Reisman, WM and Willard, AR, 'The World Community: A Planetary Social Process' (1988) 21 *University of California Davis Law Review* 807

McGuinness, D and Barrington, E, 'Immigration, Visa and Border Controls in the European Union' in G Barrett (ed), *Justice Cooperation in the European Union: The Creation of a European Legal Space* (Dublin, Institute of European Affairs, 1997)

McIllwain, JS, 'Organised Crime: A Social Network Approach' (1999) 32 *Crime, Law and Social Change* 301

Meron, T, *Human Rights and Humanitarian Norms as Customary Law* (Oxford, Clarendon Press, 1989)

Meron, T, 'Extraterritorial Application of Human Rights Treaties' (1995) 89 *American Journal of International Law* 78

Mitsilegas, V, 'Defining Organised Crime in the European Union: The Limits of European Criminal Law in an Area of "Freedom, Security and Justice"' (2001) 26 *European Law Review* 565

Mitsilegas, V, 'The Constitutional Implications of Mutual Recognition in Criminal Matters in the EU' (2006) 43 *Common Market Law Review* 1277

Mitsilegas, V, *EU Criminal Law* (Oxford, Hart Publishing, 2009)

Mittelman, JH and Johnston, R, 'The Globalization of Organized Crime, the Courtesan State, and the Corruption of Civil Society' (1999) 5 *Global Governance* 103

Moor, J, 'From Nation State to Failed State: International Protection from Human Rights Abuses by Non-State Actors' (1999) 31 *Columbia Human Rights Law Review* 81

Morselli, C and Giguere, C, 'Legitimate Strengths in Criminal Networks' (2006) 45 *Crime, Law and Social Change* 185

Mosler, H, *International Society as a Legal Community* (The Hague, Kluwer Law International, 1980)

Mueller, GOW, 'Transnational Crime: Definitions and Concepts' in Combating Transnational Crime' in P Williams and D Vlassis (eds), *Combating Transnational Crime: Concepts, Activities and Responses* (London, Frank Cass, 2001)

Nozina, M, 'Organized Crime in the New EU States of East Central Europe' in K Henderson (ed), *The Area of Freedom, Security and Justice in the Enlarged Europe* (Basingstoke, Palgrave McMillan, 2005)

Oakerson, R, 'Governance Structures for Enhancing Accountability and Responsiveness' in JL Perry (ed), *Handbook of Public Administration* (San Francisco, Jessey-Bass, 1996)

Obokata, T, *Trafficking of Human Beings from a Human Rights Perspective: Towards a Holistic Approach* (Leiden, Martinus Nijhoff Publishers, 2006)

Obokata, T, 'Illicit Cycle of Narcotics from a Human Rights Perspective' (2007) 25 *Netherland s Quarterly of Human Rights* 159

O'Connell, LM, 'State Immunity, Human Rights and Jus Cogens: A Critique of the Normative Hierarchy Theory' (2003) *American Journal of International Law* 741

Orakhelashvili, A, *Peremptory Norms in International Law* (Oxford, Oxford University Press, 2006)

Ormerod, D, *Smith and Hogan Criminal Law*, 12th edn (Oxford, Oxford University Press, 2008)

Paoli, L, 'The Paradoxes of Organized Crime' (2002) 37 *Crime, Law and Social Change* 51

Paoli, L and Fijnaut, C, 'Organised Crime and Its Control Policies' (2006) 14 *European Journal of Crime, Criminal Law and Criminal Justice* 307

Paoli, L and Fijnaut, C, 'Introduction to Part I: The History of Concept' in L Paoli and C Fijnaut (eds), *Organised Crime in Europe: Concepts, Patterns and Control Policies in the European Union and Beyond* (Dordrecht, Springer, 2006)

Passas, N, 'Globalisation, Criminogenic Asymmetries and Economic Crime' (1999) 1 *European Journal of Law Reform* 399

Passas, N, 'Globalisation and Transnational Crime: Effects of Criminogenic Asymmetries' in P Williams and D Vlassis (eds), *Combating Transnational Crime: Concepts, Activities and Responses* (London, Frank Cass, 2001)

Passas, N, 'Cross-Border Crime and the Interface between Legal and Illegal Actors' in P Van Duyne, K Von Lampe and N Passas (eds), *Upperworld and Underworld in Cross-Border Crime* (Nijmegen, Wolf Legal Publishers, 2002)

Pearce, F, *Crimes of the Powerful: Marxism, Crime and Deviance* (London, Pluto Press, 1976)

Peers, S, *EU Justice and Home Affairs Law* (Oxford, Oxford University Press, 2006)

Raghu, M, 'Sex Trafficking of Thai Women and the United States Asylum Law Response' (1997) 12 *Georgetown Immigration Law Journal* 145

Randall, KC, 'Universal Jurisdiction under International Law' (1988) 66 *Texas Law Review* 785

Ratner, S and Abrams, J, *Accountability for Human Rights Atrocities in International Law*, 2nd edn (Oxford, Oxford University Press, 2001)

Rawski, F, 'To Waive or Not to Waive? Immunity and Accountability in UN Peacekeeping Operations' (2002) 18 *Connecticut Journal of International Law* 103

Rayfuse, R, 'International Abduction and the United States Supreme Court: The Law of the Jungle Reigns' (1993) 42 *International and Comparative Law Quarterly* 882

Reinisch, A, *International Organisations before National Courts* (Cambridge, Cambridge University Press, 2000)

Reuter, P, *Disorganized Crime: The Economics of the Visible Hand* (Cambridge, MIT Press, 1983)

Reydams, L, *Universal Jurisdiction: International and Municipal Legal Perspectives* (Oxford, Oxford University Press, 2004)

Robinson, P, 'The Missing Crimes' in A Cassese, P Gaeta and J Jones (eds), *The Rome Statute of the International Criminal Court: A Commentary*, Vol I (Oxford, Oxford University Press, 2002)

Roht-Arriaza, N, 'State Responsibility to Investigate and Prosecute Grave Human Rights Violations in International Law' (1990) 78 *California Law Review* 449

Roht-Arriaza, N, 'Punishment, Redress and Pardon: Theoretical and Psychological Approaches' in N Roht-Arriaza (ed), *Impunity and Human Rights in International Law and Practice* (Oxford, Oxford University Press, 1995)

Rosenau, J, *Turbulence in World Politics* (Princeton, Princeton University Press, 1989)

Rosenau, J 'Governance in a New Global Order' in D Held and A McGrew (eds), *Governing Globalization: Power, Authority and Global Governance* (Cambridge, Polity Press, 2003)

Roujanavong, W, *Organised Crime in Thailand* (Bangkok, Rumthai Press, 2006)

Roxbrugh, RF, (ed), *Oppenheim's International Law: A Treatise*, 3rd edn (London, Longman, 1920)

Ryngaert, C, 'The Doctrine of Abuse of Process: A Comment on Cambodia Tribunal's Decisions in the Case against Duch (2007)' (2008) 21 *Leiden Journal of International Law* 719

Sambei, A and Jones, JRWD, *Extradition Law Handbook* (Oxford, Oxford University Press, 2005)

Schabas, W, 'International Crime' in D Armstrong (ed), *Routledge Handbook of International Law* (London, Routledge-Cavendish, 2008)

Scharf, M, '*The Prosecutor v Slavko Dokmanovic*: Irregular Rendition and the ICTY' (1998) 11 *Leiden Journal of International Law* 369

Schelling, T, 'What is the Business of Organized Crime?' (1971) 20 *Journal of Public Law* 71

Schelling, T, *Choice and Consequence* (Cambridge, Harvard University Press, 1984)

Shelton, D, 'Private Violations, Public Wrongs, and the Responsibility of States' (1989) 13 *Fordham International Law Journal* 1

Shelton, D, *Remedies in International Human Rights Law*, 2nd edn (Oxford, Oxford University Press, 2005)

Sheptycki, J, 'The Accountability of Transnational Policing Institution: The Strange Case of Interpol' (2004) *California Journal of Law and Society* 107

Shloenhardt, A, 'Organised Crime and the Business of Migrant Trafficking: an Economic Analysis' (1999) 32 *Crime, Law and Social Change* 203

Simma, B and Paulus, AL, 'The "International Community": Facing the Challenge of Globalisation' (1998) 9 *European Journal of International Law* 266.

Skogly, S, *Beyond National Borders: States' Human Rights Obligations in International Cooperation* (Antwerp, Intersentia, 2006)

Sluiter, G, 'Due Process and Criminal Procedure in the Cambodian Extraordinary Chambers' (2006) 4 *Journal of International Criminal Justice* 31

Smith, D, *The Mafia Mystique* (New York, Basic Books, 1975)

Sproat, PA, 'An Evaluation of the UK's Anti-Money Laundering and Asset Recovery Regime' (2007) 47 *Crime Law and Social Change* 169

Sridhar, A, 'The International Criminal Tribunal For the Former Yugoslavia's Response to the Problem of Transnational Abduction' 42 (2006) *Stanford Journal of International Law* 343

Steiner, H, Alston, P and Goodman, R, *International Human Rights in Context: Law Politics and Morals*, 3rd edn (Oxford, Oxford University Press, 2008)

Sutherland, EH, 'White-Collar Criminality' (1940) 5 *American Sociological Review* 1

Symeonidou-Kastanidou, E, 'Towards a New Definition of Organised Crime in the European Union' (2007) 15 *European Journal of Crime, Criminal Law and Criminal Justice* 8

Tunks, MA, 'Diplomats or Defendants? Defining the Future of the Head-of-State Immunity' (2002) 52 *Duke Law Journal* 651

Turnbull, P, 'The Fusion of Immigration and Crime in the European Union: Problems of Cooperation and the Fight against Trafficking in Women' in P Williams (ed), *Illegal Migration and Commercial Sex* (London, Frank Cass,1999)

Van der Wilt, H, 'Joint Criminal Enterprises: Possibilities and Limitations' (2007) 5 *Journal of International Criminal Justice* 9

Van Duyne, P, 'Organized Crime, Corruption and Power' (1997) 26 *Crime, Law and Social Change* 201

Varese, F, *The Russian Mafia: Private Protection in a New Market Economy* (Oxford, Oxford University Press, 2001)

Von Hebel, H and Robinson, D, 'Crimes within the Jurisdiction of the Court' in RS Lee (ed), *The International Criminal Court: The Making of the Rome Statute* (The Hague, Kluwer Law International, 1999)

Warbrick, C, 'Judicial Jurisdiction and Abuse of Process' (2000) 49 *International and Comparative Law Quarterly* 489

Wellens, K, *Remedies against International Organisations* (Cambridge, Cambridge University Press, 2002)

Weyembergh, A, 'The Functions of Approximation of Penal Legislation within the European Union' (2005) 12 *Maastricht Journal of European and Comparative Law* 149

Weyembergh, A, 'Approximation of Criminal Laws, the Constitutional Treaty and the Hague Programme' 42 (2005) *Common Market Law Review* 1567

Wickremasinghe, C, 'Immunities Enjoyed by Officials of States and International Organisations' in M Evans (ed), *International Law*, 2nd edn (Oxford, Oxford University Press, 2006)

Wilde, R, '*Quis Custodiet Ipso Custodes?*: Why and How UNHCR Governance of "Development" Refugee Camps Should be Subject to International Human Rights Law' (1998) 1 *Yale Human Rights and Development Law Journal* 107

Williams, P and Godson, R, 'Anticipating Organized and Transnational Crime' (2002) 37 *Crime, Law and Social Change* 311

Williams, P, 'Organizing Transnational Crime: Networks, Markets and Hierarchy' in P Williams and D Vlassis (eds), *Combating Transnational Crime: Concepts, Activities and Responses* (London, Frank Cass, 2001)

Williams, P and Baudin-O'Hayon, G, 'Global Governance, Transnational Organised Crime and Money Laundering' in D Held and A McGrew (eds), *Governing Globalization: Power, Authority and Global Governance* (Cambridge, Polity Press, 2003)

Wise, EM, 'RICO and Its Analogues: Some Comparative Considerations,' (2000) 27 *Syracuse Journal of International Law and Commerce* 303

Wise, EM, 'The Obligation to Extradite or Prosecute' (1993) 27 *Israel Law Review* 268

Wodak, A and McLeod, L, 'The Role of Harm Reduction in Controlling HIV among Injecting Drug Users' (2008) 22 *AIDS* 81,

Woodiwiss, M, 'Transnational Organised Crime: The Strange Career of an American Concept' in M Beare (ed), *Critical Reflections on Transnational Organized Crime, Money Laundering and Corruption* (Toronto, University of Toronto Press, 2003)

Woodiwiss, M, 'Transnational Organised Crime: The Global Reach of an American Concept' in A Edwards and P Gill (eds), *Transnational Organised Crime: Perspectives on Global Security* (London, Routldge, 2005)

Woods, N 'Good Governance in International Organizations' (1999) 5 *Global Governance* 39

Yeşilgöz, Y and Bovenkerk, F, 'Urban Knights and Rebels in the Ottoman Empire' in L Paoli and C Fijnaut (eds), *Organised Crime in Europe: Concepts, Patterns and Control Policies in the European Union and Beyond* (Dordrecht, Springer, 2006)

Reports and Working Papers

American Law Institute, 'Restatement of the Law (Third), Foreign Relations Law of the United States' 2 American Law Institute (1987)

Amnesty International, 'Kosovo (Serbia and Montenegro): "So Does it Mean that We Have the Rights?" Protecting the Human Rights of Women and Girls Trafficked for Forced Prostitution in Kosovo' (2004)

Amnesty International, 'State of Denial: Europe's Role in Rendition and Secret Detention' (2008)

Amnesty International, 'State of the World's Human Rights 2009'

Anticorruption and Dignity 'Çohu', 'Report on the Situation of the Justice System in Kosova' (January 2009)

Annan, K, 'We the Peoples: The Role of the United Nations in the 21st Century' (2000)

Bundeskriminalamt, 'Organised Crime: 2008 National Situation Report' (2009)

Chr Michelsen Institute, 'Corruption in Serbia 2007: A Overview of Problems and Status of Reforms' (2007)

Commission on Global Governance, 'Our Global Neighbourhood' (Oxford, Oxford University Press, 1995)

Compliance with the United Nations Convention Against Corruption: Report of the Secretariat, CAC/COSP/2009/9 (9 September 2009)

EMCDDA, 'The State of the Drugs Problem in Europe: Annual Report 2009'

European Commission, 'An Extended Report on the Evaluation of the Hague Programme, SEC(2009) 766 final EULEX, Programme Report 2009'

European Commission, 'Kosovo 2007 Progress Report', SEC(2007) 1433

European Commission, 'Kosovo 2008 Progress Report', SEC(2008) 2697

European Commission, 'Kosovo 2009 Progress Report', SEC(2009) 1340

European Commission, 'Serbia Progress Report 2009', SEC(2009) 1339

Europol, 'Europol Annual Report 2007'

EU Network of Independent Experts on Fundamental Rights, 'Opinion on the Status of Illegally Obtained Evidence in Criminal Procedures in the Member States of the European Union' (30 November 2003)

Filipkowski, W, 'Organised Crime in Poland as the Field of Research and Its Contemporary Situation', paper presented at the Research Conference on Organised Crime, Frankfurt (2008)

Gangmsters Licensing Authority, 'Annual Report and Accounts' (1 April 2008–31 March 2009)

Group of States against Corruption (GRECO), 'Evaluation Report on the Republic of Serbia' (Strasbourg, Council of Europe, 2006)

Her Majesty's Inspectorate of Constabulary, 'Getting Organised: A Thematic Report on the Police Service's Response to Serious and Organised Crime' (April 2009)

Human Rights Watch, 'Not Enough Graves: The War on Drugs, HIV/AIDS, and Violations of Human Right's (2004)

Human Rights Watch, 'World Report 2009'

Implementation of the United Nations Convention against Transnational Organized Crime: consolidated information received from States for the first reporting cycle, CTOC/COP/2005/2/Rev.2

Implementation Report 2008 of the United Nations Convention against Transnational Organized Crime: consolidated information received from States for the second reporting cycle, CTOC/COP/2006/2/Rev.1

International Harm Reduction Association, 'Civil Society: A Silenced Partner?' (2009)

International Law Association, 'Final Report on Accountability of International Organisation's (2004)

International Law Commission, 'Draft Articles on the Responsibilities of International Organisations', A/58/10 (May–August 2003)

Interpol, 'Annual Report 2008'

Long, N, 'Implementation of the European Arrest Warrant and Joint Investigation Teams At EU and National Level' (Brussels, European Parliament, 2009)

Office of the Prime Minister, Thai Country Report, submitted to the Eleventh United Nations Congress on Crime Prevention and Criminal Justice (April 2005, Bangkok, Thailand)

OHCHR, '2008 Report: Activities and Results'

OSCE, 'Special Prosecutor's Office for Organised Crime: The First Six Years' (2009)

Pearson, G and Hobbs, D, 'Middle Market Drug Distribution', Home Office Research Study No 227 (2001)

The Practice of the United Nations, the Specialized Agencies and the International Atomic Energy Agency Concerning Their Status, Privileges and Immunities: A Study Prepared by the Secretariat, U.N.Doc A/CN.4/L.118 Add. 1 and 2 (1967)

The President's Commission on Law Enforcement and Administration of Justice, 'Task Force Report: Organized Crime' (1967)

Report of the World Ministerial Conference on Organised Transnational Crime, A/49/748

Report of the meeting of the inter-sessional open-ended intergovernmental group of experts on the elaboration of a preliminary draft of a possible comprehensive international convention against organized transnational crime, E/CN.15/1998/5

Report of the Special Committee on Peacekeeping Operations on Comprehensive Review of the Whole Question of Peacekeeping Operations in All Their Aspects, A/54/839

Report of the Conference of Parties to the United Nations Convention against Transnational Organised Crime on its first session, held in Vienna from 28 June to 8 July 2004, CTOC/COP/2004/6

Report of the Conference of Parties to the United Nations Convention against Transnational Organised Crime on its first session, held in Vienna from 28 June to 8 July 2004, CTOC/COP/2004/6

Report of the Eleventh United Nations Congress on Crime Prevention and Criminal Justice, A/CONF.203/18

Report on the meeting of the Open-ended Interim Working Group of Government Experts on Technical Assistance held in Vienna from 3 to 5 October 2007, CTOC/COP/2008/7

Report of the Secretary-General on the United Nations Interim Administration Mission in Kosovo, S/2009/497

Roopnaraine, T, 'Child Trafficking in Kosovo' (Kosovo, Save the Children in Kosovo, 2002),

Save the Children UK, 'First Progress Report to UNIAP/UNOPS' (August 2002)

Save the Children UK, 'No One to Turn: The Under-Reporting of Child Sexual Exploitation and Abuse by Aid-Workers and Peacekeeper's (2008)

SOCA, 'Annual Report 2008/2009'

SOCA, 'Annual Report 2007/2008'

SOCA, 'The United Kingdom Threat Assessment of Organised Crime 2009/10'

UK Home Office, 'One Step Ahead: A 21st Century Strategy to Defeat Organised Crime' (March 2004)

UK Home Office, 'Extending Our Reach: A Comprehensive Approach to Tackling Serious Organised Crime' (July 2009)

UK Home Office, 'Public Concern about Organised Crime', Research Report No 16 (2009)

UK Ministry of Justice, 'Review of the Executive Royal Prerogative Powers: Final Report' (October 2009)

UK Parliamentary Home Affairs Committee, 'The Trade in Human Beings: Human Trafficking in the UK' (May 2009)

UNDP, 'Evaluation of UNDP's Second Regional Cooperation Framework for Asia and the Pacific' (May 2007)

UNIAP, 'Semi-Annual Project Report for the United Nations Foundation and for United Nations Fund for International Partnership' (August 2002)

UNIAP, 'The COMMIT Sub-Regional Action Plan: Achievements in Combating Trafficking in the Greater Mekong Sub-Region' (December 2007)

UNIAP, 'Phrase III Mid-Term Evaluation Report' (March 2009)

UNICRI, 'The Fight against Organized Crime in Serbia: From the Existing Legislation to a Comprehensive Reform Proposal' (2008)

UNMIK, 'Combating Human Trafficking in Kosovo: Strategy & Commitment' (May 2004)

UNODC, 'Legislative Guide to the Implementation of the United Nations Convention against Transnational Organised Crime' (2004)

UNODC, 'Alternative Development: A Global Thematic Evaluation' (2005)

UNODC Regional Office for Southern Africa, 'Terminal Evaluation Report' (2008)

UNODC, 'Independent Evaluation of Beyond 2008' (2009)

UNODC, 'Annual Report 2009'

US Department of State, 'Trafficking in Persons Report 2009', available at www.state.gov/g/tip/rls/tiprpt/2009

US Department of State, 'International Narcotics Control Strategy Report 2009', available at www.state.gov/p/inl/rls/nrcrpt/2009/vol1/index.htm

United States Government Accountability Office, 'US Government's Efforts to Address Alleged Abuse of Household Workers by Foreign Diplomats with Immunity Could Be Strengthened' report to the Subcommittee on Human Rights and the Law, Committee on the Judiciary, US Senate (July 2008)

Index